of being by cause of existence, inexistence, action, inaction, purpose or lack of purpose.

Logic 6: *Absolutes are unobtainable.*

Logic 7: *Gradient scales are necessary to the evaluation of problems and their data.*

This is the tool of infinity-valued logic: Absolutes are unobtainable. Terms such as good and bad, alive and dead, right and wrong are used only in conjunction with gradient scales. On the scale of right and wrong, everything above zero or center would be more and more right, approaching an infinite rightness, and everything below center would be more and more wrong, approaching infinite wrongness. All things assisting the survival of the survivor are considered to be right for the survivor. All things inhibiting survival from the viewpoint of the survivor can be considered wrong for the survivor. The more a thing assists survival, the more it can be considered right for the survivor; the more a thing or action inhibits survival, the more it is wrong from the viewpoint of the intended survivor.

COROLLARY: Any datum has only relative truth.

COROLLARY: Truth is relative to environments, experience and truth.

Logic 8: *A datum can be evaluated only by a datum of comparable magnitude.*

Logic 9: *A datum is as valuable as it has been evaluated.*

(continued on back end pages)

SCIENCE of SURVIVAL

PREDICTION OF HUMAN BEHAVIOR

L. RON HUBBARD

Bridge

Publications, Inc.

A
HUBBARD®
PUBLICATION

BRIDGE PUBLICATIONS, INC.
4751 Fountain Avenue
Los Angeles, California 90029
ISBN 0-88404-418-1

This book is part of the works of L. Ron Hubbard,
who developed Dianetics spiritual healing technology and
Scientology applied religious philosophy. It is presented to the reader
as a record of observations and research into the nature of the human mind
and spirit, and not as a statement of claims made by the author.
The benefits and goals of Dianetics and Scientology can be
attained only by the dedicated efforts of the reader.

Acknowledgment

IS MADE TO FIFTY THOUSAND YEARS OF THINKING MEN WITHOUT WHOSE
SPECULATIONS AND OBSERVATIONS THE CREATION AND CONSTRUCTION
OF DIANETICS WOULD NOT HAVE BEEN POSSIBLE.
CREDIT IN PARTICULAR IS DUE TO:

Anaxagoras

Aristotle

Socrates

Plato

Euclid

Lucretius

Roger Bacon

Francis Bacon

Isaac Newton

van Leeuwenhoek

Voltaire

Thomas Paine

Thomas Jefferson

René Descartes

James Clerk Maxwell

Charcot

Herbert Spencer

William James

Sigmund Freud

Cmdr. Thompson (MC) USN

William A. White

Will Durant

Count Alfred Korzybski

AND MY INSTRUCTORS IN ATOMIC
AND MOLECULAR PHENOMENA, MATHEMATICS AND THE
HUMANITIES AT GEORGE WASHINGTON UNIVERSITY AND AT PRINCETON.

IMPORTANT NOTE

In READING THIS BOOK, BE VERY certain you never go past a word you do not fully understand.

The only reason a person gives up a study or becomes confused or unable to learn is because he or she has gone past a word that was not understood.

The confusion or inability to grasp or learn comes AFTER a word that the person did not have defined and understood.

Have you ever had the experience of coming to the end of a page and realizing you didn't know what you had read? Well, somewhere earlier on that page you went past a word that you had no definition for or an incorrect definition for.

Here's an example. "It was found that when the crepuscule arrived the children were quieter and when it was not present, they were much livelier." You see what happens. You think you don't understand the whole idea, but the inability to understand came entirely from the one word you could not define, *crepuscule*, which means twilight or darkness.

It may not only be the new and unusual words that you will have to look up. Some commonly used words can often be misdefined and so cause confusion.

This datum about not going past an undefined word is the most important fact in the whole subject of study. Every subject you have taken up and abandoned had its words which you failed to get defined.

Therefore, in studying this book be very, very certain you never go past a word you do not fully understand. If the material becomes confusing or you can't seem to grasp it, there will be a word just earlier that you have not understood. Don't go any further, but go back to BEFORE you got into trouble, find the misunderstood word and get it defined.

Appendix

In authoring *Science of Survival,* LRH included an appendix providing the basic axioms and definitions of key terms upon which Dianetics is aligned (Appendix—Definitions and Axioms).

This appendix contains information invaluable to the reader, regardless of any prior study of Dianetics, as it defines the meanings of terms as they are used in *Science of Survival,* based on the discoveries and breakthroughs following the publication of the first book—*Dianetics: The Modern Science of Mental Health.* In that regard, the appendix serves not only as a reference while reading this book, but to be read in full by itself.

To aid the reader, terms appearing in the appendix are marked with an asterisk where they first appear in the book, with their LRH definition in italics at the bottom of the page.

Footnotes and Glossary

To further aid the reader's comprehension, LRH directed the editors to define other words and phrases that might be misunderstood by the reader. These are indicated with footnotes the first time they appear in the text. Each word so defined has a small number to its right, and the definition appears at the bottom of the page beside the corresponding number.

Words sometimes have several meanings, but only the meaning of the word as it is used in the text is given in the footnote. Other definitions for the word are in standard language or Dianetics and Scientology dictionaries.

A glossary which includes all footnoted definitions is also provided at the back of the book. Beside each glossary definition you will find the chapter in which the word first occurs so you can refer back to it if you wish.

SCIENCE OF SURVIVAL
PREDICTION OF HUMAN BEHAVIOR

CONTENTS

BOOK ONE: THE DYNAMICS OF BEHAVIOR

BOOK TWO: DIANETIC PROCESSING

....

GLOSSARY, INDEX & BIBLIOGRAPHY

THE GOAL
OF DIANETICS

A WORLD WITHOUT INSANITY, without criminals and without war—this is the goal of Dianetics.

For thousands of years man has struggled forward with his conquest of the material universe but he has known almost nothing about his most important weapon, his most valuable possession, the human mind. Despite this obstacle of ignorance he has made progress, but because of this obstacle he has accumulated unto himself not only the penalties of madness and disease but more important, the threat of destruction for all his works—modern war.

Dianetics is the science of thought. The word is from the Greek *dianous* (through mind). The scope of Dianetics includes all valid data pertaining to thought. Far simpler than man supposed, the workings of the human mind and knowledge itself became, in Dianetics, a body of knowledge with which any reasonably intelligent individual can work.

No civilization can progress to the stability of continuous survival without certain and sure command of knowledge such as that contained in Dianetics. For Dianetics, skillfully used, can do exactly what it claims. It can, in the realm of the individual, prevent or alleviate insanity, neurosis, compulsions and obsessions and it can bring about physical well-being, removing the basic cause of some 70 percent of man's illnesses. It can, in the field of the family, psychotherapy. Those whose "field" it invades would love to have it outlawed before their boxes of beautiful "Snake Root Oil" have been discredited.

Preventive Dianetics means more for humanity in the long run than Dianetic processing. Group Dianetics means more for these war-torn societies than any number of arthritis cures.

Dianetics is the basic science of human thought. It embraces human activity and arranges a body of hitherto uncoordinated knowledge.

Dianetics has a basic goal, a good goal, a goal which should not be discounted or thrown aside because some quack will lose his income or because some revolutionary will lose his crackpot cause. The goal of Dianetics is a sane world—a world without insanity, without criminals and without war. If our generations live to write history, let them sadly give a page to those who, in this chaotic and dark age, sought, through personal profit and through hate, to bring a truly humanitarian science down.

The goal of Dianetics is sanity. It can be stopped only by the insane.

INTRODUCTION

THIS BOOK IS BUILT AROUND A CHART. On the many columns of this chart we find the majority of the components of the human mind and all those necessary to process an individual.

In this book we will take up these columns one by one from the left to right, and explain each column. When this has been done, and you have read the book and thoroughly examined the chart, you will at least have the rudiments you need to process people.

If you desire to process individuals on a limited basis, you may specialize in Straight Memory, lock reduction and Lock Scanning. This can be done to almost anyone you would ordinarily contact without any harm and with a great deal of improvement in his general tone. If you feel a little more adventurous, you can learn how to audit secondary engrams and so become proficient in discharging grief and fear from a case. Should you desire to go the whole way and feel yourself competent, you can try running engrams on a case, with a very close regard to the kind of case on which you try to run them.

For a full education in Dianetic processing, the elements are here. But just as you went to high school to learn algebra or physics, you should take a Foundation course in order to become a truly proficient auditor. Qualification at the Foundation, coupled with any other training you may have, will permit you to become a professional practitioner. Most people, however, take a Foundation course because they want to be better educated and to function better in their own professions, for Dianetics is not just processing. That's not a thousandth of it. Dianetics deals with thought and the behavior of men and groups, and those who know the subject thoroughly survive better.

Simply reading this book, then, although it contains all the basic information, does not qualify an individual to practice professionally. But once he has thoroughly studied this book, he should be able to handle routine cases without difficulty. He should not try Dianetics on insane or severely neurotic persons unless he feels himself especially gifted in understanding or unless he has taken a qualification course at the Foundation. This particularly applies to analysts and psychiatrists and medical doctors who, having concourse with the insane and the chronically ill, could achieve remarkably better and faster results with a knowledge of Dianetics. The science was made available to them in the past, and it is again urged that they take advantage of its techniques in the best interest of mankind and the advancement of their professions. Many physicians and psychologists have already been trained by the Foundation and they, experience shows, have made good auditors.

In the same vein, the layman should be very careful whom he allows to practice Dianetics upon him. Before submitting to Dianetic processing, the individual should either look for the auditor's certificate on the wall and see that it is in good order or demand the right to give his auditor a test as to the various definitions contained in this volume. The individual who desires processing should not submit himself to a psychiatrist or a psychoanalyst or medical doctor for Dianetic treatment in the belief that they, as practitioners, know Dianetics. Only those psychoanalysts, medical doctors and psychiatrists trained by the Foundation are fully qualified to handle the whole parade of skills necessary in an auditor.

If your auditor is not qualified by the Foundation, then let him run Straight Memory, locks and chains of locks on you until you are entirely satisfied he knows what he is doing.

An auditor, by diligent study of this volume and by entering slowly into the use of his tools, making sure he understands each one of them progressively before using the next, can achieve great skill in processing. These cautionary remarks are addressed to those who, by haphazard reading of the volume may attempt to plunge into the whole array of skills at once. This would be like trying to take a plane off the ground before one learns where the throttle is located and how to bank. Dianetics is not as difficult as flying a plane, but it is a technical subject.

You can't drive anybody mad with Dianetic processing. Cases driven mad by Dianetic processing do not exist. Cases do exist where reversed techniques have been criminally used on persons. Pain-drug-hypnosis can deliver anybody into a straitjacket with greater neatness and dispatch than anything hitherto known. Dianetic processing, however, has nothing to do with restimulating or planting engrams.

So read what is written and get to know your chart. You will know more about men and women and their behavior when you have finished. If you feel you could stand some processing, come to the Foundation, or team up with somebody on whom you can rely, starting in with Straight Memory and locks and studying as you work. If possible, get supervision from a Foundation trained auditor or take a basic or professional course. You can't know too much about this subject.

No attempt is made in this volume to be literary or academic. I would happily take off a couple of years and write you something highly polished, but we're trying to get where we're going before the atom bomb gets there, and navigating the course takes a little time. So I've just written here what I know about this chart in a way I think you'll understand. The book is organized around the chart, not around the longest words in the dictionary. This is made possible by a certain difference between Dianetics and some other subjects—in those, the author has to make up in complication what he lacks in understanding of his subject, so the critics will be impressed. Damn the critics, let's get down to paragraph one and open up to flank speed.[1] There's a sane world to be won.

L. Ron Hubbard
January, 1951

---

1. **flank speed:** the maximum speed of which a ship is capable.

BOOK ONE

THE DYNAMICS
OF BEHAVIOR

CHAPTER ONE

COLUMN A

THE
TONE SCALE

F ROM FUNK AND WAGNALLS NEW Standard Dictionary, Supplement No. 5:

di.a.net´.ics noun: A system for the analysis, control and development of human thought evolved from a set of coordinated axioms which also provide techniques for the treatment of a wide range of mental disorders and organic diseases: term and doctrines introduced by L. Ron Hubbard, American engineer. (Gr. *dianoetikos—dia,* through, plus *noos,* mind)—*di.a.net´.ic adj.*

Assuming the basic idea that the sole fundamental of existence is survival, the problems of man's behavior apparently resolve rapidly. His interpersonal relations, the operation and purposes of his organizations and groups become understandable.

Science is, to many people, a sacred cow. Actually, by definition, science is only the organization of apparently disrelated facts into a useful whole. Aligned on certain basic axioms (which can be found in the appendix*) Dianetics is a useful body of knowledge by which may be resolved the puzzle of man and his behavior.

A search for an energy of life begun in 1930 has been partially resolved by the discovery of the lowest common denominator of existence: SURVIVE!

....
*See pages 539 to 555, Appendix, *"Definitions and Axioms."*

A gross error has been made by scientists in the past who sought, materialistically, to explain life on the basis of mud, chemicals and electricity. It was the contention of these individuals that matter, electrical energy, operating in space and time, combined in some incredibly lucky moment to form a self-perpetuating unit and that this item fortuitously grew and grew and one day man appeared on the scene. This childlike logic breaks down if only on the basis of the odds against it. It breaks down again when evolution, as postulated, is seen to be of only limited usefulness, being actually as full of holes as an ocarina. The main test of any "scientific" hodgepodge is its usefulness to man. The mud-to-man theory, and it is just a crude theory, has not resolved man's behavior. These schools of thought gave men unlimited weapons such as the atom bomb and yet failed to give man sanity enough to regulate his own affairs or use the type of energy released by that bomb for purposes other than destroying towns. So we can conclude and lay in a quiet grave any and all scientific theories which have not led to peace on Earth or have failed to give us a predominance of men of good will. Of course there are lots of individuals who would like to go on having man believe he is basically mud but to these we bequeath the electric shock machine and the prefrontal lobotomy,[1] the highest level of operation to which the mud-to-man theory led.

An examination of existence and the fondest hopes to which man has clung discovers for us the possibility that the energy of life is a different thing from the current flowing in a power line or the energy radiated by atomic fission. It is not necessary to have a vast knowledge of physics to conclude that life is something more than a mechanical contrivance rigged out of atoms and chemicals. In the

---

1. **prefrontal lobotomy:** a psychiatric procedure in which the frontal lobes of the brain are separated from the rest of the brain by cutting the connecting nerve fibers. *Prefrontal* means situated at the front or forepart of the brain, *lobotomy* comes from *lobe*, a roundish projection or division, as of an organ and *-tomy*, a combining form, used here to mean an incision or cutting of an organ, as designated by the initial element of the term.

first place, it follows only a few of the electromagnetic-gravitic laws[2] and at best only vaguely parallels these. Life has its own performance rules.

A further examination of life demonstrates that it is undoubtedly made up in part of matter and that it exists in space and time. This is quite certain because a dead organism disintegrates into dust. Something has obviously ceased to be a part of this organism, however, the moment it fully died. This "something" has variously been called the human soul, the spirit, the life force. Bergson called it *élan vital.*

The scientist who deals constantly with machines and chemical reactions has for some decades looked on a life organism as an oxygen-carbon motor, a heat energy machine which operated not unlike a steam locomotive. He dismissed the wild variables this introduced into any attempted solution to life and living by the expansive statement that life was simply more complicated than machines men built but that it was actually just another machine. A "too-complicated" school of thought, a scientific masquerade, took up this argument and saw that it obfuscated any real explanation, or reason for one, and began to say that the human mind, being a part of a machine which was too complicated for biology and biochemistry, was of course too complicated to understand, being a part of a too-complicated organism. It is felt that this waving aside of the problems of mind operation, this operation on the defeatist principle that the problem could not be solved, introduced "therapies" which were "too complicated." It took four to twelve years to get an inkling of these therapies and all evidence to hand, carefully compiled, shows that they do not work, that the problems of criminality, insanity and war still remained, with these systems of "therapy," far out of control. The too-complicated school of life and mind operation gives us a picture of a group of demon exorcists

---

2. **electromagnetic-gravitic laws:** a reference to the major laws manifested by the physical universe involving the interrelation between electricity, magnetism and gravity.

rushing around plague-ridden London a couple of centuries ago, telling everyone they had the solution to the plague, while some hundreds of thousands of Englishmen died the Black Death. With 19,000,000 insane in the United States alone, with nations in the grip of madmen planning conquest, the too-complicated school rushes about getting a good press on how well they are doing, while all the evidence says entirely otherwise.

Thus let us look for a simpler solution, one which does not require twelve years of schooling and practice to learn, one which will deliver to us a therapy and, more important, an understanding of life, man, and mind operation which can resolve the 19,000,000 insane, our millions of criminals and international madness.

We find the first leg of this solution in considering life force, *élan vital,* or what have you, as an energy dissimilar to electrons and molecules and mud. The laws of this "energy," once they are isolated and stated, are found to be parallel to but dissimilar to the laws of the physical universe.

Let us call this life energy by a symbol in order to identify it. We will assign to it the Greek letter *theta (θ)* and distinguish it as an energy existing separate and distinct from the physical universe as we know it.

The physical universe would be the universe of matter, energy, space and time. It would be the universe of the planets, their rocks, rivers and oceans, the universe of stars and galaxies, the universe of burning suns and time. In this universe we would not include theta as an integral portion, although theta obviously impinges upon it as life. From the first letters of the words matter, energy, space and time, we can composite a new word: MEST.

In Dianetics we are dealing then with theta and MEST. Theta is thought, life force, *élan vital,* the spirit, the soul or any other of the numerous definitions it has had for some thousands of years.

As soon as we separate these two entities, a host of problems heretofore quite complex resolve into simplicity. Theta, we could say, comes from the universe of theta, which is different from the

MEST universe. Theta has its own matter—ideas; it has its own energy and the characteristics of that energy; it has its own space of operation, as distinct from MEST space; and it has its own time.

There is an enormous amount of evidence to support theta as a postulate. Thought is instantaneous in the MEST universe so far as can be discovered. The flow of energy along nerves in an organism does not travel at light speed. Time and past, of the MEST universe, do not exist for theta.

Considering theta one finds that it, alone of observable energies, motivates and activates MEST matter and energy through space and time. Further, it computes, reasons, learns and retains what it learns. Men, building a computer with electronics which would do only a part of what the human mind can do, would have to use enough electrical power to light New York City, enough cooling system to absorb Niagara Falls, and enough vacuum tubes,[3] if they cost a cent apiece, to run up a bill of a million dollars. And the apparatus so rigged, under the existing life term of tubes, would run a split second before stopping for tube replacement. The human mind does more than such a clumsy machine, does it better, lasts a lifetime and, to cap it, is portable.

Now all a student of Dianetics needs to know and understand about all this is that theta plus MEST equals life; that theta and MEST have a natural affinity for each other and combine, linking the two universes, so to speak; that theta and MEST coming together too hard get into a turmoil which we call pain; and that the turbulence of theta and MEST under the duress of too much impact gives us a Tone Scale.

Theta crushed too hard into MEST becomes *entheta*. MEST impinged upon by entheta becomes *enMEST*. Entheta is simply a

---

3. **vacuum tube:** a glass tube normally one to six inches long and containing little to no air (a vacuum), formerly used extensively in radios, televisions, computers and other electronic devices to regulate and control electric currents or electronic signals necessary to the operation of such equipment. Because air is resistive to electrical flow, a vacuum is created in the tube so that electricity can flow inside of it.

compound word meaning "enturbulated theta." And enMEST is another word meaning "enturbulated MEST."

Consider that theta in its native state is pure reason or at least pure potential reason. Consider that MEST in its native state is simply the chaotic physical universe, its chemicals and energies active in space and time.

The cycle of existence for theta consists of a disorganized and painful smash into MEST and then a withdrawal with a knowledge of some of the laws of MEST, to come back and smash into MEST again.

MEST could be considered to be under onslaught by theta. Theta could be considered to have as one of its missions, and its only mission where MEST is concerned, the conquest of the physical universe. MEST is under raid. Theta is doing the raiding.

Theta survives by conquering MEST and retaining the conquest. Theta may have numerous other methods of survival but they do not apply to this particular physical universe where we are situate.

The survival of theta depends, as it applies to this universe, on changing MEST and organizing MEST.

Life is a manifestation of theta-conquered MEST. Theta has conquered and organized with high complexity certain MEST chemicals and energies into life forms. These forms are very diverse. They progress from the lowest orders, such as the lichens and moss, through the entire vegetable kingdom, through the animal kingdom and up to man. Each form evolved from the initial impact of theta against MEST, and each form on a higher level is supported by lower-level forms.

Without the lichen and the moss to make soil, no plant life could grow. Without plant life converting sunlight and chemicals into cellular food, no animals could live. Without the array of life forms below him, man could not support himself as an intelligent organism. Intelligence* would be more or less wasted in lower

---

*INTELLIGENCE: *the ability to perceive, pose and resolve problems. Intelligence and the urge to survive (the dynamic) are both necessary to continued existence. The quantity of each varies from individual to individual and group to group. The dynamics are inhibited by engrams which block their flow of theta, or life force, and disperse it. Intelligence is also inhibited by engrams, which enter false or improperly graded data into the analytical mind.* —LRH

forms. Evolution from lesser forms to greater forms exists in present time* and wholly in present time. Evolution traced back along the time span is evolution traced through the MEST remaining after the theta had passed over it.

Man alone of the animal and vegetable kingdom possesses the potential power of changing MEST in wholesale lots into something theta can use. Man can, by steam shovel and dynamite, move mountains and perhaps—who knows?—conquer a galaxy. Theta thus evolves toward higher and higher reason and a higher and higher ability to conquer and change the physical universe—MEST.

If we grant the cycle of re-creation, growth and decay and the postulate that theta conquers MEST by first impinging solidly into it and learning about it and then withdrawing to come back with what it has learned, we can see that theta learns by becoming enturbulated and then straightening itself out as an endless process. People have known this for a long while—one learns, they say, by hard knocks. That would be a simple way of saying that theta gets painfully mingled with MEST and withdraws to come back for an orderly conquest.

If this is the cycle—and this assumption solves problems which were never solved before—then we can see that theta would have to have a withdrawal mechanism, and so it does. Death is that mechanism. Theta and MEST are attracted to each other but when they become painfully mixed up, they become entheta and enMEST. Entheta rejects MEST. EnMEST rejects theta. Theta combines with theta or MEST. MEST combines with theta or MEST.

Here we have something not unlike a chemical reaction. Two chemicals reside placidly with each other until stirred up. Stirred they blow apart. Or we could liken this to a characteristic of some energies which, when they have their wavelengths changed, reject each other. This is death. Theta and MEST get too enturbulated and the organism dies, the remaining theta rejecting the MEST body,** the MEST body rejecting the theta.

*PRESENT TIME: *the point on anyone's time track where his physical body (if alive) may be found. "Now." The intersection of the MEST time track with the (postulated) theta time track.* —LRH

**MEST BODY: *the physical body. The organism in all its MEST aspects. The MEST body is animate or inanimate, alive or dead, depending on the presence of or absence of the theta body.* —LRH

There is nothing very complicated about this postulate, even though it solves a great many problems. One could say that when life becomes too painful, the body sickens and withers and the soul departs.

Man has for many ages inclined to a belief in free theta. Science became very unpopular when it sought to break down and abolish, by logarithmic decree,[4] the human soul.

However, we do not need a human soul to explain the theta-MEST separation called death even though evidence is growing—good evidence of a highly scientific nature on a much more practical level than parapsychology—that the human soul does exist in fact.* Recently at a major university a group of well done experiments demonstrated that living organisms had about them a field of energy which had a point source. If the energy radiated from the cells alone, according to past theory, the picture presented would have been quite different. Free theta, then, could be postulated to exist. The usual genetic line of generations begetting generations of like organisms explains, in accepted biological terms, the traverse of theta through generations.

It seems inevitable that, as theta conquered MEST and made it into higher and more complex organisms, the problem of getting enturbulated theta and MEST separated for the next generation would be resolved, at last, on an intellectual level and within one generation; theta mastering the problem of smoothing itself out within the organism itself. Actually, at a swift glance, this is Dianetics.

The defeat of death entirely is not wholly desirable. Evolution is set up to provide better and better organisms, better able to survive. Without death, all existing planetary space would soon be glutted with life which could not be supported. Death can take no holiday. But life can be much more effective at least for the species called man.

The cycle of conception, growth, decay and death, according to our postulate of theta and MEST, would be the cycle of

*A man very high in the Catholic church once said to me, "Young man, if you are not extremely careful, you will wind up by contacting the human soul as such and measuring it in ergs and dynes." —LRH

4. logarithmic decree: by mathematical or scientific decree. Logarithm is a mathematical term and a decree is an authoritative decision or order having the force of law.

"The cycle of conception, growth, decay and death,
according to our postulate of theta and MEST,
would be the cycle of pleasure-and-pain learning
by which the organism is refined so
that the new generation it begets is better
able to cope with the environment and
conquer MEST than was the older generation."

pleasure-and-pain learning by which the organism is refined so that the new generation it begets is better able to cope with the environment* and conquer MEST than was the older generation. In one lifetime, there is much accumulated pain. The cells are subjected to pain by continual forceful contact with MEST as in accidents or collision with other life forms. The whole organism as an organism is subjected to pain with every defeat in its efforts to fulfill its purposes of survival by a conquest of MEST. By pain the cells learn new methods of construction for better survival. Out of organism pain, the organism learns new skills and methods of surviving.

The hitch has been that once an organism was subjected to pain, it accumulated some knowledge but it also accumulated some entheta and enMEST. When it had accumulated enough to be highly ineffective it died, leaving the next generation to carry on. For a man, this is not efficient. There is nothing wrong with his learning by pain and pleasure what is bad and good about existence, but there is a great deal in error with his having to carry with him an excess of entheta and enMEST which hide knowledge from him and cut down his ability to function in his proper role.

Inevitably a high form of life could be expected to resolve this entheta–enMEST problem without an intervening death cycle.

The enMEST–entheta turbulence is called in Dianetics an engram. An engram is an area in time when theta and MEST have come forcefully together and have intermingled "permanently."

A small boy falls and hits his head. He is for an instant unconscious. As soon as he gets up he may think he has a complete memory of what happened to him. But there is an instant which is occluded from his consciousness. That instant contains a turbulent area of entheta and enMEST. A tiny bit of his theta and a small portion of MEST have become a part of his unreasoning mind. This moment is an engram.

There are two minds, for our purposes. One is the analytical mind, the other is the reactive mind. The analytical mind is where

---

*ENVIRONMENT: *all conditions surrounding the organism from the first moment of present-life existence to death, including physical, emotional, spiritual, social, educational and nutritional.* —LRH

theta coordinates and reasons for the organism. The reactive mind is where theta and MEST have become enturbulated. The analytical mind operates by reason. The reactive mind operates by reaction.

The reactive mind, having a different polarity than the analytical mind, has the capacity of compelling or inhibiting the organism in regard to certain of its actions. Lower forms of animals have this as their main method of thought.

The reactive mind was once called the "unconscious" mind. It is a tough, rugged mind which is alert during any moment of life, regardless of the presence of pain, and which records everything with idiotic faithfulness. It stores up the entheta and enMEST of an accident with all the perceptics (sense messages) present during the "unconsciousness" resulting from the accident. Thus the small boy who hit his head on the rock knows analytically that he fell and hit his head, perhaps, but he "knows" better with his reactive mind. Supposing the smell of dust was present in the accident. The reactive mind stored the perceptic of the smell of dust. The boy one day happens to be weary and to smell this identical smell. He becomes a little nervous. This is the reactive mind telling him to react and get out of here because when this smell is present, one gets a bump on the head. That is not logical, but that is the way the reactive mind operates. If the boy does not leave the area and the smell of dust, the reactive mind turns on the pain, in an effort to force him to leave. Finally, the boy learns to avoid the smell of dust because when he is tired this smell makes his head ache. He does not like the smell of dust, because, to the reactive mind, the smell of dust equals a bump on the head.

With an analytical mind, the organism can think complex thought and is aware of being alive. With the reactive mind, the organism reacts in accordance with data received during the highest threat to survival—unconsciousness.

So long as the reactive mind functioned in organisms which had not evolved language it was a very workable mechanism. When an animal was injured, his reactive mind picked up all the perceptics regarding this injury—sounds, smells, tactile, sights—and whenever these appeared in the environment of the animal his mind would make him run or fight. Thus he was safeguarded by past moments of pain. It is a sort of shotgun method and has a thorough workability which, while it would deny the animal pleasure at times, at least kept him alive in a tooth and claw environment. When man evolved his analytical mind into a high enough level of action to need language, trouble set in, for the reactive mind could also contain words. Words heard during moments of unconsciousness, such as those spoken during operations or around a very ill or severely injured person, are faithfully recorded along with their pain. Like hypnotic suggestions, these recordings can be brought into play by a similar word or environment and cause the individual to act as though in the presence of danger. Restimulated by the environment, these past moments of physical pain and unconsciousness force the individual into obedience.

Engrams, these moments of pain and unconsciousness stored in the reactive mind, act like hidden command posts in the mind, forcing the individual into patterns of thinking and behavior which are not called for by a reasonable appraisal of the situation. But the engram is not reasonable. It is simply a recording which has the sole purpose of steering the individual through supposed but usually nonexistent dangers.

Until Dianetics, the engram was not suspected for it was well hidden as an entity. The word, *engram,* is an old one, borrowed from biology. It means simply, "a lasting memory trace on a cell." It may be engraved on more than the cell. But, up against Dianetic processing, it is not very lasting.

Here, then, is a piece of entheta–enMEST—the engram. MEST and theta, coming together too forcefully, as in an impact or injury, or getting enturbulated through illness, are stored in the reactive mind and from there mechanically enturbulate the theta of the analytical mind into compulsive or obsessive action or enturbulate the MEST of the body into pain, deformity or psychosomatic illnesses (chronic somatics, as they are called in Dianetics).

Accumulate enough entheta in the reactive mind, and the analytical mind becomes aberrated enough to commit suicide or to undertake nonsurvival activities in order to remove the organism from the world of organisms and let another generation take up the work. Let enough enMEST accumulate in the reactive mind and the MEST of the body will enturbulate into pains and illnesses which will kill the organism and serve the same purpose.

This, then, is the basic assumption on which we are operating in Dianetics. The assumption is a workable postulate in that its application produces very advantageous results. The relatively sane person becomes more sane. The psychosomatically ill become well. The unhappy become able to obtain pleasure and lead happy lives, and we have a chance to bring about enough sanity amongst men to stop the mass murder of war. We can resolve the usual problems of behavior and set up a better organization.

The person undertaking to process another individual Dianetically is seeking only to raise the "tone" of that individual—in other words to increase his survival potential. In order to do this, the processor simply regains for the other the theta involved in the reactive mind as entheta. Theta is restored to the analytical mind, the reactive mind is left without its destructive store of turbulence and the individual being processed becomes a Dianetic Release or Clear.

Column A on the chart is graduated as a Tone Scale. Actually this scale has many more heights and levels than those we can now measure and use. How high it actually goes we have no way of knowing at this time. For our purposes, it is put to use here between the levels of −3 and 4.0.

At −3 we have simply MEST, a dead body in whatever state of decay it might be. It is different from other MEST only in that it has been organized by theta into new chemicals and compounds, for MEST is evolved into new complexities by theta just as organisms are evolved by theta.

At −1, for a short time after death, we have body cells alive. Some of these cells live for as much as a year after organism death, according to some investigators. This is, in any event, the band of cellular life, as different from organism life.

At 0.0 we have death at the moment the theta withdraws from the organism.

From 0.0 to 2.0 we have the band of operation of the reactive mind. Between these points on the Tone Scale, the reactive mind is in command of the organism. The reactive mind, in this band, directs the organism according to stored engrams and the analytical equivalent of the engram, the lock.

From 2.0 to 4.0 we have the band of operation of the analytical mind.

Above 4.0 we could postulate other mind levels such as the aesthetic mind, through other minds, to the free theta mind, if such things exist.

This Tone Scale shows the current level of survival of the organism. It shows also the potential of survival in terms of longevity of the organism (unless processing intervenes, of course).

The higher the individual is upon the Tone Scale, the better chance he has of obtaining the wherewithal of living, the happier he is, the healthier his body will be.

Actually a person fluctuates on this scale from hour to hour and day to day. He receives good news, he goes momentarily to tone 3.0. He receives bad news, he may sink for a moment to tone 1.0. He falls in love and for a month he is at level 3.5. His girl leaves him and for a week he is at tone 0.5. When he is very young he rides around tone 3.5. As he grows older his tone drifts down to 2.5. As an old man he may drift down to 0.0 and death, either slowly or swiftly.

We are interested mainly in the average level for the individual for the period of life we are addressing. The average is fairly constant. An individual's average place on the chart can be gauged by inspecting the other columns. Thus he may be an average 2.7 on the Tone Scale and yet reach 3.5 on occasion, and yet sink to 0.5 on other occasions but only for a short time.

TONE 4.0

TONE 3.5

TONE 3.0

TONE 2.5

TONE 2.0

TONE 1.5

TONE 1.1

TONE 0.5

The constant position on the Tone Scale is determined by three factors. The first is the accumulated entheta in the person—how much of his theta is enturbulated in engrams and analytical locks and so strikes back against him, forcing him into nonsurvival activities or compelling him or inhibiting him in environments containing imagined dangers.

The second factor is the amount of theta the person has as life force. This would be his volume of theta. It is the third dimension on the chart. Terror is fear with lots of volume. One person has more volume of theta than another and can thus stand to have more enturbulence, more engrams. One may have so little native theta that half a dozen engrams will convert it all into entheta, leaving the person insane. Another may have so much theta that thousands of engrams still leave him with enough actual theta to go on living a productive life in the 2.0-plus zone.

The third factor is a ratio between the analytical mind and the reactive mind. An individual may have a reactive level of 1.0 and an analytical level of 3.5. The result is that when he is in a restimulative environment he may be covertly hostile but in a more favorable environment he may be analytically very productive. These two minds average out to a constant.

All the person doing processing—an auditor, he is called in Dianetics—needs to know about this Tone Scale is that it gives the percentage of theta of the case which by engrams and locks has become chronically entheta.

To raise a person on this Tone Scale it is only necessary to recover or convert theta from entheta. Remove, in other words, the stores of turbulence from a person's life or render them unrestimulated.

An auditor is not trying to cure anything. He is simply raising tone. Incidental to raising tone, psychosomatic ills commonly vanish and aberrations* disappear. But this is incidental. The task is to make a human being happier, more effective, better able to

---

*ABERRATIONS: *irrational behavior or computation (thinking). They are stimulus-response in nature and may be prosurvival or contrasurvival. The engram is the basic source of aberrations.* —LRH

accept responsibility and aid his fellow man. That the person being processed gets "well" in the period and stays "well" is a bonus.

Anything which raises a person's tone can be considered legitimate processing. This includes, of course, nutrition, environment, and education, as well as processing. Simply taking the person to see a movie he wants to see may raise his tone. Processing achieves permanent raises in tone. If it is illegal anywhere to process people, then it must also, sequitur,[5] be illegal to make people happy. And if laws exist against making people happy, somebody had better overthrow that government, quick. For it is a death government, so entheta that it will bring about the death of the state and those within it.

---

5. **sequitur:** something that sequentially follows another thing or a conclusion that logically follows something already stated or mentioned; connected as in thought, speech, etc. *Sequitur* is a Latin word which means "it follows."

CHAPTER TWO

COLUMN B

DIANETIC EVALUATION

THE GOALS OF DIANETIC PROCESSING
form a graduated scale. Actually this scale is also the scale of sanity, for there is a parallel between the amount of life force (theta) in the individual available for his survival and the amount of sanity he displays. Turbulence of this life force decreases not only his sanity but his level of survival. The life expectancy of the individual is also proportional to his physical well-being (absence of factors which predispose him to illness) and his mental well-being.

In other words, Dianetic processing is directly concerned with increasing the ability of the individual to survive, with increasing his sanity or ability to reason, his physical ability and his general enjoyment of life.

As we look at this scale, we are also looking at the emotional tones of the individual as he reduces an engram. There is a very direct relation between this scale and natural performance. As the individual reduces an engram under processing, he may find it in an apathy tone; as he recounts it the second or third time, he is found to be hostile to the personnel in the engram but will not express that hostility. Then he begins to get angry with the personnel who have done this to him. The anger fades to antagonism. Then he becomes bored with the whole thing. Further recounting brings him into a cheerful frame of mind about it and finally he simply laughs over it. It was this sequence of behavior, of an engram being reduced with processing, which gave the clue to the existence of these points on the Tone Scale.

At the top of the chart we have levels of possible well-being which we have not yet explored and which, while we have hopes, cannot at this time be reached. Our technology does not extend as far as derivation and observation say the individual may be able to go. In this range from 4.0 to 40.0 on the Tone Scale lie many possible states of being. What is the theta being? How much can man attain toward spirituality? How can full theta perceptics* be best uncovered if they actually exist? These are some of the questions. The technology may possibly be developed which will permit man to reach a higher state than he can now attain by our current techniques of Dianetic processing.

The highest point we can at this time reach with Dianetic processing is what is called here the MEST Clear. There are probably several kinds of Clears and several conditions of being Clear. A MEST Clear would be an individual who no longer retained engrams or locks, these having been erased by Dianetic processing. The erasure of all engrams and locks in an individual restores to him a full play of his endowment of theta. His store of theta may or may not be increased by other means. That would be a matter for solution above this level on the Tone Scale.

A Clear in Dianetics, then, is simply one whose engrams and locks are erased and who does not become confused, obsessed or impelled by past moments of physical pain. This goal is far, far beyond anything envisioned by such investigators as Freud. There may be goals far beyond the state of MEST Clear.

Currently a Clear will do. Psychometry and all tests for aberration demonstrate the Clear to be unaberrated. His recalls are excellent. His mental stability is very good since environmental circumstances cannot cause him to act irrationally by reason of aberrations. His emotion and ability to enjoy life is free. By

---

*THETA PERCEPTICS: *communication with the theta universe. Such perceptics may include hunches, predictions, ESP at greater and lesser distances, communication with the "dead," perception of the Supreme Being, etc.* —LRH

becoming a Clear the individual attains an intelligence quotient far in excess of what he enjoyed before processing.

A Clear does not instantly grow wings or sprout a ten-kilowatt[1] aura. He is not superman. But he has his advantages. He has fewer accidents, and none because of his own doing. He is healthy. His education and experience are available for his use as he needs them. He acts on reason and he reasons swiftly. His reaction time is about half the normal's. What his longevity is we have no way of knowing at this time but we can only suppose that it is higher than if he had remained aberrated.

A general tendency is to regard a Clear as a sideshow piece. True, he is better than men have ever been before. But too much emphasis has been laid upon mental tricks a Clear may be able to do, his ability to recall accurately, his ability to see again anything at which he has gazed. In the business of living these things are not important.

Happiness* is important. The ability to arrange life and the environment so that living can be better enjoyed, the ability to tolerate the foibles of one's fellow humans, the ability to see the true factors in a situation and resolve problems of living with accuracy, the ability to accept and execute responsibility, these things are important. Life is not much worth living if it cannot be enjoyed. The Clear enjoys living to a very full extent. He can stand up to situations which, when he was not cleared, would have reduced him to a shambles. The ability to live well and fully and to enjoy that living is the gift of the Clear. Anyone looking for tricks can best find them in vaudeville.

The Clear has the advantage of not retaining, hidden from himself, pain and painful situations in his past which, being restimulated by the environment, enturbulate his reason and

---

1. **kilowatt:** a unit of electric power. The word *kilo* means 1000 and a kilowatt is 1000 watts. A watt is a measurement of the rate of flow of energy, that is, how much electrical energy is flowing per unit of time.

*HAPPINESS: *the overcoming of not unknowable obstacles toward a known goal.* —LRH

sicken his body. The Clear is produced simply by erasing all the engrams and locks—the pain and painful moments of the past. He is the current goal of Dianetic processing.

He is called a "Clear" because his basic personality, his self-determinism, his education and experience have been cleared of aberrative shadows.

Actual experience demonstrates that man, once socially imposed controls and domination by others have been cleared away, is basically good. He is evil only when he is aberrated. Reduction of his aberrations discovers man to be well intended toward his fellows. The highest reason, in this world of complex interdependencies, depends upon the highest cooperation of the individual with his fellows and his environment and a constructive attitude toward life. The more aberration (engrams and locks) cleared from an individual, the more independent and the more cooperative he is.

There are four valid therapies, if we wish to use the term loosely. First there is Dianetic processing. This rids the individual of the pain and painful emotion which aberrates his reason. Second there is education. This indoctrinates the individual with the culture* in which he lives and gives him the skills of survival, better enabling him to survive. The third is changing his environment into one which is less restimulative, is happier for him and in which he can better survive. This would include nutrition, medical care and recreation. The fourth is regulating the amount of MEST which the individual should control. He can be given less if he has too much, he can be given more MEST if he has not enough for his ratio of theta, or the MEST which he is trying to control may be changed for him into another kind of MEST (sublimation).

All four of these therapies do the same thing: they enhance the survival of the individual by giving him better tools of survival,

*CULTURE: *the pattern (if any) of life in the society. All factors of the society, social, educational, economic, etc., whether creative or destructive. The culture might be said to be the theta body of the society.* —LRH

better conditions in which to survive, better reasons for surviving. Any of these do one basic thing: they raise the individual on the Tone Scale. The reward of survival being pleasure, for instance, giving the individual pleasure raises his survival level. However, the last three of these are relatively ineffective if the individual has aberrations against pleasure or changing his environment or learning from life, and so we come to the conclusion that the first step toward a higher survival level would be ridding the individual of his aberrations. Within reasonable limits the rest should follow.

The auditor who is doing processing regularly and has been trained for it will use any method to raise the tone of his preclear, for when the tone is raised, processing is easier. About all one can do with a thoroughly apathetic person is raise his tone by one of the last three methods; that done, he can be processed.

Thus we have the current final goal of processing: the Clear. This is the long-range goal. It is not swiftly reached. It is reached, evidently, only by very good auditing and in the hands of an auditor who is somewhat higher on the Tone Scale than the preclear.

A considerably nearer goal is the Dianetic Release. The Release has reached a point where he no longer has psychosomatic illnesses, where he has good stability and where he can enjoy life. If one simply took all the secondary engrams off a case, one would have a Dianetic Release. The Dianetic Release is a very high above normal and, itself, has not been attained before by any past known methods of therapy. The psychometric testing of the usual Dianetic Release shows him to be in very superior mental condition.

An even nearer goal to the start of processing is the very high normal. By this is meant a person who is well above the current level of average intellect and behavior. One attains, in processing, levels one is capable of reaching by reason of genetic endowment, education and current physical potentials. One becomes the best that can be made of what one is natively. Thus, a moron by genetic endowment would reach the level of moron when processed—but he would have been, by reason of aberration, around the level of idiot when he started. An average intellect, by processing, reaches a level of stability and capability very high above the average. Hence, to reach a very high normal, one would have had to be not too much below average to begin. The use of the term *average* or *normal* is susceptible to considerable misunderstanding. It simply means the average of the population's intelligence and ability. It is remarkably low in the United States compared to what it could be. But the United States' average is considerably higher than that, for instance, of Panama.

The next level is boredom. This is borderline between what is called neurotic and what is called normal. Moderate but unused ambition, a state of mind toward life which is not discontented nor yet contented, a purposelessness in living, these mark this stratum. It is a rather sorry stratum, actually, but it is so superior to what lies below it that the auditor who can get an anger case up to boredom considers he has done very well indeed, and so he has.

Below this level we have the level of overt hostility. Here is the occasional grouch, the complaining individual who yet makes no mistake about what he finds wrong. The "blunt, honest" type who tactlessly tears up the tenderer feelings of his companions is found in this band.

At 2.0 we cross the borderline between the reactive mind and the analytical mind control. And just below this we get the anger band. Here is the person of rather continuous hatred. Here we have impulsive and destructive action.

Below anger we go into a slightly sorrier level, covert hostility. Here is the person who hates but is afraid to say he hates, who deals in treachery and who yet expects to be forgiven. At the lower end of covert or hidden hostility we have the continually frightened person, the individual ridden by fears, the person who is afraid to be or to own anything.

A far more serious level is the apathy level. Here is the suicide. Here is the person who has lost so much in life that he cannot raise to any situation but simply gives up about everything. If the auditor can bring the apathy up to covert hostility he has accomplished a rise in tone. But overt acts by the auditor are likely to drive the apathy case down toward complete paralysis or death itself. This is a very dangerous state of mind, bordering next door to death.

Finally we have the lowest band of organic life, pretended death. Some animals have developed pretended death into a survival mechanism. Pretending death says, "I am not dangerous. I am dead. Go away and leave me alone." The soldier on the battlefield who suddenly becomes paralyzed is using this mechanism. Some races, the Chinese in particular, descend into this stratum and actually die as a form of suicide self-willed. The auditor who can get a pretended death case to open and close its eyes is achieving remarkable results.

Finally we have the band below death and the MEST body and on these we can do nothing, of course.

The rightest right a man can have is to survive to infinity. The 0.0 level is death. How wrong can a person be? Dead!

The higher a person can rise on this scale, the righter he is in terms of reason, in terms of survival and in terms of general well-being. The higher he is, the happier. The lower he is, the sadder.

The whole intent of processing is to raise the individual from lower to higher strata on this scale.

C O L U M N   C

PHYSIOLOGY AND BEHAVIOR

Under this column we have data which is considerably more complex than any other section of this book but which is of considerable interest to biologists and other scientists. The auditor need not suppose he needs to know it by heart, or even understand its terms.

What one should understand about this column is that it gives a clue to behavior and to physiology in an individual or, in reverse, permits the auditor better to locate his preclear on the chart—which, indeed, is the purpose of many of these columns.

There are three main actions by which life handles itself and MEST. These are (1) Attack, (2) Retreat, (3) Neglect. These are broken down into their relative positions on the Tone Scale.

Tone	Behavior	Physiology
4.0	Motion toward, swift approach	Full control of autonomic by cortex, both craniosacral and thoracolumbar systems of autonomic functioning at optimum under direction of cortex; muscle tone excellent; reactions excellent; energy level high.

Tone	Behavior	Physiology
3.5	Motion toward, approach	Moderate control of autonomic by cortex; craniosacral functioning well, thoracolumbar slightly depressed; muscle tone good; reactions good; energy level moderate.
	Motion toward, slow approach	Autonomic functioning independent of cortex; craniosacral functioning well, slight activity in thoracolumbar; muscle tone fair; reactions fair; energy level fair.
3.0	No motion, stay	Autonomic independent of cortex; craniosacral functioning well, but no activity in thoracolumbar; muscle tone, reaction time and energy level poor.
2.5	Motion away, recede slowly	Autonomic begins to take over control; craniosacral inhibited, thoracolumbar up; slight restlessness, heightened activity, wavering attention.
	Motion away, recede quickly	Increased activity thoracolumbar, craniosacral more suppressed; increased restlessness, wavering of attention, inability to concentrate.
2.0	Motion toward, slow attack	Increased activity of thoracolumbar; inhibition of craniosacral; irritability; increased heart action, spasmodic contractions of gastrointestinal tract, respiration increased.
1.5	Motion toward, violent attack	Full autonomic mobilization for violent attack; complete inhibition of craniosacral, thoracolumbar in full action; respiration and pulse fast and deep; stasis of gastrointestinal tract; blood to peripheral vascular system.[1]

1. **peripheral vascular system:** a reference to the peripheral blood vessels of the body. *Peripheral* as used here means located at or near the surface of the body; away from the central part. *Vascular* means pertaining to vessels that convey bodily fluid such as blood around the body, and *system* refers to a related body of organs that cooperate in performing vital fundamental functions.

Tone	Behavior	Physiology
1.1	Motion away, slow retreat	Autonomic settles down to chronic rage reaction; inhibition of craniosacral; imperfect gastrointestinal action; increased peripheral vascular circulation; increased pulse and respiration.
0.9	Motion away, violent flight	Autonomic mobilization for full flight reaction; laxity of gastrointestinal tract; all blood to peripheral vascular system, especially muscles for rapid flight; breathing and pulse rapid and shallow.
0.5	Slight motion, agitation in one place, suffer	Autonomic mobilized for cry for help, grief; craniosacral on full; thoracolumbar inhibited; deep, sobbing breathing; pulse hard and irregular; discharge of tears and other bodily secretions.
0.1	No motion, apparent death	Shock reaction; thoracolumbar inhibited; craniosacral full on, gradually decreasing as organism approaches death; breathing shallow and irregular; pulse thready; blood pooled in internal organs; muscles limp, lacking tone; pallor.
0.0	Death	Cessation of organic function.

C O L U M N   D

PSYCHIATRIC RANGE

THE AUDITOR SHOULD KNOW THREE psychiatric terms, the only psychiatric terms he will find used in Dianetics as they are used in psychiatry.

These terms are: (1) *psychotic,* (2) *neurotic* and (3) *psychosomatic.*

Psychotic is really not a noun but an adjective. However, psychiatry uses it as a noun to mean an individual afflicted with psychosis. A psychosis is any major form of mental affliction or disease. In other words, a psychotic, so far as we are concerned, is an individual who cannot handle himself or his environment well enough to survive and who must be cared for to protect others from him or to protect him from himself.

The psychotic state which receives the most interest is that one which threatens the survival of the individual himself or of those around him. Such a psychotic is placed in an institution—when there is room for him. Otherwise, he roams the town or country. However, many other persons are psychotics but are not sufficiently alarming as a menace to themselves or others to be placed in an institution.

The next classification is simply a matter of degree. The neurotic individual is one who is afflicted mentally but can perform some reasonable function or other.

The term *psychosomatic* has meant an illness caused by or notably influenced by "the emotional state of the patient." Actually, more practically, one could say that it is an illness caused by the mind. About 70 percent of man's ills are psychosomatic.

In Dianetics we use these terms as follows:

Psychotic: A person who is physically or mentally harmful to those about him out of proportion to the amount of use he is to them.

Neurotic: A person who is mainly harmful to himself by reason of his aberrations, but not to the point of suicide.

Chronic somatic: A psychosomatic illness, since it is discovered that psychosomatic illness is only the restimulated somatic of some engram and goes away when the engram is contacted and reduced or erased.

As for other psychiatric classifications, these are famous, even to psychiatry, for their looseness and disorganized state. One institution, for instance, handles schizophrenics only, and so any patient who comes there is simply classified as a schizophrenic. Psychology has long laughed at psychiatry because psychiatric terminology described some manifestation and led to no cure. This was because psychiatry did not know the cause of any manifestation and could not cure either the cause or the manifestation.

This current chart gives a scale by which psychosis and neurosis can be accurately classified and described for the first time. However, Dianetics does not need a more complex terminology than it has. Definition of individual tone level by numbers, plus the citing of obviously manifested engrams, give adequate clue to what should be done for the preclear.

The individualities of psychosis and neurosis are occasioned by the engrams of a particular psychotic or neurotic. These peculiarities of behavior have as their root certain engramic commands—words contained in past moments of pain and unconsciousness. An engram can bring about a manic state wherein the individual declares hysterically and continually that he is happy or strong and yet is very low on the scale. Such a condition is brought into view by the auditor inspecting the chart for various other manifestations of the preclear. Any one column or characteristic of the chart can be altered by one pattern of engrams or severe education, but the other portions of the chart will remain constant for that level. For instance, as in the case of a manic engram, the individual appears to be happy at first glance, even says so repeatedly. But further inspection demonstrates that this person is very shy, that he gives presents to buy people off, that he is given to suspicion and hurtful lies about people. The manic engram commands a tone 3.5 be manifested, but this does not alter the position of the preclear on the chart.

This is not very complicated and it is very important. To establish the level of sanity on the chart, the auditor must only locate the level which contains a majority of the manifestations of the preclear. Almost every case will have a place on the chart which does not hold true on the chart for the majority of characteristics named. In other words, look for the majority of characteristics, the level where the preclear is found in most of the columns. Do not be upset if the preclear fails to hold true in one or two columns. A chain of engrams may command a manic or a depressive aspect in the preclear for a particular subject or column. Engrams which command, for one subject on the chart or one characteristic in life, a tone *lower* than the actual tone of the preclear may be hard on the preclear but they have a certain safety factor for the auditor. It is the manic, which commands by engrams a higher tone in one or two columns than the actual tone, that is dangerous; for then the auditor may try to use a level of processing too high on the chart for his case. If in doubt, work the preclear a tone or two lower than you estimate him by the chart. The potential manic-depressive psychotic can be hammered into a psychotic break by being worked too forcefully too high on the chart.

A saving grace in diagnosis is that a manic-depressive is not always a manic or above tone but is often depressive and well below tone.

None but a qualified auditor has any business working with a psychotic. The danger in handling psychotics is very great. This danger did not originate with Dianetics. From the beginning of man's efforts to solve the riddle of insanity, the psychotic has been a great liability to the practitioner. The percentage of psychotics who commit suicide during ordinary treatment is vastly larger than the percentage of suicides of psychotics during Dianetic processing. The conclusion one reaches is that psychotics commit suicide easily. They commit suicide oftener when in the hands of other practitioners than in the hands of those who know Dianetics. In the case of insanity almost any excuse is acceptable to the law. The inept practitioner who has just lost a patient to suicide for the thirty-ninth time can lean back, look learned and grave and say, "Well, he came to me too late. If I had had him a couple of months earlier, I could have saved him." This alibi is not recommended to auditors, if for no other reason than that it is quite shopworn. Besides, no Dianeticist to date has ever had occasion to use it and probably never will.

When a person drops below the 2.0 level he has so much entheta compared to his theta that a sudden shock may simply enturbulate the remaining theta and send him into a psychotic break. When all the theta is enturbulated, its reaction is to kick apart theta and MEST, in other words, cause death and remove the organism from the path of other organisms. Suicides are assisted normally by engrams which specifically command suicide. But suicide is a natural manifestation, apparently, a fast means of separating theta and MEST and gaining death quickly. Suicide is always psychotic.

People below the 2.0 level, no matter their avowed intention, will bring death or injury to persons, things and organizations around them, if in the anger bracket, or death to themselves, if in the apathy bracket. Anyone below the 2.0 level is a potential suicide. The fascist, for instance, is almost always, in the face of any severe reverse, a sure suicide, fascism being below the 2.0 line.

A psychotic is a threat to death for somebody or something, if not for himself. A manic-depressive, sometimes cheerful and apparently only neurotic, is actually very low on the scale and may suddenly commit suicide without any real warning.

The psychotic is a definite liability to the auditor, not so much because of processing or what unskilled processing may do, but because some factor may come suddenly into the environment of the psychotic which causes him to commit murder or suicide. This can then be laid to the processing. Every such action on the part of psychiatric patients is forgiven psychiatry as a natural consequence of handling psychotics. Handle one gently and keep him out of a nonsurvival environment and the psychotic may be very successfully treated by Dianetics. But do not be amazed if your preclear seems cheerful today and goes into a psychotic break tonight and commits suicide tomorrow, after murdering the family. Below 2.0 on the Tone Scale we have theta and MEST trying to kick apart and bring about death.*

*One of our most brilliant Instructors, David Cary, in the Los Angeles Foundation, had married, long before Dianetics, a psychotic girl. He went into Dianetics first trying to help her. He persuaded her to take a course with him at the Foundation. He tried in every way he could to give her processing but as she was actually there under protest she would not accept processing from him. Cary went on to become an Instructor, having an excellent background for teaching and a skill in it, while she separated herself from him. She was not obviously psychotic, although the training department at Los Angeles had refused her as far below student caliber on the grounds of her psychometry and a former suicide attempt and was only persuaded to take her as a favor to Cary. Some time later, in an effort to bring her some relief, Cary took a leave of absence and went home. There he was murdered by his wife, who then committed suicide. His devotion and his efforts to assist her had been unmistakable. She had been intensely inaccessible. He had been told many times by his friends in Dianetics that she was dangerous. But that danger was hidden. Cary's devotion cost him his life and cost Dianetics a brilliant Instructor and a man well loved by all who had a chance to know him. This footnote is included here not simply as a memorial to David Cary, but as information which will give pause to husbands or wives who are seeking to assist a psychotic spouse. Husband and wife auditing is difficult at best, the partners being usually very restimulative to each other. As husband and wife they will do better to make an arrangement for auditing with another couple. If one of them is psychotic, they should seek the best professional auditor Dianetics can give them. —LRH

Further, in treating psychotics, always remember that one is working with minimal theta present and maximal entheta. Thus, a sudden shock may so restimulate an engram that the remaining theta enturbulates and vanishes, leaving a lock composed of entheta. There goes sanity. Approach the lock gently and turn it back into theta with great care and caution.

No mixture of Dianetics with old treatments or practices of any kind are recommended to the auditor. Electric shock has been found to lay a severe engram into an already overcrowded reactive mind and is not truly successful in any way, other than making a few patients so apathetic that they are barely acceptable to society. Psychosurgery, removing pieces of the brain, has long been acknowledged an entire failure so far as any actual "cure" is concerned. Free association is a long-drawn-out procedure which, although it has had some success in rehabilitating patients who were not too near the bottom of the Tone Scale, is in the long run of questionable value. Restraints and cold packs only succeed in shocking the patient into a deeper state of lethargy. Do not condone such methods nor permit them to be used on your preclears, for the simple reason, aside from their inhuman aspects, that they do not work; they only sap the remaining stamina from the patient. Why cling to old-fashioned and even barbaric methods, when Dianetics provides surer, more effective and humane techniques?

Handle the psychotic gently. Respect his rights to a whole brain and a future. Do not consider that he is your toy or your experimental animal for vivisection or strange sadistic "treatment." Above all, when you are auditing, be a civilized human being. Don't try to punish your patient because he "refuses to get well." His engrams and general turbulence make your preclear very hard to reach. His basic personality is in there trying to help you. Smooth out entheta and make theta out of it and do it as gently as you can. Don't lose your temper or resort to drastic methods. Be civilized. Man can be handled only with reason, not by Hitlerianistic force. You can't beat a man into sanity. If you feel so exasperated by a preclear that you would like to scold him or hit him, stop the session and go cool down. Don't fill him full of sedatives or put him in restraints. By being as gracious and serene as you possibly can be, you will greatly increase your success in treating your fellow man. And you have to be first cousin to a saint to get the best results with psychotics.

Any effort made to hammer a patient or scold a patient into sanity will meet with failure. The proof of that is the 19,000,000 insane, institutionalized or at liberty, in the United States alone. Don't be convinced that you have rights of ownership or life-and-death powers over your fellow man. Leave that to the accomplished authoritarians, of whom we, unfortunately, have so many.

Be a human being and you'll get good results.

CHAPTER FIVE

COLUMN E

MEDICAL RANGE

THE MEDICAL DOCTOR A SHORT time ago seldom thought of his patients in terms of mental disorder. Recently he realized that some 70 percent of man's ills are of mental origin—which is to say, psychosomatic illnesses account for a high majority of sicknesses.

In addition to those commonly listed as psychosomatic illnesses many others must be suspected, because of another factor. Bacterial infection itself is assisted by the presence of engrams. Thus the percentage is possibly much higher.

The engram assists bacteria and viruses in this fashion: the physical injury (the enMEST of the engram) resides in a certain portion of the body, that portion which was injured. Let us say an engram is received by reason of a severe chest injury. This engram may not become active for many years. But keyed in then, it brings about a chest weakness in that the blood and endocrine fluids tend to avoid the area as though it were just now injured. Into this weakened area may come bacteria of one kind or another such as those of pneumonia or tuberculosis. This is a temporary infection. But now the area is restimulated by the pain of the infection and so the engram is further keyed in and reinforced, and the area of the chest cannot become resistant enough to throw aside the infection. Thus we get the chronic infections, the lasting illnesses.

Technically one can say there are three phases in a disease: (1) predisposition, (2) precipitation and (3) perpetuation. The engram accounts for these in that it renders an area of the body, or an organ such as the heart, weak, then by the key-in of the engram brings about the illness and finally, because the keyed-in pain keeps on being restimulated, makes the illness continue.

As far as injuries are concerned, engrams apparently cause the accident-prone. The engram may command the person to injure himself or others. One such engram restimulated in a preclear caused him to "unwittingly" injure his hand severely three times in one week. The engram was found and reduced and the preclear has not since injured that hand. Thus accidents of major and minor character may be chalked up to engrams. A command in an engram such as "I always have to hurt myself" will cause the individual to do just that.

The endocrine system is very sensitive to thought and is under the control of thought. A doctor who attended a series of lectures on Dianetics at length came forward and, rather disturbed, said, "For forty years of study and practice I have been using the standard concept that structure controls function. I finally see what you are saying. It is the other way around. Function controls structure. Now maybe we can solve a few more problems."

Endocrine imbalances such as reduced thyroid, overweight, reduced sexual capability, sterility and numerous others are monitored by engrams. The proof of this is simply that when engrams are reduced the glandular imbalances tend to correct themselves. Also, engrams reduce the acceptance by the body of artificial hormones, for when engrams are reduced artificial hormones can be administered with benefit.

There is a direct index between the amount of entheta in an individual and his physical health. This is manifest when one examines the state of health of the psychotic. A pretended death case is almost impossible to keep alive. Apathy cases starve and develop illnesses and cannot resist the smallest infections, just as grief shocks are so often followed by illness. The covertly hostile individual is usually a hypochondriac, is continually developing illnesses which even he knows to be false. The anger case suffers from all manner of ills, particularly arthritis and other illnesses which settle as chronic somatics and develop deposits, which enlarge glands, which alter the condition of the heart, and so forth. From there on up the scale, the less entheta and the more theta, the greater the physical health of the individual.

As an example, a young girl was in a hospital recovering from appendicitis. She was running a fever, a very serious thing in such a case. An auditor was called in and by a few questions found out she was stuck on the time track* in an earlier mumps engram. He brought her up to present time and the temperature dropped to normal within the next ten minutes and recovery then proceeded uneventfully.

A usually well but temporarily ill person slides down the Tone Scale because of temporarily restimulated engrams. Getting him into present time will often materially shorten any course of illness.

Another part of Medical Dianetics is the Dianetic Assist. Any very recent engram can be run with impunity. Picking up engrams of injuries which have just happened demonstrably shortens the term of recovery and increases life potential threatened because of the accident. Shock occasioned by operations and accidents is rendered less dangerous, according to Dianetic observation, by the Dianetic Assist.

In Preventive Dianetics, the first rule is to maintain silence around an injured or ill person. This prevents the engram from having words in it and reduces its dangerousness markedly. Several hospitals now practice this. Doctors in other hospitals would find their work much easier and more successful if they would simply make standard the practice of complete silence around operating tables.

🐟

----

*TIME TRACK: *a representation of the fact that a person exists during a period of* MEST *time. The present-life time track begins at the first moment of recording and ends at present time, or at death, and it includes all consecutive moments of "now" and the perceptics of those moments. The theta body evidently has a* MEST *time track of its own.* —LRH

THE BASIC LAWS OF THETA AFFINITY-REALITY-COMMUNICATION

THERE IS IN DIANETICS A TRIANGLE of great importance. Theta, the energy of thought and life, has as primary manifestations affinity, reality and communication.

This is the peculiarity of theta: in lieu of the cohesion, matter and force laws of the physical universe (MEST), thought (theta) has to have affinity, reality and communication to survive. MEST requires certain laws to survive—or obeys those laws in the business of surviving. Energy and matter in space and time hang together in a certain fashion, governed by certain laws. The discovery and use of those MEST laws make up the science of physics. Theta also hangs together in a certain fashion, and the discovery and use of those laws make up the science of Dianetics.

We do not know nearly as much about theta as we know about atoms and electrons, the probable parallel entity in the physical universe. Electrons, protons, neutrons and various other parts of physical universe energy flow at certain speeds and, in various combinations, exist and function in the physical universe. There is, for instance, the speed of light; there is the composition of atoms and molecules. Theta probably has various similar laws, and at this time we do not know much about them; but we know enough to know that there is a difference between theta's laws of function and those of the energies in the physical universe.

Primary amongst the laws of theta is that it has a fundamental goal, the changing of MEST. It changes MEST by constructing it into mobile units we know as life organisms and, through those, making MEST into various forms and objects or destroying those forms and objects.

Theta uses an evolutionary scale in present time. Lower forms of life support higher forms of life. We have thought of evolution in the past as something stretched out back down the eons, as a graduated scale of various species which changed as the ages progressed down to our present life forms. This concept of evolution has many limitations and gaps and is not very workable. In Dianetics, using the theta theory, we see that all theta is actually in present time and that no action is possible except in present time and that present time is a continuing series of instants in which, moment to moment, theta goes on changing MEST. It is not very complicated to see that right here in present time we have evolution operating. The lichen and moss convert crude MEST ash and rock into soil. On this soil higher forms of plant life can grow.

Vegetable life, however, is not very mobile. Theta animates organisms which are composed of theta and MEST. But trees change very little MEST. Thus, following up the scale, we find theta involved with making animals and insects. And the larger animals, unable to live on soil and sunlight, live on vegetable forms which are themselves the converters of soil and sunlight into comestibles for higher forms.

As soon as we get up to the very complex forms of life such as the mammal, we find a very large amount of MEST being converted. When we arrive at the level of man we begin to see that theta can create or destroy vast forms of MEST.

A man damming a river and installing a hydroelectric plant is, for his own survival, changing MEST. Another man turning a switch and lighting an electric bulb is shifting and altering MEST.

Theta, on this chain of evolution right in present time, exists in a state which can change a very great deal of MEST. As we learn more and more about MEST we can change more MEST. And as we learn more about theta we can control and change more MEST. The atom bomb is a case of changing a great deal of MEST in a direction which defeats a great deal of theta—thus we consider the bomb wrong. It fails to enhance survival.

Man can reasonably change large amounts of MEST. Therefore he can be considered a sort of intermediate goal. Lower life forms cannot change MEST on any grand scale. Man, potentially, can build or blow up planets. Man will evolve into more than man, probably. Educationally, he evolves a long distance when he begins to understand something about his own purpose of being.

The cycle by which theta understands MEST is a very simple one. Theta impinges heavily against MEST. This causes a turbulence. But from that confusion theta extracts some tiny law of MEST and withdraws to apply to MEST this newly learned law for the conquest of MEST. No knowledge exists without a primary enturbulation. MEST is conquered by theta taking successive laws of MEST and turning MEST against MEST to change it.

Theta, with this mechanism of turbulence, can learn much about MEST. But if theta is going to be embroiled with MEST in a disorderly fashion, then theta must have some means of becoming unenturbulated so as to profit by what it has learned through the confusion. Theta has to be able to withdraw in order to come back for an orderly conquest of MEST, using the laws of the physical universe to conquer the physical universe.

The basic mechanism theta had in the past was death. The cycle of creation, growth, decay and death was one and is one which applies to a species as a species, to an organism as an organism, or to a group of organisms. The only way theta could get free, evidently, was through death.

With the advent of a science of thought, whereby some of the natural laws of theta are understood, man can in one lifetime disenturbulate his theta and MEST and benefit from the experience gained by the enturbulence. What Dianetics does to longevity has not even been surveyed, but it certainly upsets the evident purpose of the death cycle.

In Dianetics we have much to do with affinity, reality and communication. Whatever the accuracy of the basic postulates, it becomes evident to the auditor as he uses these three points of the triangle that he has a highly useful tool.

The triangle of affinity, reality and communication could be called an interactive triangle in that no point of it can be raised without affecting the other two points and raising them, and no point of it can be lowered without affecting the other two points. The postulated reason for this is that affinity, reality and communication are component parts of theta, and thus affinity, reality and communication are three manifestations of the same thing.

This has a very high usefulness to the auditor. For instance, when his preclear has a very thorough sonic shut-off, the auditor knows that he can regain some sonic either by increasing the present time affinity of the preclear or by raising the level of reality of the preclear. Likewise, if the affinity of the preclear is markedly low, the auditor can raise that affinity by bettering the communication and reality concepts of the preclear. And finally, when the reality of the preclear is low, it can be raised by increasing affinity and communication.

This is highly useful because often the auditor cannot directly discover the suppressor on one point of the triangle. By blowing locks on the other two points he can make this suppressor accessible.

Whether or not one either understands or agrees with the theta–MEST theory of Dianetics, the affinity, reality and communication postulate which derives directly from it is of infinite use.

It is very difficult to suppress the affinity of an individual, his capacity, that is, to receive or give love, without also suppressing his communication and reality factors. Likewise, one cannot suppress the communication factor without also suppressing the affinity and reality factors. And finally, one cannot suppress reality

"The triangle of affinity, reality and communication
could be called an interactive triangle in that no point of it
can be raised without affecting the other two points and
raising them, and no point of it can be lowered without
affecting the other two points. The postulated reason for this
is that affinity, reality and communication are component
parts of theta, and thus affinity, reality and communication
are three manifestations of the same thing."

without suppressing affinity and communication. For instance, a mother telling a child that she does not love it is also forbidding the child to speak and is blunting the child's reality, since the child normally expects to be loved. To tell the child to keep quiet is also to reject the child and is to offend the child's concept of what the real world should contain. Contradicting one of the child's statements or beliefs, which is to say his reality, is also to break affinity with him and to suppress his communication. One cannot touch this triangle at any point without affecting the other two points; and yet each point is highly specific and has its own characteristics.

One must also consider in a discussion of theta that theta is measured on a gradient Tone Scale from 0.0 upwards to 40.0. At the highest range, theta could be considered to be in a pure state. It would be a clear, even-flowing river. It would be reason at its highest. It would be complete rationality. It would be complete reality. It could accomplish complete communication in its own level. And it would be purely affinity.

Descending down the Tone Scale, greater and greater dissonance could be considered to be introduced into theta. The stream, so to speak, becomes more and more tumultuous, more and more fixed within narrow banks, flowing over heavier rocks and then shoals. As a musical analogy, one could say that the note was becoming less and less a pure and harmonious vibration and was becoming more and more off-key from itself.

Descending down the Tone Scale, affinity, reality and communication form in themselves a dissonance one with the other. Also, theta is in more and more tumultuous confusion with MEST. Instead of a harmonious conquest of MEST by theta, one sees, as the Tone Scale is descended toward death, greater and greater turbulence.

The sudden impact of theta and MEST together could be considered a turbulence which creates dissonance in theta. This is registered and recorded as pain. Theta and MEST so impacted together, the characteristics of the theta are changed, according to theory and observation, and theta below 2.0 on the Tone Scale can be considered enturbulated theta—theta which has been confused and chaotically mixed with the material universe and which will lie in this confusion until death or some other process disenturbulates it. Theta below 2.0 we call entheta.

The mechanism here is a simple one. MEST, in a life form, is an orderly array above 2.0 on the Tone Scale; below 2.0 MEST is considered to be confused and enturbulated and is referred to as enMEST.

We could draw a diagram which would show theta and MEST appearing above 2.0 and entheta and enMEST appearing below 2.0. From 2.0 upwards, theta and MEST are more and more orderly mingled until MEST is left behind entirely and theta exists in its pure state. Below 2.0, entheta and enMEST are more and more enturbulated in the life form until the point of death and below is reached.

We could consider that theta gradually reverses polarity as it descends down the Tone Scale toward 0.0. We could consider that MEST reverses its polarity when it rises up the Tone Scale from −3. Entheta has a very repelling effect upon theta and MEST. EnMEST has a repelling effect upon theta and MEST. Below 2.0, MEST and theta are at best turbulently united. Above 2.0, they unite more and more smoothly as they rise up the scale, the MEST more and more under the influence of theta, the theta more and more able to do things with the MEST. Below 2.0, the theta is less and less able to do anything with the MEST. Entheta becomes almost as chaotic as MEST in its pure state.*

*It may occur to someone to ask, "What is the difference between MEST and enMEST, if both are without order or plan?" The answer is both simple and important. Pure MEST may be said to be virgin chaos, entirely innocent of plan. An organism at tone 4.0 may be said to contain MEST harmoniously planned and organized by theta. But enMEST is neither of these: it is neither organized nor virginal; it is confused and embroiled with entheta in a twisted disorganized plan. —LRH

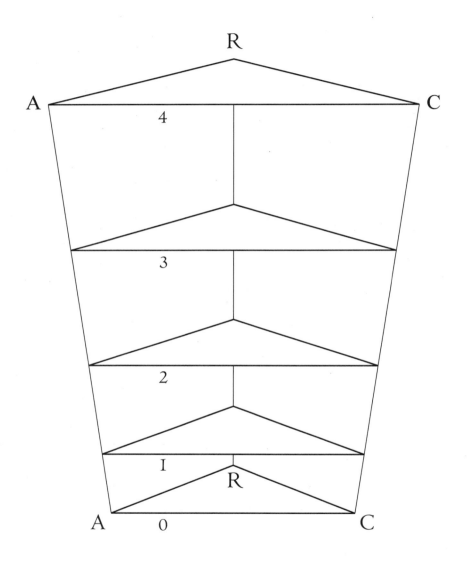

THE TONE SCALE

Affinity, Reality and Communication, the three component parts
of theta, ascend and descend the Tone Scale in unison.

Here is the mechanism of death, then: entheta and enMEST driving out from the organism the remaining theta and MEST.

This is an important postulate in Dianetics, since from this can be derived the entire Tone Scale and all the manifestations of human behavior and aberrations. These postulates are what an engineer calls a highly workable truth—for to an engineer, truth is not the absolute of the metaphysician;[1] it is simply something which has a relatively high workability.

From the theta–MEST theory also may be derived an explanation of faith healing—which is more than an explanation, being a very workable tenet for the auditor. It has been many times noted in the course of man's adventures in the realm of mental and physical healing that one individual or another, merely by his presence, or an area, by its sanctity or the belief of people in it, could accomplish the nearly entire de-aberration of mentally or physically ill human beings. In South America there is a church outside of which stands a small mountain of crutches cast away by cripples who became well merely by approaching the altar; and in Bethany, some years ago a man named Lazarus came forth from his tomb.

It is an axiom in Dianetics that a sufficient quantity of theta brought into proximity with entheta will disenturbulate the entheta and convert it into theta. This is important enough to form the basic axiom of processing. It explains to the auditor why he cannot take a psychotic who has practically no remaining theta and successfully send that psychotic into the entheta of an engram. The remaining theta of the psychotic would itself merely become enturbulated, not being sufficient in quantity, and the psychotic could theoretically become worse.

----

1. **metaphysician:** a person who is familiar with metaphysics or who creates or develops metaphysical theories. Metaphysics generally means that branch of philosophy that is concerned with the ultimate nature of existence or the nature of ultimate reality. Metaphysical expressions such as "Everything is part of one all-encompassing spirit," "Nothing exists except material particles," "Everything is a dream and nothing really exists outside our minds," have occupied various schools of metaphysics for centuries.

Thus the second axiom: Entheta in sufficient quantity brought into proximity with theta will enturbulate that theta.

Here we have a matter of quantity. When there is a great deal of theta present, a lesser amount of entheta will disenturbulate and become theta. But when we have more entheta present than theta, the theta is likely to become entheta. This is the contagion factor of aberration. Theta itself could be called reason; entheta could be called unreason. Reason in sufficient quantity brought into the presence of a lesser quantity of unreason will cause reason to prevail. Unreason in sufficient quantity brought into the presence of a lesser quantity of reason will cause that reason to become unreason. Hence the restimulative character of processing to the auditor. Hence the various kinds of processing which must be used on various cases.

The purer the theta, the more MEST will be attracted under it. Theta attempting a conquest of enMEST will become in itself enturbulated. Entheta applied to MEST will make it into enMEST.

Entheta will tend and act in the direction of death. EnMEST tends and acts in the direction of death. Theta tends and acts in the direction of survival; and MEST tends and acts in the direction of survival when it has been conquered in an orderly fashion, in an organism or by a theta organism.

As an example of entheta consider the thief. A thief is chiefly entheta and prefers enMEST to MEST. A thief will make enMEST out of the MEST he steals, which is to say cloud its title and possibly injure its form or substance. EnMEST, possessed by theta, has a tendency to enturbulate the theta. Thus, an honest man attempting to own a confused and dishonest property will himself become enturbulated.

A whole series of axioms and optimum conduct codes can be derived from these principles.

It is also observable that a high-theta-volume individual can conquer and handle more MEST than a low-theta-volume individual or an entheta individual. The psychotic, for instance, will ruin any

MEST he contacts, whereas the highly reasonable man will enhance the MEST he contacts.

Here also we apparently have some small clue as to what "luck" is. MEST moves in automatically under good theta. MEST moves out from under entheta.

When we speak of affinity, reality and communication we are talking about the three component parts of theta. These three quantities in combination playing upon MEST give us the manifestation we might call computation, or understanding. One has to have some affinity for an object, some communication with it and some concept of its reality, before he can understand it. His ability to understand any thought or object depends upon his affinity, his communication and his reality. All mathematics can be derived from affinity, communication and reality playing upon MEST.

Because affinity, reality and communication are three component parts of the same thing, namely theta, it would be difficult to increase one component without increasing the other two.

The physical universe and what we have called the theta universe* are each based upon the principle of survive and succumb. So far as life is concerned, everything above the 2.0 level is survive, and everything below the 2.0 level is succumb. Above the 2.0 level, the organism tends toward life; below the 2.0 level, the organism tends only toward death. The dynamics could actually be considered as theta applied to various subjects and in different manifestations.

Any individual, even an aberree, has occasional moments of being Clear. When he is not restimulated—when his engrams, locks and secondaries are not forcefully restimulated by his environment—the theta gradually disenturbulates, and he becomes possessed of a higher level of reason. Most people reach 3.0 part of the time, as a normal course of events. Some people, in rare

---

*THETA UNIVERSE: *thought matter (ideas), thought energy, thought space, and thought time, combining in an independent universe analogous to the material universe. One of the purposes of theta is postulated as the conquest, change and ordering of* MEST. —LRH

instances, behave and reason like MEST Clears. Hardly anyone has failed to have moments when he approximated the condition of Clear. Being Clear is a state of being possessed of all available theta, which in an aberree would be partially trapped in engrams and locks. The ordinary person, with his engrams and locks, is rarely in the happy and reasonable state of a Release or a Clear. The Release or Clear is in that desirable state rather constantly; but this does not mean that the Release or Clear are not, in the presence of an overwhelming amount of entheta in the environment, susceptible to enturbulation, for they are. They, however, do not greatly retain the enturbulence, and as soon as they are free from such an entheta environment they restore immediately to a cleared state. Further, they do not depress very far down the Tone Scale. This case is very different from that of an individual who has relatively little theta left to enturbulate and who in even a mild entheta environment sinks rapidly down the Tone Scale. It is a question of resilience and recovery ability, as well as the ability to reason constantly and clearly in most situations.

The chart should be read with the understanding that nearly everyone who does not have to be put away in a sanitarium, wholly bereft of his senses, has some available theta. There are many persons possessed of a high volume of theta but whose aberrations bring them down chronically below the level of 2.0, who can yet function, having some theta available. These people enturbulate rapidly. There are many people who are not classified as psychotic ordinarily, who demonstrate considerable quantities of theta, and who yet, on some slight setback, enturbulate rapidly down to 1.1 or 0.5 on the Tone Scale and remain there for some time after the enturbulence. These people, rested and not in immediate contact with the restimulative situation, regain some of the theta from the turbulent area.

The strength of the dynamics of an individual could be considered to be determined, first, by the native volume of theta possessed by the individual and, second, by the impeding effect of his engrams, as restimulated in the environment. One could, then, have a very high dynamic individual who yet has so thoroughly aberrated that on the least setback he would fall rapidly down the Tone Scale below 2.0. People like this, having high dynamics, attempt naturally to conquer a great deal of MEST, but in the process of conquering it are enturbulated by the MEST, the society and the environment, so that they accumulate enormous quantities of locks. And if such a person has, hidden within him, many engrams, these will rapidly become charged, and the person will become highly occluded and intensely aberrated, but will yet be able to function sometimes on a creative and constructive level.

The system of dynamics is a method of subdividing the theta of an individual to show how much theta he has available in any one sphere of activity. These divisions could be made as follows:

First: the dynamic of self, the urge for individual survival, reason toward individual survival for one's self;

Second: the dynamic of survival through sex and children;

Third: the urge to survive through groups, as a member of the group, or for the survival of the group itself;

Fourth: the urge of the individual to survive for mankind, or the urge of all mankind to survive;

Fifth: the urge of the individual to survive for life, or of life to survive for itself;

Sixth: the urge of the individual to promote the survival of MEST, either for his own benefit or for the benefit of MEST itself (manifested in the preservation of property, as such, no matter to whom it belongs);

Seventh: the urge of theta to survive, the urge of the individual to promote the survival of theta and to survive through the survival of theta.

Any of these dynamics can be broken down into the three component parts of affinity, communication and reality.

THE FIRST DYNAMIC

THE SECOND DYNAMIC

THE THIRD DYNAMIC

THE FOURTH DYNAMIC

THE FIFTH DYNAMIC

THE SIXTH DYNAMIC

THE SEVENTH DYNAMIC

On the first dynamic, one has the affinity for self, the concept of the reality of self and the ability to communicate with memory of self.

The second dynamic would concern itself with the affinity for a mate or children for the future of a race, the communication with a mate or children and a concept of the reality of these.

In the third dynamic lies the affinity of the individual for the group, or the affinity of the group for itself; the ability of the individual and the group to communicate; the general reality or agreement existing in the group and between the individual and the group.

The fourth dynamic, as ARC, would mean the affinity of the individual for all man, and of mankind for the individual; it would include the communication of man with man, and the reality concepts or agreements of man with mankind.

The fifth dynamic would include the affinity of the individual for life, or the affinity of life for other life; the ability of life to communicate with life or with the individual; and the concept of agreement and reality of life.

The sixth dynamic would include the affinity, communication and reality of MEST as itself, within its own laws as expressed in the physical sciences; but more important for our purposes, the feeling of the individual for MEST, to know it, to use it and to preserve it.

The seventh dynamic would be that of theta itself, which is composed in its component parts, according to our postulates, of affinity, reality and communication.

C O L U M N   F

EMOTION

E MOTION COULD BE CALLED THE energy manifestation of affinity. They are listed in two columns because emotion may be treated as a subdivision of the more general subject of affinity.

Emotion is not synonymous with life energy but is evidently only a part of one of the points of the triangle of affinity, communication and reality. Emotion, however, furnishes an obvious index to the psychic state, and is the quantity most easily observed by the auditor. As used in Dianetics, emotion could be called the index of the state of being.

The development of a new science naturally means the development of many new terms; and as new data is discovered, old definitions are often found to be inadequate. Thus it is with emotion. In the English language "emotional" is often considered synonymous with "irrational." One often hears the statement "Don't be so emotional, be reasonable." This would seem to assume that if one is emotional one cannot be reasonable. No more unreasonable assumption could possibly be made.

Engrams have, each one of them, their own emotional tones, just as each engram has a somatic. This is a false emotional tone which is foisted upon the aberree in lieu of the natural and reasonable emotion. Because emotion has a strong manifestation and because the less desirable kinds of emotion are displayed by people in highly tense states, emotion has been clouded as a desirable quantity.

A fully reasonable human being displays the emotion called for, rationally, by the circumstances with which he is confronted in present time. Thus if the present time circumstance requires grief, a rational and reasonable person is apt to display grief. If the present time situation demands anger, the rational human being will display anger.

Irrational emotion could manifest itself irrationally for any given situation. If the present time circumstances required grief and yet the individual displayed no grief, this would be irrational. If the present time situation seemed to indicate, because of happy circumstances, happiness, and yet the individual remained apathetic, this would be irrational.

Emotion, then, is neither rational or irrational except as it is displayed. An aberrated person seldom displays the type of emotion rationally called for by any given circumstance. To describe this we would actually need a new word, perhaps *misemotional*. Such a word would indicate that a person did not display the emotion called for by the actual circumstances of the situation. This would indicate that his aberrated condition caused him to display an emotional reaction inappropriate to the present time situation. Being misemotional would then be synonymous with being irrational. Being emotional, however, would indicate, if the emotionality agreed with current circumstances, a rational state of being.

One can fairly judge the rationality of any individual by the correctness of the emotion he displays in a given set of circumstances. To be joyful and happy when circumstances call for joy and happiness would be rational. To display grief without sufficient present time cause would be irrational.

Engrams, and the generally aberrated state of a being, generally deny emotion. Happiness and cheerfulness being the very trademark of survival, one could expect with considerable justification that as an individual became more and more aberrated he would be less and less able to be happy. Such is the case. From happiness, at the top, down the dwindling spiral through anger, grief and apathy to no reaction whatsoever would run not only emotion but the life potential of the individual. And thus we have a direct index of measurement of the aberrated state of the person.

One must remember that even a very aberrated person, in relatively unenturbulated present time moments, has considerable free theta. The fact that a person enturbulates readily, for instance, to the 1.1 level and thus reacts along that level does not mean that every waking moment finds him reacting on such a level. Until he is entirely psychotic because of present time enturbulation, he quite ordinarily demonstrates a great deal of free theta. The danger of his condition does not lie in the fact that he is always psychotic; it lies in the fact that when he becomes enturbulated, his existing free theta, which itself is capable of happiness and reason, will enturbulate down the Tone Scale to 1.1. As this individual lives longer and becomes more aberrated, when a trying situation confronts him, a situation which enturbulates his free theta, he will drop not only to the 1.1 level but below that, to the 0.5 level. Once the dwindling spiral has set in, from year to year the environment of the aberree remaining more or less unchanged, he can be expected, when enturbulated, to drop lower and lower on the Tone Scale. Dianetics can interrupt this dwindling spiral; it can restore free theta to the mind; it can erase the traps which wait for the individual when his free theta is enturbulated. Thus, a person who is a Dianetic Release or a MEST Clear is extremely resilient. Trying present time circumstances do not form heavy locks. He has no irrational reasons to experience grief or fear, but when present time circumstances strongly call for these emotions, he will display them, and yet soon afterward be fully recovered. The only thing which can enturbulate his theta and cause him to drop any distance down the Tone Scale momentarily is some circumstance in the immediate environment strong enough to influence and affect him. A person who has been freed of engrams, secondaries and locks should not be expected to remain in a state of idiotic cheerfulness in the face of any and all circumstances. This in itself would be a very aberrated type of conduct. There are certain manic individuals who do this, and they, unfortunately, are quite insane.

One of the primary things which Dianetic processing does is free the emotions of the individual so that he can experience emotion ranging from happiness, eagerness and exhilaration, down to anger, fear and grief, when these emotions are called for by present time circumstances.

Emotion is a primary index of the Tone Scale. This does not mean that emotion is all there is to theta. Emotion is used as a primary clue to the auditor of the preclear's position on the Tone Scale because it is so easily recognized. The two gradient systems, however, on the margin of the chart, one from zero to 1000, and the other from –3 to 40.0, are both arbitrary number systems. The zero-to-1000 scale exists so that psychometric percentiles can be computed on the chart. The –3 to 40.0 is the original Tone Scale of Dianetics. This original scale is preserved because it is handy for the auditor to use and is a basic part of Dianetic terminology. One quite commonly hears auditors speaking of a "1.5 case," meaning a case in chronic anger or one which enturbulates easily into anger. Or one may hear an auditor speak of a "2.5 case," which tells his indoctrinated listener that this case is rather bored with the whole thing but is fairly well advanced and comes up easily to what is known as "false four."*

The Tone Scale is not a derived scale, but one which has been constructed after observation of many preclears. An auditor can very easily observe this. Suppose he discovers his preclear to be in anger tone as he runs an incident. The auditor can expect that the anger will generally, on one recounting, abate; and on the second recounting, that the preclear will begin to express resentment; on

*FALSE FOUR: *the laughter and gaiety which the preclear exhibits when he has thoroughly exhausted an incident of charge. There is nothing really "false" about false four, except that it is often of very short duration.* —LRH

the third recounting, or fourth, or fifth, the preclear may come to boredom; then to indifference; and on subsequent recountings, rise up to perfect cheerfulness about the incident. If the auditor were to discover an incident where the preclear was in the deepest apathy, the tone of the preclear would be seen to rise during auditing through the whole span of the Tone Scale, step by step. First, the preclear would be in very deep apathy, not knowing or caring whether this incident would resolve or not. He would then go up the scale to apathy, then to grief. He would express some fear and apprehension. He would become sullen. Finally, he would become angry. Then he would express resentment, and through boredom, would gradually rise up to what is known as "false four."

Not all incidents, of course, find the preclear going up the scale step by step. He follows exactly the same scale, but he may skip or omit various stages of the emotion. Thus, starting an incident at grief, the preclear may come to boredom, and thus to complete carelessness about the incident.

Thus, the Tone Scale is based upon observation. It is a very valuable index to the state of an engram. If the preclear enters the engram in anger—is made angry by it, that is—the auditor knows that the incident will be relatively easy to run on up the line. But if the preclear is found to be in very deep apathy, the auditor knows that he has a long way to travel with this incident before he can bring the preclear entirely out of it up the Tone Scale.

Finding the preclear in a deep apathy in an incident should alert the auditor to the fact that he must handle this situation with the greatest care, that he must request subsequent recountings very gently, so that the apathy will gradually rise, with repeated recountings of the incident, up to grief; so that the grief can release and so bring the preclear up to the top of the scale, concerning this incident.

The emotional Tone Scale introduces something else as an auditor's tool. When the auditor discovers he cannot run grief out of a case, he should examine the preclear's bank a little more carefully to discover what emotional tone he *can* turn on in the preclear, since he can turn on at least one emotional tone. If he cannot turn on grief, he may be able to turn on anger; and once he has taken some of the anger off of the case perhaps he can run some of the lower levels such as fear. Having run several incidents which have fear in them, the auditor may discover that he can run grief off the case. Sometimes a case will fall so easily into an apathy that the auditor has to be very alert in order to unburden some of the higher-level emotions before he attempts to run the incidents of deepest apathy which he finds in the case.

As a working rule, an auditor can always find *some* emotional tone to run on a case. He should make it his business to discover what emotional tone is easiest to run on the case and run some incidents of that tone. Naturally, although it does considerable good to run happy incidents on a case, thus raising the preclear's tone, a new enturbulence is likely to suppress the preclear down into his original state. However, there have been instances when merely running happy incidents on a case recovered sufficient theta from the lower strata of tones of the scale that sufficient attention units were recovered to turn on sonic and visio. This trick of running pleasure moments is easily the best way to get a preclear up to present time. One runs the pleasure moment just as though it were an engram, and the attention of the preclear can be attracted to this incident so strongly that attention units are recovered.

Emotion is an integral part of every engram; but it will stand by itself in what is called a "secondary engram." There are actually three kinds of secondary engrams: affinity break or enforcement engrams; reality break or enforcement engrams; and communication break or enforcement engrams. These are called secondary engrams because they do not contain physical pain but depend, for their permanence, on a physical pain engram earlier in the bank. Thus the words *secondary engram* mean a highly charged* moment in the

---

*CHARGE: *the accumulation of entheta in locks and secondaries which charges up the engrams and gives them their force to aberrate.* —LRH

analytical mind of the preclear which depends for its force on a physical pain engram lower in the bank.

In running secondary engrams, or painful emotion, the auditor can develop considerable skill. One cannot, for instance, bluntly demand grief, nor can one bluntly demand fear. Considerable skill and tact are required to contact the necessary incident to resolve the case.

It is a working rule of the auditor that a case must be always unburdened of some emotion. Only cases in a very high range of the Tone Scale can have physical pain engrams run on them without running some secondary engrams.

If one could run off from a case all painful emotion—all expressed resentment, anger, fear, grief and apathy—one would have a Dianetic Release, whether he touched physical pain engrams or not. This is theoretically true but practically almost impossible, since, when he starts to run various secondary engrams, the auditor will often find the case sliding back into the supporting physical pain engram, which must then be run.

Running the painful emotion off a case produces the most signal improvements that are obtained in Dianetic processing.

CHAPTER EIGHT

COLUMN G
AFFINITY

IN VIEW OF THE FACT THAT THE WORD *love* has at least two outstanding meanings in the English language, a misunderstanding could result if it were employed to represent this factor in theta.

Affinity is a broad term and means simply a sympathy of feeling, an affection, the feeling of one person for another, as we use it in Dianetics. Affinity, in the theta sense, Dianetically might be compared to cohesion and adhesion in the physical universe, as applied to energy. There are degrees of affinity, according to our definition, as represented by the Tone Scale. These range from a feeling of well-being along all the dynamics down the various stages of emotion to severance of feeling from any and all of the dynamics. Affinity broadly includes emotion.

The Tone Scale of affinity, as represented on the chart, refers to the reaction of the individual at any particular time to just one or to a small number of people. But as affinity is suppressed repeatedly, the individual will begin to take on an habitual level on the affinity scale, an habitual reaction to almost all people. This is also true of the affinity scale of groups, and one can find on this scale the tone level of any nation or, indeed, of mankind, for any given period, which would be the averaging out of the general reaction of mankind to mankind.

At the top of the scale, around tone 4.0, the individual experiences love, strong and outgoing; he experiences friendliness;

this is an extroversion of affinity. One commonly finds this in children, who when growing older and receiving rejections and rebuffs, first from one or two people and then from many, will gradually experience the blunting of their affinity.

Around tone 3.0, we have the individual experiencing tolerance, without much outgoing action. The individual at this level will accept advances offered but does not readily make such advances himself.

Around 2.5, the individual begins to neglect persons, or people in general. He may even dislike them as a general rule and attempt to get away from them.

At the level of tone 2.0, the affinity is expressed as antagonism, a feeling of annoyance and irritation caused by the advances of other people toward the individual. Love is received with suspicion; it is seriously questioned and may gain as its return distaste.

Around 1.5, affinity has almost reversed itself. Its dissonance has become hate, which can be violent and is so expressed. Love offered to such a person may excite him into violent acts of repulsion. Here, actually, we have a factor of entheta repelling theta, since theta itself contains, as one of its components, love.

Around 1.1, we reach the level of covert hostility. Here the hatred of the individual has been socially and individually censured to a point where it has been suppressed, and the individual no longer dares demonstrate hate as such. He yet possesses sufficient energy to express some feeling on the matter, and so what hatred he feels comes forth covertly. All manner of subterfuges may be resorted to. The person may claim to love others and to have the good of others as his foremost interest; yet, at the same moment, he works, unconsciously or otherwise, to injure or destroy the lives and reputations of people and to also destroy property.

Below 1.0, we reach fear, which is expressed on its highest level as acute shyness, stage fright, extreme modesty, being tongue-tied among other people, being easily frightened by proffered affection. Here also we reach the strange manifestation of the individual attempting to buy off the imagined danger by propitiation. We have an interesting example of this in processing. Cases which are far down on the Tone Scale will, when they reach 1.0, quite commonly offer the auditor presents and attempt to do things for him. A crude description of this was once contained in an idea of transference. At this level we have withdrawal from people.

At 0.5, we reach the level of grief, wherein we have supplications by the individual, his pleas for pity, his desperate efforts to win support by tears. We may even have at this level extremely strange perversions of truth intended to achieve the pity and support of others. For instance, the rejected sweetheart, reaching this level of grief may invent all manner of odd and peculiar incidents of cruelty on the part of the past lover in order to win the sympathy of those around her.

Sinking below grief, one reaches apathy, wherein affinity is expressed by complete withdrawal from person or people. There is, in apathy, no real attempt to contact one's self and no attempt to contact others. Here we have a null point of dissonance which is on the threshold of death.

The auditor has a handy measuring stick with the affinity scale, since he can, by observing the preclear, establish the preclear's attitude toward people or groups and discover the position of the preclear on the chart. Further, by watching the relations of the preclear with others improve, he can see the gradual rise in tone of the case.

CHAPTER NINE

COMMUNICATION AND REALITY

THE OVERALL SUBJECT OF communication covers far more than the exchange of intelligence. Basically, communication could be called the science of perceptions. As general semantics is organized on the subject of words and ideas; so could be organized, and so has been organized in Dianetics the entire subject of perception.

Everything which we know of the physical universe and, possibly, anything which we can know of the theta universe, allowing that it exists, could be said to be embraced by perception, computation and imagination.

By perception, we mean the perceiving of entities or existences. We achieve what we know of reality by perceiving entities and existences in the physical universe, and possibly the theta universe, by combining these perceptions and computing or imagining results not in disagreement with the results obtained by others.

The channels of our perception of the physical universe are twenty-six in number. The most important of these are sonic, visio, tactile, olfactory, kinesthesia, thermal, joint position, body position, moisture, organic perceptions, and, adding one more discovered in Dianetics, perception of movement on the time track. It is with these that the auditor most vitally concerns himself, as it is through these that we learn the most of the physical universe.

With sonic we perceive, by mental mechanism, the sound waves of the physical universe, and by comparison and experience, both genetic and environmental, interpret them.

With visio we perceive light waves, which, as sight, are compared with experience and evaluated.

By tactile we perceive the shape and texture of surfaces and compounds.

With olfactory perception we perceive the minute particles of matter which register as smell.

By kinesthesia we perceive motion through space and time.

By thermal we perceive temperature, hotness and coldness, and so can evaluate further our current environment by comparing it to past environments.

By perceiving joint position we can measure space and the size of objects and know more about our physical situation.

By perceiving body position we sense our relationship with our immediate environment.

Moisture perception permits us to sense the dampness or dryness of the atmosphere and so judge further our environment.

Through organic perceptions we perceive the states of our own bodies, internally.

These and other sense messages combine to make up a body of experience. Just how much of this experience is genetic and how much of it is carried in the theta body,* if that exists, we cannot at this time accurately measure. In our environment, however, by these various sense channels we gain experience and

---

*THETA BODY: *the personal theta entity. The soul. Evidence suggests that the theta body may, through many low tone lives, become an entheta body, but that such an entheta body might be cleared by Dianetic processing. It is probable that the theta body can, in part at least, leave the organism temporarily without causing death to the organism.* —LRH

can act in the present time environment or plan for the future.

It might be said that we have potentially a sensory reception mechanism for every type of sense message which can be radiated or delivered to us from the physical universe and from the theta universe. Thus, we have hearing because there are sound waves which can be registered and interpreted; we have sight because light waves exist to be registered; and so forth. A very interesting paper could be prepared upon the probable evolution of our senses. Theta, combining with MEST to make life, reaches out in its conquest of MEST, via the sense perceptions, to exist within and control the environment and to some degree regulate the future—and, particularly in man, to adjust the environment to the organism, the species or the race.

Just what theta universe perceptics are is a subject at this time so diffuse that one cannot even be sure there is a theta universe. Such manifestations as extrasensory perception, intuition, clairvoyance, clairaudience and others make up a body of quasi-knowledge which is normally relegated to the field of psychic phenomena. The existence of God and spiritual manifestations could be classified as theta universe; contact with these would be considered a use of theta perceptics. Oddly enough, in Dianetics considerable evidence, whether we wish it or not, is accumulating in favor of not only a theta universe and a theta body but of theta perceptics as well. This has proceeded far enough to contain some evidence that certain techniques of application, already partially formed, exist by which the theta perceptics can be cleared, raising the prediction potentiality of the individual, amongst other things. Judging solely on the evidence at hand, one would say that more evidence existed in favor of the theta universe, the theta body and theta perceptics than existed to deny them. This evidence has accumulated to a sufficient extent to cast extreme doubt on the "scientific" postulate that all man would ever know was the physical universe. Indeed, science was unable to resolve mental problems and forecast behavior and invent better human technologies so long as it assumed that life and man rose from compounds and clay of the physical universe, with no other ingredient. This line of reasoning led to no advances in technology and, indeed, permitted the physical sciences to outstrip all knowledge of human behavior. This would seem more or less inevitable, however, if one considered that the primary mission of theta was to conquer the physical universe, at least insofar as the branch of theta which is ourselves is currently concerned. With such a mission, the physical universe would, of course, become the best-known sphere of reality. Perhaps theta is now in a position where it can understand more of itself. By this one does not urge upon the reader that Dianetics concerns itself vitally at this time with psychic phenomena, but it is mentioned in passing that in the course of investigation data continues to accumulate against the idea that man is a creature of the physical universe alone. The auditor, working case after case, cannot but run upon evidence strongly in favor of a relatively timeless theta body existing as a personal identity, running parallel to the genetic line of species; and if he ignores this he may bog down some of his cases. Specifically, I refer to the continuing and growing volume of reports from auditors on the subject of past deaths and past lives. This subject needs to be warily and thoroughly examined; but it remains that the auditor who runs into a past death and does not reduce it properly by Standard Procedure will find his case thoroughly bogged down; and, indeed, some cases cannot be run and will not move on the time track until these factors are taken into consideration. Some of this data has been known for two years, but a diffidence to comment upon it until the evidence was overwhelming has suppressed and continues to suppress the knowledge. As it develops, Dianetics more and more seems potentially able eventually to contact the often postulated but never thoroughly sensed, measured and experienced human soul.*

To unburden a case to the point where the individual is a MEST Clear it is only necessary to work with the avenues of perception to the physical universe.

*The subject of past deaths and past lives is so full of tension that as early as last July the board of trustees of the Foundation sought to pass a resolution banning the entire subject. And I have been many times requested to omit any reference to these in the present work or in public for fear that a general impression would get out that Dianetics had something to do with spiritualism. Further, the view has been many times expressed that in view of the fact that prenatals are so "controversial," the introduction of past lives and past deaths into Dianetics, even as an experimental investigation, would permit old schools of therapy to persist in their delusion that all is delusion. This would hardly be a scientific way of handling a science. A true scientist boldly and fearlessly reports that which he finds. A famous writer told me, a short time ago, a story about Thomas Carlyle, who upon hearing that an American lady writer named Margaret Fuller had said, "I accept the universe," said only, "By God! She'd better!" The auditor who runs his preclear down the track and suddenly finds the preclear possessed of strong somatics and a visio of A.D. 1210 scenery had better reduce the incident as an engram. Failing to get a proper reduction, the auditor had better ask for the incident necessary to resolve this weird manifestation. If the auditor is dull indeed he will invalidate the incident to the preclear and pass up running it, at which point his preclear will bog down. There are evidently three kinds of these experiences: (1) those which are dub-in and which occur only in cases which dub in, in the present life; (2) fantasies built upon reading and imagination, but without somatics; and (3) what seem to be valid and real experiences. If this data of past lives and past deaths in the theta body continues to stand up and becomes susceptible to exacting proof, it certainly threatens to radically alter our culture. At the present time, all we can do is gather evidence. The Foundation would be glad to have any and all such evidence which auditors may discover and care to submit. Never invalidate a past life or a past death, and never fail to run such somatics as actual experiences: failure to observe this enjoinder may seriously harm the case. I have given you this information because I do not believe that helping the auditor to audit and helping cases to run can seriously hurt Dianetics. —LRH

What we conceive to be reality is actually agreed-upon perception of the physical universe. There is an endless philosophic wrangle as to whether or not our perceptions perceive anything, or whether or not our perceptions are merely an illusion themselves. True enough, the physical universe can be reduced down to a zero mathematically. Matter, energy, space and time could be said to be the result of certain motions. The moment we go off into the byroad of wondering whether the physical universe is real or not we come rapidly upon many philosophic imponderables. What we know as reality, however, is an agreed-upon conception of the physical universe in which we live. You and I agree that a table exists in the center of the room; we can see it and feel it, and when we rap it with our knuckles we can hear that something is there. You and I have agreed upon the reality of the table, mainly because each of us agrees that he perceives it via his senses. Should someone come up and say that not a table but a black cat stood there, you and I would consider the man mad. Indeed, by a sort of natural selection we remove such "madnesses" from our society. When someone is in disagreement with the majority as to the sense perceptions of the physical universe, the first reaction of the majority is to have this person pronounced mad and locked up. Locked up, he does not procreate and so breaks the genetic line. This happens often enough to select out of the human race those who do not agree on the nature of the physical universe via sense perceptions. Many amusing and entertaining postulates can be formed on the subject of reality.

Certain it is that by communication—by the group of sense perceptions which make up communication—we know reality. Our affinity with that reality—our admission that we are a part of that reality, and our acceptance of our participation in it—is necessary to our communication with it; and thus we have the triangle of Dianetics: affinity, reality and communication. One cannot stand without the other two. There cannot, for instance, be communication and affinity alone; these two things would result in an agreement of some sort, which agreement would be a reality. If communication exists, some agreement can be reached, and as soon as an agreement is reached between two people or by a man with himself, there is some affinity. If affinity and reality exist, then a communication must ensue or must already exist in order to act as a channel of expression and recognition of the agreement.

An auditor, knowing the trio—affinity, reality and communication—can use any point of the triangle as a point of attack in order to enhance the other two corners of the triangle.

The overall subject of communication, as we have seen, contains all avenues of sense perception: sonic, visio, tactile, olfactory and the rest. It includes, as well, the perception of too strong a contact with the MEST universe—pain, which is itself, less directly, a form of communication. The receipt of perceptions of the real universe and the purpose of theta come about as computation. Computation creates ideas concerning reality, and this creation of ideas leads to the type of communication which is commonly and ordinarily classified as communication—conversation, messages and other methods of exchange of ideas.

The auditor must appreciate the value of communication, since if his preclear cannot communicate with his own past he cannot make an accurate adjudication of his own present and he certainly cannot compute his own future. When a man is unable to contact the reality of the present or appreciate it, and when he cannot compute his own future and act upon that computation, that man is considered in varying degrees neurotic or psychotic. The auditor, then, does well who knows this subject thoroughly.

C O L U M N   H

SONIC

BY THE WORD SONIC IN DIANETICS
is meant sonic recall, rather than hearing sounds outside the body.
Sonic means hearing the sounds which have been remembered.
Those sounds which the individual has heard in the past are all
recorded, either in the analytical standard memory bank or in the
reactive bank. Those which are recorded in the analytical standard
memory bank are all available to the recall mechanisms of the
individual—to his "I."* Those which have been recorded in the
reactive bank have been received by the individual while he was
unconscious—in a hypnotic state, while drugged, while delirious,
while unconscious from a severe injury, or even while unconscious
momentarily because of a light injury. Such perceptics as sonic
were not thought, before Dianetics, to be recorded at all during a
period of unconsciousness. One of the basic discoveries of
Dianetics was that these perceptics were recorded during periods
of unconsciousness of an individual, and that this material was
available for recovery, and that this material, so received and so
recorded, had an aberrative effect on the individual.

Whether the sound has been heard while the person was
awake, or asleep, or unconscious, that sound is available to the
recall mechanism of "I." The fantastic storage capacity of the mind

---

*"I": *the awareness of awareness center. Organisms are aware of their environment. Higher
organisms are aware, also, of this very awareness. The "I" of the human being may be said to be
the center or monitor of this awareness of awareness.* —LRH

has no structural explanation at this time. But every sound, whether a voice, an auto horn, the click of tableware, footsteps, the wind, every sound which the individual has heard in his lifetime is recorded. Thus recorded, it is available to the "I" of the individual. Dianetic technique sends the individual back through his life, and by the perceptics of sonic, visio, and so forth, enables him to recover information which has been occluded from him.

There are very many gradations of the quality of sonic. A case on which there is much grief and other types of charge may or may not have sonic recall. A case which is generally occluded from one end of the track to the other may be so occluded by charge, valence trouble, sonic command shut-offs, or being stuck out of present time, that it has no sonic at all. This condition may be so bad that it renders the individual unable to remember anything that has been said even shortly after it has been uttered, as well as back along the time track. The charge, valence troubles and command shut-offs of sonic may be relatively light, under which circumstances the individual will receive what are known as sonic impressions; he can get impressions of the voice tones in which the words are being uttered, as he travels along the track, but he does not hear the sounds clearly. The case may have, however, so little sonic shut-off, valence trouble and charge that clear sonic, just as it was heard in the first place, is available as the person travels on the time track, as well as in near present time.

Sonic shut-off may be quite selective: the individual may be able to hear sounds but not voices; he may be able to hear an entire symphony orchestra and yet be unable to hear again what his wife asked him to bring home for dinner. Selective shut-offs are caused both by charge on the case and by selective sonic shut-off commands, such as "You cannot hear your wife" or "You pay no attention to me."

A primary concern of the auditor is the turning on of sonic; therefore, he must know what turns it off. According to present theory, which works out relatively well in practice, the most severe source of sonic shut-off is being stuck on the track: in that the individual cannot move on the track, he cannot, of course, move through incidents and hear them. The next most severe interference with sonic comes from valence-shifters: the person's identity is confused with that of another person; he is not in his own valence, and he is off his own time track. The next most severe source of sonic shut-off is the command phrase which says specifically "You can't hear anything," "You never listen to a word I say," "You have to keep still," "I'm as deaf as a post," etc., etc. Sonic is additionally affected somewhat by grief and charge on the case, but not as much as might be expected, since cases which have enormous grief and charge on them in general yet retain sonic recall in the absence of valence-shifters.

The most severe sonic shut-off would be that caused by a combination of factors, which would include not only being stuck on the track in an engram but also having the track itself collapsed by groupers which are active.

There are cases which have fake sonic—sonic dub-in. According to theory, this dub-in is caused by demon circuits, which is to say, heavily charged portions of the analytical mind which have been captured by the reactive mind and do its bidding, walled-off by charge into separate entities. These are very easy to spot, however, since dub-in sonic usually is inane and does not make sense. Furthermore, when the individual with dub-in has gone through an incident once, he cannot return through the incident with the same words. One should not regard a dub-in recall case as something hard to detect; it is very simple, even for the beginner, to detect dub-in, since it will not repeat or bear repetition but alters markedly, and it is not particularly sensible, and it does not run at all like an engram. The dub-in sonic case, after it has been worked for a short time, can be expected to lose the dub-in, once the circuit causing it is contacted. A nonsonic case results. This should not be confused with a case which has sonic but which has experienced severe auditor breaks of the Code, has had engrams run partially but not reduced and has had groupers triggered so that the time track is collapsed. The way to differentiate these is that the case which had dub-in that has turned off will still run as easily and ably on the time track as formerly; from a nonsonic condition, as valences shifters and sonic shut-off commands are run out of the case, sonic impressions will become available, and then sonic itself should return.

The subject of sonic recall is one which requires an enormous amount of study before final adjudication can be made by anyone as to its total ramifications. Experience in Dianetics has demonstrated that recalls in general are very fully recovered by the Clear, and this is true of sonic.

As may be seen on the chart, the gradient scale of sonic does not show it to be a phenomenon by which the position of the preclear on the chart may be established, save only in the broadest sense. The Clear, at the top of the scale, has, ordinarily, full sonic recall. But such may have been his aberrated condition that over large areas of the track his analytical memory bank has received no adequate or sharp recordings. From the moment a person is Clear or nearly Clear, on forward in his life, he will have sonic recall; during his period of aberration, however, he may not have registered sounds here and there on the track.

There is much misunderstanding about sonic and visio recalls in the state of Clear. These recalls are not eidetic in all cases, as photographic or phonographic recall are a matter of training, and a person not trained into them will not necessarily register sights and sounds with sufficient concentration to have all the material available for immediate recall. A very large number of tests must be undertaken on the whole subject of recalls and a great number of cases must be observed before we can clearly and scientifically evaluate recall potentials in every individual when cleared. The recalls, however, are good in those cases so far observed but are not necessarily eidetic.

A person may have sonic recall of an accurate nature at any place on the Tone Scale, providing the person can move freely on the track and is in valence. Ability to recall in sonic is not an index of neurosis or psychosis. Sonic recall is affected by factors which, in themselves, are not such an index. The amount of free theta available for analytical perception and computation is itself actually the only index.

However, in the lower portions of the Tone Scale one ordinarily expects the reasonable person not to have sonic recall or any other recall and one expects the true psychotic or neurotic individual to have sonic recall. This has misled practitioners of the healing arts in the past to believe that sonic recall was only to be found in idiots and morons, an entire falsity based on limited observation.

The influencing mechanism on sonic recall is whether or not the mind has sufficient power (structurally, most likely) to cut off and wall up charge and the general results of engrams and still reserve a portion of the analyzer for free thought with the remaining free theta. The psychotic or neurotic individual does not have the power to reserve for clear thinking some portion of the analyzer, and so, when enturbulated by engrams but still in valence, becomes analytically completely and wholly enturbulated, with no reserved portion of the analyzer not subject to that enturbulation. Where a person has a psychosomatic illness and sonic recall one should expect to find a near-psychotic individual, the psychosomatic illnesses telling of many engrams and the sonic recall stating that the analyzer has not the power to wall up unhappy and painful memories. Where one finds psychosomatic illnesses and a sonic shut-off, one may find a person who is potentially low on the Tone Scale but who yet has enough free theta to respond on a high analytical level—and yet who may perform in life in a very aberrated fashion, for all this.

The thinking on this subject in the past has been entirely too short. The observation has been, in past schools, that a great deal of aberration meant a great deal of thrust and drive and, therefore, that an individual who was neurotic could be expected to perform in the arts and in other directions more ably than a person who was sane. This, by derivation and observation and much experience, is an outright fallacy. The individual with a great deal of free theta is apt to be more robust than his fellows. He may or may not have more engrams; but he tries, from his earliest days, to take in more area than his fellows and to adjust his environment to him rather than follow the sheeplike course of trying to adjust himself to the environment. He is, therefore, continually rebuffed, and his engrams will gradually charge up, by the process of affinity, reality and communication breaks, until he responds rather neurotically to his environment. Such a person is, normally, rather thoroughly shut off so far as sonic and visio are concerned. His theta, what is left of it in a free state, operating in what small portion of his analyzer is still available, is still greater than the theta available to the average human being. When we take this individual and Dianetically process him and turn the entheta into theta, he becomes more and more powerful and able to cope with and adjust his environment. He will not have sonic and visio until he reaches a released or a cleared state. Such individuals are difficult to process only because the mind has so expertly walled itself in from the charge on the case. However, such an individual is very worthwhile to process, since when the auditor has finished, or even if the auditor never does finish, one has left a strong, creative asset to the society. The auditor who, because they seem easy, works near-psychotic or psychotic cases which have sonic, may have when he is through an individual who, no matter if structurally intelligent, is yet possessed of so little theta that his worth to the society is small. These conclusions are highly generalized, but have been borne out in a large number of cases.

Cases exist in which the individual is so unaberrated that, though he is endowed with enough free theta to make him a tremendous asset to the society, he still has sonic and visio, being already at the 3.5 range on the Tone Scale. It is far from true that a person, to be of worth to the society, must be highly aberrated and must have his recalls cut off, since in such an aberrated state he is likely to be so low on the Tone Scale that his positive worth to the society, which would be realized were he at 3.0 on the Tone Scale or above, becomes a liability, and his aberrations violently affect his environment and bring about its destruction. Such persons are the dictators who lead their countries to ruin through war; the artists who, through their grossness and vulgarity, destroy the mores of a race, and so destroy the race.

What the auditor should know, principally, about sonic recall is that it makes a case easier to run, and that a case without it, properly processed, will eventually pick it up. The auditor should never despair of sonic recall shut-off cases; impressions will get stronger; and sonic recall will eventually turn on. But the individual has to be very high on the Tone Scale before he regains sonic, if he began with complete shut-offs. Further, there is a technique, which sometimes turns on sonic, known as running pleasure moments.

Pleasure moments can be run on a case just as the auditor runs engrams, going through the moment over and over again. Attention units are attracted to the pleasure moment, since it is one of the missions of the mind to attain happiness and pleasure along the various dynamics. By returning the preclear to a moment of pleasure and running that moment, the auditor will be able to regain a few attention units out of areas of enturbulence; this will make it a little easier for the preclear to move on the track, and in so moving he may pick up sonic recall. In any event, the running of pleasure moments is highly beneficial to a case.

The running of future pleasure moments sometimes tunes up the perceptics. These are actually imaginary incidents, so far as can be told. The tone of the individual goes up when running moments of pleasure, and so when moments of pleasure existing in the past are run, or when moments of pleasure in the future are imagined, the tone of any individual may be expected to rise.

Affinity breaks often depress sonic; so that a preclear who has sonic on Monday and a quarrel with his sweetheart on Tuesday, may be found to have much less sonic recall on Wednesday. Further, when the sonic recall of an individual is invalidated, his reality is depressed, so the recall reduces. ARC locks and secondaries markedly influence sonic or any other type of recall. Heightened affinity, reality and communication may, by themselves, turn on sonic.

C O L U M N   I

VISIO

RECALLING A SCENE BY SEEING IT again is called, in Dianetics, *visio,* by which is meant visible recall.

There are two kinds of visio which the individual may encounter. One is imaginary visio, by which is meant the scenery which the imagination constructs. The other is actual visio, by which is meant recall of actual and authentic scenes. In Dianetic terminology, *visio* usually means valid recall of past scenes; the word *dub-in* is used to characterize visio which is imaginary.

Visio may occur in present time, of past scenes, which would be the process of visually remembering. Or it may occur as the preclear is returned on the track, seeing again in recall scenes which he has recorded in his past. Dub-in visio may work in much the same way.

Possibly the most exact borderline between sanity and insanity would be that between knowing that one was imagining what had happened and not knowing that one was imagining. All recalls can become short-circuited through the imagination, so that the "I" is led to believe that it is recalling an actuality when really it is having furnished to it from the memory banks an imaginary sequence. When ARC is very low on a case, usually below the 2.0 range, the condition obtains with the case that many of his recalls, no matter how authentic "I" considers them, are imaginary. As an example of this, consider the person in an anger state who is recounting a conversation or a quarrel he has had. People who are angry almost never tell the truth. People who have sunk to the covert hostility range become so confused between reality and imagination that even their small talk is utterly untrustworthy, and yet these people may believe they are telling the truth. This is a case of recall being short-circuited through the imagination and "I" being furnished imaginary data which is yet labeled as authentic data. Possibly the most flagrant breach of truth occurs in the apathy range or slightly above it, where fear, mingled with grief, can cause the wildest perversion of recall.

The best example of dub-in visio would be the scenery which the preclear gets when he is returned on the track into the prenatal area. He may get very clear and active, but exteriorized, pictures of the scenery around his mother—which views and scenes are entirely false and are not to be attributed by the auditor to extrasensory perception. They denote a 1.3 to 1.0 position on the Tone Scale. Circuitry, about which much will be said later, is the cause of this visio. When the case has been unburdened of many secondary engrams this visio will cease, and the actual visio of the prenatal will take its place. Actual prenatal visio, of course, is black, except at such times when a light may be entered into the area for surgical purposes, at which times the light is sometimes recorded.

A person who is found to be on the Tone Scale between 1.5 and 0.5 should not be expected to have accurate visio—or any visio at all, as in the occluded case.

Visio and all other recalls follow the same pattern as sonic, and in considering any recall the data which is given on sonic may be used interchangeably.

In the 4.0 range, the individual, when in present time, sees what he remembers, and when returned on the track, gets accurate and clear pictures of the scenery just as he saw it when he was looking at it. He is inside himself, which is to say, in valence, and does not get a view of himself as a part of the scenery. This condition normally obtains down to the 3.0 band. Here we begin to get occlusions* and exteriorizations in areas which contain highly charged engrams which themselves contain command phrases that shift the person out of his own valence, such as "I can't be myself around you," etc. Around 3.0, the person is, in most cases, on the track; he can get visio on pleasure moments and he is able to be inside himself except when in secondary engrams.

Around 2.5 the occlusion becomes marked. Large areas of the track may be missing because of charge and valence-shifter engrams.

From 4.0 down to 2.0 it is relatively easy to run out occluded areas and discharge secondaries so that visio returns easily. Below 2.0 the auditor begins to get into trouble and must use a great deal of patience with his preclear, because the visio may be either absent or exteriorized. The auditor, when working such a case, should be very careful at all times never to call any of these oddities to the preclear's attention, as this would be an invalidation of the preclear and would do him much damage. The trouble with a preclear from 2.5 down is that life has invalidated him too often. When the auditor, who is attempting to maintain high ARC with the preclear, seems to rank himself with those factors in life which have already suppressed and hurt the preclear, what little visio has survived may very easily fold up, so that the auditor causes himself a great deal of work in rehabilitating the ARC and getting the visio or other recalls back.

Around the anger band we begin to enter the potentially psychotic area. This does not mean that a person who is at 2.0 is a psychotic. It means that when the free theta of the individual enturbulates momentarily, he finds himself easily along the 2.0 band, and that he conducts himself generally, in his reactions toward life, along this band.

It is possible for a case to be in valence all the way down the track and to get good, moving visios and still be in the 2.0, 1.5, 1.1 band and be thoroughly psychotic. Here again we have an

---

*OCCLUSION: *a hidden area or incident on the time track. The existence of a curtain between "I" and some datum in the standard memory banks. Occlusions are caused by entheta.* —LRH

individual whose structural mechanisms are insufficient to bar out existing charge on the case; thus the person's theta is continually and entirely enturbulated, having no free portion of the analyzer in which to operate. His theta is always under the influence of the charge on the case because he has made for it no protecting partitions.

By partition, compartmentation and occlusion are not meant valence walls; these are something else. The valence wall can actually exist in the individual to a point where he can be either one of two persons, himself and another person. In the very highly charged case, in the case of the obvious psychotic, these valence walls are so well defined that the auditor can almost watch the person click from one valence to another. The schizophrenic of psychiatry, the person who shifts from one identity to another, in Dianetics, we call a valence case. And when these valence walls are so well defined that a whole new personality emerges with the shift, we have a person, of course, below the 2.0 band. Such people ordinarily run in Dianetics quite noisily and are called screamers. The visio of such people is normally present for the valence in which the preclear is at the moment. If he is in Father's valence, he will get the same view of the scenery that Father would get. Or he may be in Mother's valence, in which case he would have a view of the scene just as Mother would see it. Or he may be in a synthetic valence, the valence of no actual person, which might give him a view of the scene looking down from the ceiling. Such cases almost never have their own point of view.

Even valence walls are a sort of protective mechanism by which the charge of the case is compartmented to permit the individual to work at least some of the time. The truly low-power individual merely continues to accumulate charge until he is suppressed to the near bottom of the scale without ever developing a mechanism to overcome the charge. As far as his recalls are concerned, he is continually in his own valence, and in visio will get the scene just as he himself saw it.

Just as in sonic, visio manifests itself all the way down to the bottom of the case when the mental structure is insufficient to compartment off, for the use of "I," any portion of the analyzer.

Dub-in visio actually has two subdivisions: (1) where the actual scenery is approximated and (2) where entirely new scenery is substituted. The first is caused by valence shifts; the visio the person gets of the scene when he is being acted upon by a valence-shifter, highly charged up, as in any secondary engram, is exteriorized—which is to say, he sees himself as part of the scene; he may be in the valence of another person, or he may be merely out in the blue, looking at the scene. When the charge is run off of this particular scene by repeating it over several times (providing any release takes place in the first four or five recountings) the engram on which this secondary is depending and which, of necessity if it creates such an illusion, must contain a valence-shifter command, loses some of its charge, and the individual is then able to get inside of himself and get a view of the scene as he saw it at the time. Any engram in which the preclear is exteriorized cannot be fully discharged until the visio is restored to the scene as it was viewed by the preclear. In other words, if the preclear continues to be exteriorized, the whole charge is not off the engram. However, if any charge at all can be gotten off a secondary, the auditor should run it to exhaust all possible charge.

If visio persists in being exteriorized in spite of many runnings of the incident, there is usually later charge on the case, a later secondary which has to be tapped and discharged first; since physical pain runs from early to late, and secondaries have to be discharged from late back to early.

Imaginary exteriorizations are most chronic around 1.1. In such cases the auditor may sometimes use the mechanism of running the preclear on somebody else's track, which is to say, on Father's track or Mother's track or Grandfather's track, in order to contact scenes. In such cases it is as if the person's track had been swallowed up, leaving available only the tracks of other valences around the individual. This mechanism is of very limited use.

In any apathy secondary the preclear may commonly be found to be outside himself until the charge is off the incident, at which time he becomes interiorized. There is always a valence-shifter* somewhere in a physical pain engram which creates this illusion. Charge itself will not cause a person to be exteriorized, as evidenced by people who have highly charged tracks and who yet remain in valence all the way to the bottom of the scale.

In the very occluded case, visio is the most notably absent thing. The preclear may think that visio is necessary for him to scan locks, but this is not true. He can scan through locks "in the dark," with no visio whatever, and yet bring to his consciousness phrases or incidents which can be run. The auditor must not make the mistake of believing that visio is necessary for the individual to move on his track.

Very little is known of the reasons for visio, and no large body of observation exists to determine the state of visio in all persons that have been cleared of their engrams. This much has been observed, however, that visio does return in a Clear; and any effort to palm off as a Clear an individual who yet does not have an interiorized visio on his track is a dishonest one.

Most children have visio, for the simple reason that their engrams are not yet charged up to a point where secondaries can be formed and so occlude visio or thrust the child out of valence. In a case which has many valence-shifters, affinity, reality and communication secondaries will result in a chronic exteriorized visio case. In a case which has an analyzer sufficiently able to block off charge, visio starts to disappear in the presence of repeated secondaries. After a major ARC break, such as the loss of a sweetheart, visio may cut out, in such a case, entirely. Also, in the

---

*VALENCE-SHIFTER: *You're just like your father, don't be like Uncle Rudy, you're just like everybody else, you're exactly like Rover, you're nobody, you're not human, you're out of this world, you can't ever be yourself, I'll just have to pretend I'm somebody else or I'll never be happy again.* —LRH

case of an individual who is stuck in a prenatal engram, visio is blocked off by the simple fact that the prenatal visio of black is present through all of his memories. He is not, of course, moving on the track, and so cannot pick up the scenery.

Visio is not a good test of the tone level of a case, except in the generality that when visio is present and accurate, and other columns on the Tone Scale agree, the person can be said to be above the 2.0 line. But in view of the fact that visio can exist all the way down the track, such a test must be considered only cursory.

CHAPTER TWELVE

COLUMN J
SOMATICS

THE WORD SOMATIC MEANS, actually, *bodily* or *physical*. Because the word *pain* is restimulative, and because the word *pain* has in the past led to a confusion between physical pain and mental pain, the word *somatic* is used in Dianetics to denote physical pain or discomfort of any kind. It can mean actual pain, such as that caused by a cut or a blow; or it can mean discomfort, as from heat or cold; it can mean itching—in short, anything physically uncomfortable. It does not include mental discomfort such as grief, which would be misemotion. Hard breathing would not be a somatic; it would be a symptom of misemotion suppression. Somatic means a nonsurvival physical state of being; it is distinguished, on the one hand, from a nonsurvival mental state of being and, on the other hand, from a physical action or prosurvival perceptic, such as kinesthesia or tactile, or visio.

An engram has several component parts: the two main components, of course, are entheta and enMEST. Free theta has come into collision with MEST, with resultant enturbulation. In a living organism, the enMEST component would be the manifested somatic.

The chief difference between the analytical and reactive minds, aside from their functions, is that the reactive mind registers pain and the analytical mind merely records the fact that pain exists. This gives the reactive mind an additional perceptic; this perceptic is called a somatic.

In the presence of *any* physical pain the analyzer goes off. Even if the pain is very mild and brief there is still a moment of analytical shut-off. In Dianetics this is called *anaten,* an engineering type of abbreviation for "*ana*lytical *atten*uation." The anaten buries the somatic, and, unfortunately, buries with it all the perceptics present when the somatic was received. It may be difficult to realize that anaten is present with every somatic, until one has mildly injured his finger, for example, and has gone back over the incident a few times. He will discover that there was an incident during the injury, which became occluded because of anaten; and by running the incident two or three times, he will find some additional perceptics which he may not before have noted. Thus the somatic is buried by this mechanism of anaten. This is a workable mechanism in a life organism which is not analytically capable of recovering pain and running it out; but it is not workable in a rational organism possessed of considerable analytical power, since the perceptics of the painful moment can then react back against the analytical power, and the organism is then victimized by its somatics rather than trained into the avoidance of danger by the avoidance of pain—the evident primary use of somatics.

A severe physical pain causes considerable analytical attenuation, shutting off the analyzer thoroughly for a period of time. This, technically, is an engram, although any incident, painful or not, contained in the reactive mind and occluded by anaten can be considered an engram.

Once an engram exists, analytical experiences can restimulate it by approximating its perceptics or breaking the dramatization demanded by the engram. These analytical moments are called *locks,* and they charge up the engram. There are, technically speaking, two types of such locks: those which merely restimulate the engram, which is then dramatized by the individual; and those which break the dramatization. The first type are not as severe as the second type, since the second type, by making it impossible for the individual to obey the "mandates" of the engrams, cause the physical pain to turn on and the individual gets what has been known as a psychosomatic illness.

A psychosomatic illness, according to Dianetic findings, is the somatic side of the engram, turned on by continual suppression of the dramatization. Thus, in Dianetics, psychosomatic illnesses are not regarded as such but are called *chronic somatics,* since they disappear once the engram and its locks are discharged from the case.

Another manifestation than anaten occurs with regard to a physical pain. The somatic enturbulates theta, and if the analytical incident which forms a lock on this engram contains considerable misemotion, as caused by fear or loss, the presence of the physical pain earlier in the bank makes it possible for a secondary engram to be formed. Misemotion is actually a conversion of physical pain, according to Dianetic findings. There is much more that could be discovered about this mechanism of conversion of physical pain to, for instance, terror or grief or apathy; and the discovery probably lies in the field of further examination and understanding of free theta, but it is certain that secondary engrams, with their misemotion, occlude somatics. When the misemotion is discharged, the engram itself then becomes available.

Indeed, so intimate is the relationship between misemotion and physical pain that the case is run by "layers." One may discover, early in the case, many physical pain engrams which easily discharge when recounted. This brings to light a long series of secondary engrams, later in the case. One is unable to find any further physical pain engrams until one has discharged these secondaries of their fear, grief and apathy. Having done this, the auditor will find that he has a new series of physical pain engrams available for running.

A somatic, then, may be said to be buried beneath anaten and beneath misemotion or secondary engrams. Thus, somatics in a case can be seen to "hide."

Somatics can be turned on by Dianetic auditing only when the anaten and the misemotion are not too heavy for the particular somatic the auditor is trying to reach.

A very heavily charged case (by which is meant a case with a very heavy burden of secondaries) may be found to have no somatics available for auditing.

A very occluded case, in which the mind has compartmented off charge, will also have blocked off the majority of the somatics.

The case which is stuck thoroughly on the time track may have in constant restimulation the somatic which was present at the moment he received the engram in which he is stuck.

The characteristic of the psychotic is that the entheta side of the engram is in constant action and that the somatic side of the engram is not particularly active.

The case which was formerly referred to as the psychosomatically ill case would be said to be one in which the entheta side of the engram is suppressed and the somatic side of the engram is in restimulation. These chronic somatic cases are usually found to be cases which have been subjected throughout life to breaking of each and every dramatization, cases, in other words, which have been denied the MEST control irrationally directed by the engrams, as well as the MEST control rationally directed by theta.

The Tone Scale of somatics could begin, at the top, with the MEST Clear at 4.0, who would have *no* somatics left to be run. This is the technical definition of the MEST Clear, that each and every incident that contained physical pain, during his entire lifetime from conception forward to present time, has been erased, thus freeing the theta which has been held as entheta in the bank by freeing the body of pain or potential pain. This does not mean, by the way, that the Clear cannot receive new pain and new engrams. It does mean that new incidents of pain will have much less effect on him than they would were he not a Clear; and he can ordinarily run out such incidents by himself, unless he has been from the start a very low theta-power individual.

In the 3.5, 3.0 and 2.5 bands, somatics are sharp and readily available to the auditor. Almost any engram on the case can be run, providing the basic on its chain and other preceding engrams have been erased before it. Slightly above 2.0, engrams begin to be suppressed by charge and anaten on the case.

In a heavily occluded case, who is yet in the 2.0 band, somatics may all but be absent. In a less occluded case in the 2.0 band somatics may be very light. In a case which is in valence, and yet in the 2.0 band, and which can move on the track, somatics are available and can be run.

Around 1.1, the heavily occluded case will have no somatics available. The auditor must here work solely for the discharge of locks and secondaries before he can find somatics on the case. In the less occluded case, however, some light somatics will be found available. And in the unoccluded case, which is yet at 1.1, somatics will be found to be extremely light, and, again, will not discharge adequately until locks and secondaries are run.

At the 0.5 level, somatics in the occluded case, the partially occluded case or the wide-open case will be found to be so light as to be practically nonexistent, according to usual experience.

Below this level somatics do not exist at all.

The auditor should very thoroughly recognize, then, somatics for what they are—the physical pain of past injuries. He should recognize, further, that it is the somatic, in the first place, which makes locks and secondaries possible. And he must further realize that somatics are buried beneath anaten and misemotion, when these are present. He must not believe, however, that just because somatics make locks and secondaries possible his primary mission is to run somatics off the case. Of course he is trying to get the physical pain engrams off the case, but where somatics are not easily available he must be very chary of trying to find them, and should devote himself to locks and secondaries rather than somatics. He will discover that by discharging locks and secondaries he can very often relieve what have been called psychosomatic illnesses.

Running somatics is the act of putting the case into permanent good shape. Running locks and secondaries is a much more rapid way of raising the tone of the case; however, that tone can fall again so long as engrams remain. It is theoretically possible to bring a case up to 3.0 or 3.5 without ever running a somatic, but this is not possible in common experience, and one has to run physical pain engrams when they offer themselves, save in those cases where so little free theta is available that by running a somatic the remaining free theta may become enturbulated and involved with the engram, forming a new lock in auditing. Such an act can take the borderline psychotic down into the psychotic band. This is prevented by addressing locks and secondaries on the borderline case, rather than somatics.

The auditor should not try for specific somatics in the case in the hope of relieving chronic illnesses. He can best address a specific chronic somatic by running locks and secondaries involved with that somatic.

Merely by running the preclear through various parts of his life, up and down the track, the auditor may relieve enough anaten and misemotion from the case to permit somatics to occur. This was once upon a time known as "greasing the track." However, one should not run a preclear into a somatic unless one intends to reduce it or to discover the basic on the chain and reduce that. Once somatics are contacted they must be reduced; if they do not easily reduce on a few recountings, an earlier engram or a chain of locks or a secondary should be found which inhibits the somatic from reducing.

It is the somatic which predisposes a case to illness. An old physical pain in an area of the body weakens that area, to the extent that there is a remembered injury in it; body fluids approach the area with caution. When that old injury is restimulated, the approach of body fluids is inhibited even more, and so the area is denied, more and more, the nourishment, support, repair and protection which the general flow of fluids in the body is designed to bring about.

Bacteria are then able to enter the area and maintain themselves, and an illness can result, according to theory, and according to what has been observed while working with Dianetics on many people. If the somatic in the area is heavy, the presence of bacteria may further restimulate it, and so the illness is perpetuated and becomes a chronic infection. In the case of a simple pain—known to doctors as "strange, bizarre pains"—or of rheumatoid arthritis, it may only be that the somatic itself is restimulated, and the reduction of the somatic is often attended by the sudden loss of the psychosomatic illness. This is not to make the claim that removing the somatic cures a psychosomatic illness: such a claim is specifically forbidden by law, as applied to past healing arts. Clinical experience, however, law or no law, demonstrates this to be a workable theory in practice. Any law which would seek to force people to remain ill when they might be well would be an evil law. Furthermore, the laws of man have never been able to do much to suppress the laws of God.

C O L U M N   K

SPEECH: TALKS
SPEECH: LISTENS

Pᴿᴼᴮᴬᴮᴸʸ ᴛʜᴇ ᴍᴏsᴛ ᴀᴄᴄᴜʀᴀᴛᴇ index for the auditor of the preclear's position on the Tone Scale is speech. Here is a generalized manifestation of perceptic communication.

Engrams can induce, by specific command, too much talking, too little talking, too much listening to other people, or too little listening. Throughout the chart there is this liability that the individual is operating upon compulsive or obsessive commands regarding one or more of the columns. The average position on the columns is the most important. A manic, telling a person to talk continuously, or a suppressive engram, requiring a person to do nothing but listen, will produce such behavior; but unless a person talks openly and listens receptively he cannot be considered very high on the Tone Scale.

There are double boxes in the speech column: one set referring to talking, the other to listening. It may not have occurred to some people that communication is both outgo and income. An observation of how a person both listens and talks will make it possible to form an opinion as to whether or not the person is operating on an engramic command either about listening or about talking: because usually one or the other—talking or listening—will be an accurate indication of his position on the Tone Scale. A person who is not operating on engramic commands which deny or enforce either talking or listening, will talk and listen more or less equally.

Mind operation being what it is, as a person drops lower and lower on the Tone Scale his affinity potential, his reality potential and his communication potential also drop. Thus, by entirely mechanical means, we get reduction of visio, sonic, somatic recall, all other perceptics, and talking and listening. The highest level of the scale contains the faculty of communicating completely and withholding nothing; also the ability to communicate with complete rational selectivity; also the ability to be conversationally creative and constructive.

At this high level of the scale, the individual is able to listen to everything which is said and evaluate it rationally. He can listen to entheta communications without becoming severely enturbulated. He can receive ideas without making critical or derogatory comments. And, while receiving another person's ideas, he can greatly aid that person's thinking and talking.

At the level of 3.5, the individual is capable of communicating deeply felt beliefs and ideas to others and can communicate with others selectively, which is to say, he can cut off entheta lines, and hold back or give forth conversation according to the rational or pleasant circumstances of the moment. The individual at this level can listen without becoming critical and can aid and assist others in conversation, but he is apt to become enturbulated slightly if given entheta conversation.

Between 3.5 and 3.0, the ability of a person to talk to others decreases to a tentative expression of a limited number of beliefs and ideals and borders on the conservative. He may have a very conservative reaction toward people who have highly creative and constructive ideas. He is critical of flagrant irrationalities. In other words, from 3.5 down to 3.0, we are in a band where injury from life has created a defensiveness on the part of the individual.

At 3.0, the speech of the individual becomes more casual and reserved. Here is the level of small talk, about weather and good roads. At this level the individual has a resistance toward ideas which are too massive. An analytical fear is expressed here of being not quite at ease.

At 2.5, we have the level of indifference to conversation with others, a "let's not argue about it" attitude, a dismissal of communication, a carelessness as to whether one's conversation is being received or is even understandable.

Between 2.5 and 2.0, we have a level where communication from other people is refused, and where one does not talk.

At 2.0, we reach a level of antagonistic conversation. The individual is apt to nag or to make derogatory comments to invalidate other people. On this level the individual can only be roused by nagging, nasty cracks, invalidations and other antagonistic communication.

At the 1.5 tone level, we have a shutting off of other persons' conversation, a complete refusal to listen and efforts to destroy incoming conversation. The conversation which is given forth by an individual at this level is forthrightly destructive and is given without any thought of the possible retaliation which may result from this destructiveness. Conversation on this level could hardly be called *con*versation, as it is a forward motion toward destruction and a refusal to accept anything which might prevent that destruction.

Below this level, before we reach 1.1, the individual sinks into stubborn silence, sulks, refuses to talk. He will not listen to any communication of any kind from other people, except that which encourages him in his attitude.

At 1.1, we have lying to avoid real communication. It takes the form of pretended agreement, flattery or verbal appeasement, or simply a false picture of the person's feelings and ideas, a false facade, an artificial personality. Here is the level of covert hostility, the most dangerous and wicked level on the Tone Scale. Here is the person who smiles while he inserts a knife blade between your vertebrae. Here is the person who tells you how he has stood up for you, when actually he has practically destroyed your reputation. Here is the insincere flatterer who yet awaits only a moment of unguardedness to destroy. The conversation of this level is filled with small barbs which are immediately afterwards justified as intended compliments. Talking with such a person is the maddening procedure of boxing with a shadow: one realizes that something is wrong, but the guardedness of a 1.1 will not admit anything wrong, even as, all the while, he does his best to upset and wreak havoc. This is the level of the pervert, the homosexual, the turncoat. This is the level of the subversive. From such a person one should never expect an outright frontal attack; the attack will come when one is absent, when one's back is turned or when one sleeps. Any luckless person married to a 1.1 is, literally speaking, in danger of his life and sanity, for such a person is incapable of any real affection; such a person is so introverted that any demonstrated affection is a hectic sham. Such a person will opportunistically take any avenue which leads to his own security and will leave in the lurch anyone he has pretended to call his friend. A 1.1 is the most dangerously insane person in society and is likely to cause the most damage. Because of the covert nature of this insanity, it is completely beside the point whether such a person is pronounced insane by any agency. On this level there is no concept of honor, decency or ethics; there is only desperate, death-bent thought of self and of damage to others. Society can handle the angry man; it knows what to expect from him. Society can handle the apathy case; his insanity is obvious. But the 1.1 is a skulking coward who yet contains enough perfidious energy to strike back, but not enough courage ever to give warning. Such people should be taken from the society as rapidly as possible and uniformly institutionalized; for here is the level of the contagion of immorality and the destruction of ethics; here is the fodder which secret police organizations use for their filthy operations. One of the most effective measures of security that a nation threatened by war could take would be the rounding up and placing in a cantonment, away from the society, of any 1.1 individual who might be connected with government, the military or essential industry; since here are people who, regardless of any record of their family's loyalty, are potential traitors, the very mode of operation of their insanity being betrayal. In this level is the slime of society, the sex criminals, the people whose apparently rational activities are yet but the devious writhings of secret hate.

A 1.1 can be accurately spotted by his conversation, since he seeks only to enturbulate those around him, to upset them by his conversation, to destroy them without their ever being aware of his purpose. He listens only to data which will serve him in his enturbulations. Here is the gossip, here is the unfaithful wife, here is the card cheat, here is the most undesirable stratum of any social order.[1]

No social order which desires to survive dares overlook its stratum of 1.1s. No social order will survive which does not remove these people from its midst.

The 1.1 is so low on the Tone Scale and yet so active mentally, as a rule, that he is very difficult to process. The longest and most arduous course of therapy may still leave the auditor baffled by a mind which is so full of circuits that no real desire for improvement on the part of the preclear can make itself felt. The auditor may feel that only an offer of an obvious present time advantage, like being let out of confinement, would tempt this preclear into genuine cooperation. The auditor may feel that this case is just not salvageable. But if, in the case, the auditor can manage to remove some of the circuits or destimulate them he may be able to make progress. It takes a very clever Dianetician to do anything with a chronic, computational 1.1.

---

1. **social order:** the totality of structured human interrelationships in a society or a part of it; the manner in which society is organized at a specified time, the constituted social system.

The 0.5 talks dolefully and hopelessly in terms of bad things which are happening and will happen and for which there is no remedy. He listens only to such conversation. He cannot be heartened or cheered up but will slump immediately into his apathy. Here is hopelessness.

At 0.1, we have an inability to talk, and an individual who is completely unresponsive to conversation.

It is interesting to note that the auditor can, with this column, conduct what we call a "two-minute psychometry" on the preclear. The trick is simply to start talking to the preclear at the highest possible tone level, creatively and constructively, and then gradually drop the tone of one's conversation down to the point where it achieves response from the preclear. An individual best responds to his own tone band; and an individual can be lifted only about half a point on the Tone Scale by conversation. In doing this type of "psychometry" one should not carry any particular band of conversation too long, not more than a sentence or two, because this will have a tendency to raise slightly the tone of the preclear and so spoil the accuracy of the test.

Two-minute psychometry, then, is done, first, by announcing something creative and constructive and seeing whether the preclear responds in kind; then giving forth some casual conversation, perhaps about sports, and seeing if the preclear responds to that. Getting no response the auditor starts talking antagonistically about things about which the preclear knows—but not, of course, about the preclear—to see if he achieves a response at this point. The auditor may then give forth with a sentence or two of anger against some condition. Then the auditor can indulge in a small amount of discreditable gossip and see if there is any response to that. If this does not work, then the auditor dredges up some statements of hopelessness and misery. Somewhere in this range the preclear will agree with the type of conversation that is being offered—that is, he will respond to it in kind. A conversation can then be carried on along this band where the preclear has been discovered, and the auditor will rapidly gain enough information to make a good first estimate of the preclear's position on the chart.

This two-minute psychometry by conversation can also be applied to groups. That speaker who desires to command his audience must not talk above or below his audience's tone more than a half a point. If he wishes to lift the audience's tone, he should talk about a half a point above their general tone level. An expert speaker, using this two-minute psychometry and carefully noting the responses of his audience, can, in two minutes, discover the tone of the audience—whereupon, all he has to do is adopt a tone slightly above theirs. In Italy and Germany, when an entire people were at the level of 1.0 or slightly below, two death talkers, Mussolini and Hitler, were received by great crowds with wild enthusiasm. A powerful saint could have come forth and talked to these people in the most creative and constructive terms and would have had no response from them at all. This phenomenon has led historians to believe erroneously that individuals were created by the moment and that the moment was not created by the individual. Some instinct prompted these extinct leaders of Europe to seek and find the point on the Tone Scale at which they could most rapidly seize the attention of their audiences. It so happens that anyone in the 1.5 band will bring about disaster regardless of his stated intentions. A death talker can bring an entire people up to anger and hold them there long enough to destroy them, as did Mussolini and Hitler during the second phase of World War II.

C O L U M N   L

Subject's Handling of Written or Spoken Communication When Acting as a Relay Point

As in speech, it is a mechanical fact that a person at a certain position on the Tone Scale tends, unless affected by engrams specifically demanding different action, to follow a definite pattern in handling messages when acting as a relay point.

This is mentioned here because it is important to organizations, but mostly because it is a good diagnostic point for the auditor. What does the subject do with letters he is given? Does he answer them or does he put them away? When you give him a message to give to somebody else, does that other person receive the message which you wanted him to receive, or is it twisted or altered in some way, or is it not delivered at all?

The handling of messages approximates the ability of the individual to contact his own standard memory bank—which is to say, he will handle in the external world various communications from one person to another just as his own circuits handle information between his standard memory bank and himself. At the highest level of the Tone Scale we have complete communication, and at the lowest level we have no communication at all.

At 4.0, the individual passes communications freely, contributes to them, normally, and rather tends to cut entheta communications—which is to say, lines he knows are vicious or slanderous he is not likely to assist.

At 3.5, the individual passes communications but resents and hits back at entheta lines—by "line," of course, is meant communication line, which is any sequence through which a message of any character may go.

At 3.0, we begin to get a breakdown of the communication line on which our individual is acting as a relay point, because an individual at this level is likely to be slightly suspicious of 4.0 construction and creation and is likely to tone down the message considerably. Here we have conservatism, and conservative communications are most rapidly relayed at this level. Here the individual does not readily lend himself to either an entheta line or to a heavy theta line.

At 2.5, the individual devaluates emergencies. He is not likely to believe a very highly constructive message or a destructive message. He handles communications above or below his level poorly, but passes communications which are at the boredom range.

An individual at 2.0 deals mostly in hostile or threatening communications. He lets only a small number of constructive communications go through, tends to select out theta communications, and tends to pass entheta communications—which is to say he will make himself a party to slander but will not make himself a party to a high endeavor unless it happens to fit his own antagonistic purposes. Here we have a very poor relay point but one which, when pressed, will function.

At 1.5, we run into a relay point level which is a dangerous one in any organization or nation or family, since here all good, constructive, theta communications are stopped or perverted in some way. Suspiciousness and other entheta elements are added to the communication before it is sent through. This level favors, and most readily passes, angry communications which will cause destruction. Giving a communication to such a person to give to someone else will most certainly bring about different results than one intended, when that communication has been relayed.

At around 1.3, all theta communications are cut, and malicious communications are most readily relayed. Communications that are passed are twisted and perverted.

Around 0.9, we have an individual who tends to cut communication lines and who, on one pretext or another, will not relay communications. At this level we have the individual who specializes in secret communications and is apt to give the classification of secret or confidential to the most banal matters.

At 0.5, the individual takes very little heed of communications. He cannot see the necessity of passing anything to anybody—it's "hopeless" anyway, and so there is "no point in doing anything about it."

At 0.1, of course, the individual is unaware of communications of any kind and so does not relay them.

This subject is much more exhaustively covered in the field of Group Dianetics, since it applies, with enormous importance, to the conduct of business, governments, armies and other organizations. One might safely say that 95 percent of an executive's trouble is with communication lines. This index on the Tone Scale will give him some idea of what to expect from certain of his subordinates. If any executive is surrounded by individuals who will not pass communications or who pervert communications, he can be very certain of trouble in the organization, caused by this point alone.

The auditor can establish his preclear's position on the Tone Scale by observations and inquiries about his preclear's handling of written and spoken communications when acting as a relay point. He may best do this by giving the preclear a message to relay to someone else, in order to see what happens to that message—the preclear, of course, thinking not that this is a test, but that it is a sincere effort to relay a communication.

CHAPTER FIFTEEN

COLUMN M
REALITY
(AGREEMENT)

As HAS BEEN SAID IN EARLIER chapters of this book, the quantity known as reality exists, so far as we know, mainly because we *agree* that it exists.

The entire physical universe, according to the tenets of nuclear physics, is reducible to near zero, if we think in terms of an actuality that can be sensed, measured or experienced. Matter and energy exist in space and time; but matter is composed of energy; and energy seems, at best, to be a motion rather than a substance. For a motion to take place, one sees that space and time are necessary, but that space and time are themselves such strange entities, according to Einstein and others, that they are also reducible and expandable and are not sharply defined entities. Much could be said on this subject, all more or less of a confusing and indecisive nature. Philosophers for many centuries have been debating over the reality of reality, and each one has come to the final admission that man agrees that he perceives something with his various senses and that man has agreed to call this reality.

For our purposes, the lowest common denominator of reality could be called, then, agreement. If you and I both agree that we are gazing at an automobile, then that automobile has reality for us. If another person comes forward and says that it is not an automobile but a barrel of olives, then you and I are apt to suppose him crazy. Majority opinion rules, where reality is concerned. Those who do not agree with the majority are commonly pronounced insane, or are exiled, and thus we have a sort of continuous natural selection which gives us a social order that has agreed upon certain definite realities. Anyone who seeks to alter those realities in any way is attacked, unless the strength and force of his reason are such that they carry into the minds of men a new reality on which those men can agree.

There are, actually, two kinds of reality. There is the reality which can be sensed, measured and experienced in the physical universe. This MEST reality is so thoroughly constructed into a human being genetically and is so uncompromisingly consistent in its behavior, as in the science of physics, that man finds it unwieldily consistent and so works, as in the science of physics, to discover certain natural regularities of behavior of the physical universe. When new data about the physical universe is discovered to compare favorably with what the current age is accustomed to sense, measure or experience, a high order of agreement is attained.

A second type of reality is *postulated reality,* which is brought into being by creative or destructive imagination. This reality borders over into the still unexplored field of aesthetics. There are men, usually in the fields of the arts and philosophy, who postulate new realities for the social order. Social orders progress or decline in ratio to the number of new realities which are postulated for them. These postulates are made, usually, single-handedly by men of imagination. Social orders are normally very conservative and seek to hold hard to old realities. The reason for this is a simple one. In the absence of wide communication networks by which new realities can be generally offered, it takes considerable time for the new reality to become known. Indeed, a new reality postulated by some individual becomes known in direct ratio to the velocity and magnitude of the idea. There undoubtedly exists a formula for the speed and advance of ideas. For example, a man named Ibsen, by writing a few plays, wildly altered single-handedly the entire cultural aspect of Scandinavia within a few years. Ideas, and not battles, mark the forward progress of mankind. Individuals, and not masses, form the culture of the race. On a lesser scale actors and other artists work continually to give tomorrow a new form. Hollywood makes a picture which strikes the public fancy, and tomorrow we have girls made up like a star walking along the streets of the small towns of America. A Hollywood interior decorator dresses a set which takes the eye of the American audience, and tomorrow that set is seen as the apartments of Miami Beach and other resorts. A culture is as rich and as capable of surviving as it has imaginative artists, skilled men of science, a high ethic level, workable government, land and natural resources, in about that order of importance.

One might postulate two more realities. The first is that of the Supreme Being. No culture in the history of the world, save the thoroughly depraved and expiring ones, has failed to affirm the existence of a Supreme Being. It is an empirical observation that men without a strong and lasting faith in a Supreme Being are less capable, less ethical and less valuable to themselves and society. A government wishing to deprave its people to the point where they will accept the most perfidious and rotten acts abolishes first the concept of God; and in the wake of that destroys the family with free love; the intellectual, with police-enforced idiocies; and so reduces a whole population to an estate somewhat below that of dogs. A man without an abiding faith is, by observation alone, more of a thing than a man. Modern science, producing weapons for the annihilation of men, women and children in wholesale lots, has solidly run itself aground on the reef of godlessness. Modern science has gone so far as to advocate the rise of man from mud and clay alone, has denied to him even a semblance of a soul, and so has not only solved none of the problems of the humanities, but has aided and abetted a godless government which seeks nothing less than the engulfment and enslavement of all men and the extinguishment of every spark of decency in the breast of every human being. These two tracks which have led away from the affirmation of the existence of a Supreme Being are both bringing man into a machinelike state of being, where the ideal has become a lump of muscle, greasy with sweat, or a grimy mechanic serving a howling monster of steel. The arts, the humanities and the decencies are fallen away from, until they are like tiny stars shining across a great, black void. The abandonment of the admission of a Supreme Being as a reality, intimate to the life of man, makes prostitution the ideal conduct of a woman, perfidy and betrayal the highest ethic level attainable by a man, and obliteration by treachery, bomb and gun the highest goal attainable by a culture. Thus, there is no great argument about the reality of a Supreme Being, since one sees, in the failure to countenance that reality, a slimy and loathsome trail, downward into the most vicious depths.

The theta universe is a postulated reality for which there exists much evidence. If one were going to draw a diagram of this, it would be a triangle with the Supreme Being at one corner, the MEST universe at another and the theta universe at the third. Too much evidence is forthcoming in research to permit us to overlook this reality. Indeed, the assumption of this reality is solving some of the major problems of the humanities and fills in many gaps which existed formerly in the theory of the engram.

It has long been considered beneficial in psychotherapies for a person to be able to face reality. However, none defined what reality was, and so the individual found this rather difficult.

There would be two realities with which the individual was most intimately concerned. The internal reality, of his own existence and past, and the external reality, of his present time environment. To this could be added, of course, his future reality.

The reality Tone Scale on extroversion–introversion would be, at a glance, that around tone 4.0 the interior world was sufficiently comfortable so that the individual's thought and perception was mainly directed toward the exterior world and his computation had to do with present time and the future. And as one descended the Tone Scale, one could see the gradual involvement of free theta with enMEST, with less and less concern with the exterior world and the future and more and more involvement in the interior world and the past, until the majority of the theta was enturbulated and death ensued. There would be, then, an extroversion–introversion scale which would mark very sharply the position of the person on the Tone Scale. The position of the person would, of course, be determined by the amount of free theta with which he was endowed and the percentage of that theta which had become entheta.

Yet another reality scale could be postulated on the basis of the theta perceptics, but that is beyond the scope of this work.

The general attitude of the individual with regard to reality, as shown on the Tone Scale, would be as follows:

At 4.0, the individual would be creatively and constructively inclined toward reality. He would be more likely to adjust reality to him and to postulate new future realities than he would be to adjust himself to existing realities. He would search for different viewpoints and changes in reality in order to broaden his own reality. He would have a complete flexibility and understanding in relating and evaluating different realities.

At 3.5, the individual would have the ability to understand, relate and evaluate realities, regardless of the difference in viewpoint; moderate flexibility about realities brought to view, without eager search for new ones. A little lower on the Tone Scale, the individual would be involved with attempts to reconcile his own reality with conflicting realities, and he would have a limited flexibility.

At 3.0, the individual would possess an awareness of the possible validity of a different reality without relating this to his own reality.

At 2.5 would ensue an indifference to conflicting realities, a "maybe—who cares?" attitude. Below this would be a refusal to match two realities, rejecting conflicting realities.

At 2.0 would be found verbal doubt, defense of one's own reality and attempts to undermine the reality of others. Here is the critical level, and criticism intensifies from here on down to 1.0 and then dies out.

At 1.5, the individual is mainly concerned with the destruction of opposing realities, wrecking or changing them, knocking apart the realities of other people. The environmental reality would be attacked, with destruction in view. The only change that would take place would be a destructive change.

Below this would be doubt of the opposing reality, a nonverbal disbelief, a refusal to accept the disbelief of others, a refusal to accept conflicting realities without trying to fight back.

At 1.1 on the Tone Scale would ensue the doubt of one's own reality, insecurity and attempts to gain reassurance. In the sphere of MEST realities there would be appeasement of gods or elements.

At 0.5, we would have shame, anxiety, strong doubt of one's own reality with a consequent inability to act within it. If the person is to act at all he must be told what to do. He is afraid to act of himself since he has no way to assess the consequences.

Below this is a complete withdrawal from conflicting reality and a refusal to recognize the existence of any reality but one's own, in which one is rigidly locked.

At tone 0.0, the only reality is death.

C O L U M N   N

CONDITION OF TRACK AND VALENCES

Everyone has a time track. To some preclears, this may not be immediately apparent.

The time track consists of all the consecutive moments of now, from the earliest moment of life of the organism to present time. Actually, the track is a multiple bundle of perceptics; and it might be said that there is a time track for each perceptic, all tracks running simultaneously. The track might also be considered as a system of filing recordings made of the environment and the organism, filed according to time received. All the perceptions of the environment and the organism during the entire lifetime, up to now, or present time, are recorded, faintly or deeply, upon the time track.

It was not generally known, before Dianetics, that the time track existed for an awake and conscious person and that the individual could move upon it. In the field of hypnotism something was known of the phenomenon, but it had been indifferently studied and was thought to be available only to a hypnotized person. Experiments conducted by experts in hypnotism have demonstrated that the person, awake, moves more readily on his time track than a person in a hypnotized state.

There is actual perception of movement on the time track, if the individual is moving. Present time is an ever extending moment; and a person who is free on his time track is generally in present time, moving forward through the consecutive moments of time.

A primary concern of the auditor is to keep the case of his preclear in such good condition that the preclear can continue to move upon the time track and contact locks, secondaries and engrams in order to recount them at the place they occur a sufficient number of times to reduce or erase them. It is possible for the auditor, by failing to conduct his preclear properly through locks, secondaries and engrams, to cause the preclear to stick upon the time track in some moment of the past. When this happens the preclear is not able to move upon the time track, and the auditor should make it his first concern to return mobility to the preclear.

Various things can happen to the preclear with relation to the time track. The most upsetting of these is when a grouper, a phrase such as "Pull yourself together," "It all happens at once," "Everything is against me," "It all comes down to this," and other action phrases* which would tend to bunch all incidents in one place, creates the illusion that the time track is collapsed and that all incidents are at the same point in time. A case must be heavily charged and the action phrases in the case must have considerable effectiveness with the preclear before this can happen. The auditor can detect its occurrence rather easily, and at the first difficulty with the time track, the auditor should suspect a grouper.

The question of how early the time track goes has not been completely resolved. The auditor, in the absence of such resolution, should take into account the fact that considerable experimental evidence exists that the time track continues into the past earlier than the life of the present organism. There is a possibility that the time

---

*ACTION PHRASES: *words or phrases in engrams or locks (or at 0.1, in present time) which cause the individual to perform involuntary actions on the time track. Action phrases are effective in the low tone ranges and not effective in the high ranges. As a case progresses up the scale, they lose their power. Types of action phrases are bouncer, down-bouncer, grouper, denyer, holder, misdirector, scrambler and the valence-shifters corresponding to these.* —LRH

track is a portion of what we call the theta body rather than of the organism itself. There could be a genetic time track which would go back through the generations preceding the organism, but experimental evidence has not borne out this possibility uniformly, as it has the existence of the theta body. Thus, the auditor should be prepared to discover some astonishingly early incidents; and if and when he does discover them he should be very careful to run them and to erase or reduce them or if they will not reduce, to find an earlier incident which can be erased or reduced, in order to relieve them. It is not in the province of the auditor to question the data of the preclear in any way; and it is in the province of the auditor to reduce any and all engrams which he recovers in the case.

In addition to the grouper, there can be other troubles with the time track. The most common of these is for the preclear to be stuck in an incident of the past. A holder existing in an engram has seized him at some earlier age, and he is not in present time but is locked in an earlier period of his life, which also contains pain and unconsciousness or heavy grief or fear charges.

Lock Scanning or running earlier engrams generally remedies this condition. This condition is checked for very simply, by the use of the flash answer. As will be covered elsewhere, the auditor uses the file clerk of the preclear. The file clerk uses automatic response mechanisms which are not "thoughtful" mechanisms but instantaneous replies, the first thing that flashes into the preclear's mind at the snap of the auditor's fingers. The auditor asks the preclear for a date and snaps his fingers. The preclear may not give the present time date; if he does not, he is giving the date of the moment where he is stuck on the track. Simply asking various people around you their age will give you considerable data on this mechanism. Tell these people to give you the first number that comes into their heads when you snap your fingers, and then ask them "How old are you?" *(snap!)* In a number of instances you will get ages much earlier than present time. Asking them to remember what happened at that period will very often bring them up to present time, where they may not have been for years. An auditor could walk through any sanitarium and simply tell patient after patient "Come up to present time," and he would find that some very small percentage of the "insane" people would come up to present time and would begin to be sane; this has been done several times, with some astonishing results. This is mentioned to give the auditor some idea of the importance of having the preclear in present time and the importance of being in present time. Flash answer checks can also be done by the following mechanism: the preclear is asked to give the first answer that flashes into his head, yes or no, to each of the following questions; the auditor then says "Hospital?" to which the preclear answers yes or no; the auditor then says "Nurse?" and the preclear gives him a yes or no. When the preclear is unable to recall anything having happened at the age he gives in lieu of his present time age, by flash answer, this yes-or-no check will serve to tell the auditor the nature and character of the incident in which the preclear is held. The preclear's memory can then be more ably directed toward discovering whether it was an accident, an injury or an illness in which he was concerned and who it was who gave him the holder which keeps him in the incident. Sometimes merely remembering the incident will free the preclear so that he can come to present time. Sometimes in a case which has been nonsonic there is sonic at the exact moment where the preclear is held, and the sonic is the holder by which the preclear is held.

Simply directing the preclear's attention to a pleasure moment and running him through it many times, over and over, particularly one in which the preclear was victorious as himself, will often snap the preclear out of an engram in which he is held and permit him to come to present time. It is common procedure to end all sessions by running the preclear through some pleasure moments in order to bring him easily and completely to present time.

Another mechanism which gives the auditor trouble in bringing the preclear to present time or moving him on the track is the call-back. Such phrases as "come here," "come back," and other action phrases which would, in present time, cause the preclear to move back to another position in *space,* act, when contained in engrams, to pull the preclear down from present *time* into the engrams. It often happens that the auditor tries to bring the preclear to present time, and every time the preclear nears present time he is pulled back down the track to an earlier age. This is caused by a call-back.

Another mechanism which keeps the preclear early on the track is the "down-bouncer." This type of phrase is one which tells the person to "get down" or "get back" and keeps the preclear below the actual incident in which he is held.

Another difficulty on the time track is the "bouncer." The bouncer always bounces the preclear up. The preclear may be in an engram and yet be bounced into present time. This creates a situation in which the preclear seems to be in present time but is actually under considerable tension, being held in an engram.*

Another difficulty with the time track is the "misdirector." This would be a phrase which, when the auditor sends the preclear in one direction, makes the preclear go in another direction. Such a phrase as "You do everything backwards" causes this situation. When the auditor tells the preclear to come up to present time, if such a phrase is active the preclear may go back to basic-basic.** Any case in which phrases are this active is a highly charged case, and it will be necessary for the auditor to get rid of many locks and secondaries before he can run engrams.

It is not possible for an individual to be stuck in present time. He is always stuck in an engram. Some people who find it very difficult to move on the track seem to be stuck in present time, but they are not. Lock Scanning or the running of a secondary or the location of the actual engram in which the preclear is stuck will serve to get the preclear moving on the track. —LRH

BASIC-BASIC: *the first moment of pain, anaten or discomfort in the current life of the individual.* —LRH

Another difficulty which affects the time track, but is not exactly a time track difficulty, is the matter of valence.

A valence is a false or true identity. The preclear has his own valence; then there are available to him the valences of all persons who appear in his engrams. A valence-shifter is a phrase which causes the individual to shift into another identity. The phrase "You ought to be in his shoes" and the phrase "You're just like your mother" are valence-shifters, which change the preclear from his own identity into the whole identity of another person. There are, then, many valences open to the preclear. The valence is a whole identity. If the preclear is in his grandfather's valence, the preclear may be expected to have all the troubles Grandfather had and most of the peculiarities and characteristics. These characteristics do not have to be contained in engrams themselves; they are simply part and parcel of the valence. The preclear may be in several valences at once, in a synthetic valence or in no valence at all. Or he can be in his own valence. If the preclear is not in his own valence, every effort should be made in the course of processing to cause him to find his own valence. Running pleasure moments very often brings the preclear into his own valence.

Being out of valence is a primary cause, evidently, of sonic, visio and somatic shut-offs. The auditor may be running an engram in which the preclear has sonic, visio and somatics which suddenly disappear. The first thing he should suspect is a valence-shifter. He asks for a yes-or-no flash answer as to whether a valence-shifter is present, and if the answer is yes, he asks for the wording of the valence-shifter, and when he gets the words he has the preclear repeat them, and the preclear will go back into his own valence and visio and sonic will turn back on. Most cases which are occluded are out of valence.

Valence is a survival mechanism, one of the means used by the mind to escape too painful an existence; therefore, in order to get the preclear into his own valence much of the charge has to be unburdened from the track. Locks can be scanned with the individual out of valence. In most secondaries, where terror and apathy are present, the preclear will be found to be out of valence. It is necessary to run such an incident several times before the preclear can get into his own valence and so get a proper discharge of the grief, fear or apathy.

On the Tone Scale we see that we are, again, involved with two different types of cases. The first is the case which is wide open, in valence, with sonic and visio, although highly charged; being too weak structurally to cover up charge, this case stays in its own valence though that valence is too painful to bear. The other type is where the mind has the ability to get out of valence and so occlude painful moments in the past. The mind ordinarily chooses winning valences. Valence-shifters, however, can force the individual into the valence he abhors. Continued repetition by a parent that the preclear is "just like Grandfather" but that he "must not be like Grandfather" because "Grandfather is detestable" will bring about a conflicting situation in which the preclear is forced, by valence-shifters, to occupy a character he feels is abhorred. This is the primary mechanism which causes an individual to "detest himself"; he actually does not detest himself at all; he detests the valence in which he has been forced to live.

The chart is self-explanatory for the occluded case. It goes without saying that in a wide-open case the person is in valence from top to bottom, wherever he is on the Tone Scale. From this it should not be adjudicated that it is either desirable or undesirable to be a wide-open case; such cases are relatively easy to work. The occluded case, when finally in his own valence, with sonic and visio and with most of his engrams gone, is in excellent condition, with a very high mental potential.

The condition of the track is normally regulated by the factors of charge, valence-shifters and action phrases. In view of the fact that action phrases are not active unless there is heavy charge on the case, it actually comes down to the fact that the condition of the track and of the valence of the preclear is regulated by charge. By charge, of course, is meant anger, fear, grief or apathy—misemotion—contained in the case. This form of entheta (there is other entheta, in the form of communication and reality secondaries, as well as misemotion secondaries) charges up the track so much that the action phrases become very active. It is charge which makes action phrases act. The charge must be very heavy on a case before engram action phrases—action phrases contained in engrams themselves—can be active. The charge must be much heavier for action phrases to be active in secondary engrams, which are those containing misemotion and communication and reality breaks and enforcements. The charge on the case must be extreme indeed for action phrases to be active in locks.

Thus it can be seen that the condition of the track and valences is mainly a matter of charge. In the wide-open case, a tremendously heavily charged track brings the individual into a psychotic level. The inability of the mind to occlude and encyst charge gives us the strange picture of an individual who can move on the track and who can run through engrams and who has sonic and visio but who is psychotic. These people are relatively easy to work; but the primary target should be the removal of charge, regardless of the temptation to run engrams, because such people will lock up on the track if the auditor makes the mistake of running engrams because they are easy to reach.

CHAPTER SEVENTEEN

COLUMN O

MANIFESTATION OF ENGRAMS AND LOCKS

Human conduct, in the absence of engrams, can be considered to be *good,* from the viewpoint of the individual and his group, as modified by the education and environment of that individual. The individual without engrams seeks survival along all of the dynamics, in accordance with his breadth of understanding.

This does not mean that a Zulu who had been cleared of all of his engrams would not continue to eat missionaries if he were a cannibal by education; but it does mean that he would be as rational as possible about eating missionaries; further, it would be easier to reeducate him about eating missionaries, if he were a Clear. Being a Clear does not mean being a reeducated or a reenvironmented or a regeneticized individual; but it does mean that all possible free theta in the case can be brought to bear on the problems of the environment and the future and that all the data in the analytical memory bank is available for the solution of those problems. Engrams and their secondaries and locks inject unalterable conclusions into the mind, so that computation becomes much on the order of trying to add two and two when an unseen hand is always adding another two to the column, unknown to the computer. An engram makes it impossible for a person adding two and two to get four; furthermore, it makes the individual do strange and irrational things, which is to say, it makes him act along nonsurvival lines and causes him to do things although he "should know better."

The engram, with its secondaries and locks, alters behavior by inhibiting action or thought or imagination or by causing the individual to dramatize. So long as an individual can actively dramatize an engram, however, the engram does not become particularly charged. When the engram commands such nonsurvival activity that the environment censures or brings further pain to the individual, that engram begins to charge up. If an engram commands an individual to walk three times around the block every morning for his health, the engram may be effective but not troublesome so long as the individual is permitted that walk. Let him, however, move into an environment such as the army, where he is not permitted to take this "constitutional" every morning but must stand muster[1] instead; the dramatization is broken and, as a consequence, the action potential of the individual is observed by his analytical mind to be cut down, and the individual feels reduced in scope. When an engram in a thief commands that he steal, he may be cheerful and happy so long as he can go on stealing; then the law may step in and jail him because he steals; this breaks the dramatization and reduces him in scope and well-being.

There are two sides to an engram: entheta and enMEST. So long as the thought can be dramatized, the enMEST remains quiet; but when the dramatization is broken, the enMEST, or physical pain, turns on in an effort to force the individual to do what the engram commands. Engrams monitor individuals in this unseen way. In lower organisms than man there is a survival value to this type of reactive action. In the environment of a lower organism, the receipt of pain normally comes about because the organism is not following a survival course; therefore, if the organism attempts to

1. **stand muster:** to undergo a formal military inspection.

do the same thing again, the pain threatens to turn on and the organism is forced into another course of action which, presumably, is better survival.

Much could be written about human behavior and about the engram as the cause of aberrated behavior, but this is a book about auditing. What the auditor wishes to know is how to audit his preclear and how to find his preclear on this chart so that he will know what type of entheta to address in the case, whether to run engrams, secondaries or locks, and how to run them.

An engram is a moment of physical pain and unconsciousness. A secondary is a moment of misemotion where loss is threatened or accomplished. A lock is an analytical moment in which the perceptics of the engram are approximated, thus restimulating the engram or bringing it into action, the present time perceptics being erroneously interpreted by the reactive mind to mean that the same condition which produced physical pain once before is now again at hand. Secondaries contain only misemotion and communication and reality enforcements and breaks. Locks contain mainly perceptics; no physical pain and very little misemotion. These are all types of entheta. Secondaries and locks charge up engrams; it is not possible to run engrams in a case which is very heavily charged with secondaries and locks.

By observing his preclear, the auditor should be able to establish fairly rapidly what the preclear does with locks. In surveying the case, he may find that the preclear acts very aberratedly on the subject of religion, and yet all he can find as a cause is a scolding by a minister when the preclear was a child; the human mind is a very tough mechanism, and this is insufficient cause for aberration in a sane person. If the conduct is remedied merely by running this lock, the auditor can see that this preclear will dramatize locks, which is to say, he will act as though locks were engrams. This denotes a very highly charged case.

The auditor may discover that the preclear dramatizes secondaries, which is to say that the preclear is a "coffin case," which lies in the position of a dead man, with arms folded. This is a grief engram having to do with the death of some loved one, and with the preclear in the valence of the loved one. The auditor will see many examples of the "coffin case." This means that the preclear will dramatize secondaries and that the track is very heavily charged, but less heavily charged than that of the preclear who will dramatize locks.

Finally we have the preclear who will dramatize only engrams. He is fairly high up the scale; is more or less normal.

The column on the chart about the manifestation of engrams and locks is self-explanatory if one understands these basic principles.

There are three types of locks: broken dramatizations, restimulations and ARC locks.

It is a principle of theta that it desires to carry to completion any cycle of action once begun. When such a cycle is interrupted, as in the breaking of a dramatization, turbulence is entered into the theta, and entheta is produced.

The restimulation lock merely brings to the person perceptions which approximate those of an engram. If the individual is tired or weary, these perceptions, sights, sounds, smells, or whatever they may be, will restimulate the engram which has similar perceptics; and the incident becomes a lock on the engram and charges it to some small degree.

The third type of lock results when affinity, communication or reality is forced upon the individual by the environment when he does not want it, when it is not rationally necessary, or when one or more of these is inhibited or denied to the individual by others in the environment.

Some of these ARC locks which occur in a person's life are so intense and cause so much charge to enter into the engram that they are considered secondary engrams. We have, then, as well as misemotion secondaries, the secondaries of enforced or denied ARC.

CHAPTER EIGHTEEN

COLUMN P

SEXUAL BEHAVIOR ATTITUDE TOWARD CHILDREN

THIS IS THE COLUMN DEVOTED TO the second dynamic. This dynamic would normally be called sex. In Dianetics, one considers sex to be divided into two parts: the sexual act; and the product of sex, children.

Any dynamic can be considered to be a flowing line of theta. The power of theta along any dynamic varies from individual to individual. Engrams can be considered to lie across the dynamics in such a way as to cause dispersion. When the engrams are removed the dispersion, which would be theta turning into entheta and the inhibition of the flow of free theta, disappears and the natural flow of free theta can begin again.

One sees this dispersion and entheta effect most markedly on the second dynamic. It is so clear-cut that some psychotherapies, in the past, placed the entire emphasis of aberration on the second dynamic. Naturally, these psychotherapies were not very workable, since they left out the other six dynamics, and were, indeed, severely criticized by their contemporaries for not being sufficiently comprehensive. Sex, however, is an excellent index of the position of the preclear on the Tone Scale. It is the excellence of this index which probably brought so much attention to the second dynamic.

In this current culture, sexual aberration is very high. Anything which is hidden and highly regulated in a culture will become aberrated. There is considerable confusion in the American and European cultures about sex; since there was so much perversion and promiscuity and maltreatment of children that the erroneous conclusion was reached that the remedy for this lay in further regulation; whereas, in reality, it was the regulation which caused the derangement of the dynamic.

It will be noted, in observing the behavior of human beings, and on this chart of the Tone Scale, that promiscuity, perversion, sadism and irregular practices fall far down the line. Free love falls, also, in this very low band; since man is relatively monogamous and since it is nonsurvival not to have a well-ordered system for the creation and upbringing of children, by families. A society which falls into this 1.1 band of the Tone Scale can be expected to abuse sex, to be promiscuous, to misuse and maltreat children, and to act, in short, much in the way current cultures are acting. It is of vital importance, if one wishes to stop immorality, free love and the abuse of children, to de-aberrate this dynamic for the whole group of the society, to say nothing of individuals.

At the highest MEST point of the Tone Scale, 4.0, one finds monogamy, constancy, a high enjoyment level and very moral reaction towards sex; but one also finds the sexual urge acting to create more than children, and so comes about a sublimation of sex into creative thought.

At 3.5 on the Tone Scale, we have a high interest in the opposite sex, and constancy, but we do not have so great a sublimation.

At 3.0 on the Tone Scale, we have some falling off in sexual interest, but we have an interest in procreation and children.

At 2.5, we have some disinterest in procreation, not for any reason beyond a general failure to be interested in much of anything. The sexual act can be adequately performed, given the physical ability.

At the band of 2.0, we begin to get a disgust for sex, a revulsion toward sex, mostly when irregularly practiced.

At the 1.5 band of the Tone Scale, we find sex appearing as rape; we find the sexual act being performed as a punishment.

At 1.1 on the Tone Scale, we enter the area of the most vicious reversal of the second dynamic. Here we have promiscuity, perversion, sadism and irregular practices. We have here no enjoyment of the sex act, actually, but a hectic anxiety about it. The sex act cannot truly be enjoyed whether performed regularly or irregularly. Here is the harlot, the pervert, the unfaithful wife, free love, easy marriage and quick divorce, and general sexual disaster. People at this level on the second dynamic are intensely dangerous in the society, since aberration is contagious. A society which reaches this level is on its way out of history, as went the Greeks, as went the Romans, as goes modern European and American culture. Here is a flaming danger signal which must be heeded if a race is to go forward.

At 0.5, we have impotency and anxiety about sex, with only occasional efforts to procreate. On the second dynamic we get occasional resurgences, from 0.5 up the scale, which quickly relapse.

It is interesting to note here the application of the principle of the dwindling spiral to the second dynamic. On any of the dynamics and on any column of this chart, when the individual sinks below the 2.0 level, the dwindling spiral rapidly carries him down through 1.5, 1.1, 0.5, to death. This is particularly evident on the second dynamic. The 1.1 individual, engaged in frantic pseudosexual activity today, will in a very near tomorrow, much nearer usually than he suspects, find himself or herself at the 0.5 level of impotency and anxiety.

The organs of sex, at the 0.5 level, become relatively useless; indeed, this second dynamic Tone Scale is closely applicable to the endocrine activity of the individual and the form and condition of the physical body. The woman who in her teens was at the 1.1 level of the scale will not have a well enough developed pelvic structure or endocrine system to permit her bearing children with ease. Difficult births are a normal result of too long a residence in a low band of the Tone Scale during the formative period of the body. Easy births can only be expected with women who are relatively high on the Tone Scale.

It is noteworthy that the 1.1 to 0.5 area of the Tone Scale finds the muscles, particularly the sexual muscles, without tonus. The nymphomaniac and the satyr are extremely slack-muscled, and the tonus around 0.5 is almost nonexistent.

In the pretended death band there is, of course, no effort to procreate.

Along the −1 band, where the organism as an organism is dead but the cells still survive, it is interesting that ejaculation and sexual activity occasionally take place immediately after the death of the individual, which gives some index of the strength and force of this dynamic.

Life is defined, in cytology, as an unending stream of protoplasm from the beginning of life itself until now. Down through the ages as a continuous genetic stream, this protoplasm is modified by natural selection and environmental conditioning, as well as by what seems to be outright planning, from generation to generation. Because life is so dependent upon this lifeline, it is very easy to place too great an emphasis upon the sexual act, the thing which keeps this lifeline in a continuous stream.

The second part of this dynamic concerns itself with children, the product of sex. There is a gradient of reaction toward children, from the top to the bottom of the Tone Scale, which the auditor can use in order to place his preclear properly on the chart.

At 4.0, there is an intense interest in children, which extends to both the mental and physical well-being of the children and the society in which these children will live. Here are efforts to add to the culture so that the children will have a better chance for survival.

At 3.5, we have a love of children, a care of them, an understanding of them.

At 3.0, we have an interest in children.

At 2.5, we have a tolerance of children, but not too great an interest in their affairs.

At 2.0, we have nagging of, and nervousness about children.

At 1.5, we enter the band of brutal treatment of children, heavy corporal punishment, the forcing of the child into a mold with pain, breaking his dramatizations, upset about his noise or clutter.

At 1.1 on the Tone Scale, there may be two reactions to children. There may be an actual and immediate desire for children, as a manifestation of sex. But we also may have the use of children for sadistic purposes. And we may find both of these in the same individual. We have a long-term general neglect of children, with an occasional sporadic interest in them; we have very little thought for the child's future or the culture in which the child will grow up.

At 0.5, we have mainly an anxiety about children, fear that they will be hurt, fear of this and fear of that concerning children, and a hopelessness about their future.

At 1.1, a mother will attempt the abortion of her child; and any woman who will abort a child, save only if the child threatens her physical life (rather than her reputation), lies in the 1.1 bracket or below. She can be expected to be unreliable, inconstant and promiscuous; and the child is looked upon as evidence of this promiscuity.

At 0.5, we have abortion with the specious reasoning that the world or the future is too horrible to bring a child into. With the parent at 0.5, all the natural gaiety and happiness of the child will be suppressed, and we have as unhealthy an atmosphere for childhood as one could postulate.

At 0.1, there is not even awareness of children.

It is notable, as one glances down this column, that an interest in children includes an interest not only in the bearing of the child but in the child's well-being, happiness, mental state, education and general future. We may have a person on the 1.1 level who seems very anxious to produce a child; very possibly this person is following an engram command to have children. Once the child is born we may have, in this 1.1 bracket, an interest in it as a plaything or a curiosity, but, following this, we get general neglect and thoughtlessness about the child and no feeling whatsoever about the child's future or any effort to build one for it. We get careless familial actions, such as promiscuity, which will tear to pieces the family security upon which this child's future depends. Along this band, the child is considered a thing, a possession.

A half a tone above this, in the anger band, the child is a target for the dramatizations which the individual does not dare execute against grown-ups in the environment—a last-ditch effort to be in command of something. Here we have domination of the child, with a constant warping of its character.

The whole future of the race depends upon its attitude toward children; and a race which specializes in women for "menial purposes," or which believes that the contest of the sexes in the spheres of business, action, and politics is a worthier endeavor than the creation of tomorrow's generation, is a race which is dying. We have, in the woman who is an ambitious rival of the man in his own activities, a woman who is neglecting the most important mission she may have. A society which looks down upon this mission, and in which women are taught *anything but* the management of a family, the care of men, and the creation of the future generation, is a society which is on its way out. The historian can peg the point where a society begins its sharpest decline at the instant when women begin to take part, on an equal footing with men, in political and business affairs; since this means that the men are decadent and the women are no longer women. This is not a sermon on the role or position of women: it is the statement of a bald and basic fact. When children become unimportant to a society, that society has forfeited its future.

Even beyond the fathering and bearing and rearing of children, a human being does not seem to be complete without a relationship with a member of the opposite sex. This relationship is the vessel wherein is nurtured the life force of both individuals, whereby they create the future of the race in body and thought. If man is to rise to greater heights, then woman must rise with him, or even before him. But she must rise *as* woman and not as today she is being misled into rising—as a man. It is the hideous joke of frustrated, unvirile men to make women over into the travesty of men which men themselves have become.

Men are difficult and troublesome creatures—but valuable. The creative care and handling of men is an artful and a beautiful task. Those who would cheat women of their rightful place by making them into men should at last realize that by this action they are destroying not only the women but the men and the children as well. This is too great a price to pay for being "modern" or for someone's petty anger or spite against the female sex.

The arts and skills of woman, the creation and inspiration of which she is capable and which, here and there in isolated places in our culture, she still manages to effect in spite of the ruin and decay of man's world which spreads around her, must be brought newly and fully into life. These arts and skills and creation and inspiration are her beauty, just as she is the beauty of mankind.

CHAPTER NINETEEN

COLUMN Q

COMMAND OVER ENVIRONMENT

IT MAY BE POSTULATED THAT THE mission of theta is the conquest of MEST. The organism controls as much MEST as it has theta with which to control that MEST.

One could envision command over the environment, for a man or for a group, as a series of concentric circles. The widest circle would demonstrate the individual's or the group's considered belief in its ability to have an effect on the physical universe. The next circle, just inside, would be the individual's or the group's belief in its ability to affect all of Earth and life. The next circle inside would be the individual's or the group's belief in its ability to affect a section of life, a nation or a smaller group. The next circle would be the belief of the individual or the group in its ability to affect some other species and the men in its environ. The next inside circle would be the belief the individual or the group has in its ability to affect a few people or a small portion of its environment. The next circle would have to do with the individual's and the group's belief that it could affect the individual and the group. The next inside circle would be the individual's or the group's inability to affect self.

One cannot say what would be the normal command area, but certain it is that when the command area comes to the point where the individual can barely affect the individual and the group can barely affect the group we reach a point where the only MEST (and for their purposes, as a matter of viewpoint, the individual and the group often consider life and life forms as MEST, subject to their control) which can be changed by theta is the MEST of the individual or group. Here psychosomatic illnesses set in, theta acting only within the organism, to destroy it; a group at this stage will tear itself apart. It is just slightly wider than this circle that we enter the 2.0 area of the chart. The wider areas could be said to be those where theta could act freely enough to be constructive and creative within those spheres of influence; and very close to the center of the spheres would be where entheta exists. A much more complex system, which would possibly tell us a great deal about theta and MEST, could be worked out on this gradient scale, and probably should be.

The auditor is primarily interested in spotting his preclear on the chart. In order to do so he should establish what the preclear thinks he can control in terms of life, MEST, people and groups *and* what the preclear thinks he would do with these if he could control them. If the preclear has constructive and creative plans in mind for the sphere he outlines, one can see that he is above the 2.0 band and that one is working with the amount of theta the individual has as his endowment, since not all men believe they can control the entire universe but should not necessarily be suspect of being psychotic should they entertain such a notion, even though it is a manifestation of psychosis to have grandiose ideas because of manic engrams. Men have existed who could control enormous spheres and be creative and constructive within those spheres, but these were not men of the sword; they were men of ideas.

Should the preclear postulate for himself a rather wide sphere and then appoint for it a destructive end, one can be sure that one is dealing with a preclear below the 2.0 level.

The auditor should keep in mind the axiom that all creation carries with it a small amount of destruction; just as one may not be able to construct an apartment building without destroying the tenement which sits there; just as one may not be able to publish a newspaper without destroying forests to obtain newsprint; it is the ratio of creation to destruction which counts.

In view of the postulates laid down in this chapter, the column on the chart is self-explanatory. Some comment, however, should be made on the political ramifications contained in this column. It will be seen that the democratic area—where one deals with Jeffersonian democracy—lies in the bands at 3.0 and above. This postulates a belief in the goodness of men and the good sense of men in council. It postulates the belief that men should be free to decide things for themselves. It outlaws tyranny as undesirable, and relegates government to the service of the group rather than the group to the service of the government.

One has to go well down the Tone Scale in order to find the next stopping point for politics, and here he locates fascism as existing between 2.0 and 1.5. Fascism is an absolute control, for destructive purposes, of an environ, with forthright and strong-armed means employed in seeking that control. There are intermediate stops between democracy and fascism, such as monarchy; they are not of major interest in the world at this time, and are not within the scope of this work but belong in Group Dianetics, which will be covered completely in another volume.

In today's world, the next stop down the Tone Scale politically is the subversive, who belongs in the 1.1 to 1.3 bracket. Most theoretical subversion pretends to be very high on the Tone Scale, and so has had its appeal to the liberally inclined individual; but there is a wide gap between theoretical and destructive liberalism, and the unthinking liberal confuses the theory with the practice. He finds himself keeping company with 1.1s, since an inspection of any brand of politics which oversweeps the world because of the general apathy of societies shows that it falls exactly into this position on the scale: communication lines are cut; affinities are flagrantly used and perverted; reality is twisted; the level of cabal as seen in hate propaganda, compares with lowest gossip; and the treatment of human beings is without any regard to the respect an individual human being should have. Psychometry on subversives places them uniformly in this 1.1 bracket. They have no respect for the wit and sanity of anyone; they hold promiscuity as a high virtue; they have no belief in family. They are about as safe to have for friends as an adder—but probably this is unfair to the honest adder.

Subversion receives its main support from such individuals as lie in the vicinity of 1.1; and the reason it gains so many volunteer agents in lands which it wishes to overrun lies in the desire of the 1.1 to have good cause and reason to flaunt flagrantly and place himself "above" existing morals and the laws of the land in which he operates. He gains through his warped philosophy a very fine excuse to believe himself above such things as law and decency, and it is very possibly this appeal alone which brings so many recruits to ruthless politics.*

*In this column on the Tone Scale chart, brief reference is made to certain political philosophies and attitudes in the world today. While this subject will be taken up at length in Group Dianetics, the present chart would be incomplete if it did not show that these political systems have their own tone positions and that their general methods of operation can be seen to conform with the methods and operations of individuals at those levels. At 3.5, we have the liberal. The liberal reasons well, accepts wide responsibilities, and is guided by the high ethical principles. He is eager to seize upon any new idea which will improve the society, and he is not suggestible, being swayed this way and that by any propaganda, but reaches conclusions extremely rationally. He has a high regard for individual freedom, for property, and for the right of the powerfully productive person to be allowed to contribute to the society without hindrance, spontaneously and efficiently. At 3.0, we have the person who is democratic, but who is somewhat more conservative in his attitudes and more given to social regulations, being more in need of them. The term democratic is a somewhat loose one, but at this level it signifies the individual or system which allows personal freedom and has moderate regard for property and productive ability but is not particularly inventive or enthusiastic about refining and improving and enriching the social order along all of the dynamics. The next familiar political level is the 1.5 level of fascism. The activities of Hitler and Mussolini

154

and the social orders they produced are, of course, the examples which come to mind. The open declaration of intention to conquer, kill and control by the most obvious and forceful methods is the mark of fascism. Justification is limited to the bluntest, most baldfaced lies. Invalidation of other persons and social orders is straightforward, angry and lacking in any subtle pretense of reasonableness or moderation. The next political level is the 1.1 level of communism. The literature of communism, particularly in the works of Lenin, sets the tone of secret, flexible, deceptive operation which is observable in the methods of communism throughout the world. In its strongholds such as the Soviet Union, in times and sections where it is not threatened, communism will sometimes rise for brief periods to the level of 1.5, but in its normal action it partakes of all of the characteristics of the 1.1 level as they are outlined in this present work. The willingness to devote an unlimited amount of time to accomplishing secretly a destructive action which the fascist would accomplish immediately by force is implicit in communism. Communism has an endless patience in tearing down by subtle propaganda a society or an idea which it never openly opposes in all that time, and an unwillingness ever to use open methods which would betray interest or activity. Communism, like the individual 1.1, makes an initial pretense of giving great assistance and help, and it keeps up this pretense in the face of any and all contradictory evidence, blandly giving forth soothing justifications and assurances of the most sincere and deeply felt interest in the good of all. The reader who will examine these various political manifestations in the light of the Tone Scale chart will find, undoubtedly, that from time to time mysterious actions of various political factions become predictable and understandable. —LRH

C O L U M N   R

Actual Worth to Society Compared to Apparent Worth

In Dianetics we have some means of establishing the worth of a human being. In the past, the worth of individuals or groups was judged by the amount of MEST they owned. If a man had money, he was said to be worth so much money; if a group had control of property, it was said to be worth so much control of property. However, this is a nonsurvival definition. Whereas every individual should be entitled, unconditionally, to whatever he can earn in a society, since this is a blunt measure of his value to the society, and one should never make the mistake of believing otherwise; by means of inheritances and strange effects to which money can lend itself it can become badly perverted as a yardstick. When it becomes perverted, men of money begin to be damned by a society and are sought out as the scapegoats for all its ills; whereas a goodly number of them are the very pivots on which the society is turning. The subversive appeals to the indigence and poverty which is the lot, unfortunately, of a majority of populaces in these days of poorly advanced culture by promising to murder every man of property once a land is taken. The whole cult of anticapitalism is something less than a sound philosophic postulate and rather more than a gross appeal to those who have no property and no hope of attaining any. As this philosophy has no concept of any individual worth, of whatever kind, and rather tends to operate on the maxim that "five morons make a genius," it can afford to overlook any means of evaluating any human being and would rather not do so, since its practice when entering a country is to corral and murder every man of worth to that country and leave it pauperized as a race.

In the handbook,[1] an equation was written which caused people some puzzlement; it was to the effect that potential value was equal to intelligence multiplied by the dynamics of the individual to a certain power. This might be restated as meaning that the potential value of any man was equal to some numerical factor, denoting his structural intelligence and capability, multiplied by his free theta to a power. This was written in the handbook in an effort to encourage some psychologist to discover what the power of the dynamic might be and conclude some means of establishing potential value by psychometry. Actual worth, then, of the individual would be his potential value as modified by the direction that potential value took with regard to the survival of his group or of himself. One might have an individual of very high potential value who yet, by education and engrams, was a distinct liability to himself and his group.

In this column on the chart, anyone, regardless of his potential value, below the line of 2.0 as evaluated by other columns, has a negative value to the society. Anyone above this line goes from zero value upward in a positive direction.

This whole scale is postulated on the fact that the brain and brawn of an individual serve the other dynamics. The remark has been made that social orders are carried upon the backs of a few desperate men. If the social order were being carried forward

---

1. **handbook:** a reference to *Dianetics: The Modern Science of Mental Health.*

toward higher levels of culture by these few desperate men, they could be considered and, indeed, upon inspection would be found to lie well above the 2.0 level. When the desperation is expressed in terms of death and destruction, the individual lies below this 2.0 level and, regardless of what his actions are, will bring the society lower on the Tone Scale.

The auditor's main interest in this column lies, again, in the estimate of the preclear's position upon it; and this column makes it possible to estimate position by examining both the actual worth and the potential value of the preclear in his environment. If the preclear normally injures—makes enMEST out of—those things which he seeks to control or which he owns, he can be said to lie below the 2.0 line; and if he is fairly successful in his use of MEST he lies above that line.

This column is otherwise self-explanatory.

As a member of his own social order, the auditor should take into account, when deciding which of the people around him he will take as preclears, the actual worth of those people to their family, group and society. He will do well to spend his efforts upon those who show the highest promise, in terms of current activity while aberrated, even though these may not be the easiest cases to work. While all men are created with equal rights under the law, an examination of the individuals in the society rapidly demonstrates that all men are not created with equal potential value to their fellows.

CHAPTER TWENTY-ONE

COLUMN S
ETHIC LEVEL

T HE WHOLE SUBJECT OF ETHICS IS one which, with societies at their present low position on the Tone Scale, has become almost lost.

Ethics actually consist, as we can define them now in Dianetics, of rationality toward the highest level of survival for the individual, the future race, the group and mankind, and the other dynamics taken collectively. Ethics are reason. The highest ethic level would be long-term survival concepts with minimal destruction, along any of the dynamics. A reasonable examination of this subject demonstrates immediately that dishonest conduct may serve, on a short-term basis, the advantage of an individual or a group, but that a continuous line of dishonest conduct will bring the individual or the group down the Tone Scale. Thus, dishonest conduct is nonsurvival. Anything which is unreasonable in the conduct of interrelations among men could be considered unethical, since those things which are unreasonable bring about the destruction of individuals and groups and inhibit the future of the race. The keeping of one's word, when it has been sacredly pledged, is an act of survival, since one is then trusted, but only so long as one keeps one's pledged word.

To the weak, to the cowardly, to the reprehensibly irrational, dishonesty and underhanded dealings, the harming of others and the blighting of their hopes seem to be the only way of conducting life. Unethical conduct is actually the conduct of destruction and fear; lies are told because one is afraid of the consequences should one tell the truth; thus, the liar is inevitably a coward, the coward is inevitably a liar. The sexually promiscuous woman, the man who breaks faith with his friend, the covetous pervert are all dealing in such nonsurvival terms that degradation and death commonly ensue. A "love" clandestinely conducted and based on lies which will bring harm to others denotes a cowardice low enough to bring nausea to any decent man. Thus, one has the ethical or unethical aspect of sex.

In the modern dictionary we find that ethics are defined as "morals" and morals are defined as "ethics." These two words are not interchangeable. Morals should be defined as a code of good conduct laid down out of the experience of the race to serve as a uniform yardstick for the conduct of individuals and groups. Such a codification has its place; morals are actually laws. The origin of a point in a moral code comes about when it is discovered, through experience, that some act is more nonsurvival than prosurvival. The prohibition of this act enters into the customs of the people and may eventually become a law. This is the natural process of creation of all law. Morals are, to some degree, arbitraries, in that they continue beyond their time. This far from states that laws are bad, as uniformity and regulation are vital to the conduct of all groups, but only that laws become outmoded now and then and need to be revised. Many things which were moral in the past were moral only because they were hygienic; and, indeed, as has been said, all morals originate out of the discovery by the group that some act contains more pain than pleasure.

In the absence of extended reasoning powers, moral codes so long as they provide better survival for their group are a vital and necessary part of any culture. Morals, however, become onerous and protested against when they become outmoded; and a revolt against morals normally has as its target the fact that the code no longer is as applicable as it was before; although revolts against moral codes actually occur because individuals of the group or the group itself has sunk on the Tone Scale to a point where it wishes to practice license against these moral codes, not because the codes themselves are unreasonable.

If a moral code were thoroughly reasonable, it could, at the same time, be considered thoroughly ethical, but only at this highest level could these two be called the same. Theta, in its action against MEST, is reason itself; and the ultimate in reason is the ultimate in survival.

In the light of the above, the column on the chart is self-explanatory, but the additional comment should be made that at the level of 2.0 and below, destructive arbitrariness, called, for lack of a better word, authoritarianism, sets in; and that all laws made at this level, and on down the scale, will have nonsurvival results.

Criminals lie in the band from 2.0 down the scale, as a generality; but most criminals are found from about 1.3 downward; there is nothing very glamorous about the criminal, the breaker of his pledge, the betrayer of his friend or group. Such people are simply psychotic.

This does not say that individuals who lie potentially along tone bands from 2.0 down are actively criminal, chronically, or that they are actively unethical, chronically; but it does say that during periods of enturbulence they are unethical and immoral, and refrain from being so only in ratio to the amount of free theta they still have available. They normally enturbulate easily and often, however, and while for days and weeks together they may appear to be rational, insofar as the current normal is concerned, they are a serious liability to any employer or mate or family or group. Here again we have the condition of the acute psychotic state as opposed to the chronic psychotic state; in the acute psychotic state the person becomes temporarily insane for short periods; in the chronic state, he remains insane. If a person can enturbulate easily down to a level below 2.0, and has not enough free theta to refrain from aberrated action, he should not be given more freedom in the society than the chronic psychotic, since he is as thoroughly psychotic in his acute state of enturbulence as any constantly insane individual. Society, recognizing that the greatest danger from an individual lies in the band from anger down to 1.1, has sought to safeguard itself by suppressing these people permanently into an apathy level; this control mechanism, however, is as unworkable as it is widespread, since individuals in the apathy strata can rebound sporadically up into the active strata and so are still thoroughly dangerous. The only answers would seem to be the permanent quarantine of such persons from society to avoid the contagion of their insanities and the general turbulence which they bring into any order, thus forcing it lower on the scale, or processing such persons until they have attained a level on the Tone Scale which gives them value.

In any event, any person from 2.0 down on the Tone Scale should not have, in any thinking society, any civil rights of any kind, because by abusing those rights they bring into being arduous and strenuous laws which are oppressive to those who need no such restraints. And particularly, none below 2.0, chronically or acutely, should be used as witnesses or jurors in courts of law, since their position in regard to ethics is such as to nullify the validity of any testimony they might essay or any verdict they might offer.

This does not propose that depriving such persons of their civil rights should obtain any longer than is necessary to bring them up the Tone Scale to a point where their ethics render them fit company for their fellows. This, however, would be a necessary step for any society seeking to raise itself on the Tone Scale as a social order. A fundamental of law already provides for this step, since sanity, in law, is defined as the ability to tell right from wrong. The rational, and therefore, the ethical, state of persons acutely or chronically below the point of 2.0 is such that it is impossible for them to judge right from wrong. Thus, by bringing forward a simple definition not only of right and wrong but of ethics, the existing fundamental can be put into effect, should it happen, by chance, that anyone cares whither our social order is drifting. It is simpler to do psychometry on 150 million people than to bury a culture for which we and our fathers have striven these past 175 years.

CHAPTER TWENTY-TWO

COLUMN T

THE HANDLING
OF TRUTH

THE METAPHYSICIAN WAS CONCERNED with absolute truth and considered that it transcended the limits of human experience. The social orders of his day must have been not much better than our own.

Truth is actually a relative quantity; it could be said to be the most reasonable existing data about any body of facts. Truth, as a manifestation of human conduct, would be the holding or voicing of facts as one knows them and refusal to utter or hold statements contrary to what one knows.

Creative and constructive imaginings about the future are not untruths but are postulated new realities. Few mothers there are who do not have untruths and imaginative postulates thoroughly confused, thus suppressing the necessary imaginative instincts of the child and giving the child, in fact, a confusion about the truth itself.

Truth may also be confused with tactlessness. Many 1.1s blatantly "pride themselves" on their honesty, and so license themselves to make destructive statements "for the good of" somebody else which are actually lies. There is an ethic about the handling of truth. While it may be true that something is destructive or that a person is bad, if it serves no purpose to make the statement the issuance of this "truth" is in reality the establishing of an entheta line. The highest concept of truth, then, has a certain aesthetic about it, in that it is creative and constructive.

In common human experience we all know something about the truth and that we cannot deal in a black-and-white breakdown between the truth and lies. Truth is concerned in the issuance and acceptance of facts. Some people favor truthful facts; some favor facts which are not so truthful; some prefer to twist facts; some prefer to hide facts; and some prefer to lie about facts. Some favor high and powerful facts; and some favor only apathetic facts. As one examines this whole subject, one then discovers that the Tone Scale itself, from 4.0 down to 0.0, postulates the selection of various types of facts; and that the most reasonable facts are the most constructive ones; and that, as one falls away down the Tone Scale, the facts selected are less and less rational and more and more contrasurvival. It could be said that life was made to be lived, not died out of; and that facts which encourage a high level of living would be, for man, the most truthful facts; and that those which encourage his demise would be the most untruthful facts. Those things which are truest for man are, then, those things which most powerfully aid his survival, in theta, life and MEST.

This column of the Tone Scale might also be considered the column of preference of facts. At 4.0, we would have a preference for creative and constructive facts. Around 3.0, we would have a preference for conservative and less optimistic facts. At 2.5, we would have a carelessness of facts. At 2.0, we would have a preference for facts which were twisted well away from truth in order to serve antagonisms. At 1.5, we would have a preference for destructive facts, twisting all true facts which were constructive so that they would become destructive facts. At 1.1, we would have a preference for artfully twisted facts which hid a desire to destroy. At 0.5, we would have a failure to select facts, to evaluate them one way or the other, but a preference for hopeless facts. Below this level there would be no reaction.

The auditor can do psychometry on his preclear and locate him on the Tone Scale simply by discovering the type of fact which the preclear likes best or by discovering what the preclear does with facts.

The individual accepts or gives forth truth or untruth according to his position on the Tone Scale. If you know, from other columns, the probable position of the preclear on the Tone Scale, regardless of his convincingness or even his ability to "prove" what he is saying, by rather artful "evidence," you can correctly and properly evaluate the facts he gives you or the facts he will receive. The rather horrible part of this is that it admits of no great variation. A man at 1.5 deals in destructive facts and twists them so as to make them more effectively destructive; his data cannot be believed; and, indeed, any data from individuals at the 2.0 level or below has discard value only.

At 4.0, the individual has a high concept of truth and prefers constructive and creative truths. He seeks for new truths.

At 3.5, the individual is truthful but prefers not to deal in entheta facts.

At 3.0, we begin to get an onset of conservatism, a cautiousness about receiving or uttering truths and a shortsighted program of social lying in order to "avoid hurting people's feelings." One should, by the way, beware of placing in charge of anything people who are "afraid of hurting other people," for this is not a virtue but a form of cowardice and propitiation and denotes a fear of people; people are not so easily hurt as such persons believe.

At 2.5, we have insincerity and carelessness of facts. The modern American newspaper exemplifies this level on the Tone Scale, or perhaps the various magazines which could be named.

At 2.0, we get the first willful twisting of facts to suit purposes, and here facts will be twisted to suit antagonisms the person holds.

At 1.5, we achieve the ultimate reversal in facts; any white fact will be turned into a black fact; here we have blatant and destructive lying. Did you ever hear an angry man tell the truth?

At 1.1, truth receives her severest drubbing; for here truth is confused, upset, used and twisted, hidden for fear somebody may make retaliation, until one understands that data from this level of the Tone Scale has only two purposes: to wreak the most harm upon others and secure the greatest safety for self. Here we have lies used to hide lies amid the most frantic protestations of honesty and a noisy advertising campaign about the ethics of the speaker. Beneath the facade of honor, honesty, ethics and "one's sacred word," one is apt to find a writhing cesspool of vicious and malicious lies calculated to do the greatest possible harm. Early in the studies of the Tone Scale which resulted in this chart the lengths to which the 1.1 would go in advertising his virtuous character, while performing his knife-in-the-back tricks, were not wholly understood. Because such persons said so often that they were honest and ethical, it was, for a while, accepted that a person could be at a low level on the Tone Scale in other columns and still be able to tell the truth. Experience demonstrated that, whatever the advertisement of honesty, the 1.1 is completely incapable of truth but lies out of some horrible mechanical compulsion. Not one of the people for whom this allowance was made succeeded in being worthy of it, but each was discovered to be so deeply enmeshed in chicanery, all the while appearing so honest, that the depths to which aberration can suppress man were, for the first time, clearly understood. Bluntly, anyone takes his life and his reputation in his hands when he believes a 1.1, no matter the evidence. In this band we have fantastically accomplished actors, who may weep and plead and decry with contempt and disdain, asserting their honesty and their sincerity and demonstrating them with such consummate conviction that even the most critical observer may be unable to detect the slightest falsehood; and yet, in the 1.1, a deep and exhaustive inspection of the motivations and goals reveals a snake pit of lies and insincerities, of pretenses and unrealities. Such people can turn on tears and other emotions at will and use the language of highest honor to serve the most despicable ends.

At 0.5, we have no less dangerous but certainly more obvious levels of untruth. Just as fear drives the 1.1, grief drives the 0.5; and while the grief itself may be perfectly honest, the facts and evaluations which it collects to itself certainly are not. Since here we have an individual who is making a cry for help, supplications, pleas for pity, all facts stand magnified. The dead are found to be suddenly, utterly, without faults; the lover who abandoned the sweetheart is found to be a black-hearted villain. The 0.5 may be given sympathy, but never believed. People who are commonly in this band of the Tone Scale and are yet able to reason somewhat, to carry on some of the routine of life, are perilous to be around, since they demand enormous quantities of affection, and at the slightest rejection, fancied or real, dive in the direction of death, perhaps only as a demonstration of how badly they need aid, but, nevertheless, fatally; and such dives toward death inevitably affect others around them, since this individual has no responsibility of any kind toward other human beings and is so thoroughly introverted that however pathetic he may appear he only absorbs and never responds; he is an unsaturable sponge for sympathy and he is a chronic potential suicide. The tendency toward death will communicate itself toward all the aspects of life around this individual; he will make enMEST out of any MEST; he will prefer sordid and squalid quarters; he will drive ancient and rickety cars; he will dress only in the most ragged clothes; all these things are pleas for pity. When audited, his case, like the 1.1, commonly dubs in. The auditor must be particularly careful of the 0.5: not to run too much dub-in; not to give too much sympathy; not to give too little sympathy; and not to make an error in auditing which will depress the preclear's tone, since the 0.5 has so little distance to go to attempt death, either by sickness or by actual violent self-destruction. The 0.5 is near the end of the road and by contagion he much more markedly enturbulates the free theta of those around him than does even the 1.1 or the 1.5.

The validity of engrams run and the preclear's concept of truths are in direct ratio. The auditor can be guided thereby. But the auditor should never be critical of the facts the preclear brings forth; he must only attempt adroitly to guide the preclear toward running the highest level of fact the preclear can attain. Cases which are very low on the Tone Scale achieve their best advance, not by running data, but by running off charge, through boil-offs, yawns, false-fouring and other mechanical unburdening. The data the individual runs when below 2.0 may be interesting but it is quite often untrue, and it is less and less true the lower the individual drops on the scale.

The lowest point on this scale, for a life organism, is, of course, pretended death; and here is an untruth among untruths; for the organism is obviously alive and it is saying that it is dead. But the untruth is here modified by the fact that the organism requires but the slightest thrust to be dead in actuality.

CHAPTER TWENTY-THREE

COLUMN U

COURAGE LEVEL

COURAGE MIGHT BE CONSIDERED the theta force necessary to overcome obstacles in surviving.

One has, as a definition of happiness, the process of overcoming not unknowable obstacles toward a known goal, or the momentary contemplation of the completed task. It can be seen that this is a definition for happiness; and indeed this definition works. But courage is necessary if the individual is to be happy. And so it works out on the Tone Scale; the more free theta an individual has, in comparison to the theta he has enturbulated, the happier that individual can be, and the more courage he will demonstrate in his forward actions in life and in the face of adversities.

The courage level of an individual is actually a direct index of the free theta–enturbulated theta, or the theta–entheta, ratio of that individual. The courage level is also an index of the safety with which one may associate with a person or a group. A person of high courage is a valuable associate and group member, but a coward is a dangerous liability as a friend.

There is some strange mechanism in some men, an aberration of a decadent age, which causes them to seek out and help and protect the pitiful and weak amongst women. The reverse is sometimes found amongst women, a woman of strength seeking out and defending a weak and pitiful man. In either case, a failure is postulated at the beginning of such an association. However much the weak member may be raised on the Tone Scale by this association, the person on the higher level is inevitably lowered. Indeed, when two people occupy different positions on the Tone Scale and yet are in association with each other, the person at the higher point on the scale will become somewhat enturbulated to a greater or lesser degree by the person at the lower point on the scale; and the person at the lower point will become unenturbulated to a greater or lesser degree. People, then, who are low on the Tone Scale instinctively seek out people who are high on the Tone Scale; and if the people who are high on the Tone Scale have any thought for their own survival and efficiency, they will take adequate steps to understand the liability which they are incurring and to prevent themselves from being lessened in substance by such an association.

The auditor, in processing, is continually encountering entheta in any preclear. Thus it is necessary for the auditor, if he is doing constant processing, to keep himself adequately processed elsewhere. Otherwise, the auditor will find himself coming down the Tone Scale in a dwindling spiral, until he is at last unable to handle the entheta he is encountering in cases.

Courage level has a great deal to do with auditing. The auditor who has a low courage level is apt to let the preclear get into such a thing as a fear or terror engram and, justifying the action as sympathy, let the preclear out without having run the incident. This will most rapidly and certainly snarl the case. The auditor of low courage level who encounters for the first time a "screamer" and who fails to persevere in the face of the obvious and shrill agony of the preclear will make the preclear very sick. So far as courage level is concerned in auditing, any auditor must have the courage to take anything from a preclear and to run a preclear through anything without quailing. Courage has a great deal to do with auditing. A coward has no business in the auditor's chair, and if he is so placed, his preclear can expect to have his case ruined. In a later column on the chart you will see the tone level required of the auditor in order to handle preclears; the data most pertinent to this is courage level.

There are three ways of handling a problem: one is to attack it, directly or indirectly; one is to flee from it, directly or indirectly; and one is to neglect it. It is a matter of reason which method the individual selects to handle which problem. Continuous attack, bluntly and directly, on a problem is not necessarily a courageous address but may only be an angry and destructive address. A persistent address to the problem, however, requires courage, since one of the components of courage is duration of effort.

At 4.0, we have the high courage level of free theta itself.

At 3.5, we have courage displayed on reasonable risks.

At 3.0, we have a conservative display of courage where the risk is small.

At 2.5, we get neither courage nor cowardice but a definite neglect of danger.

At 2.0, we have blunt, undisguised, unreasoning thrusts at danger.

At 1.5, we get what would normally pass as "bravery," as distinct from courage. Here we have the hammering, destructive rush at danger. This often results in damage to self and to the cause for which the person is fighting.

At 1.1, we have reached fear, on the Tone Scale, and when the individual rises above fear we have underhanded displays of action. Suddenly addressed by danger, however, we have cowardice.

At 0.5, we have complete cowardice, no attack upon any problem, no reason, and only defeat.

In fighting, the best tactic is to strike such a sudden, unexpected and hard blow that one's enemy is instantly shot down the Tone Scale to apathy. Japan, receiving an atom bomb, descended instantly into apathy and surrendered. Hard but long-drawn-out blows or shocks harden resistance as in the bombing of London or Madrid. Shock and courage level are intimately connected.

CHAPTER TWENTY-FOUR

COLUMN V
ABILITY TO HANDLE RESPONSIBILITY

THERE IS NO MORE CERTAIN INDEX of the theta–entheta ratio and of the free theta endowment of an individual than the ability to undertake and execute responsibility.

By responsibility is meant the area or sphere of influence the individual can rationally affect around other people, life, MEST and the general environment, as represented in column Q, Command over Environment. The emphasis should be placed on *rationality,* since engrams are perfectly capable of placing a person in a manic state which causes him to believe he can handle a larger sphere than his capabilities permit, but when this is the case the effect of the individual on the sphere of influence betrays the fact that an engram is acting, because the sphere of influence will be affected destructively; this might have been called, in older terminology, a superiority complex.

The word *responsibility* is seen, then, to have a finer definition. If it is to be used it must include the shading that a truly responsible person works toward the survival of his environment, which would include action along any and all of the dynamics, himself, his children, his family, his group, mankind, life, MEST, theta and the Supreme Being. Where he falls short in advancing and aiding the purposes of any of these dynamics he is falling short of his responsibilities.

The operation of free theta would be the complementing of its component parts in others and the remainder of the dynamics, since each individual has, as the component parts of his own free theta, all of these dynamics. A high affinity level is necessary, then, in any individual, by which is meant his partnership with the dynamics as existing in others. Where the individual has had many affinity breaks with the other dynamics (and an engram is an affinity break between the theta universe and the MEST universe) the concept of partnership reduces, and the individual is more and more concerned with responsibilities which are nearer and nearer at hand, until he can barely be responsible for himself. This narrowing of the sphere of responsibility is analogous to the descent down the Tone Scale. When the individual cannot be responsible for himself any of the time he is a chronic psychotic and is institutionalized. When he cannot be responsible for himself except part of the time he is an acute psychotic and passes in this society for normal.

It is not the magnitude of the sphere of responsibility of the individual which should take the auditor's eye as he attempts to evaluate the individual on the Tone Scale, but it is the quality of responsibility along each of the dynamics.

The fully responsible individual bears certain definite marks which are unmistakable.

On the first dynamic, he takes good care of himself; he gives a well-kept appearance in accordance with his means and pursuits; his personal effects are tidy and in reasonably good condition.

On the second dynamic, he attempts to give adequate support and assistance to his mate and to provide the future with a happy and successful new generation. He is loyal to and takes good care of his family.

On the third dynamic, he takes orderly care of his own affairs as related to his group and members of his group and seeks to increase the survival potential of his friends and group.

On the fourth dynamic, he is concerned for the survival of man, within the limits of his education.

On the fifth dynamic, he demonstrates an affinity with other life forms. He will be found to engage himself, given opportunity, in raising plants or animals and will prefer to have living things in his vicinity. He will not be given to wanton destruction of life, but will use life for his own sustenance. The individual who will not kill for food he needs is actually on the propitiation level of the Tone Scale, since it is a natural arrangement that higher forms of life have to support themselves by the ability of lower forms to translate sunlight and chemicals into the food required by the higher forms.

On the sixth dynamic, the individual will encompass MEST in ratio to his endowment of free theta, his property will not have confused titles, the inanimate objects around him which are meant to serve him will be in good repair, he will have an accurate idea of how much MEST he encompasses, in terms of matter, energy, space and time.

He may or may not have some consideration in the direction of theta, this depending upon his own advancement.

He will ordinarily be considered to have a reverence and respect for a Creator.

As the individual drops down the Tone Scale, the orderliness in the various dynamics decreases. One by one his concept of affinity between himself and these dynamics decreases; and so decreases his responsibility in the field of these dynamics.

At 4.0, we have an inherent sense of responsibility on all dynamics, and a care for the entities on those dynamics.

At tone 3.5, the individual is capable of assuming and carrying on responsibilities along the various dynamics but may show some shortsightedness of responsibility along one or more of them.

At tone 3.0, the ability to handle responsibility along the various dynamics has decreased markedly, but responsibility is demonstrated, if in a slipshod fashion. Above this level the individual will execute orders given to him in as reasonable a fashion as possible, but at this level the individual accepts and executes orders only if they are enforced by blunt threats of punishment which are unmistakable. However, at this level, one or more of the dynamics may remain quite free, and responsibility may be full along this dynamic.

At tone 2.5, the individual is very careless and not trustworthy, although one may find that the individual took good care of himself so far as his dress was concerned. He falls markedly short in his concept of what is required of him in order to maintain a high survival level. The manifestation of this level is only that of carelessness, however, and not that of revolt, as it is on the lower levels.

At tone 2.0, we find the individual not executing responsibility for its own sake but assuming responsibility only when self or group interest can be served. We have the individual executing responsibility not reasonably toward creativeness and construction, but exercising responsibility on a punishment-drive basis. The individual orders things to be done in threatening tones.

At 1.5, we have the individual assuming responsibility much more often and more widely than he can possibly manage in order to bring about destruction along the dynamics. He will play one dynamic against another. He may talk as if he is saving something or give very preservative motives for his actions, but no matter what he does the end result will be destruction. This is a phenomenon which has been too little understood in the past. Here is the death talker who is going to save something from destruction by creating great havoc. This person will not listen to a creative and constructive plan unless he can see ways and means of using it to destroy. Warmongers and dictators are markedly in this band, but one finds 1.5s in all business organizations. When the amount of theta with which an individual is endowed is high, and when more of that theta is enturbulated than remains unenturbulated, according to the 0.0 to 4.0 ratio, the midpoint of 50 percent enturbulated theta and 50 percent unenturbulated theta being at 2.0, the thought and action of the individual begins to partake of the nature of MEST force. He will use MEST force for hammerlike actions and blasts of destruction; he will oppose reason with MEST force. Such an individual assumes responsibility for the purpose of destruction by giving out dour and terrible news. Even though he has good news to give forth he will not give it, but prefers to broadcast tidings of alarm and death. His is the assertion that all is about to be destroyed and that destruction alone can prevent destruction from taking place. Unfortunately, it is all too often true that suppressors to a creative action must be removed before construction and creation takes place. Any person very high on the Tone Scale may level destruction toward a suppressor. The individual at 1.5, however, does not add any creation or construction into his computation except as a tool to trump up further power to destroy. The rather horrible thing about this particular band is that it is above the current band of civilized societies around the world; and societies will not be led by governments more than half a point above the general social tone.

At 1.1, the attitude towards responsibility is capriciousness. The individual is irresponsible and incapable. The responsibilities assumed by a 1.1 are surface manifestations only. The individual may seem to be carrying out a program and may seem to be useful, but the end results of all these programs and responsibilities will be disastrous, since underneath this veneer so many crosscurrents and cabals exist that chaos will result. A 1.1 with a superiority engram which demands that he take responsibility may make an excellent show and be very convincing, but the show he is making and the conviction he seeks to implant in others are not the things intended, and a glance below the surface will discover an entirely different program aimed solely toward malicious destruction.

At 0.8, 0.5, to talk of anything like responsibility is nonsense unless one begins to change the direction of responsibility. From 2.0 down, the individual seems to have a "responsibility" toward death. It is a duty, one might say, for persons from 2.0 down to cause death, failures or disaster or to die. And it is an additional "responsibility" to mask this "duty" with apparent constructive goals or merely denial of that "duty." The "minions of the Devil" and the "Devil and his dark angels"[1] are descriptions of persons engaged on 2.0 down activity. The concept of sin as destructive practice containing more pain than pleasure stems from observations of the activity of low-tone persons. How *real* these concepts become to one who is himself enmeshed with another who is responsible to death and not to life. *Death* is such a blunt, if hidden, taskmaster!

1. **Devil and his dark angels:** a reference to Satan and the fallen or rebellious angels that work for him. Throughout history the Devil has been portrayed as an evil angel who was banished from heaven and became the archenemy of God. Other corrupt, wicked and evil angels who were cast down from heaven joined the Devil and he became their prince. Used here the *Devil and his dark angels* refers to those individuals with such characteristics.

CHAPTER TWENTY-FIVE

COLUMN W
PERSISTENCE ON A GIVEN COURSE

ANOTHER INDEX WHICH THE AUDITOR can use to place his preclear on the chart is the persistence of the preclear along any given course of action toward a goal.

It has been advanced that there are two kinds of individuals, so far as persistence is concerned. The individual who has sufficient theta endowment and sufficient structural ability to keep his free theta and his enturbulated theta relatively separate may, but not always, have a good persistence level even when the factors and conditions in his environment are such that they continually hammer him away from his given course of action. The other type would be the person who is knocked by life from one course to another and who will persist on any given course only so long as no new factor introduces itself. This is characteristic of the potential psychotic.

The persistent individual keeps going toward his goal; he may go slower and slower, and he may die on route, but he does not deviate. The potential psychotic, on the other hand, is not very apt to have a goal in the first place but is apt to follow any goal which comes into view, and then only so long as no environmental factor enters to make him deviate from that course.

One must recognize that the exterior world of the environment, in its action on the individual, and the interior world of the inmost obsessive engrams are working on the same "I," and that if the individual is not deviating very markedly on his course toward his goal even when confronted by heavy environmental factors which seek to move him in other directions, neither is he reacting heavily to his engrams in proportion to the severe reactions he might manifest were he less persistent. An individual may be known by his persistence, but this index is not a sharply defined one, since there are, evidently, two types of personalities, in general, or one might even say, two types of mental structure.

The persistent individual who normally carries forward toward his goal despite environmental suppressors and deviators, in the absence of processing and during the normal course of life, because of the dwindling spiral, will drop down the Tone Scale. More of his free theta will become enturbulated and the balance will gradually shift until, most likely, there is far more enturbulated theta than free theta. The persistence of this individual may continue, but the methods he uses to gain his goal will match the various points on the Tone Scale on the way down. The individual may begin with a high enthusiastic thrust and may through experience become less blunt and open about his creative and constructive efforts and may assume conservatism and caution; he may enter a stratum where he is bored with the goal and may dawdle on his way toward it; lower than this he becomes antagonistic toward factors which do not permit him to reach his goal; below this he becomes angry and destructive toward suppressors, and although he is still apparently going toward his goal, the majority of his time is absorbed in combating suppressors. Losing here and there in his battles, his tone will drop, and he will become more and more covert, even to the point of pretending that he is not any longer persisting toward his goal, while at the same time continuing to do so. Only when he reaches the level of apathy will he give up. When a man has been defeated too often, when too many of his dreams have been broken, he sinks into the apathy band and thereafter no longer struggles toward his goal. Truly enough, he dies with the last of his dreams.

The individual who has a low theta endowment and seems structurally incapable of concentration when at a low point on the Tone Scale may yet increase his persistence to the point where he can win the minor goals of life with great ease when he has been released or cleared.

It is an observed fact that an individual's attitude toward Dianetics and an individual's attitude toward life in general are parallel. The better Dianetic processing can approximate the mechanics of the mind the better that processing is: this is another parallel.

When the auditor takes a preclear who is in the apathy level, all too common in this present social order, he can expect the preclear to depend exclusively on the auditor for any persistence as to the processing of the case. The auditor, incidentally, must take the responsibility of doing the processing. As the preclear comes higher on the Tone Scale and reaches 1.1, the auditor can expect the preclear to propitiate him by giving him presents or being very flattering. Ordinarily, however, the preclear is operating on mechanisms which tell him he is not supposed to go anywhere or get well, and the auditor must be even more persistent, since the only persistence toward the goal of getting well or cleared will still be from the auditor, regardless of what the preclear is saying. Women, by the way, reaching this level of the Tone Scale, may propitiate by offering sex and are very easy to seduce; an auditor who is a wise auditor will steadfastly refuse sexual relations with a preclear. The auditor who yields to temptation at this level finds himself in a bad situation because his preclear is on the way up and will shortly pass this propitiative level and achieve more honorable levels of the Tone Scale. Auditors who, knowing this, permit themselves such actions are themselves at the 1.1 level and have no business auditing; none but a despicable cur would seek to benefit from this phenomenon; none but a chronic or acute psychotic would find enjoyment in it. The person who does this, by the way, usually stops or discourages all processing beyond this point, realizing that as the tone of the preclear rises some honesty will come into the preclear's reasoning. Where you spot a sudden cessation of auditing, the barring of a person from auditing or a refusal to audit, you can be certain that the person responsible for this cessation of auditing or the refusal to permit or encourage it has a selfish profit to make or is hiding something. A person like this is such a menace to himself and to others around him that auditing is much too good for him; he should be shot on sight.

Every case has to get angry before it can get well. The auditor must never discourage a case when it begins to breathe fire and destruction toward its enemies. It is quite common for a preclear to go through a phase of desiring murder or sudden death for both parents for what they have done. The auditor who discourages this anger is inhibiting the ability of the case to get well. This phase will pass; and the auditor should take care, during it, to prevent the preclear from making overt acts against his enemies for which he will have to apologize a few weeks later when the anger phase has gone away; yet, the anger phase must be encouraged, nevertheless. The hypnotist who implants suggestions to the effect that one must treat one's fellow man kindly is actually driving his client down toward apathy.

Rising on the scale, at 2.5 the preclear finds it difficult to concentrate on the force and fury of engrams and is liable to be slack in persisting on his case. He is apt to be too busy about other things. This is a difficult period in any case; but there is so much to be gained above it that somehow the preclear must be raised even higher on the Tone Scale. There is only one way to do this: not by suppressing the preclear back into anger, but simply by getting enough locks and other bric-a-brac off the case to bring the preclear up to a 3.0.

At 3.0, for the first time the preclear will begin to demonstrate self-determinism. Self-determinism should never be confused with refusal to cooperate or willfulness in nonsurvival directions. At 3.0, the preclear is willing to proceed in the most orderly possible fashion toward a thorough and complete swamp-up[1] of his case.

At 3.5, the persistence of the preclear is such, ordinarily, that he begins to knock out engrams in chains.

At 4.0, the persistence of the individual will be the persistence with which he is natively endowed; all the theta that he possesses will be free.

As a word of caution, authoritarian auditing, rather than affinity auditing, will not produce any marked rises on the Tone Scale even though many incidents be run, since the hammering auditing itself keeps the preclear so thoroughly enturbulated that free theta is not able to manifest itself. The preclear must always be coaxed through affinity, communication and reality into being processed. This is the reason why auditors who are low on the Tone Scale do not achieve good results; their very position on the Tone Scale demands that they use forceful methods, apathetic methods or spurious methods.

---

1. **swamp-up:** a cleaning up or clearing out; a moving out of the way or road.

CHAPTER TWENTY-SIX

COLUMN X

LITERALNESS WITH WHICH STATEMENTS OR REMARKS ARE RECEIVED

IT IS AN ASPECT OF THETA THAT THE more it is enturbulated the easier it is to enter enturbulence into it.

The highest level of reasoning is complete differentiation. The lowest level of reasoning is complete inability to differentiate, which is to say, identification. On the highest levels, the individual can understand that the thing is not its name, and that objects are similar to each other but never equal to each other. In the reactive levels, from 2.0 down, the individual more and more identifies, until finally all things are the same thing, and this is complete inability to rationalize. Rationalizing is, in essence, differentiation; reacting is, in essence, identification.

The literalness with which the person receives statements is an index of the amount of enturbulence in a case.

At 4.0, we have high differentiation, good understanding of all communications, as modified by the Clear's education.

At 3.5, we have a good grasp of statements made and a good sense of humor—a sense of humor depending, to a large degree, upon the individual's ability to differentiate and to see and reject situations which do not fit.

At 3.0, we still have good differentiation of the meaning of statements made, but here orders have to be explained a little more carefully, since less reason is going to be applied to them.

"*The highest level of reasoning
is complete differentiation. The lowest level
of reasoning is complete inability to differentiate,
which is to say, identification. On the highest levels,
the individual can understand that the thing
is not its name, and that objects are similar
to each other but never equal to each other.*"

At 2.5, the individual accepts very little, literally or otherwise. The sense of humor of this individual is liable to be very literal, dealing to a large extent in puns rather than in situations.

At 2.0, there is no sense of humor that one could call a sense of humor, but there is laughter over the misfortune of others, which is a demonstration of antagonism. This individual will accept remarks which are antagonistic remarks literally; but he will reject remarks which are lower on the Tone Scale and be able to differentiate on those remarks. He does not pay much attention to remarks higher on the Tone Scale, and if remarks are made to him from persons higher on the Tone Scale he is apt to interpret them into antagonism, if they can literally be so construed.

At 1.5, the individual accepts alarming remarks literally, and when statements on the higher tone levels are made he will alter these statements to his own understanding so that they are alarming or destructive. The sense of humor, again if it can be called such, of individuals at 1.5 consists of laughter at very painful misfortunes.

At 1.1, we have a lack of acceptance of any remark. The individual is likely to seem to have difficulty in hearing; he corrects remarks made to him; he is very concerned sometimes about the rightness of words in remarks. The sense of humor at this level is forced to counteract the tendency to accept remarks literally.

Here is a continual nervous necessity to reject almost any remark for fear that it will register literally and be a command, hence anxiety or fear of conversation of a serious nature. Rather underhanded efforts are made at this level to knock apart serious statements or plans from higher levels on the Tone Scale.

At 0.5, we have an individual who literally accepts any remark which matches his tone and ignores remarks of any other tone. Apathy statements made to this individual have the force of hypnotic suggestions.

Anything at all which is said to a person at the 0.1 level is recorded directly in the lowest strata of the reactive mind.

CHAPTER TWENTY-SEVEN

COLUMN Y

METHOD USED BY SUBJECT TO HANDLE OTHERS

THE MEANS USED BY THE PRECLEAR to control or live with the people around him make an easy and accurate index of the preclear's position on the Tone Scale. This is, unfortunately enough, a precision column. No matter the guise used on the lower levels of the Tone Scale, observation indicates that individuals at these levels use these methods uniformly, to the considerable harm and detriment of their families, friends, associates and the entire social order. If any column on this Tone Scale chart should carry more emphasis than the others from the standpoint of human behavior, this column would be so marked.

The auditor can expect to be treated by the preclear according to the preclear's position on the chart.

The methods of handling others could be assigned to three general categories. The highest category would be one of enhancement, where the individual seeks by example and good reasoning to lift the level of those around him to the point where they will partake of the projects of living with him. This would extend from 4.0 down to 3.0. The second category would be that of punishment drive. Here the individual uses alarm, threats and the general promise of pain unless compliance is given by the others around him. This area extends from 2.0 to around 1.3. The third category is that of nullification, wherein the individual seeks to minimize individuals, to be more than they and so to be able to control them. This category would rather see a man sick than well, because sick men are less dangerous than well men according to the "thinking" that takes place in this band. Three other names for these areas would be enhancement, domination and nullification.

The unfortunate part of the conduct of the lower levels of the Tone Scale toward others is that it has as its invariable end the lowering of the tone of the family, associates, friends and society of the subject; yet the subject by no reason or education, below the point 2.0, could use any other means; forcing the subject to use other means only drives him down the Tone Scale, and as he descends he uses the means of the lower levels he attains.

Here we have the dwindling spiral at work upon the environment of the subject and upon the subject's associates, friends and social order.

It is not danger by violence from the low-toned individual about which the social order or the family should worry; it is this insidious adoption of domination and nullification methods. This enturbulates the theta of the individuals in the subject's environment and brings them down the Tone Scale, gradually, hardly noticeably, but nevertheless inevitably.

From 2.0 down, the individual uses a great deal of justification. He has to explain his acts since the social order normally questions the rationality of many of these acts. For instance, a 3.5 operating in good order may be offering nothing but good to a 1.5 in his vicinity. The 3.5 will yet find himself the target of anger which has no cause in the conduct of the 3.5 but is simply emanating from the 1.5 position of the other on the Tone Scale; the 1.5 would act this way toward the 3.5 regardless of anything the 3.5 might do.

The 3.5, in the vicinity of a 1.1, may find himself descending down the Tone Scale toward anger without any apparent reason.

The 1.1's efforts to nullify are so well veiled and so carefully calculated to annoy that any target for correction or reason by the 3.5 is unavailable, and as reason fails the 3.5, continually subjected to nullification which he cannot locate, will eventually become angry. The 1.1's reply to this anger will not be a return argument or anger, but an apparent continuation of the status quo, while at the same time he does everything possible which can still remain veiled and hidden to reduce and nullify the 3.5. These hidden efforts will become stronger and stronger until nullification or destruction takes place. Or the 1.1, quailing before the anger, will drop into apathy and so use every ally available anywhere who can be coaxed or deceived into supporting the 1.1's efforts to destroy the 3.5.

The reasonable man quite ordinarily overlooks the fact that people from 2.0 down have no traffic with reason and cannot be reasoned with as one would reason with a 3.0. There are only two answers for the handling of people from 2.0 down on the Tone Scale, neither one of which has anything to do with reasoning with them or listening to their justification of their acts. The first is to raise them on the Tone Scale by unenturbulating some of their theta by any one of the three valid processes. The other is to dispose of them quietly and without sorrow. Adders are safe bedmates compared to people on the lower bands of the Tone Scale. Not all the beauty nor the handsomeness nor artificial social value nor property can atone for the vicious damage such people do to sane men and women. The sudden and abrupt deletion of all individuals occupying the lower bands of the Tone Scale from the social order would result in an almost instant rise in the cultural tone and would interrupt the dwindling spiral into which any society may have entered. It is not necessary to produce a world of Clears in order to have a reasonable and worthwhile social order; it is only necessary to delete those individuals who range from 2.0 down, either by processing them enough to get their tone level above the 2.0 line—a task which, indeed, is not very great, since the amount of processing per case might be under fifty hours, although it might also be in excess of two hundred—or simply quarantining them from the society. A Venezuelan dictator once decided to stop leprosy. He saw that most lepers in his country were also beggars. By the simple expedient of collecting and destroying all the beggars in Venezuela an end was put to leprosy in that country.

The methods used by individuals on various levels of the Tone Scale in order to live with their fellows are as follows:

At 4.0, the individual uses enthusiasm, serenity, confidence and his personal force to inspire those around him to reach up to a constructive level of action. Indeed, the presence of a 4.0 or above, if the theta endowment of the individual is high, unenturbulates an area.

The 3.5 begins to employ communication and reasoning in order to invite the participation of others but still believes in bringing people up to a level where they will work with him.

At 3.0, we have the level where conservatism begins to enter the reasoning and where persuasion and social graces begin to be employed to invite the participation of others. Safety, security and somewhat better survival conditions are the arguments used along this level of the Tone Scale.

At 2.5, the individual is relatively careless of the participation of others in his projects.

At 2.0, we begin to enter the domination band, which extends downward to about 1.2. Here theta force can be seen to be distinguishable from MEST force. Theta force is reason; and MEST force is simply that—force. Here we have efforts to hammer and pound and dominate by physical strength, threats, anger and promises of vengeance. Here compliance is commanded, and lack of compliance is stated to mean death. Here we have emergencies being more important than constructive planning. Here we have all manner of undesirable things which, indeed, seem to be the primary business of men and nations today.

Nullification actually begins with domination but becomes very pronounced at about 1.3. A 2.0 might demand of another that he demonstrate enough "guts" to carry forward a project, but from 1.3 down, the modus operandi is any and every effort to convince another human being "for his own good" or "for the good of others" that he has neither the force nor strength to be dangerous. By rendering the individual undangerous, the 1.3, 1.2, 1.1 and on down, seeks to dominate him with the pitiful strength which still remains to the 1.3 and down. The 1.2 and down is most comfortable around sick people, around people who are in apathy, since the 1.1 mistakenly believes these people not to be dangerous because they are obviously weak. This is so far from good reasoning that the results are catastrophic—but little if any reasoning is done from 2.0 down; in its stead are excuses and justifications. Here in a social culture from 1.2 down is the welfare state at its worst, the creation of indigence in the populace to make it easier to control, the nullification of strong individuals in the society, the removal of all constructive persons, and the preservation of the idle, the hopeless, the helpless and the weak. This is actually a social or an individual mechanism to accelerate death. The 1.1 wife who has a strong and able husband keeps on living so long as he keeps breathing the force of life into her. At her position on the Tone Scale, her direction is toward death. Every action she takes, regardless of its surface manifestation, will tend toward a nullification of any life source in her vicinity. Every conceivable mechanism is used in this area of the Tone Scale to make nullifications of others seem valid, to make them stick. Here we have raillery against people who refuse to accept criticism "for their own good." Here we have painstaking efforts to "better people" by showing them their faults. Here we have attempts to "educate" people to adjust to their environment—in other words, to stop being vital and active and go somewhere and lie down, where they will be no menace. Here we have confusions introduced into any situation which are given the most adequate "reasons" and which are yet only nullifications.

From 2.0 down to 1.2, efforts to change people or dominate them are recognizable as such. From 1.2 down, all forthrightness vanishes, and the most devious and insidious and complex methods are employed to nullify. The individual in this area of the Tone Scale very often has a complete belief in his or her superiority, which is a justification for using the methods he uses. Such people commonly fasten themselves on strong personalities well up the Tone Scale and then continue to assert their superiority, without ever giving, of course, and demonstrating that the superiority exists, until the higher level becomes nullified. The individual in this area seeks death not only for himself and his own projects but also for his entire environment. At this level we have murder, by slow erosion, of individuals and the culture, and the actions are masked with voluminous "reasoning." Here is the snake pit of human behavior, and from this area comes the venom which will gradually destroy any individual or culture. Heretofore, people in this area have not been seen to be dangerous, and the word *psychotic* has been used to designate only those who were helpless or overtly destructive. However, this area never becomes overtly destructive, tending if anything toward suicide and rarely toward murder, save on a long-term basis of murder of the personality or the projects of others. Yet this area of the Tone Scale is far more dangerous than any other.

Here we have perversion of anything and everything, so that the surface manifestation will never match the undercover purpose. In sex we have no facing of the purpose and use of sex as something to be enjoyed and for the creation of children, but we have all manner of anxieties and irregular practices which do anything but tend toward the creation of children. And where we may have in such a person a hectic obsession with the performance of the act and an avowed interest and enjoyment in the act, we have actually no enjoyment of it. Sexual efforts tend not toward enjoyment but toward the pollution and derangement of sex itself so as to make it as repulsive as possible to others and so to inhibit procreation. Here is the promiscuous woman, the inconstant lover, the pervert and the sadist. With a great deal of advertisement about sex there is only an effort to destroy sex. In this area of the scale we have avowal by the individual at times that sex is free and must be enjoyed, and a continuous stream of accusation toward others that they believe sex to be a hideous thing and that their attitude must be reformed. Sex is stained and soiled under the guise of being protected. Here we may have an advertisement as to the proper attitude toward children, and strange practices concerning children.

In handling people around them, persons in the 1.2-down bracket deal in reversals of fact. One can take it as a rule of thumb, which is too often workable to be ignored that whatever this person says he is doing, he is actually doing something else. Whatever this person says is true is actually false. Whatever this person says is false is actually true. Making allowance for the fact that much of such a person's conversation is without purpose, one can beware of this contrariness between manifestation and actual purpose.

In keeping with the avoidance of any surface statement of what is actually going forward, we have here the hypnotist. The hypnotist normally ranges from around 1.8, where he uses it as straight dominance, to around 0.6, where apathy has become strong enough to prevent active efforts to dominate or nullify others. Hypnotism never has and never will raise an individual on the Tone Scale. A manic hypnotic suggestion making one feel that he feels better and is better could be implanted. But the act of hypnotism actually enturbulates the free theta, and it can be easily shown by psychometry that a manic implantation leaves the individual less able than he was before, regardless of its content. Hypnotism is the entering of the hypnotist's personality and desires below the choice level of the individual. It is nonsurvival, save only when used as a temporary anesthesia for an operation and picked up and run out in processing immediately after the individual is well—not to pick it up would be equivalent to continuing a general anesthetic forever after the operation. Civilized cultures of today are unaware of the widespread use of hypnotism. It is the favorite tool of the pervert and the sexually deranged. An individual at this level of the Tone Scale may very well have the permission of a partner for the sex act but will actually prefer to accomplish the act in an undercover fashion, as provided by hypnotism. Hypnotism is used in some base religions and is commonly employed by old schools of mental healing, which should make plain the level of these cults on the Tone Scale. When a "therapy" on this level of the Tone Scale (1.3 to 0.6) is employed, it is only to render the individual under treatment more tractable, less "liable to be harmful to others" and to wreck self-determinism in the individual. This is the exact reverse of what it takes to make people well and sane. Empirical evidence should have demonstrated long since that such methods do not work, but this level of the Tone Scale is not much given to reasoning. Here is the prefrontal lobotomy, the transorbital leukotomy,[1] electric shock, insulin shock,[2] directive therapies[3] and all the rest of the unworkable claptrap with which modern civilization has been victimized. True enough, an individual by such methods can be made less dangerous to his fellows and easier to handle, since he is made into more MEST and less theta. But it is equally true that this treatment decreases, often permanently, any ability of the patient to be of service to his society.

The processing methods which raise a person on the Tone Scale are so very simple to apply that one wonders, or perhaps does not

---

1. **transorbital leukotomy:** a psychiatric procedure in which the frontal lobes of the brain are separated from the rest of the brain by cutting the connecting nerve fibers. *Transorbital* means measured or drawn across between the orbits (the bony cavities of the skull containing the eyes; the eye sockets); occurring by way of or passing through the eye socket. *Leukotomy* comes from the French *leucotomie, leuco* referring to the brain's white matter (nerve tissue, particularly of the spinal column and brain) and *-tomy,* a combining form, used here to mean an incision or cutting of an organ, as designated by the initial element of the term.
2. **insulin shock:** a form of shock treatment commonly used by psychiatrists. The purported treatment consists of a series of shots, injecting an excessive amount of insulin into the body, thereby inducing a coma.
3. **directive therapy:** a form of supposed "treatment" used in psychotherapy where the therapist takes an active, often authoritarian approach towards the patient, giving advice, suggestions, interpretations and demands for the patient to follow.

wonder, at the continued insistence on destructive "therapies" in institutions. These institutions often use sedatives, and yet one of the worst things that an individual who is in a disturbed state can be given is a sedative; it makes him quieter and less dangerous but it does not make him more able; furthermore, an individual under sedation receives sounds and sights in his environment as positive suggestions and therefore is continually receiving new locks and more enturbulence, although it may appear momentarily that his condition is better. *A preclear must never be audited under sedation.* This is a strong injunction, since preclears audited under sedation or under the influence of alcohol become worse, and a psychotic treated when he is under such influence (as in narcosynthesis)* may very well have all of his free theta enturbulated and so be sent into a "permanent" break. The auditor should be very careful when working with anyone to ascertain whether or not that person is taking any drugs, since medical doctors will very often issue sedatives to patients without telling the patient that he is taking a sedative. Sedatives have been around for many thousands of years. They have certain uses, in light doses, but such uses are extremely temporary in duration. Continuous application of sedatives to an individual, as they make him more suggestible—make it easier for him to receive locks—wreaks considerable harm upon his mind. This, however, can be remedied unless it has gone to a point of no return.

Politically, the area of 2.0 to 1.4 is the area of fascism, where dominance of others is continually preached, where safety and safeguarding are continually stressed and where destruction and threats of punishment are used to force others.

---

*NARCOSYNTHESIS: *a complicated name for a very ancient process quite well known in Greece and India. It is drug hypnotism. And it is generally employed either by those practitioners who do not know hypnosis or on those patients who will not succumb to ordinary hypnotism. A shot of sodium pentothal is given intravenously to the patient and he is asked to count backwards. Shortly he stops counting at which the injection is also stopped. The patient is now in a state of "deep sleep." That this is not sleep seems to have missed both narcosynthesists and hypnotists. It is actually a depressant on the awareness of an individual so that those attention units which remain behind the curtain of his reactive bank can be reached directly.* —LRH

From 1.3 down to 0.6 we have the general area of the subversive, who promises a people freedom and equality and gives them a slaughter of their best minds and cultural institutions, to the end of a totalitarian dominance. Because it exists in this tone band, the subversive leader can use as his personnel only people in this tone band; if this tone band were to be removed from a society he would have no recruits. To such people the perfidious and twisted practices of subversion have an enormous appeal. It gives them the "right" to practice free love and general promiscuity and sets them above, by destroying the church and other institutions or by holding these as nothing, any necessity to conform to an existing social order. Thus the recruit is exhilarated by having a new justification for doing on a wide scale what he has been doing on a narrow scale, nullifying by hidden and insidious means all the strong and the orderly in the environment. In any relatively low-toned social order the idea of having the right to do hidden and vicious things for a "glorious cause" is so attractive to persons in this area that they automatically support this political idiocy. As reason is absent in this area of the Tone Scale, it never occurs to these recruits that the most zealous amongst them will be the first to go down under firing squads, since even a totalitarian regime, in attempting to run any kind of a state, must compel severe conformity to its own "codes," no matter how depraved these "codes" might be; and the recruit in the land which was about to be conquered was selected because of nonconformity. Thus, immediately after a complete totalitarian conquest of a country we invariably witness an extensive slaughter of individuals. One can select with ease the individuals marked for liquidation in the solidation[4] of the conquest. The selection is not made according to the position the individual occupies but by his individualism, his strength and his reasonableness, or by his continuing revolutionary desire not to conform to set and regimented patterns. A considerable percentage of the people slaughtered in any new

4. **solidation:** a strengthening or consolidation; the act of making firm or solid.

conquest consists of the agents and tools used by the conqueror to soften up the country before the conquest took place. The morbid fear of any totalitarian regime is counterrevolution, because they, best of all, understand how perfidious revolution can be. The 1.1 may take a 1.1 as a bedfellow and political mate and may make a 1.1 group, but this group has to continue to be faced by a strong and dangerous foe to remain consolidated. This is the condition of a subversive cell. These people continue in association with each other only so long as they are in the presence of and are busy undermining a worthy opponent. Because a 1.1 will act in handling people only as a 1.1, however, the cell, once the pressure is taken off of it, devours itself.

If the auditor is processing anyone known to have been in continual association with a 1.1, he can readily and rapidly assemble the pattern of aberration of this unlucky preclear, since it will consist of the surface display by the 1.1 that all was being done for the preclear's good and a continual and insidious underhanded campaign to hit the preclear at his weakest points.

The apathy band of the Tone Scale is only less dangerous to the social order than the 1.1. The apathy band has a definite procedure for handling people and the environment. Apathy is attempting to tend toward death; here is the suicide. And the apathy case will actually thoroughly enturbulate those around him in an effort to cause death along the other dynamics. There was once a whole political philosophy about apathy, known as Zeno's Apatheia,[5] which was embraced in the last death throes of the Roman Empire. The apathy case will try to discourage anyone from doing anything. Hopes and dreams are destroyed merely by claiming that they are hopeless and impossible.

----

5. **Zeno's Apatheia:** a reference to one of the central themes of the school of philosophy founded by the Greek philosopher Zeno (ca. 334–ca. 262 B.C.). It taught that man should be free from passion and indifferent to emotion, pleasure and pain, but not without rational feelings. It also taught that the universe is governed by divine will and happiness lay in conforming to such will. *Apatheia* means without feelings.

It has been fashionable to "feel sorry" for individuals on this band of the Tone Scale. This is exactly what this band of the Tone Scale demands of associates in the environment. Here we have cries for pity, supplication and any and every means to gain sympathy. These are actually enturbulative mechanisms rather than real requests for help. The entheta of the apathy level does not want to be helped but merely wishes to enturbulate further and to die, causing at the same time as much death as possible in the environment. Nearly any human being confronted with the loss of a friend or loved one dives momentarily into the grief level, and the acute state of apathy is thus seen commonly, if sporadically, in the society. This state can be easily remedied by processing when it is a momentary, environmental restimulation. The chronic apathy case is a different matter and is intensely dangerous to the environment. It is fashionable to feel sorry for the apathy case, and yet the apathy case never feels sorry for anyone. Despite all the tears and moaning, the apathy case, on a substratum, is quite cunning and attempts to produce through tears the maximum enturbulation possible. If the 1.1 is considered to have manifestations of one kind and motives and actions of an entirely different kind, then the apathy case is a direct reversal. The apathy case will declare all past kindnesses to have been the most sadistic cruelties and the cruelties to have been kindnesses. Facts are not simply distorted by an apathy case; they are reversed. By reversing all visible evidence and declaring everything to be the exact opposite of the reality, maximal enturbulation can be produced. The apathy case, by insisting that every white is black, so tries the reasons of others in his vicinity that they, lost in this confusion, also become apathetic, since there seems to be no possible method of reasoning. Apathy is more than hopelessness: it is death in a very forthright form. The apathy case talks about death, threatens personal death and will actually attempt suicide. There is not enough courage on this level to forthrightly attempt the death of others, but by enturbulation the apathy case can effect this and will do so if not understood. The apathy case quite commonly sets an example of death by fake suicide in a vague effort to be mimicked by another and so bring about another's death. The apathy case that is threatening suicide, however, cannot be disregarded, since a sudden enturbulence may actually bring about an attempt. Here, the command over the environment is recognized by the apathy case to be limited to the individual's possessions and body alone. We get various types of neglect of possessions, which quietly and undramatically lead to their destruction. Here we get neglect of the feelings of other people and their concerns. Here we have neglect of person which may, dramatically or undramatically, tend toward the destruction of person. The apathy case is so reversed on reality that he will declare things, which are normally ugly and horrible, to be beautiful, and things which are beautiful to be ugly and horrible. An insidiousness is present at about 0.7 wherein the apathy case seems to support beautiful things and art but spoils them, in so supporting them, for others in the environment. There is a gruesome obscenity in the admiration such people give to beauties in life.

Below 0.7 there is not enough activity to lend active support for any purpose save the attainment of death for self and others. Valuable objects, assets and projects are in considerable peril in the vicinity of an apathy case even though the apathy case may not seem to be very active. It is this inactivity which is deceptive. A slight surge in tone can cause an apathy case to despoil anything in the vicinity which is normally considered survival. Apathy cases have destroyed great works of art, organizations and individuals for the most specious and spurious reasons.

The apathy case is so self-centered that it is very difficult for the auditor to gain any cooperation. Indeed, every effort the auditor makes to invite hopefulness will be rejected. It will not be so thoroughly rejected that the auditor is rebuffed, but will be met with new reasons why the auditor should feel sorry for the apathy case. Most of these reasons are outright lies, and the apathy case commonly runs floods of dub-in as well as spurious tears. Auditors, and indeed a society, not understanding the true motives of apathy are placed in considerable peril since a natural mechanism exists in the higher levels of the Tone Scale to aid and support one's fellows. The apathy case is actually perverting and destroying this mechanism by inviting it toward unworthy causes. This is a death action intended to destroy the mechanism of cooperation. The self-centeredness of the apathy case is appalling to any reasonable being once he examines it. A great deal of the conduct of the apathy case is, knowingly or unknowingly, pretense or act. At the 0.6 level, one may even occasionally catch an apathy case peering hawklike but covertly from under the veil of tears to be sure that the show is still receiving the attention of the audience.

Much experience with apathy teaches the auditor that there is nothing very noble about grief or apathy. The actual grief should be run out of a case as soon as possible. But when he is auditing an apathy case the auditor will find himself running a great deal of specious incident all of which contains grief. The invitation for sympathy knows no bounds. The demands for pity will become shortly, even to the most patient, trying beyond endurance. Although one may at first feel an active urge to help an apathy case, when one has penetrated the depth of speciousness of the data, an impulse toward contempt and ridicule will result, for no reasonable man finds an impulse toward death a reasonable thing, and the apathy case has no other impulse. The cry for pity and the supplication for aid *seem* to require the assistance of others. Actually these are demanding the enturbulence and death of others. No apathy case wants to be helped but will use any and every means to keep from being helped. As courage is absent, the apathy case will dodge any incident which contains real impact, just as the apathy case will dodge any factor in the environment which contains real help or aid and will go inevitably toward environmental factors which are destructive. The apathy case, thus, avoids any good auditing and will actually seek out and encourage very bad auditing.

It is a certain mawkish sentimentality in our current society, encouraged by generations of literary men who were attempting only the strongest impact and thus the greatest sale for their works, which makes us brook, tolerate and countenance the apathetic. Perhaps because each of us feels his importance demands that someone feel sorry for him when he is hurt or dead we countenance a continuing grief in others. By Dianetic processing this grief is very easily dispensed with, and anyone who has long experience in the handling of apathy cases would be more likely to feel sentimental about running sores or venereal disease than to feel long and enduring sympathy for apathy.

As an admonition to auditors: never give support to the whims and ideas of an apathy case, and do not give the apathy case sympathy, but give it gentle processing. Don't believe the data obtained from an apathy case, but work mechanically with the case, actively getting up as much free theta as possible to raise the case on the Tone Scale at least to covert hostility. Apathy cases enturbulate one very easily, because one can so easily feel that grief over lost ones is something which should be supported and assisted as a worthy mechanism. An apathy case will say or do anything to gain sympathy. Utter immorality is present. The apathy case will surrender his or her body as readily as anything else as a price of a little sympathy. The "love" one receives from an apathy case is actually the extreme depths of propitiation, and the "loving" apathy case will deliver one up to the hangman with as little compunction as he or she would feel in drinking a glass of water. No reason, no codes, no ethics, no decency, no truth, no life are the hard and fast rules of the apathy case. And because justification can be given forth by the apathy case wild and alarming enough to justify his condition one is often tempted to accept this propitiation as actual affinity, when actually it is an invitation to be killed. Because this propitiation can be mistaken for love one is often tempted, out of sympathy and a desire to assist or to become closely associated with an apathy case, but one should be apprised that his name on a marriage certificate coupled with that of an apathy case constitutes a death warrant more certain than that of a court of law. His home, if he ever manages by strenuous effort to assemble one, will be a shambles. His position will be lost and his dreams will be shattered. His self-respect will be slaughtered and his concepts of morals and decency will be destroyed. These statements are made without compromise after long and close observation of apathy at work in an individual. Apathy is only half a point above death, and apathy will bring death to anything and everything in the environment.

A social order in the apathy band will take any unreasonable course which leads toward death. It will follow any leader who claims that life is not worth living and that things and people should be neglected until they cease to live. Here is no outright destruction of entities. Here is insidious destruction through neglect, overuse and accelerated decay. The American Indian, for instance, when pushed by defeat into the tone band of apathy, adopted program after program which was acclaimed as a salvation program but which was always a death program. There was the matter of the ghost dancers,[6] who avidly received the falsity that their cotton shirts could stop bullets. There was the wave of dog killing, whereby it was asserted that the buffalo would come back if all the dogs were dead.

The body itself cooperates in the apathy band by becoming easily sick from any slightest cause, by involving itself in accidents of devious and various kinds and by failing in endocrine function. One can expect the apathy case to become ill from bacteria even when bacteria are not present.

One should be extremely chary of using authoritarian auditing, any violent means or hypnotism on cases from 2.0 down, since such cases are very easily driven into the apathy level. Apathy is apparently, and only apparently, more tractable and easier to

----

6. **ghost dancers:** members of an American Indian religious movement in the western United States, called Ghost Dance. The religion, based on the belief that the white man would disappear and dead ancestors and buffalo would return to life, centered on the ghost dance. The dancers chanted and wore special shirts, called ghost shirts, decorated with sacred symbols, such as stars, eagles and moons, believing they were protected from enemy bullets.

manage, since the apathy case to some degree is in a permanent hypnotic trance and will listen to and believe anything said no matter how ridiculous it may be. This is a highly dangerous state and will result not only in the suicide of the person, on occasion, but also in the death of the concerns and persons of others in the environ of the apathy case. This is the reason why there are so many suicides pursuant to the practice of hypnotism and old-school techniques. These, by asserting control over the individual, depress him down the Tone Scale. The apathy case is capable of such thorough lying that the individual may even claim to be better and appear to be better, until one morning he is found a suicide. The apathy case can be very deceptive.*

The auditor should be warned not to employ any authoritarian methods in processing. We in Dianetics are only interested in raising people on the Tone Scale, and are not at all concerned with psychosis, neurosis or psychosomatic illnesses. The auditor should be

*The death of James Forrestal,[7] who had been driven into apathy by overwork and fears, is an illustrative case not only of what happens when authoritarian methods and incarceration are used as "treatment" but of the complete deceptiveness of which the apathy case is capable. Forrestal had not seemed so pleasant and relieved for some months as he did an hour before he threw himself from the tower of the Bethesda Naval Hospital[8] and fell sixteen flights to his death on the concrete and glass below. Thus perished one of the most brilliant managers and champions of the United States Navy. And other suicides, great and not so great, stack like cordwood before the back alleys that block Dianetics. —LRH

....

7. **Forrestal, James Vincent:** (1892–1949) American banker and government official who, in 1940, became the undersecretary of the United States Navy. During World War II (1939–1945) he directed huge naval expansion and procurement programs and was responsible for readying a peacetime navy to meet the enormous demands of global war.
8. **Bethesda Naval Hospital:** a reference to the National Naval Medical Center, a large governmental hospital founded in 1942 in Bethesda, Maryland, USA. It is run by the US Navy and services navy personnel.

careful not to enturbulate persons below the 2.0 line any further than they already are, but should be as nondirective in approach as possible to produce results. For, if the auditor permits his preclear to drop into apathy he has on his hands a much more difficult and a much longer case than a 1.1 or a forthrightly, howlingly angry 1.5. Remember too that in this social order people from 2.0 down the scale are accepted commonly as sane so long as they can perform any seemingly rational acts in the environment.

At 0.1 or 0.3, the individual also has a method of handling others around him. This mechanism is based upon the reasoning that if one disavows all possible dangerousness, the dangerous people in his vicinity will go away and leave him alone. As a matter of fact, hunters and soldiers rationally employ this mechanism as a last resort, and the mechanism occasionally works. Certain animals have this built in as a habit pattern. By an abandonment of all appearance of life they hope to arrest the urge of the attacker to produce death.

One should realize that all individuals below 2.0 have a tendency to look upon family, friends and associates as menaces to life or aids to death. Real affection is impossible, but propitiation and pretense of affection are mechanisms by which one invites pity or disclaims dangerousness. People from 2.0 down live in an atmosphere, according to their own viewpoint, of potential death and murder. At 1.5, the mission is to cause the death of the "dangerous" entities by forthright acts of destruction. The 1.1 considers the family, associates and environ even more potentially deathly and so, seeing greater danger in them, uses more covert and devious methods to cope with and disarm these "dangerous" entities, and puts forth a smokescreen of helping and doing good for family, associates and environ. Here also one finds the mechanism of championing the underdog. The underdog is not dangerous and may be an ally one can use against one's very deathly environment. Anyone championing the underdog is projecting himself into the underdog and is making a covert plea for the rights of underdogs to live, in the usually not realized hope that he as an underdog will be permitted to go on living regardless of his acts against others.

Following this ratio of the dangerousness of the environment as viewed by the individual, the environment to the apathy case is literally crawling with death threats. Every person, every object and every act is considered to have in it a death intent. The kindest word, though apparently accepted by the apathy case, is yet received deviously in the "full understanding" that death lurks but a small distance behind that proffered help. This encourages the apathy case to act in a murderous fashion and seems to him to give him license to pay no attention to any moral code or feeling of decency. The apathy case lives in a cesspool of impending slaughter and interprets anything done for him or her as something to be accepted warily. The apathy case quite commonly speaks of being killed, either of killing himself or of being killed by others. His attention may be so fixed in its unreality that he chooses but one murderer who is about to kill him; or his concentration may be so scattered that he chooses many men, organizations or things as potential murderers.

The pretended-death case has come to a point where he considers the environment so fraught with menace that nothing in the environment has any intent save to kill him and that death is immediate. He has insufficient energy or reason remaining even to appeal for help, and, indeed, he considers that there is no person or object to which he can so appeal, and so he attempts to demonstrate to anything in the environment that it has won and that he is already dead. By posing as dead he imagines he can survive at least long enough to die a little less painfully than he considers he will die if he moves. Old and decadent races are commonly found to have the practice of willing death. An individual merely goes and sits on the edge of his grave until he dies and falls in. One can find such people any day on, for instance, Coal Hill,[9] near Peking.

---

9. **Coal Hill:** a man-made mound more than a mile in circumference, approximately 210 feet high (64 m), in Peking, China, covered with trees and temples and which was also the site of a burial ground.

The pretended-death case has abandoned even trying to find any one menace and considers everything a menace. This state has the peculiarity of being unfixed. Possibly the most signal effect to rouse this case can be made by concentrating the attention of the individual upon a single and definite threat of death. Indeed, observing an honest and active source of death, by raising the necessity level, brings anyone up the Tone Scale at least for a brief time. Thus in war, cities which are under sporadic bombardment show a lower incidence of psychosis than cities which, far behind the lines, only read about the deaths in newspapers. The source of death has been so pinpointed as artillery and bombardment planes and the source is so dramatic that attention can be fixed upon it. The source is also so simple that it requires very little effort to comprehend it. Further, such destruction brings with it many dead and disabled over whom the erstwhile psychotic can loom and so cease to occupy the tail end of the procession as target number one for all dangerous entities in the environment. For, in treating wounded and dead he can observe without having to reason very much that he is more dangerous to them than they are to him. An additional reason for this sudden upsurge of a city under threat is the uniting toward a common goal of resisting or overcoming a common menace. Nations which engage in war so unify their populaces, and this is an immediate revelation of the position on the Tone Scale of those nations which suppose they have to resort to war. For any reasonable and active nation need not engage in MEST destruction to secure the cooperation of another nation: this is an insanity, brought about by a position of 2.0 or below on the Tone Scale.

The text corresponding to this column is long because it is actually a coverage of interpersonal relations. The rough rule regarding interpersonal relations, from which other matters may be deduced, is that reason and cooperation exist in an increasing quantity from 2.0 up and that the direction of effort is survival. From 2.0 down domination and control, overt or covert, are employed in handling people, and the direction of effort is toward succumb. People above 2.0 on the Tone Scale suffer from any and all association with people at 2.0 and down on the Tone Scale. And people from 2.0 down benefit, so far as surviving is concerned, from any association with people above 2.0. But the purposes are crossed, since individuals from 2.0 up do not want to be made to succumb and will combat any effort in that direction. And the individuals from 2.0 down do not wish to be made to live or create, and so resist any effort in that direction. Where reason will not swiftly resolve an argument between two human beings, an inspection of the position each of those two occupies on the Tone Scale will probably demonstrate that one is arguing to survive and the other is arguing to succumb, or one is arguing to create and construct and the other is arguing to destroy or neglect.

Because a person's position on the Tone Scale can be acute or momentary due to enturbulence in the environment or can be chronic due to entheta "permanently" (except for Dianetic processing) enturbulated, one can observe in people below 2.0, when less enturbulated, efforts to survive, and one can observe in people above 2.0 occasional efforts to succumb.

It is worthy of note that the environment of the individual may have its own position on the Tone Scale. His school, the office in which he does business, his family may occupy as a group a certain position. This position of the environment on the Tone Scale comes about because of the influence of certain persons or the nature of the organization or the existing state of culture, and it cannot be neglected in estimating both the personality of the preclear and the methods he will use in handling others.

Actually there are three kinds or conditions of theta below the 4.0 line. The first is free theta. The next is temporarily enturbulated theta which, left alone for a short time, will unenturbulate. And the third is frozen entheta, which is held in place in the case by the nature of engrams, secondaries and locks. Environmental impacts, of course, charge up the engrams in the case and keep any person, unless a great change in environment takes place bringing much better survival factors, continuing on down the Tone Scale throughout his lifetime. The environment impacting upon the individual thus alters "permanently" (except for Dianetic processing) free theta into frozen entheta, but this is a gradual process, cumulative and deadly though it may be. As a child he may have a very large number of engrams, but the environment has not acted upon him with sufficient impact to charge these engrams up with entheta in secondaries and locks. When he is an old man the track is almost completely entheta, in the usual case.

There is another kind of enturbulation. The free theta is enturbulated by the environment, and although the majority of the free theta may become temporarily enturbulated, only a small portion of it freezes into the locks, secondaries and engrams. Thus a person, because of the enturbulation of free theta on a temporary basis, can be moved up and down the Tone Scale by his environment. It is this surface manifestation and volatility of misemotion which has masked the nature of free theta. The environment impacting against the individual may, for instance, inflict 1.5 factors on him to such an extent that he becomes momentarily 1.5. If the quantity of free theta remaining to him is great he will rather rapidly unenturbulate and regain his higher position on the Tone Scale. Free theta can only be enturbulated downward, and the case can only be enturbulated downward on the Tone Scale. The 1.1 does not go up to 1.5 because of enturbulation, he goes down to apathy. The apathy case, when his free theta is enturbulated, flashes quickly into pretended death, or may even die, his margin of operation is so slight.

The environment, then, has a marked effect upon the individual, from hour to hour and day to day. An individual who lives in a family which has a chronic tone of 1.1 may himself be potentially a 3.0 and outside the family may manifest the qualities of a 3.0, but in the family his enturbulation is so constant that he is little by little losing free theta into lock, secondary and engram entheta and will gradually decline down the scale. The only thing which would remedy this is for him to have at the same time another environment which is higher on the Tone Scale than he is which would tend to unenturbulate the free theta that becomes enturbulated in the vicinity of the family.

Thus is it important to the auditor that his handling of the preclear has as high a tone level as possible, and he should attempt to arrange the preclear's environment so that it has as high a tone as possible. An auditor who is attempting to work a preclear who is being mishandled by a 1.5 environment will find himself working day after day with nothing but temporarily enturbulated theta, and he will make very small progress with his case. It is necessary for him to get this case out of the 1.5 environment so that the free theta can unenturbulate and thus be available to free the frozen entheta in the locks, secondaries and engrams, in order to add constantly to the preclear's free theta and not just keep it from becoming less by daily environmental enturbulation.

It is also of interest to the auditor and to people in general that education has its own positions on the Tone Scale. Education designed to inhibit and restrain, to create conformity in the individual to the social order, has the unfortunate effect of reducing the individual on the Tone Scale. This would be authoritarian education and would be from 2.0 down. Education which invites and stimulates reason and seeks to accelerate the individual toward a successful and happy level of existence and has enough faith in individuals to assume the good usage of the education raises the individual on the Tone Scale. One can by reviewing the education of any individual discover much supportive evidence for this, since it will be found that those subjects in which the individual is able will be those which were taught by methods from 2.0 up, and those subjects in which the individual is poor, lacking accuracy or self-determinism, and failing in his reason with them, were taught by methods which would be found from 2.0 down on the Tone Scale. As a society declines, it more and more resorts to authoritarian teaching and attempts increasingly to impress upon the individual that he must adjust to his environment and that he cannot adjust his environment to him. The educational process becomes one of semi-hypnotically receiving doughy masses of data and regurgitating them upon examination papers. Reason and self-determinism are all but forbidden.

When we speak of people using various methods to handle other people we must also speak of the methods which have been used to handle our preclear. We are interested in Dianetics in what has been done to an individual, not what the individual has done. This is not an effort to escape or alter moral standards but is simply a statement of fact; the auditor who becomes interested in his preclear's motives and evaluations of his preclear's reasoning is not only wasting his time but is trying to perform authoritarian therapy.

What has been done to a person educationally is of very great concern to the auditor, since education can be so thoroughly suppressive that it and it alone, given engrams to charge up on the case, can move the individual considerably down the Tone Scale, as witnessed by the many vapid, will-less and idle graduates of our universities. Knowing that education can be such a strong factor in the aberrating and suppressing of the human being is helpful, in that by Lock Scanning he can pick up and deintensify an education wholesale, with a resultant rise of his preclear on the Tone Scale and without touching anything which could be dignified as locks, secondaries or engrams. The whole of a person's education may be a lock. No words bitter enough or strong enough could be leveled at authoritarian educational systems, which even though they witness in their parades of graduates destroyed artists, hopeless and apathetic women, stupid and dull engineers, yet have made no great effort to establish and remedy the cause—their own authoritarian methods of education. Fortunately, a college education can be picked up out of a preclear who is in fair working condition in ten or fifteen hours. Wastebasketing this enormous and onerous effort on the part of mentally constipated straw men and would-be Little Caesars on their lecture platforms would, of course, be an enormous benefit to the whole society, but in the absence of this highly desirable measure, the auditor can at least regain the free theta which has been tied up in the individual's education. The college is not the only destructive element in the educational system. High-school systems are as bad, but they have as their subjects people who are still well enough up the Tone Scale to be able to resist, since youth is resilient. Grade school educations, particularly in their first years, are very likely to be authoritarian, and as they form the basis of formal education they should also be addressed.

Entheta is best freed out of locks and secondaries from late to early, so that one should actually address present time and then earlier times and then earlier and earlier in his scanning and running of locks, in order to arrive at the earliest possible times. Complete recall of childhood is so reached, and efforts to reach childhood without treating the rest of the life by scanning are normally defeated. By treating childhood alone, out of the mistaken reasoning that it was a highly aberrative period (an aberration which was planted by amateur philosophers and schools of mental healing half a century ago), one sends the preclear against the occluding force of the late locks and secondaries without giving him a chance to reduce them. One should not expect to be able to run a case by addressing the early portion of the case first, unless the case is in such a condition that he can get to basic-basic and reduce it with most perceptics on.

Education, then, must be run from last to first in order to recover it. Now, one does not ordinarily think of parental training in terms of education, and yet the whole business of gaining experience could be lumped under the heading of education. Common usage of the word denotes formal instruction, but it is no less education that Mother, Father, nurses and other people in the home administer to a child. It is in the early portion of life that the most checks and the strongest authoritarian measures are used, since the child, through lack of data, is least capable of reasoning. These restraints compound continually and much free theta becomes frozen "permanently" in locks during early childhood. This is along the educational line and is best cleared up by picking up the instruction closest to present time and lock-scanning it thoroughly, then picking up an earlier period of instruction such as college, then picking up an earlier one such as high school, then an earlier one such as grammar school and finally parental training, as being the same general type of lock chain. In such a way one will recover the general restraints imposed upon children and the general unreasonableness of most adults toward children.

You can discover the way your preclear was handled as a child by investigating the way he handles children, but this has a limited value since he is normally, if he had a bad childhood, in an ally's[*] valence and the methods he uses may be those of the ally rather than the overall methods of the family. But in many cases the preclear is following the advice of doing unto others as has been done to him, and this is true in other things than childhood.

Educational systems which have been used on your preclear had their own positions on the Tone Scale and tended to freeze the individual at those same positions on the Tone Scale. Thus we could have a child whose home life made him a potential 3.0 but who was educated in a 1.1 school. The education would tend to bring the individual down the Tone Scale to 1.1. The values he has been given for various facts and actions of other people and the methods he has been taught to use in the handling of other people have been educated into him by some educational system. Thus, if you attempted to clear an individual and bring him up the Tone Scale without giving a thorough address to his education, you would have, even with the bulk of his engrams and secondaries gone, an individual who hung very low on the Tone Scale. It requires a very little bit of work to correct this, and the work should not be

---

[*]**ALLY:** *a person recorded in the reactive mind of the preclear about whom the preclear makes the reactive computation that this person is necessary to the preclear's survival.* —LRH

neglected. Otherwise, your individual will continue to handle people and to act in his environment along the tone level where he was educated. It is highly doubtful that any preclear exists in the civilized world today who has been educated by a system above 2.0 on the Tone Scale.

In keeping with this educational theme, its aspects in processing, and the way it influences the preclear in his handling of other people, one should carefully scout every case for the lowest-toned individual in the environment of the preclear at any time during his life and find any later individuals who approximated the earlier individual. Scan out the later individual, then find and scan out the early individual, and much will have been done to increase the tone of the preclear. Association with persons low on the Tone Scale is always depressing, and a long and continuous association creates many and severe locks.

You will have as one of your better indexes of how your preclear is progressing the changes in his handling of those around him.

The auditor would do well to examine his own general method of handling people, with a highly critical eye, and adjudicate for himself where his auditing is therefore likely to lie on the Tone Scale, and by the educational process of knowing the consequences and knowing how to get results, simply raise his necessity level up to a point where he achieves a more desirable attitude, if he thinks one is necessary. If the auditor should happen to find himself in that band of the Tone Scale where one is afraid of hurting people he should be very wary not to demonstrate any lack of courage in running the case.

The preclear should examine his auditor for his position on the Tone Scale, and if he finds his auditor in the apathy or covert hostility range, he had himself better work the auditor or else render himself liable for inevitable "mistakes" in the handling of his case, sudden and unexpected affinity breaks and a general confusion. The moral of this column is that auditors should not audit and preclears should not permit themselves to be audited unless they are certain of an above-2.0 handling of the case and of people in general.

As an emergency measure, where none other is available, two persons can co-audit each other, step by step up the Tone Scale, but unless a parity is maintained, one of them will suffer, and a good Release or a Clear will be impossible to attain—which is thought to be the difficulty so far experienced in Dianetics, where the making of Clears is concerned.

CHAPTER TWENTY-EIGHT

COLUMN Z

COMMAND VALUE
OF ACTION PHRASES

THE SUBJECT OF ACTION PHRASES has been covered earlier in this book. Action phrases are those which seem to order the preclear in various directions. If the preclear were standing in a room obeying orders, and if he had means of raising and lowering himself, action phrases would act on him as follows. If he were told to go up, he would go up; if he were told to go down, he would go down; if he were told to go in two directions at once, he would become confused; if he were told not to move, he would not move; if he were told to pull himself into himself, he would try to shrink; these, in essence, are action phrases.

The action of the individual on his time track, back through his past, is sometimes directed by action phrases appearing in his engrams. He does not have to obey these phrases in order to be processed; indeed, the auditor should discourage him from obeying them; it is not necessary to prove the validity or value of an engram by proving that one can react to an action phrase.

The action phrases are: bouncers, such as "get up," "get out"; holders such as "stay here," "don't move"; misdirectors, such as "don't know whether I'm coming or going," or "everything is backwards"; down-bouncers, such as "get under" or "go back";

groupers, such as "everything happens at once," "pull yourself together"; call-backs, such as "come back," "please come"; and one other, the denyer, which states that the engram does not exist, such as "there isn't anything here," "I can't see anything." There is also the valence-shifter, which shifts the individual from his own identity to the identity of another; the valence-bouncer, which prohibits an individual from going into some particular valence; and the valence-denyer, which may even deny that the person's own valence exists; and the valence-grouper, which makes all valences into one valence. These are all the types of action phrases. A dictionary of these phrases could be made up and might be of some use, but with a little experience the auditor will learn what these phrases are. It is mandatory that he understand what these phrases are, since when he finds his preclear doing strange things on the track, he had better remedy the condition rapidly by asking the file clerk for the type of phrase, and then asking for the phrase, and then getting the preclear to repeat the phrase in order to lessen its effect, so that the preclear can continue moving on his track in the proper fashion.

At 4.0, there are no engrams. Present time phrases have no reactive value.

At 3.5, if a whole chain of incidents remains in a case, the action computation of the chain may be effective. Individual phrases are mildly effective sometimes in very severe engrams.

At 3.0, the action phrases in severe engrams are effective on the preclear.

At 2.5, phrases in engrams and in secondary engrams cause the preclear to respond.

At 2.0, engrams, secondaries and chains of locks all contain phrases or computations which produce action in the case as the preclear runs on the time track.

At 1.5, action phrases in engrams, secondaries and locks matching the tone of the preclear are very effective, and control phrases are very effective. The individual is usually still dramatizing his circuit control phrases, seeking to control others.

At 1.1, action phrases in engrams, secondaries and locks are very effective, and valence-shifters are very effective. Down to this point valence-shifters are not very effective, but at this point they become extremely effective, unless one is running a wide-open case, which normally, by the way, has few if any valence-shifters.

At 0.5, present time action phrases—that is to say, action phrases just heard in the environment—are effective on the preclear to some slight degree; engram, lock and secondary action phrases are all effective, of course.

At 0.1, groupers are particularly effective and one can expect the track to be in a collapsed condition. Indeed, groupers are possibly effective anywhere on the scale, being just another type of action phrase; however, from 1.5 up, the time track will not collapse because of a grouper; from 1.5 down, it may do so.

The use of this column is apparent. After a short run, the auditor will see how the preclear behaves toward action phrases, and this will help him to determine the preclear's position on the Tone Scale.

BOOK TWO

DIANETIC PROCESSING

CHAPTER ONE

THE BASIC PRINCIPLES OF PROCESSING

In practice, in Dianetics, the auditor is doing a very simple thing. He is recovering theta which has become confused with MEST by reason of physical pain and emotional shock. He is by Dianetic processing converting entheta to theta.

A fundamental axiom of Dianetics is that life is formed by theta compounding with MEST to make a living organism. Life is theta plus MEST.

Another axiom is that theta conquers MEST by first becoming enturbulated with it and then withdrawing, possessed of some of the laws of MEST, and returning over the MEST for an orderly conquest.

Another axiom is that theta, in its conquest of MEST, has followed the cycle of contact, growth, decay and death, repeated over and over, theta each time using the data gained during the cycle to better adapt the organism for the further conquest of MEST.

Theta is thought, an energy of its own universe analogous to energy in the physical universe but only occasionally paralleling electromagnetic-gravitic laws.

The three primary components of theta are affinity, reality and communication.

Theta has the strange power of animating and directing MEST and bringing it into an orderly, mobile and self-perpetuating unit known to us as a life organism.

Theta and MEST in a disorderly collision bring about enturbulation in both the theta and the MEST which actually changes or reverses the polarity of the theta and the MEST. This reversed polarity permits the rejection of theta by enMEST and of MEST by entheta, so that death can ensue and a new organism can be begun.

Theta acting upon MEST with affinity, communication and reality takes on an aspect known as reasoning or understanding. All mathematics can be derived from ARC acting upon MEST.

Theta may have considerable residual knowledge of its own, but the knowledge in which an organism is interested is information concerning theta and MEST laws as applied to the organism, and each and every organism develops in the ratio that it utilizes and understands these laws.

In the cycle of the organism, from conception to death, theta and MEST are many times brought together in disorderly collision. This creates the phenomenon known as physical pain. Perception of threats to survival and dwindling position on the Tone Scale "charge up" these moments of physical pain as a mechanism to force the organism into, at first, greater survival activities and then, these failing, into death activities in order to free the theta from the MEST to begin a new cycle. The break point, where the organism is no longer driven upward toward survival but begins to go downward toward death, is 2.0 on the Tone Scale.

Death has been a vital mechanism in theta's conquest of MEST, since in no other way could the theta become sufficiently unenturbulated to be able to use the information received through enturbulence to create and construct new organisms or new species. Inevitably through this evolution theta, seeking according to theory wider and wider conquest of MEST, would construct an organism which by force of reason could actively handle large quantities of MEST. Man is such an organism. No lesser organism can rationally arrange any large quantity of MEST exterior to the organism, although many lesser organisms have genetic habit patterns which do permit the handling and altering of small amounts of MEST.

All learning springs from disorderly enturbulences where theta has impinged too suddenly and sharply upon MEST. All reasoning is done by freed theta returning over the MEST for an orderly conquest, utilizing the lessons learned in the disorderly conquest. This applies not only to the formation of organisms but to all adventures of man, according to observation.

It is possible that Dianetics, if these theories continue to prove correct as they have in the past, forms an evolutionary bridge which minimizes death as a mechanism for new learning and conquest and maximizes the conversion of entheta to theta, or disorderly experience to reason, within one life span. Should this prove to be the case, the acceleration of conquest of MEST by man should be very marked, and indeed at this time it can be observed that through a past lack of knowledge of the humanities his social orders have been for some time on a dwindling spiral, even though his knowledge of the physical laws increased. Man, according to these theories, could be said to have learned a great deal about the physical universe without learning enough about theta.

An interesting series of experiments recently done by the Foundation seems to bear out the theory that heightened reason-ability is contained in theta which has been newly recovered from an enturbulence with MEST. Individuals were given psychometry for a few minutes in order to measure their existing intelligence. They were then sent back down the track into an engram by an auditor and the engram was thoroughly restimulated. Immediately afterwards, the engram not reduced, these experimental subjects were ordered to do a second psychometry. In this condition of stress the second test was taken, and it was found that the score on the second test was uniformly higher than that gained on the first test. Considerable additional experimentation must be undertaken, and these results are very far from conclusive, but they would seem to indicate validity in some of the theta–MEST postulates. Other explanations can, of course, be found for the results of these experiments; however, the theta–MEST postulates have permitted new Dianetic processes to be derived and have markedly increased the ease of processing and have decreased the length of time necessary to bring about a Dianetic Release. Further, the theta–MEST postulates shed much light on the third dynamic, and with them it was possible for me to bring into being a new technology of groups which, when tested on pilot projects with groups, was found to have a uniform workability.

To learn anything about MEST, theta must become enturbulated with it, but to utilize the changes in it caused by the enturbulation, the theta must be freed from MEST in order to accomplish a reasonable conquest of further MEST. Death has been an answer, of sorts, but is not satisfactory to the unit organism. Dianetic processing offers a much less drastic theta recovery. The theta–MEST theory, as it applies to the increased reason-ability of theta which has been recovered from entheta, is pronounced in the many psychometries gathered by the Foundation. These show swift rises in intelligence and marked betterment of personality in ratio to the amount of processing done. As locks, secondaries and engrams are reduced, more and more free theta could be said to exist in the individual.

Inspecting a time track at the beginning of a case one ordinarily finds many occluded areas about which no reasoning can be done. It could be said that these areas, as in engrams themselves, contain entheta. Any of several processes which can free this entheta and convert it into theta will increase the reason-ability of the individual, as witnessed by many long series of psychometric tests taken before and after Dianetic processing. The restoration of recall of the areas hitherto occluded, in that the data contained in these areas is valuable as experience and information, could be said therefore to increase the health and reason of the individual. But the recovery of the theta which could be said to lie in these areas as entheta could also be postulated to increase the reason of the individual.

The Tone Scale is actually a chart of the ratio of free theta and entheta in the individual. Above the 2.0 line, the individual could be said to have more theta than entheta. Below the point 2.0, the individual could be said to have more entheta than theta. Simply by converting entheta to theta the auditor can cause the individual to rise on the Tone Scale.

It will readily be seen that the ideal condition would be all theta recovered and no entheta remaining in existence in the individual. The attainment of this ideal is called in Dianetics a "cleared" state. This would be, at this time, the end goal of processing. Just how often it can be completely attained by skilled or unskilled auditors is open to question. That it can be neared and that cases grow markedly better under processing is not open to question, since regardless of any wonder about the cleared state none who have associated with the Foundation or who have practiced Dianetics with any knowledge at all have any smallest doubt of the ability of Dianetic processing to improve cases 100 percent more than was ever before possible. If Clears cannot be created easily and swiftly, Dianetic processing is still very far from invalidated. Actually, Clears have been and are being produced, but their total potentialities remain relatively unexplored.

The Dianetic Release is more understandable than the Clear and has been produced and studied in sufficient numbers to admit of little doubt about the desirability and stability of the state. This is a nearer and more easily obtainable goal.

The simple alleviation of pain, worry and general unhappiness is routine to the Dianetic auditor. He can accomplish these goals in anything from a few hours to a few weeks on most preclears. These are much more easily obtained goals and are quite ordinary in the vicinity of the Foundation, so that these, which some say might have been considered miracles two years ago, hardly cause comment. Occasionally some Foundation auditor is startled into advertising a result to his fellow auditors in a processing unit, but these successes are generally taken for granted.*

A considerable study of the production of Clears is in progress at this time. The most pertinent factor which has come to light is the evident requirement that the auditor must be higher on the Tone Scale than his preclear in order to produce good results. Just as we have the ratio of theta to entheta establishing the sanity or insanity of the individual, so do we have the ratio of free theta in the auditor to the free theta–entheta ratio in the preclear establishing the swiftness with which the entheta can be unenturbulated in the preclear.

An examination of this theory will demonstrate that there are three valid processes. The first and the simplest of these processes consists of changing the environment of the preclear. His old environment possibly contains many restimulative objects and persons, so that his free theta is in continual enturbulence by reason of the restimulation. Shifting the preclear to an unrestimulative environment permits him to "settle out," which is to say, permits entheta to settle down in his reactive mind and convert, in some small portion, to free theta. Part of the environmental change process would be, of course, the bettering of affinity, reality and communication in the environment of the preclear. This by itself could produce a rise in his tone. Falling in love, being an increase of affinity, can make a well man out of a

---

*The most recent case under casual comment at the Foundation was an elderly woman who had been bedridden for sixteen years and who was sufficiently disabled with locomotor ataxia to be unable to take a single step. She was processed for four weeks by a student, as an extracurricular activity, and at the end of this time had lost her symptoms and was walking by herself. However, this case was rendered interesting to Foundation personnel mainly because of the charm and gratitude of the lady. —LRH

sick man. Being rejected or falling out of love, being a decrease of affinity, can make a sick man out of a well man. Bettering a person's communication, even if it only consists of a new pair of glasses, will also raise his tone. Validating his realities which were in question can raise his tone. All these things could be considered environmental changes.

A special part of environmental change would be changes in health, by reason of nutrition or better living conditions. This process must not be overlooked, since it has been our experience that some preclears who were not doing as well as could have been desired were deficient in their nutrition. The preclear who lives on coffee and sandwiches does not do as well during processing as one who has an adequate and balanced ration, with proper vitamin supplements. Good physical exercise can by itself markedly increase the individual's position on the Tone Scale, and a whole therapy to aid psychotics could easily be worked out along the lines of exercise alone.*

*Probably the worst thing that can happen to a psychotic is to be placed in the atmosphere normally provided for him by the state. Only a sane, healthy environment where he gets proper exercise and where he has unrestimulative individuals around him could do much to improve his condition. The psychotic will sometimes improve if he is given command over more MEST and, indeed, a fundamental in the production of psychosis is denying the individual a command over MEST.

No better method of tailor-making psychotics could be devised than the usual institution, and it is probable that if the normal person were placed in such an institution, in such an atmosphere, he would become psychotic. Indeed, the incidence of psychosis overtaking attendants and psychiatrists in attendance in such institutions is alarmingly high, a sign which one would have thought would have meant something some time since. This is second only to psychosurgery and shock treatment in the worsening of psychotics in a psychotic state. Rather than give psychotics such treatment and sanitariums it would be far kinder to kill them immediately and completely, and not partially as does psychosurgery and electric shock. —LRH

The second process which is valid in producing results is education. Education, if defined as the process of making new data available to the individual and causing his mind to attend to and use that data, itself brings reason into the case. Education usually provides new areas of concentration in the environment of the individual and translates many of his unknowns into knowns. Unreason could be classed in two categories: too wide a zone of attention, and too fixed a zone of attention. In the first, the mind wanders over large areas unable to select pertinent data. In the second, where the mind is fixed, it cannot wander far enough to find pertinent data. In neither case can the mind resolve the problem about which it is concerned, due to the absence of data. Superstition is an effort, for lack of education, to find pertinent data in too wide a zone or to fix the attention upon irrelevant data. Personal experience in one's environment gives one what might be called a personal education. A man has become embroiled with MEST, has freed himself, solved problems, has become embroiled again, has drawn back and solved problems anew, so that he has accumulated a fund of personal data about his task of living. Education might be said to be the process by which the individual is given the accumulated data of a long span of culture. It can, no less validly than personal experience, solve many of his problems. And so free theta, confronted by too many problems can, just by this, become enturbulated. Good education can in this way convert some of the entheta of an individual into theta, with a consequent rise on the Tone Scale. A very sharp proviso, however, must here be entered. Authoritarian teaching, by which the facts are impressed upon the individual and his self-determinism in his utilization of those facts is suppressed, can reduce the free theta in the individual by involving it in a fixed state in the memory bank. Theta is reason. Fixed theta is entheta. Many a man with a college education hammered home by authoritarian professors has been reduced so far down the Tone Scale that he behaves in life more or less like an automaton. His self-determinism and hence his persistence and ability to handle responsibility are so reduced as to unfit him for his role in life. Further, concentrating on educational processes past the midteens, after which a person should be solving problems of living, has an inhibitive effect upon the mind. An artist specifically is hindered by authoritarian education, since his must be the highest self-determinism if his work is to have any value. Authoritarian education has more or less the same effect upon the individual as hypnotism, depressing him down the Tone Scale, and indeed, at this time most education is leveled as hypnotic commands rather than invitations to reason. An education which invites reason and the comparison of taught data with the real world can raise the individual on the Tone Scale.

The third process which can be considered valid in raising the individual on the Tone Scale is individual processing, by which is meant any method which will turn his entheta into theta by addressing him as an individual.

It seems to be one of the characteristics of theta that when the theta present exceeds to a very high degree the entheta present, the entheta will tend to disenturbulate and become theta. In other words, if we considered these matters in terms of polarity and energy, a positive field if sufficiently strong would inhibit and then convert a negative field near it. A very large magnet placed close to a small magnet will change the poles of the small magnet. When a very large amount of entheta is placed in the vicinity of a lesser amount of theta, the theta may rapidly become entheta. When theta and entheta exist together in more or less equal amounts, or when the disproportion is not large, a relatively stable condition exists, the theta tending to remain theta and the entheta tending to remain entheta. An example of this in the group is the phenomenon of mass hysteria, where one or two members of the group become enturbulated and very rapidly the remainder of the group becomes enturbulated.

This is the basic law of the contagion of aberration. Entheta will enturbulate theta. Misemotion will change emotion into misemotion. Poor communication will change good communication into poor communication. Poor reality will change good communication into poor communication. Poor reality will change good reality into poor reality. The engrams in a case enturbulate theta into the entheta of secondaries and locks.

Amongst people one sees this exemplified when a person who is relatively insane enters a group which is relatively sane. The relatively sane may attempt to raise the sanity level of the relatively insane person, and it may occur in this group that the relatively insane person becomes more sane. At the same time, however, the relatively sane people become less sane, unless they have some means or technology for preventing this phenomenon from occurring.

In the case of a husband and wife, it is easy to observe that the mate who is higher on the scale will during the marriage association drop lower, and usually the mate who is lower on the Tone Scale will come slightly higher as a result of that association. As a further example, the mate who is lower on the Tone Scale will demand more affection and give less than the mate who is higher. The mate who is lower will demand more communication and give less and will assert more reality but will actually have less.

It can thus be seen, as represented in column AQ on the chart, that the auditor must have a higher ratio of theta to his entheta than has the preclear. A condition must exist where much more theta is available than entheta. An auditor whose theta–entheta ration is around 2.5 could, with skill, handle individuals lower on the Tone Scale by not more than one point. A 2.5 auditor attempting to handle an apathy case would find his already badly enturbulated condition worsened so much by the case that the case, having very little free theta, would not get much better. A 2.5 auditor attempting to create a Clear begins to work uphill as soon as his preclear reaches 2.5, and the hill very rapidly becomes too steep to climb. The ideal auditor is one who has a very high endowment of theta and who is at 4.0 on the Tone Scale. Thus, at the beginning of Dianetics, where we have the usual auditor operating between 2.5 and 3.0, we find it very simple to pull preclears up to 2.0 or 2.5, more difficult to bring them up to 3.0. Where auditors are being heavily employed in processing people they tend to neglect their own processing, and being constantly in the vicinity of and handling entheta, they begin to encounter difficulties with a preclear as soon as the preclear reaches 2.5. It is incumbent upon the auditor to keep himself continually processed and keep his own tone coming up the scale. Where a co-auditing team exists, one person auditing the other, it is considerably more than a fair exchange for each to give due attention to the state of the other's case, for the moment one begins to appropriate the bulk of processing his own case will slow down in its progress.

Dianetic processing, then, by the theta–MEST theory, attempts only one thing: the recovery and conversion of entheta into theta. Any processing which does not accomplish this in an orderly fashion is therefore not valid Dianetic processing.

Theta is many things. For a description of it as it applies to the MEST organism you need only read the 4.0 band of the Tone Scale chart. Theta is reason, serenity, stability, happiness, cheerful emotion, persistence and the other factors which man ordinarily considers desirable. Any practice which enturbulates theta suppresses the case. The Auditor's Code is actually a list of the things one must or must not do to preserve the theta-ness of theta and to inhibit the enturbulation of theta by the auditor.

Where the preclear has a small amount of theta and a large amount of entheta, the auditor must be particularly careful not to enturbulate the existing theta, since it is in the proximity of so much entheta that it enturbulates rapidly. The auditor mishandling such a case, using brute force, invalidations, hypnotism, sadism or devil worship, can send the free theta still in existence down the track and lock it up in an old secondary or engram and so find himself with a temporarily completely enturbulated preclear on his hands. To avoid this danger, one should mark the preclear well on the chart and be guided accordingly. This gives him an estimate of the amount of free theta he has with which to unenturbulate the existing entheta in the case. It may happen that so little theta exists in the case that the auditor must use the lightest and most pleasant methods of which he

"The auditor might liken his job to removing the rocks and shoals from the hidden depths of a turbulent river and making of it a smooth-flowing and powerful stream."

is capable in order to make enough theta available even to start down the time track.

The percentile column (the scale from 0 to 1000) is an index of the amount of organism theta available to work the case. At 4.0, 100 percent is available. At 2.0, the amount of theta and "permanent" entheta are more or less equally balanced, but environmental enturbulation leaves the preclear with very little theta. Below this point is the death zone, and here as the tone lowers increasingly more danger exists that all the remaining theta will suddenly at one fell swoop become entheta, thus changing the occasional psychotic into a chronic psychotic, at least until rest, good food and exercise permit the not seriously enturbulated portions of the entheta to become theta again. It takes very poor auditing to accomplish this, and the danger is hardly a danger at all if one follows the chart.

The least forceful processing produces the best results. As Dianetic processing evolves it becomes less and less directive, the preclear being allowed more and more latitude in his actions. This should not go so far as to permit the preclear to free-associate or ramble on endlessly and uselessly, but it does go as far as never driving a preclear hard when he balks, unless he is in the middle of a secondary grief or terror engram and is refusing to go on through with it, where if the auditor permits him to leave it the possibility exists that much skilled auditing will elapse before the auditor will have his preclear back into the secondary.

The auditor might liken his job to removing the rocks and shoals from the hidden depths of a turbulent river and making of it a smooth-flowing and powerful stream. The auditor is not changing the preclear's personality or attempting to improve the preclear by evaluations and suggestions. He is simply making it easier for the mind to do what basic personality naturally wants the mind to do. This might be said to be the total end and goal of processing.

THE AUDITOR'S CODE

THE FIRST THING ANY AUDITOR should know and know well about processing is the Auditor's Code. This has been called the code of how to be civilized. It is much more important than knowing mechanical techniques to know well the attitude one should have toward a preclear. This is not for courtesy but for efficiency. No preclear will respond to an auditor who does not adhere to the Auditor's Code.

It must be remembered that the mission of the auditor is not to reduce engrams, not to run out secondaries, not to eradicate psychosomatic illnesses, psychoses or neuroses, but to raise the preclear on the Tone Scale. It happens that these incidentals of removing neuroses, psychoses and psychosomatic illnesses as well as increasing the persistence and general responsibility of the individual follow in due course so long as the auditor attends closely to his primary mission of raising his preclear on the Tone Scale. If he does not give this his first attention, he is not freeing theta and converting entheta, and if he does not do this he cannot efficiently accomplish the other goals. The index of how well he progresses with the preclear's case is the Tone Scale. Mechanical, lackadaisical and careless auditing can actually remove psychosomatic illnesses and yet not raise the preclear on the Tone Scale. This may be paradoxical, but what happens is that the entheta in the engram

"It must be remembered that the mission of the auditor
is not to reduce engrams, not to run out secondaries,
not to eradicate psychosomatic illnesses, psychoses or neuroses,
but to raise the preclear on the Tone Scale."

causing the psychosomatic illness is converted into another type of entheta which is not physically painful to the preclear. It is, nevertheless, entheta, and the preclear is not raised on the Tone Scale. Thus, the auditor must closely attend to every means which will raise the preclear on the Tone Scale and should disregard the immediate and short-term goals of the eradication of specific "illnesses," bad habits, neuroses, psychoses, obsessions and compulsions. The auditor must remember that even such a degraded practice as hypnotism can, by the implantation of positive suggestions, suppress certain physical and mental disorders. Though these are suppressed in one quarter they may very well manifest themselves as something entirely different. A person is saner to have "psychosomatic illnesses" than he is to have mental aberrations. Hypnotism can in a small percentage of cases eradicate the "psychosomatic illness" but will produce in its stead a lowered tone in the individual. Electric shock and psychosurgery may alter the behavior pattern of the individual and may suppress him into some tractable condition, but the result is inevitably harmful to the ability, efficiency and general worth of the subject, with the added detraction that they cause damage to the brain from which the individual never completely recovers.

Simply by addressing processing from the viewpoint that one is changing entheta to theta and freeing up all available theta in the case one will make the most rapid progress with the preclear. Experience in the field has demonstrated that irascible, authoritarian auditing can continue for as long as five hundred hours, that actual "psychosomatic illnesses" can be removed and that some small improvement can be seen in the general tone of the preclear, and yet that neglect of emphasis on raising tone might permit such a case to continue on another thousand hours without producing a Clear, the entheta being transferred from one part of the bank to another, endlessly.

The auditor should give attention to the environment of his preclear. Here he may find that his preclear is in the vicinity of such restimulative people, situations and objects that the free theta in the case is continually in a turbulent condition. In such a case the auditor has every right to recommend a change of environment for the duration of processing. In this alone he has gained free theta for his preclear, and much of the turbulence he observes in his preclear will settle out. Cases have been observed in which the preclear was in the vicinity of a marital mate who produced such constant tension, so many invalidations, and who had so little thought for or belief in any possible gain for the other that the processing was only of small benefit and the auditor was wasting ten hours of auditing time for every one which was effective.

The auditor should not draw back from educating his preclear, so long as the education is not on a command basis but is done as an invitation to the self-determinism of the preclear to manifest itself, an invitation to the preclear to reason things out on a basis of his own adjudication. This is particularly beneficial with children. Indeed, children are surrounded by such ordering about and restrictions that their self-determinism is often too slight to cope with anything like their personal situations. In such a case it is definitely the role of the auditor to invite the child to think things out for himself, occasionally redefining words or situations for the child. Actually, an auditor can take two or three preclears and form an educational group wherein mutual discussion of their own problems will result in a rise of tone in the preclears.

The third method of processing, of course the most lasting method, is auditing by Dianetic processing, wherein the auditor concentrates on freeing all available theta in the case and converting as much entheta as possible to theta. The auditor's first step toward accomplishing this, should he consider the environmental situation compatible, is to promote affinity, communication and reality with his preclear and to found a group of two—himself and his preclear.

The auditor must recognize that he is dealing with a person, in every case, whose conduct is not as good as it will be. Thus, the auditor must practice much self-restraint and must form an example for his preclear. To do this the auditor must never under any circumstances or for any reason break any part of the Auditor's Code with the preclear.

Breaking the Auditor's Code, at first glance, may not appear to be a very great sin. But an auditor has undertaken to aid a fellow man, and his dedication to that purpose must be sincere to the point of sacredness. An auditor, by misusing his position through what he knows about the human mind, can bring havoc upon an unsuspecting preclear. Carelessness alone, if it is backed with good intention, can seldom do much harm. But malicious intent, wherein an auditor expects to "gain" heavily by use of deception and misuse of the sacred trust he has taken unto himself in helping his fellow man, can cast a preclear far back down the Tone Scale.

If one does not feel that he can keep the Auditor's Code wholly and completely, he should not under any circumstances audit anyone, nor should he permit himself to be persuaded to audit anyone, and any preclear should be very wary of permitting himself to be audited by anyone who potentially would break the Auditor's Code. The preclear who finds himself confronted with an Auditor's Code break should instantly and finally terminate his processing with that auditor and should find another who can keep the Code. A man who will break this Code once will break it many times, and the preclear should never persist in the arrangement out of the argument that he can get only one auditor. Anyone who breaks this Code is under 2.5 on the chart and should not be auditing but should be in the process of being audited himself.

An openhearted and sincere effort to practice Dianetics, after a thorough study of the principles contained in this book, should the student adhere to these principles, will produce marked and beneficial effects upon human beings never before attained in man's history. To produce these effects the auditor must permit himself to be embraced by the Auditor's Code and to keep these principles as sacred as if they were the vows of priesthood.

The auditor conducts himself in such a way as to maintain optimum affinity, communication and agreement with the preclear.

The auditor is trustworthy. He understands that the preclear has given into the auditor's trust his hope for higher sanity and happiness, and that the trust is sacred and never to be betrayed.

The auditor is courteous. He respects the preclear as a human being. He respects the self-determinism of the preclear. He respects his own position as an auditor. He expresses this respect in courteous conduct.

The auditor is courageous. He never falls back from his duty to a case. He never fails to use optimum procedure regardless of any alarming conduct on the part of the preclear.

The auditor never evaluates the case for the preclear. He abstains from this, knowing that to compute for the preclear is to inhibit the preclear's own computation. He knows that to refresh the preclear's mind as to what went before is to cause the preclear to depend heavily upon the auditor and so to undermine the self-determinism of the preclear.

The auditor never invalidates any of the data or the personality of the preclear. He knows that in doing so he would seriously enturbulate the preclear. He refrains from criticism and invalidation no matter how much the auditor's own sense of reality is twisted or shaken by the preclear's incidents or utterances.

The auditor uses only techniques designed to restore the self-determinism of the preclear. He refrains from all authoritarian or dominating conduct, leading always rather than driving. He refrains from the use of hypnotism or sedatives on the preclear no matter how much the preclear may demand them out of aberration. He never abandons the preclear out of faintheartedness about the ability of techniques to resolve the case, but persists and continues to restore the preclear's self-determinism. The auditor keeps himself informed of any new skills in the science.

The auditor cares for himself as an auditor. By working with others he maintains his own processing at regular intervals in order to maintain or raise his own position on the Tone Scale despite restimulation of himself through the process of auditing others. He knows that failure to give heed to his own processing, until he himself is a Release or a Clear in the severest meaning of the terms, is to cost his preclear the benefit of the auditor's best performance.

This is the Auditor's Code. It has been discovered that the two most important aspects of the Code are the preservation of the preclear's sense of reality and the trustworthiness of the auditor. An invalidation of the preclear's data, no matter how outrageously that data may assault the auditor's own sense of reality, can be severe and will go so far as to shut off the preclear's sonic and visio, all in a moment. Most preclears are uncertain enough in the presence of their own past. They quite commonly invalidate themselves, a practice from which they should be discouraged. When the auditor invalidates the preclear's data the shock to the preclear can be very great. In the matter of trustworthiness, the auditor must never take advantage of the preclear, either in using his data or in using a temporary state of apathy, propitiation or restimulation in order to possess himself carnally of the preclear or to gain materially.

Any two people in constant association who will conduct themselves according to the Auditor's Code will soon find not only that they are Clear or almost Clear as a group of two but also that their knowledge of and joy in human relationships have been immeasurably increased.

THE MECHANICS OF ABERRATION

ACCORDING TO THE BASIC THEORY of Dianetics, theta, by which is meant the life force, life energy, divine energy, *élan vital,* or by any other name, the energy peculiar to life which acts upon material in the physical universe and animates it, mobilizes it and changes it, is susceptible to alteration in character or vibration, at which time it becomes enturbulated theta or entheta.

A description of pure theta acting in a harmonious control of MEST is to be found along the 4.0 band of the chart. Here we see theta as reasonable, persistent, responsible, with an affinity very high in all spheres of attraction, capable of high communication both "perceptically" and with ideas, and with a high sense and appreciation of reality. An individual whose theta is unenturbulated in his current environment, whose education is not enturbulated by poor data and bad teachers in an unreasonable culture, and from whose life has been deleted all the physical and mental pain, given an average genetic background, would be a very high order of Clear.

The things which reduce the individual down from the state of Clear and bring him lower on the Tone Scale would be a turbulent and unhappy environment, a poor and unreasonable education in a not too rational culture, poor physical endowment and, what is most important to the auditor, theta trapped as entheta in past moments of physical pain and further theta trapped as charge as later consequences of that physical pain.

So far as the immediate address to the case is concerned, the auditor might conceive of a case as being *potentially* relatively pure theta, as modified by environment, education and physical endowment, but that this theta has in past moments of pain and sorrow become, at least some portion of it, converted to entheta which is held at various moments of a person's past. By methods of processing, the auditor frees the entheta, which automatically converts to theta and becomes available to the individual's general action in life and so raises him automatically on the Tone Scale.

Physical pain could be said to be the alarm reaction to theta that the organism has been too heavily impinged upon MEST. Physical pain is an abrupt and sharp warning of nonsurvival. Without a mechanism of physical pain no organism could be warned of physical dangers through experiencing pain, and so no organism could survive, since no organism would have a perception of destruction. Thus, physical pain is actually a perceptic, just as sight and sound are perceptics. Physical pain as a perception mechanism lies immediately behind every other perception mechanism, since too much light can cause pain, too much sound can cause pain, too much motion can cause pain, and so forth. MEST, which is to say the physical universe of matter, energy, space and time, is perceived by the theta of the organism by the various perceptions of sight, sound, motion, organic sensation, and so forth. The moment any of these grows too intense, theta's orderly and harmonious control of MEST undergoes a shock of interruption. The theta and MEST brought too closely together in turbulence thus form entheta and enMEST.

Every individual has a time track. This is simply all of the perceptions of a lifetime from conception to present time—the organism time track. Every moment of now—present time—finds the organism registering by perception some portion of the physical universe. These perceptions are stored in what is called the standard memory bank if they are analytical and not physically painful or in the reactive memory bank if they contain physical pain. Thus, these perceptions are stored in an unending continuation from the first moment of cellular life forward to present time. The time track is a consecutive series of nows, through day and night, week, month and year for all the lifetime.

Each time the perceptions, by reason of severe turbulence, record as physical pain, the theta present could be said to be converted and held there static by enMEST. Every physically painful recording is missing from the time track so far as standard memory is concerned and is filed instead in the reactive bank. Each time this occurs less theta is apparently available to the analyzing and conscious portion of the person's being and becomes a debit on the entheta side of the ledger. So long as the individual possesses proportionately more theta than entheta he is fairly well up the Tone Scale, but when the trapped entheta begins to outweigh the theta the individual is brought down the Tone Scale to a nonsurvival level. The position of the person on the Tone Scale determines not only his potential for happiness but also his longevity. Immortality* can be measured in many ways. The higher a person is on the Tone Scale the more he tends toward immortality. The lower a person is on the Tone Scale the more he tends toward death. The amount of theta in the case determines the amount of survival potential of the individual and the amount of entheta in the case determines the amount of nonsurvival potential.

The auditor by processing frees the entheta from the case, thus increasing the survival potential of the individual. The processes which free entheta and convert it into theta may be formidable in

*IMMORTALITY: *infinite survival, the absolute goal of survival. The individual seeks this on the first dynamic as an organism and as a theta entity and in the perpetuation of his name by his group. On the second dynamic he seeks it through his children, and so on through the eight dynamics. Life survives through the persistence of theta. A species survives through the persistence of the life in it. A culture survives through the persistence of the species using it. There is evidence that the theta of an individual may survive as a personal entity from life to life, through many lives on Earth.* —LRH

theory but in practice are quite simple and may be done by rote, since it is the nature of theta readily to convert back to its free and unenturbulated state when given simple assistance.

It should be thoroughly understood by the auditor that according to theory, confirmed by observation in practice, no entheta exists unless it has as its basic cause physical pain.

It should be no less well understood that entheta, when it contacts small quantities of theta, makes that into entheta as well. Further, theta contacting smaller quantities of entheta converts the entheta into theta. This is a two-way conversion. Theta, in proximity to entheta, makes theta out of it. Entheta, in proximity to theta, makes entheta out of it. From this we have the contagion of aberration, a principle of considerable importance in Dianetics. Theta, in the vicinity of entheta, becomes enturbulated and made into entheta. It was once thought that insanity was inherited. It is true that a genetic endowment in terms of structure or an endowment of too small a quantity of theta may predispose one person more than others to insanity, but only in the vicinity of entheta. Of course, there can be the insanity of malformed brains, where some of the perception and computation mechanisms are absent, but this type of insanity results only in inability to think, not in aberrated thinking. It is not true, then, that insanity is hereditary. Insanity, apparently, comes about wholly by contagion. An enturbulated culture or environment can keep an individual in a continuous state of turbulence, but, lacking engrams, that individual would cease to be enturbulated as soon as he removed himself from the source of the turbulence. People who are insane bring those around them markedly down on the Tone Scale and could be said to be responsible for all the existing insanity in the race. If one associates with badly aberrated individuals one will himself in consequence become badly aberrated, if only while in the vicinity of the badly aberrated associates.

There is an apparent family line of aberration. It was previously thought to be carried genetically, but this is evidently not the case.

It is carried on the thought channel of the family. The confusions of domestic life get into the moments of physical injury of the child, and the child as a consequence becomes liable for the family aberrations and will manifest them.

The principle of the contagion of aberration is broad in scope. One can observe in any group of men that one or two may be much more aberrated than the others. One can make the simple experiment of removing the one or two aberrated persons from the group, and he will then see that the general tone level of the group will rise, since the source of the group's main turbulence has been removed.

By examining the life of any preclear, his case history, and without examining any of the preclear's own aberrations, the auditor can make a good estimate of the preclear's aberrations simply by discovering what manner of people the parents were. It is an inexorable fact that these aberrations, one way or another, will manifest themselves in the preclear.

The auditor should fully understand the principle of contagion. Fortunately, the conversion works in both directions. Sanity is also contagious. Thus, by observing the Auditor's Code and providing a sane environment for his preclear, the auditor can bring some of the entheta in the preclear's case back into the state of theta without any processing. This is particularly valuable in the treatment of psychotics.

There could be said to be three divisions of entheta. Basically, the only way entheta comes into being in any life form is through physical injury, but after the physical injury is present the entheta in it contages into the theta involved in circumstances that approach or approximate those of the physical injury. When this happens we have another kind of entheta; locks formed by restimulation. The shocks of conscious moments, the griefs and sorrows, the fears and angers, the breaks of affinity, communication and reality which one has with life would be the third kind of entheta, which would be temporary entheta if it were not for the presence of physical injury and its entheta in the case. To make this plainer, first there is the engram. This is physical pain, enMEST and entheta held at a specific point on the time track. This might never become serious but for restimulation by the environment. When this engram becomes restimulated it makes much of the existing free theta in the organism turbulent. Some of this turbulence remains as additional frozen entheta, some of it unenturbulates and becomes theta again.

The engram, a moment of physical pain, forms the basis for entheta, and having formed it, little by little by contagion, steals free theta from the individual and makes it into entheta "permanently" in the form of secondary engrams and locks. At the moment of restimulation, perhaps nearly all of the individual's theta becomes enturbulated, but this more or less rapidly unenturbulates, or settles out, and becomes theta again.

One could, then, have a picture of a time track as a straight line from conception to present time. At some early point on this time track there is a moment of physical injury. At a little bit later on the track this moment is approximated by the environment. This would be a key-in. Actually, the individual has to be more or less enturbulated by the general environment when the key-in takes place, which is to say he would have to be worried or tired or perhaps only annoyed about something.

This key-in now gives the engram more power and strength. The next time the engram is restimulated, another lock is added and would be marked as a third point on the track. Then, let us say, that some loss takes place which approximates in some way or ways this original engram. If it were such a thing as the death of a loved one, an enormous amount of enturbulence would take place. The turbulence, by its very magnitude, approximates the nature of physical pain. A very large amount of theta becomes trapped by the physical pain. This would be called a secondary engram. The difference between a secondary engram and a lock is the order of magnitude of the trapped theta, that is, entheta. Each time a secondary occurs the whole of the theta of the individual may be temporarily enturbulated, but only a small portion remains frozen as entheta, and the remaining enturbulated theta converts back into free theta.

Thus one can see that as life progresses, more and more theta becomes fixed as entheta in locks and secondary engrams, and less and less theta is available to the organism for purposes of reason. This is called the dwindling spiral. It is so called because the more entheta there is on the case, the more theta will be turned into entheta at each new restimulation. It is a three-dimensional "vicious circle" which carries the individual down the Tone Scale. In a child, very few locks and secondaries have been formed and so the child's theta is free and the child's tone is high, yet even though this child receives no more engrams for several years, the engrams he already has may gradually be charged up by locks and secondaries until he had less free theta than entheta, at which time he would be very low on the Tone Scale.

It may also happen that some enormous success in life, an extremely happy marriage or association with high-theta individuals will work on the reactive bank to convert it without processing, at least in part, back into free theta. Here is the calmness of the aberrated person who quits the turbulent world, for instance, and takes the vows of the Church. In this new environment he has fewer approximations of his old locks and engrams, but more importantly, he is in the vicinity of far more theta, and he will as a consequence disenturbulate, and therefore rise on the Tone Scale.

Similarly, that person who is idle, without goal or direction, may find his accumulation of secondaries and locks is far greater, since his theta, being idle, is already slightly enturbulated. This individual may become very busy in the pursuit of some definite and worthwhile goal, and his theta, thus unenturbulated, will rob his locks and secondaries of some of the entheta they contain.

An individual who in one environ may have been living under extremely unhealthy conditions may change his mode of existence so as to include exercise, sunshine and fresh air, and this change, bringing about a better physical condition, will itself unenturbulate the individual to some degree.

Dianetic processing does simply this: It uses the theta of the preclear, as aided by the theta of the auditor, to disenturbulate the theta contained in the preclear's locks, secondaries and engrams.

The goal of the auditor is to disenturbulate entheta, not necessarily to run engrams or to concentrate on locks or secondaries, one more than another. In various cases various conditions exist which make it necessary to address first one and then another of these three types of entheta. The auditor should thoroughly understand the anatomy of the engram, as well as that of the secondary and of the lock.

An engram comes about when the individual organism suffers an intense impact with MEST. This is actual physical pain. It may occur in any portion of the body and may be from simply too intense a reception of light or sound, erosion as in chafing or sunburn, cuts, contusions, fractures, organic derangements, overdoses of poisonous substances, attacks by bacteria and viruses, or any usual or unusual cause of physical pain. Every moment of physical pain contains with it a partial or major shutdown of the analytical function of the mind. Consciousness may be interrupted for a moment or for days by physical pain, but regardless of the duration, physical pain always brings about lowered consciousness. One may not realize this completely until one has had erased from him an instant in which he burned his finger or something equally inconsequential. He will learn that while he had supposed he knew everything that happened during that moment of pain, some data yet remained hidden concerning the incident. This missing data is the content of the reactive mind.

The engram contains all of the perceptions present during the period of its receipt. Before Dianetics, this was not realized. It was thought that an unconscious person was simply unconscious and that things which were said to him and that other perceptible entities which impinged upon him went unrecorded. No matter the depth of unconsciousness in the presence of physical pain, the reactive mind records fully and completely all the perceptions possible in the environ, including the physical pain. During an operation involving anesthesia, for instance, all the physical pain, the doctor's words, the smell of the ether, the nurse's footsteps, the feel of the table and the functions of the internal organs, amongst other things, are recorded in full in the reactive mind of the individual, as an engram.

If one is acquainted with hypnotism, one can readily understand the compulsive or obsessive character of data which is out of sight of the conscious mind but which is yet forced upon it from below by the drive of physical pain. Hidden data and hidden pain cause identity thinking, so that the power to differentiate and thus to reason is reduced. An individual obeys engrams literally. When an engram is restimulated the individual may dramatize the engram or go through the cycle of action demanded by the engram, if it can be dramatized. Dramatized or not, the engram, containing unconsciousness, reduces the analytical awareness of the individual, and a person who has many engrams in restimulation is ordinarily less than one-quarter analytically aware and can still be considered normal.

The entheta of the engram makes it possible for locks to form. The engram is restimulated in the individual when he is less analytically alert than ordinarily, by reason of weariness or other nonoptimum conditions. The engram may contain certain perceptics which are duplicated in the immediate environ of the individual. This approximation of the environ to the engram brings about an identification of the exterior world with the interior world of engrams, and so brings about restimulation of the engram. This restimulation manifests itself in the enturbulation of the individual. The process of enturbulation fixes into the engram some of the individual's theta, "permanently" converting it to entheta. The first time an engram is restimulated (and one may lie dormant for forty years without being restimulated) is called a key-in. A key-in is merely a special kind of lock.

The secondary engram takes place when the turbulence of the individual is very high. Anger, fear, grief or apathy may be occasioned by the environment, and if a physical pain engram underlies this situation and even vaguely approximates it in perceptics, enormous quantities of theta are trapped as entheta in the secondary. The secondary engram is enormously important. It is run exactly like a physical pain engram. If one could remove all the secondary engrams from a case without touching physical pain engrams, he would have a Release. The secondary stores such large quantities of entheta that remarkable results are often obtained by running one simple secondary engram. The auditor should understand thoroughly, however, that no secondary engram can exist unless a physical pain engram underlies it. In running a secondary engram the auditor may often discover that with it he is running also a physical pain engram.

Affinity, communication and reality enforcements and breaks in a case are not specialized types of secondaries or locks but are only the component parts of secondaries and locks. Any physical pain engram is a break of affinity between theta and MEST and is, indeed, the basic affinity break. The break of affinity brings about reduction of communication since the theta no longer wishes to approach this type of MEST as avidly as before. And as the theta is not in harmonious agreement with MEST, the reality is reduced. Here we have, in affinity, communication and reality breaks, the basic cause of trouble in any organism. The intent of theta is harmoniously to conquer MEST, and when MEST reacts suddenly and without warning against the theta organism the basic impulse of that theta is thwarted. Thus, this could be said to be the basis of all aberration, and by observation and experience this postulate seems to be adequately confirmed.

The engram becomes charged up with entheta through the process of the individual's acquiring locks and secondaries. An engram which is too highly charged not only cannot be run but ordinarily cannot even be contacted, until secondaries and locks are reduced. Thus, in most cases the first address of the auditor is to locks and then secondaries and then engrams, with the treatment of more locks and secondaries to make available more engrams.

The whole purpose of the auditor is to change entheta to theta as rapidly and as efficiently as possible. Where he gets the entheta, whether out of engrams, secondaries or locks, is of no basic concern. Theta is theta.

THE DYNAMICS OF EXISTENCE

BEHIND DIANETICS THERE IS considerable technology concerning knowledge itself and general philosophies about thinking without which Dianetics could not have come into existence.

The major postulate of Dianetics is:

THE DYNAMIC PRINCIPLE OF EXISTENCE IS SURVIVE.

Theta (where its purpose is the conquest of MEST), life and organisms have no other principle than *survive* as their motivation. The opposite to this motivation is succumb.*

The failure to survive is to succumb.

Two basic axioms about knowledge are as follows: Axiom One: A datum is as important as it is evaluated in terms of survive or succumb. Axiom Two: A datum can only be evaluated by data of comparable magnitude.

The basic unit of both the theta and the MEST universes is Two, not One. Dymaxion geometry,[1] the three-dimensional mathematics of space, has comparable axioms and values, evidently, in the theta universe. The basic unit of One as a postulate is impossible, since it has nothing by which it can be evaluated; therefore, the basic unit of Two is necessary. Attempting to postulate anything on the basis of One as the basic unit brings about considerable disorder in thought. The Supreme Being, for instance, has as the second datum for evaluation the Devil. The Supreme Being is Survive. The Devil is succumb. The basic postulate of Dianetics contains as an understood portion the fact that survive is matched by succumb. —LRH

....

1. **dymaxion geometry:** a reference to a philosophy of construction and design developed by American engineer and inventor Buckminster Fuller (1895–1983). Fuller devised a system of architecture, based on specific geometrical units, resulting in the invention of large domes which had no supporting members except a frame made of these units. Fuller's dome encloses a greater volume with less material than any alternative form.

Theta as an energy, insofar as we observe it in organisms which are partially MEST, survives or succumbs. MEST, in accordance with the most fundamental physical laws and the conservation of energy, survives or succumbs. It will be noted in both cases that succumbing is apparently the conversion of the energy into another form. Theta converting into entheta travels from survive to succumb, but the energy is not lost, and death is one of the freeing mechanisms by which the theta is able to become momentarily independent of MEST and so combine again with MEST, forming another organism to carry along the generations. In the physical universe, energy survives but the forms the energy takes often succumb and change into other energy forms.

The chart of the Tone Scale divides at 2.0. Above this point the direction of dynamic action of the organism is toward survival. The organism will seek higher levels of survival, will try to live as long as possible and as well as possible, both of which are components of survival, since in general the more bountiful the existence, the better the potentials of survival.

Below 2.0, the dynamic action of the organism tends toward succumb. The individual may apparently engage upon survival activities but will do something to bring about a nonsurvival end, regardless of what activity the individual engages upon. Below 2.0, the individual will tend toward the death of himself, sex, the future, groups or mankind. He is destructive toward life. He makes enMEST out of any MEST he may have at hand or can influence. He repels theta and attracts entheta.

This is the band of the immoral, the promiscuous, the criminal, the fascist, the godless, the suicide and other undesirables. Whatever action is taken by the individual who is acutely or chronically below 2.0 will tend toward the death of himself or anything with which he is associated. His avowals may be entirely different, and he may even himself believe that he seeks higher survival levels, but the end product of his actions, whether these actions apply to a business, to a marriage, to a friendship, to a group or to a religion will be death or some undesirable nonsurvival situation, which, of course, itself tends toward death.

It is not realized generally that the criminal is not only antisocial but is also antiself. Anyone below 2.0 is a potential or active criminal, in that crimes against the prosurvival actions of others are continually perpetrated. Crime might be defined as the reduction of the survival level along any one of the eight dynamics.*

The old adages about the forces of good and the forces of evil are amazingly apt when one studies men from the standpoint of the theta–MEST theory. In order to understand this further perhaps one should offer the Dianetic Axioms for good and for evil.

Good can be considered to be any constructive survival action. It happens that no construction can take place without some small destruction, just as the tenement must be torn down to make room for the new apartment building. Good is further modified by the viewpoint of the individual. To be good, something must contribute to the individual, to his family, his children, his group, mankind or life. To be good, a thing must contain construction which outweighs the destruction it contains. A new cure which saves a hundred and kills one is an acceptable cure. What is good from the viewpoint of one person may be bad for another person. In the case of A, who gets a

*Police are continually baffled by the irrationality of the criminal. Since police officers are, ordinarily, rational men and tend themselves toward survival, they sometimes cannot readily comprehend that the criminal habitually takes the route of nonsurvival for himself and his group. No matter the criminal's IQ he will leave obvious clues on the scene. He will flee from crimes at a rate of speed calculated to attract the attention of any traffic officer. Trapped in a criminal act which has as its penalty as little as thirty days in jail, the criminal may attempt to use weapons against police, and thus commit suicide at the expense of some worthy officer's life. The most baffling thing in police work is an attempt to deduce motives using any kind of a rational yardstick upon the criminal. The only motive the criminal has is destruction along any one of the dynamics, including the first. It sometimes happens that if a criminal is promised nonsurvival in return for information, he will gladly make the trade, whereas he refuses to give information in return for liberty and continued good health. Those who aid criminals or deal with them know, to their sorrow, that the criminal ordinarily repays a helping hand with destructive actions. Parole boards are rendered particularly dismayed by the numbers of times their extensions of liberty, on certain conditions, is repaid by destructive action. Police have for some time looked for a proper definition for a true criminal. Men should be removed from society only when they constitute a continual or occasional threat to that society. An answer to this problem may be found in the accompanying chart. —LRH

new job, this is good for A, but perhaps bad for B, who was released so that A could have the job. Good is survival. Good is being right more than one is wrong. Good is being more successful than one is unsuccessful, along constructive lines. Things are good which complement the survival of the individual, his family, children, group, mankind, life and MEST. Acts are good which are more beneficial than destructive along these dynamics, as modified by the viewpoint of the individual, the future race, the group, mankind, life or MEST.

Evil is the opposite of good, and is anything which is destructive more than it is constructive along any of the various dynamics. A thing which does more destruction than construction is evil from the viewpoint of the individual, the future, group, species, life or MEST that it destroys. When an act is more destructive than constructive, it is evil. When an act assists succumb more than it assists survival, it is an evil act in the proportion that it destroys. A thing is evil which threatens more destruction than construction for the individual, future, group, mankind, life or MEST.

Good, bluntly, is survival. Evil is nonsurvival. Construction is good when it promotes survival. Destruction is bad when it inhibits survival. Construction is evil when it inhibits survival. Destruction is good when it enhances survival.

An act or conclusion is as right as it promotes the survival of the individual, future, group, mankind or life making the conclusion. To be entirely right would be to survive to infinity.

An act or conclusion is wrong to the degree that it is nonsurvival to the individual, future race, group, species or life responsible for doing the act or making the conclusion. The most wrong a person can be is dead.

The individual or group which is, on the average, righter than wrong (since these terms are not absolutes, by far) should survive. An individual who is wronger than right, on the average, will succumb.

All conclusions are modified by time, since one conclusion made wrong during an emergency can cause the nonsurvival of the individual or the group.

Individuals above 2.0 on the Tone Scale are more and more right in their actions and conclusions than they are wrong, as they rise up the Tone Scale. Individuals below 2.0 are, on the average, increasingly more wrong than they are right, in all fields, as they descend the Tone Scale.

Accepting these postulates and axioms, it can then be observed that one can predict to some degree what he may expect from individuals above or below 2.0 on the Tone Scale. A reasonable individual attempts to read into the acts of others some reason. An individual who is tending toward survival tends to evaluate the conduct of others in terms of efforts to survive. He may see in an individual below 2.0 what he thinks is merely an aberrated inaccuracy or an occasional mistake, but closer observation will demonstrate that the individual below 2.0 is aggregating numerous mistakes, even while being occasionally right, and is tending to bring about the nonsurvival of himself, of the future, of the group, and by contagion, the mankind of which he would like to be a part. Below 2.0 lies fatality. That fatality may be manifested on a gradient scale. It may only be nagging or forgetfulness or occasional gossip, but it is destructive and it is evil. In an older time a stern voice could have said that those who lie below 2.0 are the servants of evil and the minions of the Devil.

These few axioms should give the auditor some ability to predict actions and to know the reasons he should expect certain actions on the part of preclears.*

*Very little experimental evidence exists with regard to many aspects of the theta body or, as it might otherwise be called, the individual soul. It is distinct from cellular or genetic line and apparently has its own personality and follows in a continuing line along the various generations, possibly, now and then advancing to a point where it separates itself from the race and joins the theta universe, if this can be considered to exist as such. The data accumulated would also seem to indicate that some entheta is carried forward along the line of the generations, since engrams in the theta body exist, if to a much lighter extent, specifically the death engram, where the theta body is very much in evidence—so much so that if the auditor neglects to run the death engram of a past life when it is presented by the preclear, he will without fail bog down his case. There seems to be a distinct possibility that the theta body might begin, through the generations, to carry a preponderance of entheta by being too continually in the lower area of the Tone Scale. It could be postulated that the theta body might become an entheta body entirely, and so drop out of the survival concatenations, to what destination one cannot surely say. —LRH

GENERAL DESCRIPTION OF PROCESSING

Dianetic processing is relatively simple. The auditor usually assists the preclear, provided with an easy chair and a couch. The preclear at first normally sits up and answers the questions of the inventory. This actually is the beginning of processing, although it may appear that the auditor is merely seeking information which he can later use. During the inventory, the interest of the auditor in the preclear builds up affinity between them. The discussion of the case increases communication. And the auditor's acceptance of the preclear's first evaluations of his own case builds up a sense of reality.

The auditor can tear down these desirable ARC conditions by being bored, uninterested in his preclear, peremptory, demanding that less time be consumed, criticizing the preclear in any way, or in general breaking the Auditor's Code.

The auditor then makes a test of the case, finding out whether or not the preclear can move on the track, finding out whether the preclear's memory is good, and estimating what level of the Tone Scale his preclear probably occupies.

CAUTION: THE AUDITOR UNDER NO CIRCUMSTANCES SHOULD TELL THE PRECLEAR WHERE HE THINKS THE PRECLEAR LIES ON THE CHART. HE SHOULD NOT BE INVEIGLED IN ANY WAY INTO DISCLOSING WHERE HE THINKS THE PRECLEAR LIES ON THE CHART, SINCE A

LOW VALUE ON THE CHART FOR THE PRECLEAR IS, IN EFFECT, AN INVALIDATION OF THE PRECLEAR HIMSELF. (The auditor does not have to disclose this information even by the way he starts in his processing, for any case can be expected to be given Lock Scanning and Straightwire. A case may be actually well up the Tone Scale but so occluded that Lock Scanning and Straightwire must be employed.)

The auditor furthers his investigation of the case by asking the preclear to lie down on the couch and close his eyes. In the past there was some confusion about the condition called reverie. The only difference between being in reverie and being awake is actually being in or out of present time. Reverie is not even a cousin to hypnotism. The auditor, contrary to any early practice, does not count the preclear into a state of reverie or concentration. The moment he asks the preclear to close his eyes and the preclear complies, the auditor can consider the preclear to be in reverie. If the preclear does not move on the track, this is not caused by a failure to be in reverie, but by being stuck in an engram or having a heavily charged case.

The auditor tests out the perceptics of the preclear by simply asking the preclear to go back to a recent meal he has eaten or a recent pleasure moment and having him recount this moment over several times, not as a concept of the moment, but as if he were right on the scene doing the things again which were done before. This is called testing or tuning the perceptics. The auditor here is attempting to discover whether or not the preclear can actually taste again a steak he has eaten, see again the scene he has seen exactly as it was, feel again the knife and fork in his hands, hear again the conversation around him, feel again his weight upon the chair, and in general reexperience the incident. Running several such pleasure moments, it occasionally happens that some of the occluded perceptics tune up and turn on. In any event, running pleasure moments is very good for raising the tone of the preclear.

Having run a perceptic test, the auditor takes the preclear, merely by asking him to go to a moment when he was very slightly injured, to a point on the track where he has a somatic. The auditor runs the incident. The somatic, if felt at all, will ordinarily reduce. This should be a recent moment of physical pain and should be a very minor one such as a cut finger or a stubbed toe. This gives the preclear some idea of what he is expected to do.

The auditor should pay particular attention to the fact that he is actually educating his preclear into track movement. The preclear may have to be coaxed several times before he gets the idea of being back in an incident and reexperiencing it. He may try to give merely the concept of the incident instead of perceiving it as though he were right there going through it again. He might try to free-associate and so wander around all over the track getting odds and ends and bits of information which are relatively valueless.

After estimating the perceptics, the auditor should continue according to the chart, on which by this time he should have thoroughly located his preclear. (Questions of almost unlimited variety will have been asked by the auditor. Simply by using the data in various columns and levels on the chart, he can avoid a stereotyped approach and be sure of turning up the information he needs.) The most significant points on the test run are movement on the track and the ability of the preclear to feel somatics. The auditor continues processing according to the chart, occasionally checking the preclear for any rise on the Tone Scale, and if he finds a rise in tone he may use additional methods, as delineated on the chart. The auditor should be particularly chary of using on the preclear methods below the preclear's tone level. Those individuals who are relatively low on the Tone Scale have so little free theta available for processing that it must be preserved and added to by the gentlest and lightest methods possible for some time until the preclear's tone rises.

Should the auditor discover that the preclear lies high in one column and low in another column he should take an average and by this discover the approximate position on the Tone Scale.

If the auditor is unable immediately to establish the preclear on the Tone Scale it is, in general, safe to use Lock Scanning without much investigation of the case. Even a case which is stuck on the time track can be lock-scanned. If the preclear is scanned through his locks and sticks in one of these locks, the auditor can generally free him by running pleasure moments or scanning pleasure moments, if he does not want to run the incident in which the preclear is hung up. Even when stuck in an engram preclears usually can be lock-scanned.

The auditor should not be beguiled or sent astray by the wide-open case. This case is a very peculiar thing, as discussed elsewhere. Sonic and visio can be on full from the top to the bottom of the Tone Scale, but trying to run engrams on a wide-open case, as engrams, when the case is at 0.5 or 1.1, will bring about a long and arduous course of processing in which the preclear will remain more or less static on the Tone Scale regardless of how many engrams are run out of the case. When such a case, or any case, is low on the Tone Scale, the running of engrams absorbs free theta. Further, the preclear will consistently combat running engrams, since when any preclear is below 2.0, his tendency is toward death, suicide or further decline. No plans or hopes for the future, no coaxings, nothing will persuade this preclear to do anything very arduous to help himself. A preclear low on the Tone Scale may, however, be persuaded into some of the milder methods of processing, since they do not occasion much effort and actually do not seem to threaten his intended decline—since, make no mistake, the preclear below 2.0 will, one way or another, by knowing or unknowing intent, bring about failures and consequent death to himself, his associates and his group. The wide-open case must be established on the Tone Scale by columns other than visio and sonic. It is best located by its sense of reality, sexual behavior, other manifestations and the condition of the somatics. The wide-open case which is low on the Tone Scale must be handled with great care, since here we have, unlike the occluded case, a persistence so low that the individual drifts at the command of any engram or changes course at the slightest pressure from the environment. The wide-open case low on the Tone Scale has no feeling of responsibility toward self, future or group, save aberrated ones. Persistence is so slight that any auditing errors can cause the case to withdraw from any processing. Here is an individual who climbs molehills as though they were mountains. This case can be the greatest trial to the auditor and will render, unfortunately, the most unsatisfying final results. The wide-open case can, of course, be low on the Tone Scale only temporarily, because of some environmental situation. If so, the auditor had better extend himself if he can to clear up this situation before he begins auditing.

This case is also a great liability to the auditor, when low on the Tone Scale, because of the vagaries of behavior. If a woman, she may offer herself freely to the auditor, disregarding her position in life, her husband, the future she may blast by doing so, the fate of any children she may have or any other consideration. Woe betide the luckless male auditing such a case who involves himself with this bundle of destruction, since as she would betray another so she will betray him; as she will be dishonest with another so she will be dishonest with the auditor. The dishonesty will extend not only to treachery and betrayal, wherein she may freely surrender to the auditor and then go directly to the police to have him arrested for seduction, and wherein she may promise the greatest secrecy around any liaison and yet strew all about evidence of that liaison, but she will also be dishonest when being run and will, for no other reason than to confuse the picture, deliver up the most twisted and perverted scenes of her own life. Raised amid riches, she will represent herself as having been a pauper. Raised a pauper, she will represent herself as a princess. She will normally have pride in her ability to act, and will commonly writhe and moan and weep over some incident that she quite consciously knows to be imaginary. No trust of any kind can be placed in a wide-open case when it is below 2.0 on the Tone Scale, and for that matter no trust can be put in an occluded case below 2.0 on the Tone Scale, but the wide-open case is far more deceptive and far more prone to wide vagaries in behavior and delusion.

The male wide-open case is no less difficult and trying, but strangely enough seems by observation to be far more persistent, either toward destruction or in efforts toward survival, than the female case.

The auditor will have his problems with preclears who want attention but not processing. These preclears are automatically classifiable as below 2.0. This is the quickest chart location which can be done. The preclear who wants no kind of processing whatsoever, even though he understands some of the principles involved and knows they will not be harmful, and the preclear who wants no processing but to be hovered over are both headed toward succumb and will do their best to pull the auditor with them. As a shooting and quick burial for such people is frowned upon, at least at this time, the auditor should employ his ingenuity, if he will continue processing them. He should use very light methods and a catfoot approach, and he may be able to raise his preclear enough above 2.0 to cause a continuing direction toward survival.

It should be borne in mind by the auditor when he is doing his inventory and when he is locating his preclear on the chart that people below 2.0 may not be immediately obvious. Their acceptance of processing may be only a method of securing attention. However, the auditor by using light, routine methods can produce the necessary rise on the Tone Scale to get the case to resolve itself.

The auditor should remember that the contest is between his own theta, his reasonableness, his serenity and his persistence, and the entheta of the preclear, the preclear's locks, secondaries and engrams. The moment the auditor permits his own entheta to attack the preclear, turbulence is produced and a reduction of the preclear on the Tone Scale will ensue. Thus, becoming angry, critical, stupid, avaricious, destructive or malicious toward the preclear reverses processing. The preclear is not responsible for his engrams. The auditor is concerned with what has been done *to* the preclear, not what has been done *by* the preclear. The auditor should exhibit no morbid curiosity about the acts of the preclear. He should not inquire into the preclear's own doings unless he needs to find in the dramatizations of the preclear a clue to the engrams which caused the dramatizations. Getting angry at the preclear because the preclear will not run an engram is certain to lower the preclear on the Tone Scale. The auditor, poor fellow, must retain his patience even under upbraidings from the preclear. The auditor must *never* justify himself when the preclear thinks he has made a mistake. For the auditor to explain how it was not a mistake is only to further enturbulate the situation.

When the preclear is returned to some point prior to present time at the auditor's request, the auditor should under no circumstances use more words than are absolutely necessary, and should at this time in particular be careful to observe the Auditor's Code, since the incident may contain anaten and the preclear may be receptive to hypnotic suggestions. This is also true of a boil-off. The auditor should not talk to the preclear during a boil-off, should not try to wrestle the preclear into alertness out of the feeling that the preclear is merely trying to go to sleep.

Sessions may be of whatever duration and frequency during the week as are agreed upon by the auditor and preclear. Two-hour sessions are usually considered minimum, since it occasionally takes that long to contact and run out enough engrams or to do enough Lock Scanning to make the session worthwhile. Six hours of processing a day may be done without loss of efficiency, and this can be done seven days a week without harm to the preclear. It could be added that medical doctors advise that under such heavy processing a balanced vitamin ration be used by the preclear, who otherwise may suffer nightmares, since it is apparent that the running of engrams reduces the amount of vitamin B_1 in the system.[*]

The general progress of the case would be to use Straightwire, then use some Lock Scanning, then to run some secondary engrams to relieve some grief or fear, and then to begin an erasure of the case by contacting the first moment of pain or discomfort in this lifetime, which is ordinarily found somewhere in the vicinity of conception. If enough entheta has been converted to theta on the case, this first engram will erase. If it will not erase, then too much charge still exists in secondaries and locks. When the first engram in the case, known as basic-basic, has been erased, the next consecutive engram should be contacted and erased in its turn, and so on up the bank toward present time. Somewhere up the line it will be found that new grief has presented itself and it will be necessary to run out some more secondary engrams. When this has been done, the preclear is sent back again to the first moment of pain or unconsciousness which can then be found on the case. Basic area[**] engrams will probably have presented themselves. These are erased

[*]*Experience at the Foundation demonstrates some additional precautions which should be taken with preclears. The auditor should make sure that the preclear is not audited when he is tired or ill, that he is not audited late at night when by habit he would be sleeping, that he has adequate rest, and that he is not audited during periods when his present time environment is intensely restimulative to him. Those preclears with whom the Foundation has had any trouble were found to have been audited late at night, having inadequate food and B_1 intake, during intensely restimulative environmental circumstances (which might in any case have caused them to drop on the Tone Scale) and when they were physically weary. All of these people had psychotic histories. While such trouble has not been had by the Foundation to a tenth of a percent of that, proportionately, experienced by practitioners of non-Dianetic methods, the Foundation has instituted a careful program to avoid such conditions and circumstances.* —LRH

[**]**BASIC AREA:** *the time track from the first recording on the sperm or ovum track to the first missed menstrual period of the mother.* —LRH

consecutively toward present time until further trouble develops. Then more secondaries are run, more locks are scanned, and the preclear is returned again to the basic area, where an erasure is continued. Sooner or later this erasure will continue all the way forward to present time. Then, after running a few isolated missed engrams, the auditor will have on his hands a Clear, provided the auditor was far enough up the Tone Scale in the first place to encourage the de-enturbulation of this case to the point where it could run engrams.

The auditor may find an occluded case so heavily charged with engrams that the case can only boil off. This will appear to be a form of sleep, and the auditor may feel that he is being cheated of his opportunity to perform. In such a case, no matter how many hours of processing are consumed by this apparent sleep, the "sleep" must not be disturbed, but when the preclear comes out of it, the phrase on which he went into the boil-off should be repeated again, thus putting him back into the "sleep." In such a way, enormous quantities of anaten are unburdened from the case.

The auditor may find himself confronted with a preclear who will run only phrases and cannot seem to get a whole incident anywhere. Much Lock Scanning should be done with this preclear, but it is also of benefit to permit the preclear to run these fragments of aberrative phrases, since sooner or later one of them will cause the preclear to boil off or to suddenly hit a grief charge.

No case of any kind should dismay the auditor. With these presented techniques of Lock Scanning, running secondaries, running engrams, boil-offs, Straight Memory and even running disjointed phrases, any case which can be persuaded to work at all will resolve.

The auditor should be particularly wary of running his preclear into any heavily charged secondary unless the auditor intends to run the preclear through it again and again and again until the charge is reduced regardless of how much the preclear wants not to continue it and regardless of any trick the preclear may use to get out of it. This sometimes requires much courage on the part of the auditor, since the terror and agony of the preclear or the extremity of the grief may cause the auditor, out of misguided sympathy, to relent in the face of such a secondary engram.

The auditor should be careful of running a heavily charged case into more than the case can handle. Processing should be as nondirective as possible, the auditor saying only enough to get the case running. Most auditors talk too much.

The auditor should never confuse his role with psychotherapy or with medicine. The medical doctor is important in the society: bacteria are bacteria. Bruises, contusions, broken bones and obstetrics will be with us for a long while. The auditor, because he can sweep aside with ease most of the manifestations which were formerly called psychosomatic illnesses, should not discount the reality of many kinds of physical disorders. The auditor is trying to bring the individual up the Tone Scale. Incidentally, this bypasses the individual around the majority of physical troubles and complexes and obsessions, but it does not obviate the occasional necessity of medical treatment for the preclear, and it certainly does not obviate the institutionalization of the obviously insane, no matter what Dianetics can do for these people. The auditor, then, should work in close unison with medical doctors, helping them to understand what he is doing and helping them to understand Dianetics, and trying to educate medical doctors into planting fewer and lighter engrams. The auditor should ignore the hundreds of conflicting psycho-therapies and ignore any of their practices, since the auditor will learn, in the realm of experience, that giving advice to his preclear about how he should think about his engrams and other aberrative manifestations is highly detrimental to the mental health of the preclear.

The auditor should realize he is working in a relatively low-toned and unenlightened society. Dianetics will be invalidated to him continually, as with any constructive or creative activity. If the auditor simply goes forward, yanking cases up the Tone Scale, he will win his battle. He has in his hands tools more powerful than those which existed before. He should use them.

The auditor should not despair of any case. He can do something for any case which will even remotely give him its attention. There will be moments in the progress of any case where environmental circumstances hit a case hard or where an engram of unusual force is on its way to the surface, when the case will apparently go into a decline. The auditor should not despair because of this, since he only needs to revert to the types of processing marked out for lower levels of the Tone Scale, and so he may restore his preclear to the proper level. The auditor should appreciate that any case progresses upwards, not in a steady line, but by swoops and jerks, and that the average advance alone is steady. In olden times antiquated therapies occasionally triggered a manic engram. Not knowing about the cause of human aberration, they were content to assume that this sudden elation of the patient was indicative of an advance. The auditor will learn that these sudden surges to new highs of well-being are simply symptomatic of an engram which has as its content some highly complimentary phrases. An auditor will often find his preclear claiming in high euphoria that he is now Clear, only to have the case regress within two or three days to a depressed state. The auditor, by Lock Scanning and running out the causative engram, can remedy this with ease.

The auditor will behold, in the progress of any case, certainly while it is returned on the time track, some alarming manifestations. Running an engram which contains fever, the preclear's temperature will rise. Running engrams early in life, the preclear's facial structure will change. Running engrams which are very highly charged may cause the preclear to scream, to the point where the neighbors a block away will be phoning for the police. None of these manifestations should worry the auditor. The only way the auditor can harm the preclear is to refrain from running off what has been contacted. If the auditor becomes alarmed because the preclear's heart is beating at twice its normal speed or because the preclear is

"Results are what are desired.
Well, clear-thinking, strong individuals
are highly necessary in this society at this time.
They are so remarkably few."

moaning and weeping and so tries to bring the preclear up to present time, the auditor is inviting trouble. The manifestation of an engram while the preclear is returned may be slight. Brought to present time without the engram being reduced, the manifestation is many times increased. The somatic, at the point on the track where it occurred, may not be very great. In present time, the somatic is greatly intensified. Thus, the safest course is to run out whatever one contacts, even if one has to hold one's ears or when one's observation of the preclear seems to clearly demonstrate that here is a person become very suddenly ill. The reduction of the engram or incident will bring about a complete revival of the preclear.

Above all else, the auditor should have faith in his tools. When he tells the preclear to go back to the time when he was five years of age, he should not then sit there and wonder whether the preclear has returned to that time. Certainly some portion of the preclear's mind has gone to five years of age. The auditor deals with certainties. The auditor does not wonder about the actions of the somatic strip and the file clerk. He takes what they give him. He runs whatever is necessary to resolve the case. He has complete confidence in his tools and in his own ability. With this complete confidence, which is in itself a manifestation of theta, the auditor can produce marked and remarkable results. If the auditor dillydallies with the case, wonders whether or not Dianetics works, wonders what's happening, wonders whether he shouldn't read chapter sixteen again, then looks at the preclear and thinks perhaps these prenatal engrams are illusion or delusion, and begins to question people around the preclear, wondering if that was what happened to the preclear, and is in a high state of doubt about everything in general and the case in particular, he will not produce results. Results are what are desired. Well, clear-thinking, strong individuals are highly necessary in this society at this time. They are so remarkably few.

BOOK TWO
CHAPTER SIX

C O L U M N   A B
PRESENT TIME

ONE OF THE PRIMARY CONCERNS of the auditor is present time. By *present time* is meant the current "now" on the time track. Actually, the entire time track is only a consecutive progress of present times.

When a preclear returns to an incident by going down the time track, he is returning to a present time which once existed. Because of action phrases such as groupers, bouncers, denyers, misdirectors, and because of the heavy charge which can be on a case it occasionally occurs that he is continuously in some past present time. Further, when one fails to reduce an incident a case may be difficult to return to current present time. For these reasons the auditor must understand clearly both the value of being in present time and the methods of returning his preclear to present time at the end of a session.

The value of present time has been illustrated by the fact that if one went through a sanitarium and told patients one after the other, "Come up to present time," a certain low percentage of the inmates would thereupon become sane. The simple fact of being in present time is in itself a factor of sanity. At a certain sanitarium, some medical doctors made this test with the patients, and one of these, who had been insane for a considerable period, who ordinarily refused to talk, and whose face was a mask of acne, responded to this command, and as a result of no other ministration returned to present time and to sanity. That night, according to report, she attended a sanitarium party and gave a speech about how glad she was to be there. Within three days the acne had disappeared from her face, and while her sanity was of course far from being a good risk, she manifested and was continuing to manifest sanity many weeks afterward. It is much simpler to invite someone to return to present time than it is to hack up portions of his brain or shatter him with high voltages.

There are, according to Dianetic classification, two types of insane. The first type is the dramatizing psychotic. The second is the computational psychotic. The dramatizing psychotic goes through the engram in which he is stuck, over and over and over. It is acutely or chronically in restimulation, and his reactive mind causes his vocal cords and his body to go through the dramatization demanded by the engram. He is generally imprisoned in two or three engrams and goes from one to another of them ceaselessly. Such a case, of course, is heavily charged, and it does not do much good to try to run out the engrams. It is necessary to take charge off the case and bring the case to present time. This is not very difficult if one can gain the psychotic's attention. The other type of insanity is computational. Here, the engram has walled up a certain portion of the analyzer as captured territory, and a circuit causes this portion of the analyzer to be the whole of the being. The remainder of the analyzer is shut off, and the "I" of the individual is not in evidence. The paranoiac is usually computationally insane, which is to say he does not dramatize like a phonograph, but actually appears to think up things. The schizophrenic is an individual who has several portions of the analyzer segmented off by different circuits, which are actually valences, and who goes from one to another of these portions of the analyzer, only occasionally, if ever, becoming himself. Both the dramatizing psychotic and the computational psychotic have the bulk of the analyzer completely shut off by anaten and by being out of present time. Present time perceptics are not rationalized, since they are entering upon an engram area. Probably the crux of the treatment of all psychotics is getting them into present time and stabilizing them there. All psychotics have heavily charged cases, and it is necessary one way or the other to reduce this charge. While this may appear an oversimplification of the problem, it also might well be that the problem is simple. The most difficult thing in the treatment of the psychotic is establishing enough affinity, reality and communication between the psychotic and the auditor to persuade the psychotic to do something to help himself. This can be done by mimicking the psychotic, which is a form of establishing affinity, or by bringing the psychotic into some contact with the present world.

This short dissertation on the psychotic is given to illustrate the importance of present time. The auditor should not believe, however, that he can easily get his preclear out of present time and cause his preclear to go insane. The case would have to be a borderline psychotic in the first place, and the auditing would have to be in such flagrant violation of the chart that it could be presupposed that the auditor who would accomplish such a psychosis would himself be a moron or a psychotic in the first place.

Any preclear is less alert out of present time than he is in present time. People go through their whole lives far out of present time and never suspect it. If they should be returned to present time they would be far more able to cope with their problems and would be considerably happier, since evaluating the current environment in terms of, let us say, the environment of five years of age, is not conducive to good computation. The percentage of people who are chronically out of present time would astonish you if you were to test it out. The test is a simple one and is, indeed, the standard mechanism used by the auditor in returning his preclear to present time. If you were to use this mechanism on a number of your friends you would find that many of them are stuck somewhere on the time track and are not in present time. You should find it relatively easy, if you are dealing with people above 2.0, to return anyone to present time whom you find out of it. The person need know nothing about Dianetics, and, indeed, this is an excellent way to introduce the subject to a stranger.

Discovering where the individual lies on the time track may be done in two or three ways. The first method is the age flash. To understand this, one should also understand something about the file clerk, a subject which will be covered in a later chapter. The first flash response, the first impression a person receives in answer to a question is called, in Dianetics, a *flash answer.* This is assisted by the auditor's snapping of his fingers immediately after he asks the question.

The age flash is obtained, then, in the following fashion: The auditor says, "When I snap my fingers, an age will occur to you. Give me the first number that comes into your mind." He then snaps his fingers, and the preclear gives him the first number which comes into his mind. This may be the preclear's actual age, but in this current civilization, it usually is not. Sometimes it is a circuit response. The preclear has, through continual answering of this question, set up a circuit which replies instead of the file clerk. Such a person can be detected as running on such a circuit simply by asking the question whether or not at the beginning of every year he has difficulty putting down the date of the new year. If he carries over the past year into the new year for some days, or if he carries the past month into the new month, or if he simply has trouble in knowing what date it is, he can be considered to be out of present time; and if his flash answer is his current age, he can be considered to be running on a circuit. The usual response, however, will be an honest one. And the circuit response can be set aside and another answer gained by another mechanism. Using the flash answer, one will discover at what point on the time track the preclear has most of his attention units.

The second mechanism by which the individual is discovered to be in or out of present time is the date flash. The auditor says to the preclear, "When I snap my fingers, the date will flash. Give me the first response which comes into your mind." *(snap!)* The preclear then gives the first date which comes into his mind. In all these flash answers a new preclear will ordinarily give the second or third answer which comes to him, and therefore the auditor must ask whether this was the first number. The preclear may give the present date, but on further questioning may admit that some earlier date flashed first and that he corrected it. This earlier date is where the bulk of the preclear's attention units are located on the time track.

Another method of detecting whether or not the individual is in present time is also on a flash-answer basis, but this time one asks for a flash of the scene. The auditor says, "When I snap my fingers, the current scene will flash before your eyes." *(snap!)* A visio may then flash in the mind of the preclear and is quite often not the visio of present time but of a much earlier period.

It also occasionally happens that a preclear, not too heavily charged by entheta, will be stuck in an engram exactly on the point of the only sonic he will get on the track and the only visio he will get on the track. Merely by telling him to close his eyes and listen the auditor may get him to come up with a holder which is holding him out of present time. This is not general but happens often enough to be remarked.

There is yet another method of detecting whether or not the preclear is out of present time. This is by auditor observation. The preclear who holds on relentlessly to tokens of a certain period of the past is normally partially in that period, either because of a grief charge or some other type of entheta which holds him there. The old lady who surrounds herself with the trappings of 1910 and who wears an outmoded gown will usually be found on the time track at the moment of the death of her husband or son or some other loved one. The secondary engram is run out or enough entheta is converted elsewhere on the case, and the auditor can return her to present time, at which moment she will recognize, for the first time perhaps, that her keepsakes and her gown are a trifle out of the mode.

There is an additional auditor observation which establishes whether or not the preclear is out of present time. The auditor learns rather rapidly to observe the physiology of his preclear and judge from this where the preclear is stuck on the time track. At the period of birth, the baby is equipped to put on considerable fat and weight, and a person who is stuck in the birth engram is usually somewhat overweight and usually has some physiological characteristics which remind one of an infant. This is only one example of one period on the time track. The auditor will find preclears who look like twelve-year-old boys and who are actually stuck at twelve years of age in some operation such as a tonsillectomy or in some grief charge.

The auditor will find girls who appear to be four or five years of age although they are grown up and who retain some mannerisms and physiological characteristics of the earlier age. And then there are those people, not too lovely to look at, who are arrested in the prenatal period. They bear some slight hint of the period of life at which they are arrested. Their mouths and the condition of their skin seem to remind one of the condition of the zygote, embryo or fetus. Such people have a tendency to be formed in the curved position of the prenatal period, are round-shouldered and are apt to draw up into a ball when they sleep. This condition becomes very pronounced in the insane, where a call-back in a prenatal engram has taken all the attention units of the individual and placed him exactly at and only at some portion of the prenatal period. There is no argument concerning the existence of prenatals. They have been known for the past thirty years and have been adequately proven by experiments at Rutgers University[1] and are so common in Dianetics that one considers the practitioner who questions them rather poorly read

1. **Rutgers University:** the State University of New Jersey, founded in 1766 and named in honor of a local benefactor, Henry Rutgers.

on his own literature. The auditor who does not recognize prenatals will never have very well preclears, and the auditor who does not see in his potential preclear the symptoms of being stuck in the prenatal area may have a difficult time with his case.

There is the postulate of attention units. It could be considered that an attention unit is a theta energy quantity of awareness. Any organism is aware in some degree. A rational or relatively rational organism is aware of being aware. Attention units could be said to exist in the mind in varying quantity from person to person. This would be the theta endowment of the individual. One person, assigning merely arbitrary numbers, might have a thousand attention units and another person might have but fifty. If all of a person's attention units could be free in present time for recall, enjoyment, perception and direction of body activities and for computation, that person could be said to be most excellently cleared. People below the level of Clear have fewer and fewer attention units in present time as they descend on the Tone Scale. The percentile scale on the chart might be interpreted also as the number of attention units which the person has available in present time. The normal person probably has about 25 percent of his attention units in present time. In view of the fact that these attention units are what he enjoys with and thinks with and works with, this can be seen to be not quite optimum. The rest of his attention units are caught somewhere back down the time track in one incident or another in the form of entheta.

When an individual is out of present time, it can be said that he has more attention units existing at some past moment on the time track than he has existing in present time.

The auditor, by failing to reduce engrams or secondaries, can induce a momentary condition in his preclear of being out of present time. The preclear, after the session, if he is not in present time will look rather groggy, will not perceive very readily and will be, as a matter of fact, much more suggestible than when he is in present time. It is symptomatic of being out of present time that present time perceptions find no attention units to handle an evaluation of the perceptions, and so make a much deeper or unrationalized impression on the individual.

In every session the auditor, even when he is doing only Straightwire, takes his preclear somewhat out of present time. It is the concern of the auditor to get the preclear back into present time. This is done best by running pleasure moments as though they were engrams. These moments of pleasure will assemble the attention units and unenturbulate them, so that they will easily return to present time and the preclear will stabilize in it.

It is a general rule that the more entheta there is on a case, the more the individual is out of present time.

It is possible for entheta itself to be in present time, but this is where the environment itself is enturbulative, where the individual is upset or angry because of contagion from the environment. Thus, all the attention units in present time can be seen to be not necessarily theta. But entheta on the time track is not itself in present time. In the absence of environmental restimulation, then, it can be seen that these attention units which should be in present time in a Clear, but in a person lower on the Tone Scale are not, are actually entheta units wrapped up in locks, secondaries and engrams.

When the preclear does not return to present time and cannot be persuaded by any coaxing or cajoling to return to present time easily, the auditor has either tied up too many attention units in some past moment—a situation which will remedy itself in the course of a few hours, usually—or there is so much charge on the case, which is to say so much entheta, that present time is unattainable.

In cases below 2.0, the auditor has to be very careful how many attention units he sends out of present time, how much he restimulates his case, as these cases are so heavily entheta that any existing theta will enturbulate swiftly, thus taking the preclear far from present time into dramatizations or engramic computations. In working the usual case, not the psychotic, one still must be aware of the methods by which one may stabilize the preclear in present time.

This rule can be applied to every case: The conversion of any amount of entheta to theta will increase the preclear's ability to come to present time and stabilize there. The auditor should work to convert entheta into theta until he can get his preclear into present time. He can do this by Straight Memory, by scanning locks, by running pleasure moments or even by running an engram on cases which are high on the scale.

There is no cause for panic because the individual is out of present time. Most of the society is out of present time. Any national army or navy, for instance, is so far out of present time that it is always ready to fight the war before last. Moral codes are ordinarily two or three centuries out of present time. Governmental systems are usually a couple of thousand years out of present time. So, for an individual to be ten or fifteen years out is not very serious, unless the case as a whole is extremely serious. The auditor ordinarily finds his preclear out of present time and finds it necessary to leave him out of present time for the first few sessions, being unable to do enough processing during these few sessions to convert sufficient entheta to return his preclear to present time.

The auditor's first and primary concern in any case which he finds out of present time is to return that case to present time. He should work with light methods, session after session, concentrating only on one thing: getting the preclear back to present time. He does not attempt to drive the preclear to present time or command the preclear to present time, since driving and commanding will only turn theta into temporary entheta. Once he has his preclear in present time and has his preclear very stable in present, the auditor can start worrying about specific incidents and the vaster difficulties of the case. Trying to work somebody who will not come to present time or who cannot stay in present time once he is there should not be a trial to the auditor. The auditor should not run engrams on such a case since, obviously, any person who cannot stay in present time does not have enough free theta to work engrams.

Various manifestations take place concerning present time in preclears. The first manifestation, of course, is being chronically out of present time. The preclear is usually held in some operation, accident or sorrow back on the track somewhere. Or the preclear comes to present time and then slumps back out of it because of some restimulated engram which, one way or another, by literal command, contains a call-back, a phrase which says, "Come back here" and which the preclear obeys by returning back down the time track right after the auditor has gotten him to present time. This indicates a rather heavily charged case, and it is the charge itself which should be addressed, which is to say simply converting entheta to theta rather than the specific engram which is doing the calling back. Then there is the case which is all the way out of present time all the time. This case is not in contact with the environment in any way whatsoever and is, of course, psychotic. Then there is the case which is apparently "stuck in present time." No one could actually be stuck in present time but is stuck somewhere on the track in an incident which carries with it the illusion that it is present time. Christmas, for instance, is a time when presents are given, and as the preclear is brought back up the track he may hang up at any point on the track which contains the word "present." The habit of medical doctors during operations of saying "That's all for the present" will create the illusion of putting the preclear up in present time and making it difficult for the preclear to return. Then there is the preclear who is in a chronic bouncer. Some engram in the case has in it a "get up" or "go up there," and the preclear is thus bounced to the extremity of his time track and even into the future of his time track. Obedience to such phrases indicates a heavily charged case, and the auditor, again, should address himself to the charge on the case rather than to the specific engram which is producing the manifestation.

There is a flash answer method of discovering the incident in which the preclear is located. The auditor asks a series of questions which will identify the incident and receives flash answers on a yes–no basis. The auditor says, "When I snap my fingers you will answer yes or no to the following question: Hospital?" *(snap!)*, and the preclear answers yes or no. Such a series of questions and answers might run as follows: "Accident?" "Yes." "Hospital?" "No." "Mother?" "Yes." "Outdoors?" "No." "Fall down?" "No." "Cut?" "Yes." "Kitchen?" "Yes." And suddenly the preclear may remember the incident or get a visio of the scene and remember or get a sonic recall of what his mother said to him, which might be something like, "You stay right here and hold on to it until I come back." If the case was not too heavily charged, remembering this might permit him to come to present time. In this way, using the names of people who might have been around the preclear and things which might have happened to the preclear, the auditor can, on a flash answer basis, bring enough data about the incident to light to allow the preclear to remember a hidden or forgotten engram or secondary, and simply by recalling it, to return to present time.

Getting the preclear to recall by Straight Memory the incident where he is stuck on the track is sometimes sufficient to get him to return to present time. However, any preclear who is out of present time and who has to be coaxed into a memory of where he is stuck on the track is usually a rather highly charged case, and the auditor should, generally, concern himself with the conversion of entheta to theta rather than the location of the actual incident. One case was under processing by a rather poor auditor for many months for an hour or two a week. This case was hung up in a serious operation at the age of thirty-one. The auditor eventually became bright enough to inquire whether or not there was an earlier operation, and an almost duplicate operation was suddenly located by the preclear, at which moment he returned to present time.

In getting people to present time it is a necessity to understand the principle that the earlier the engram is the easier it is to reduce.

Later engrams on a case contain their own force plus the force of all similar previous engrams on the case. Engrams exist in chains, and there may be anywhere from one to forty or a hundred engrams on one chain. The preclear is quite ordinarily stuck, not in the first engram on the chain, but in some later engram. Thus, the identification of the point on the track where he is stuck is ordinarily insufficient to free him. An earlier moment of a similar nature must be discovered before he is able to return to present time. The use of Straight Memory to discover such an earlier moment is a simple operation.

As will be seen by an examination of the Tone Scale on the subject of present time, the more heavily charged the case, the more likely the preclear is to be out of present time or to stay out of present time. The whole question of returning the individual to present time is the question of converting entheta to theta. It would be a very simple thing if all one had to do was to run the engram in which the preclear was stuck and so get him to present time. This usually doesn't happen. The engram in which the preclear is stuck is quite ordinarily unreducible, in the existing state of the case.

Thus, getting the preclear to present time necessitates running pleasure moments, scanning light locks, running secondaries or simply making present time so thoroughly attractive that the preclear's attention units return there.

The auditor should not neglect the fact, nor should the preclear, that present time itself may be desirable or undesirable. The preclear who is faced with a divorce or whose child has just died or whose wife has suddenly been discovered to be a harlot may find present time so thoroughly undesirable that attention units shun it, just as they, being theta, would shun any other entheta area on the track.

Engrams, secondaries and heavy locks become buried and hidden from recall because they are entheta and, by theory, have a repelling effect upon theta. The area at the age of twelve, in which the individual was told he was going crazy because he was discovered to be masturbating (along with the remainder of the human race) will be difficult to approach. The entheta of the scolding and upset will cause theta to shy away from the area. Other nonsurvival periods of one's life, where one was down on his luck, where one found that college girls do not make good wives, where one discovered that one's husband, of an evening, liked to take off his shoes and read the paper rather than conquer dragons for his lady fair, as he promised to do so often before the wedding, and other periods of great travail are quite normally shunned as the preclear goes back down the track. This is very well evidenced by the number of new incidents which turn up during Lock Scanning. At first there appear to be only one or two incidents on a lock chain, but when the preclear has been scanned through the chain many times it is discovered that there are several hundred incidents on the chain. Entheta incidents, then, vanish so far as the theta of the conscious or analytical mind is concerned. One should not overlook the fact that present time can be such an area, and so may be shunned. The auditor should do what he can to remedy this situation by providing a friendly atmosphere, or even a refuge, for his preclear and so make present time, at least during the session, palatable.

As a summary, then, the more entheta in ratio to theta there is on the case the less likely the preclear is to move on the track and to be in present time. The more entheta there is in present time the less likely the preclear is to enter it—and this includes the fact that a cross, authoritatively inclined auditor will make present time unpalatable to his preclear. A primary mission of the auditor is to get his preclear into present time. The fundamental principle of getting the preclear to present time lies in improving the theta–entheta ratio of the case by Straightwire, running or scanning locks, and in cases which are well up the Tone Scale, running secondaries or engrams. As is shown on the chart, the Dianetic Clear is highly stable in present time and does not leave it. All his perceptics are clear. This does not mean that the Clear cannot leave present time. With "I" in control of the entire analytical mind, instead of some circuit or telephone switchboard of circuits, the Clear can run on his track entirely at will, but he almost never needs to do so, since his memory mechanisms can be counted on to furnish him with accurate data without recourse to return mechanisms. Here is the difference between memory and returning, where it is best manifested. Memory would be, for instance, sending two attention units to the standard memory bank to bring up information for the use of the analyzer, and returning would be sending 50 percent of the available theta back down the track for a full reexperiencing of the incident. The Clear ordinarily does not fully reexperience incidents, simply because he doesn't have to, and he ordinarily finds present time palatable. Theta units in present time offer a resistance to the entheta coming in from the environ. The impact of the environ is combated by the theta unit reasoning and evaluation. If there is a great deal of entheta on the case and the present time environ is entheta, the present time perceptics will go toward the entheta and will restimulate it whether it be in the form of locks, secondaries or engrams, and so enturbulate the whole case. This does not happen to the Clear. But that does not mean that the Clear cannot be enturbulated. Given a very low-theta-endowment Clear and a very heavy entheta environment, such as the slaughter of a thousand Christians, the Clear will temporarily enturbulate. He does not, however, have large areas of frozen entheta on his track which could trap the temporarily enturbulated theta, and so he will completely disenturbulate the moment the entheta environ is no longer present. A Clear is very definitely in present time.

The 3.5, the Dianetic Release, is quite stable in present time, and he is very alert to his environment. He gets the full beauty out of any scenery he observes, he is not disturbed by extraneous noises or upsets, but because he still has frozen entheta on his case he is susceptible to heavy enturbulation if the present time environment is enturbulative. Nevertheless, he is stable in present time.

The 3.0 has no definite difficulty in reaching, returning to or maintaining himself in present time. He snaps back to present time very rapidly when he is being processed and is very alert when he gets there. However, he can be enturbulated to the point where he will hang up temporarily somewhere on the track and will possibly dramatize the point where he has hung up, if sufficiently hit by enturbulation.

The 2.5, when once brought to present time, will easily remain there until the next processing. He has perhaps 30 to 40 percent of his theta in present time, as an ordinary rule, and an auditor has to be very careless to hang this preclear up on the track. However, this preclear can be hung up on the track, and the auditor will have to run pleasure moments at the end of the session and do some Straightwire when he has had a very enturbulative session, in order to stabilize his preclear in present time.

The 2.0 requires considerable care on the part of the auditor in order to return him to present time and stabilize him there. Pleasure moments have to be run, if any can be found. Some Lock Scanning must be done. Some future pleasure moments may be run. But the 2.0 may respond to a call-back, and once brought to present time may slump back down the track to an earlier period. Dealing with 2.5s and 2.0s the auditor should always check at the end of the session at least twice to see whether the preclear is in present time. At the first check he may find that the preclear is in present time, but ten minutes later the preclear may have slumped back down the track in answer to a call-back in some early period of entheta. Here we have a case where there is far more entheta on the case than theta, and the individual tends strongly to go toward the entheta of the past or the entheta of present time rather than toward theta. Theoretically, he would rather come up to present time for a fight than for anything else; however, this is not recommended as a processing procedure, and the auditor must use much skill in getting the preclear to present time.

The 1.5 is usually in some dominating valence somewhere out of present time. He is very difficult to get to present time and once in present time will almost always slump back. Here is the chronically angry case, and he goes toward angry entheta more readily than toward any theta in present time. The auditor will find efforts to bring this preclear to present time very difficult until he has raised this preclear's tone up above the 2.0 level.

At 1.1, the preclear stays out of present time most of the time. When he reaches present time he nearly always slumps back immediately. A tremendously inviting situation, covertly hostile, devious or perverted in present time will bring this preclear to present time but little else will. The balm and persuasion of an auditor's personality will not by itself do the trick. The auditor working a 1.1 should not worry if he cannot get the preclear to present time at the end of the session, since the preclear is usually out of present time anyway. Still, the auditor should be careful not to pull down any of the preclear's theta into entheta areas, since there is very little left to pull down. Very light processing methods should be used.

The 0.5 can always be requested to come to present time and sometimes will. But he slumps back immediately into some apathy incident. This case requires considerable skill on the part of the auditor, who is working with somebody so far out of present time all the time that it is difficult for him to get the preclear's attention. If the auditor acts particularly sad, sometimes this preclear will come to present time.

At 0.1, the preclear's perceptics can, at best, be directed to present time concepts. One can ask him to observe a cup, or a saucer, or a bright colored object, or some music, or an emergency situation. But here one is very lucky to be able to get the preclear merely to perceive something which exists in the present time environment.

The auditor's primary concern with any case is whether or not the case is in present time.

C O L U M N   A C

STRAIGHT MEMORY

IN DIANETICS, STRAIGHT MEMORY is a specific technical process. It should not be confused with "free association."

Straight Memory is also called Straightwire. It is so called because the auditor is directing the memory of the preclear and in doing so is stringing wire, much on the order of a telephone line, between "I" and the standard memory bank, plowing through all occlusions and circuits.

There is something about Straight Memory which is very validating. Once a person really remembers something it seems real to him, and this sense of reality greatly promotes the ARC of the case. Straight Memory thus has a certain advantage over Lock Scanning and running engrams. The preclear using Straight Memory very thoroughly associates the past event in terms of the present time environment. When the preclear is returned on the track he often evaluates the past event only in terms of its own environment, and while repeated recountings of the incident may bring about reduction of the entheta in it, the validation factor is still much lower than in Straight Memory.

Straight Memory was developed in Dianetics on the basis that if one knew the fundamental mechanical cause of insanity one should be able to do better than the various older therapies, since it is known that "free association" produces some minor alleviation of tension and anxiety. The mechanisms of why this came about were thus explored. It was found that the heightened reality of Straight Memory and the knowledge of why locks, the usual target of Straight Memory, were aberrative combined to make an orderly and fast type of processing, valid in the ratio of several hundred to one over old therapies.

All by itself Straight Memory is an excellent method of processing. The busy doctor or consultant who has but a few minutes to spend with every patient can employ Straight Memory to great advantage. One specialist in Parkinson's disease in New York City, although he did not understand very much about Dianetic processing, used Straight Memory to achieve the alleviation of Parkinson's disease at least temporarily in three cases out of five on which it was employed.

The importance of Straight Memory should not be underestimated. Preclears low on the Tone Scale can sometimes support only Straight Memory.

In the Foundation, various people have become Straight Memory experts, since Straight Memory has its own peculiar skills.

Straight Memory can be used on anyone without any danger. It is a slightly directive process. The auditor does not permit his preclear to wander around and free-associate and generally waste time and energy. The auditor knows exactly what he wants and he directs the preclear's attention to it. Thus, a Straight Memory expert must be able to sum up more or less what is wrong with the case. After he has summed this up he can do a very good job of resolving the case by Straight Memory.

Originally, Straight Memory required considerable perspicacity on the part of an auditor. However, in late 1950, recognizing the great skill necessary to a good Straight Memory auditor, I postulated what became inelegantly called the "hurdy-gurdy" system. The use of this system demands the minimum of the auditor and extracts the maximum of aberration from the preclear. It at least gets things done.

The first thing one should know about Straight Memory is the phenomenon of the human mind that a fact asked for today and not received may be received tomorrow or the next day. The mind, on facts long laid away, has a one- to three-day refresher period. If one were to give an examination on history to a number of forty-year-old men on Monday one might expect many low grades. But by giving another examination to this same group two days later one would find that higher grades were attained. This experiment has not been broadly conducted, but its basics seem to be borne out in the practice of Straight Memory. The mind, in short, refreshes itself, and the repetitious request by the auditor for certain facts from the preclear's standard memory bank will eventually elicit those facts. The auditor, if he does not get the information he wants from the preclear on Monday, should ask the same questions on Tuesday, Wednesday, Thursday and Friday, and he will find that the preclear will eventually remember.

Because so many people in our society seek to profit by the failure of others to remember, memory is a generally reduced quantity in the current culture. The mother who has many times attempted abortion upon her child is quite anxious that the child should not remember anything. The mother instinctively knows, although the culture has taught her that the child could not possibly remember such early incidents, that she had better suppress any possible recall. Thus, mothers, by contagion, have encouraged bad memory. There is something triumphant in having a better memory than the other fellow. This is based on the formulation that being right is to survive and being wrong is not to survive. By being right in memory one demonstrates the fact that one has a greater survival potential than the fellow who is wrong in memory. Memories come into conflict continually, and one will find unthinking people quarreling as to which one remembers the best and as to which fact is correct. This is an additional befuddlement in the society which suppresses memory.

There are cases on record, well authenticated, of individuals who have remembered back into their prenatal period. One eight-year-old girl who was under processing by a Book Auditor recently stunned her parents by remembering back to the third month after conception, when "Mama squeezed her tummy and hurt me." In the presence of non-Dianetically oriented individuals, this memory would have been immediately suppressed, but in view of the fact that it agreed with the memories of the parents, and in view of the fact that both parents had, to their benefit, experienced Dianetic processing, the little girl was permitted to go on remembering, and Straightwire was done with considerable profit into the prenatal bank—a profit so considerable that the child's school grades went up 50 percent, on the general average. Many instances are on record of Straight Memory back to birth, and it is too ordinary for comment for an individual to remember into infancy. The society, of course, because of the contagion of aberration of mothers who have practiced extracurricular sex relations and attempted abortions, holds memory this early in considerable question. It has been held in such question, prior to Dianetics, without anyone's being scientific enough to examine any evidence on the subject, or even to accumulate any, that outmoded therapies branded all memory earlier than about three years of age as delusion and were thus able to promote a large clientele of individuals driven into aberration by being invalidated.

Memory of infancy does not depend upon memory of how to talk. Befuddled professors and practitioners in the past believed that the ability to talk had something to do with the ability to remember, but this is not the case. There have been objections to prenatal engrams on the basis that "no one would be able to understand language before he was born," despite the fact that Sigmund Freud *stressed* traumatic prenatal incidents. The syllables, meaningless though they are, are recorded in a prenatal engram, along with all other perceptics. When they are keyed in, in a person past two years of age who has learned to talk, they are evaluated in terms of the meanings the person has learned to give those syllables. Thus, it is possible to recall as far back as one pleases.

Forgotten incidents were postulated by Sigmund Freud, to whom, through Commander Thompson, one of his students and the friend and mentor of my youth, I am much indebted, to be a considerable factor in human sanity. The release through recall of any incident which is forgotten, hidden or off the track and which contains considerable turbulence, will produce a tone rise in the individual.

Many individuals undergoing processing—in fact most individuals—cannot "remember" any earlier than eight years of age, much less into infancy. The more entheta there is on a case, the less theta is available to the analyzer. The more entheta there is along the time track, the harder it is for the existing theta to disenturbulate it enough to get the data out of it. The more aberrated the individual, the more entheta there is on the case. Entheta does not necessarily lie in childhood, but key-ins can ordinarily be expected to lie in childhood, and the key-in is sometimes difficult to remember, but when remembered will produce the most marked change in the case. After a person has been processed for a while and considerable free theta exists for the use of the analyzer, Straight Memory back to early periods is very possible.

One can also get into early periods in a person's life by the use of repeater technique.* This is not Straight Memory technique, but is an archaic technique of Dianetics independent of Straight Memory. Repeater technique has its uses, but anyone using repeater technique

---

*Some misunderstanding has resulted on the part of some individuals about repeater technique, what it is, and how it was used. In the handbook Dianetics: The Modern Science of Mental Health there is a discussion of repeater technique, but simply defined, it is this: The repetition of a word or phrase in order to produce movement on the time track into an entheta area containing that word or phrase. Repeating or "rolling" a phrase in an engram in order to deintensify the phrase or reduce the engram is not repeater technique. Repeater technique almost invariably causes a temporary enturbulation, as an inevitable consequence of contacting an entheta area of the time track, and therefore should obviously not be used unless the auditor feels that he can disenturbulate the area so contacted. Repeater technique is a forcing technique, and now that more delicate and more effective means have been developed, it has limited usefulness. Allowing the preclear to repeat isolated phrases which he himself presents may be of benefit by taking him into a boil-off or a grief charge which is ready to reduce. Feeding the preclear random and arbitrary phrases to repeat will produce nothing but trouble. —LRH

at random on a case will quite commonly find his preclear hung up in an engram which cannot be contacted and run out. Repeater technique causes trouble. But by the use of repeater technique, barring accidents, the preclear can be pulled back into a return into periods of infancy, if the auditor is lucky enough not to get the preclear into an engram. (Repeater technique on holders, such as "stay there," will almost certainly wind the preclear's attention up in engrams, attention which will not be freed until the auditing is scanned out.) This should not be confused with Straight Memory. Straight Memory consists of the preclear staying in present time with his eyes wide open and being asked to remember certain things which have been said to him and done to him during his lifetime. He is not asked to return to these incidents. He is asked only to recognize their existence. He is not commanded to accept the fact that such incidents existed, and minimal aid should be given to his memory mechanisms.

The auditor may get a preclear who has difficulty remembering yesterday, to say nothing of the time when he was two years of age. The auditor may be assured that when he has worked with this case long enough to restore a considerable amount of theta, converting it from entheta, the preclear will be able to remember things which he has never been able to remember before, since one of the first things which improve in Dianetic processing is memory. When an auditor has a preclear who has difficulty remembering, the auditor should be careful to start with things that are rememberable. If the preclear says bluntly that he cannot remember things, it is up to the auditor to encourage and validate this preclear's memory. If the preclear says, "I can't remember names," the auditor says, "Well, what is the name of your business associate?" The preclear says, "Oh, his name is Jones!" The auditor has proven to the preclear that the preclear can remember at least one name. If the preclear is in such bad condition that he cannot even remember this at will, the auditor says, "What is my name?" The preclear, having just heard the auditor's name, may be able to remember it with ease. If he cannot, the auditor says, "What is your own name?" The preclear tells him, and the auditor says, "You see, you can remember one name. Now let's see if you can remember others." In such a fashion, the preclear can be assisted to remember from the most obvious incidents or facts back to more and more obscure incidents. This is the common progress of Straight Memory, to begin by remembering the obvious and finally to be able to remember the aberrative.

A whole and entire method of processing can be made out of Straight Memory. Time spent on Straight Memory is usually time well spent. Straight Memory might also be considered a pair of stilts by which the preclear, persuaded to remember incidents later and later in his life, can be brought back up to present time. That Straight Memory does free theta, or convert entheta to theta, is beyond question. It is, however, a rather lengthy process, and it would take an auditor fifteen hours of Dianetic processing by Straight Memory to accomplish what would take two or three years with non-Dianetic techniques. Thus, Straight Memory should be used only as indicated on the chart, or to get the individual back up to present time, or by auditors who are so rushed for time that they have only a few minutes to attempt to rid a preclear of some specific somatic or aberration.

The primary rule of Straight Memory is this: Whatever the preclear thinks is wrong with himself, his family, his group, or mankind, life or MEST, has generally been told to the preclear by somebody else at an earlier period of the preclear's life. This is modified by the fact, of course, that things can be wrong along these various dynamics which are perfectly rational observations. The auditor is looking for irrational beliefs about these things.

The second rule about Straight Memory is that the preclear, at least at this time, is surrounded by very aberrated individuals and has been so surrounded since conception. It is symptomatic of any aberrated individual that he is acting upon his engrams and is dramatizing those engrams. Thus, there is a consistency of performance. The rough rule of thumb is that if an aberrated person says something once he will say it hundreds or thousands of times. Once you have isolated the fact that a certain individual in the preclear's past, for instance, complained about his stomach, you will have discovered a whole chain of such complaints, and a conversion of entheta to theta on this subject will take place.

By Straight Memory one can easily discover the dominant or the nullifying individuals in the preclear's family. From the dominant individuals, those who attempted to dominate and command and control the others around them, the preclear will have received the circuit phrases, which are the control phrases, in his bank. From the nullifying persons he will have received the nullification phrases. The auditor, by locating these persons and their habitual statements, finds the preclear's circuits.

Those things which are found in the locks of a preclear are normally found in his engrams. Thus, if one finds Mama, at the preclear's tenth year, saying, "Men are no good," one can expect to find Mama shortly after the preclear's conception making the same remark in an engram. If one discovers the lock by Straight Memory, he can then find the engram.

Difficulties arise in Straight Memory in cases where the preclear has not been raised by his own parents. A preclear whose parents have died shortly after his birth does not have in his post-speech period the same phrases which are in his early engrams. A lock must have an engram below it in order to exist, but here the auditor is confronted with a person whose locks do not, as far as phrases are concerned, match his engrams. This would appear at first glance to be a fortunate condition for the preclear, since the engrams would never be repeated as to voice tone or content later in the preclear's life, which is the case with the usual preclear. But something else has been interrupted here which is very important to the preclear's life and that is parental care. It may be the common, shallow and collegiate remark that parents are only biological. This does not happen to borne out by the facts. There does not seem to be any substitute to a child for the proximity and care of his own parents. Preclears who have been raised by nurses and maids do not demonstrate the same alertness as those who have been raised by their own parents. Preclears who have been raised by foster parents, no matter the quality of those foster parents, do not seem to be as well off as preclears who have been raised by relatively indifferent and unaffectionate actual parents. There is more here than the biological production of new organisms, and the affinity of parent for child, even when clouded by maltreatment of the child, is apparently superior to nonparental care of the child, even when this is near optimum. Thus, the severance of the parent–child relationship after birth is a more solid break of affinity, reality and communication than the summation of locks which would occur in the usual case by the approximations of incidents later in life to early engrams. This is not theory, but observation of many cases, since no case processed to date which had been raised by maids rather than parents was found to be as high on the Tone Scale as cases which had been raised by indifferent parents, much less those who had been raised by parents who loved them dearly. Russian pseudoscientists to the contrary, there is more to man than biology and environment. Training women extensively in political economy, symbology or the care and cleaning of rifles is not conducive to a forthcoming sane generation.

Straight Memory, as a technique, strikes toward seven types of incidents: the enforcement of affinity, communication and reality, by command; the implantation of circuits; and the inhibition of affinity, communication and reality, by command.

Affinity, communication and reality exist as they exist, under the self-determinism of the individual. What is wrong with the preclear is what has been done to the preclear, not what he himself has done. Basically, man is intended to survive as an organism.* An individual who has been subjected to enforced affinity, reality and communication has an interrupted self-determinism. By enforced affinity, reality or communication is meant the demand on the individual that he experience or admit affinity, reality or communication when he has not felt it. The child who has been forced to "love" a parent or guardian has been subjected, when he

---

*The matter of the modification of the organism by the theta body has been very far from fully investigated. This reservation in regard to the possibility of entheta bodies must be included, out of scientific honesty, in these observations. —LRH

did not feel that love but was forced to admit it, to an enforced affinity. This is aberrative. The wife who has been continually subjected to demands from a lower-toned husband that she tell him she loves him, when she does not, and who yet accedes to this demand, has been subjected to enforced affinity. Lower-toned people than the preclear commonly command his affinity, and when affinity is given but not felt locks are formed which are quite enturbulative should engrams underlie such an enforcement.

What child is there who has not had a reality forced upon him which he did not feel? He has been told that it was very important for him to go to school, when he himself did not have sufficient reason to believe this. In the limited sphere of his experience, he sees that it is desirable to play, to get sunlight, to eat, sleep, have friends and to exist in harmony in the bosom of his family, but he does not see that it is necessary for him to study. Nearly all grammar school education is an enforced reality. The grown-up can see that it is necessary for the child to have some slight command of the three Rs, but the child has not agreed to this. Agreement has been forced upon him, and thus, aberrative locks are formed upon any existing engrams. School is very far from being the only enforced reality. Any time a person is made to agree, by force or threat or deprivation, to another's reality and yet does not feel that reality himself, an aberrative condition exists. When engrams are present which can be restimulated by this situation, a certain amount of theta is trapped as entheta. The most insidious of all these enforced realities is where the individual knows the truth or is told the truth and is then made to confess that what he knows to be the truth is a lie. He has said that such and such is the case and then he accedes to the demand that he deny this assertion. This very commonly happens to children and forms bad locks. Whenever an individual is forced to agree to something to which he would not agree if left to his own reason, a lock is formed, where underlying engrams exist.

Enforced communication is productive of all manner of aberration and physiological changes in the individual. Of course, any lock has to have an engram underlying it, but it is fairly certain that what the parent says in the lock has already been stated in an engram earlier in the case. Communication, of course, includes all perceptics as well as conversation and messages, and when an individual has been forced to look at something which his self-determination says he should not look at, his sight to some degree is impaired. When he is forced to listen to something to which he would not ordinarily listen if left to his own self-determinism, his hearing to that degree is impaired. When he has been forced to touch something which he would not ordinarily touch, his tactile is thus impaired. When he has been forced to talk when his self-determinism says he should remain silent, his speech communication is impaired. When he has been forced to write when he would not ordinarily write if left to his own devices, his ability to write or to communicate messages is thus impaired. These are enforced communications and, in the presence of engrams, become very aberrative locks.

Circuits occupy a later column. But any circuit is simply a control or nullification "you" phrase which makes the individual compute differently than he ordinarily would and which walls up a certain portion of the analyzer for use against the individual. A circuit, for instance, can be critical, so that thoughts that criticize him occur to the individual whenever he thinks or acts. The circuit "I've got to protect you from yourself" can wall up a large portion of the mind. The individual in this society is surrounded by people who would either dominate or nullify, and thus many locks are formed of the circuit variety, where people are by the "you" phrase attempting to dominate or nullify the individual. Locks can only exist, of course, when engrams exist, and so these are normally received in their most aberrative form from parents, guardians and other individuals who have been around the early portion of the person's life, when the bulk of the engrams are received. Circuits are quite peculiarly resolvable by Straightwire. When an auditor strikes a circuit during the running of an engram very occasionally the whole engram blanks out or a strange visio turns on. When the auditor strikes a circuit in an engram he can expect the preclear to go out of the auditor's control into the control of some past and even dead individual's phrases, since the circuit takes over control from the auditor. Individuals who go around auditing themselves and running engrams and phrases ad infinitum are running because of circuits. Individuals whose banks cannot be entered in any way are in that condition because of circuits which bar the auditor. By Straight Memory it is possible to discover the dominant or nullifying individuals of the family and so recover the dominant or nullifying circuits in the form of locks. Once these locks are "blown" the engrams containing these circuits are to some degree discharged. Further, the auditor is forewarned of what he might find in the engram bank of the individual. Every case is to some degree a control case, which is to say a case which has circuits of one kind or another. One of the best ways to find out what circuits the preclear has is to give him Straightwire on the statements of the people by whom he was surrounded in very early life and childhood.

It is interesting to note, on the subject of circuits, that as one goes down the Tone Scale, from the top to the bottom, one finds that people on lower and lower levels are more and more surrounded by dominant and nullifying individuals. Thus, Straightwire becomes more and more indicated the lower one drops on the Tone Scale for the location and blowing of circuit locks.

The inhibition of affinity, communication and reality is no less serious than their enforcement.

The inhibition of affinity comes about when a desirable similarity of the preclear to another person is denied or rejected or when the love and affection of the preclear is rejected. In the presence of underlying engrams considerable turbulence is created by these nullifications of affinity. The wife who is commonly answered with "You don't love me" every time she attempts to express her affection, is undergoing an inhibition of affinity. The individual who is told that nobody in the office likes him is undergoing an inhibition of affinity. The person who is rejected from a group because of some fault, or otherwise, experiences a major break of affinity. When such breaks of affinity overlie engrams, which they commonly do, they become highly aberrative and serve to charge up the engrams considerably. Straightwire reaching such incidents can unburden the case of considerable enturbulence. The individual who is not permitted to feel that he is loved or that he may love, the person who is denied any common ground with the universe, with man, with his group or family, or even with himself is experiencing an inhibition of affinity.

The inhibition of reality requires considerable attention. Left to his own devices and reasoning on his own data, the individual decides what is reality for him and with what he can agree. When he is informed that he cannot agree with those things he thinks he should agree with, he experiences an inhibition of reality. When engrams underlie this, these locks can be very serious and can tie up considerable theta on a case as entheta. One might say that this is the most serious influence in reducing the individual on the Tone Scale—the inhibition of the individual's reality. This is invalidation, and invalidation is the most serious break of the Auditor's Code. What a person, by his own observations, has come to believe real becomes then a part of the conclusions and observations which a person uses to guide his future actions and to evaluate himself with regard to his environment. A sudden challenge or denial of the reality of these conclusions comes as a severe shock to the individual, when it is underlain by engrams, and will shake his reality, in any event. The reality of an individual can be so thoroughly shaken that he will be doubtful of anything he does or says, since he is not sure of his conclusions. Reality, together with affinity and communication, is a basic in the computations which an individual makes with regard to the courses he should take in the pursuit of his own survival. The reality of children is very ordinarily threatened or knocked to pieces by parents. The child has very little data with which to evaluate his current environ and to plot his future. In comparison to his conclusions that he should survive, that he needs food and clothing and shelter, and that he needs affection, the aberrated culture into which he is born is often a very strange reality to him. Grown-ups have agreed upon this culture, but this agreement is not ordinarily the most sensible one which could be made, and the child is often faced with realities which are to him, dealing in the basics with which children deal, quite unreal. Thus, children are being disagreed with continually. The little baby believes it should have its own control of MEST, that it should be permitted to crawl about at will (which is its command of space), that it should be able to take its own time about what it is doing (which is its conquest of time), and should be able to expend energy in whichever direction it desires (which is its control of energy), and should be able to pull about and do as it pleases with matter such as mud pies and precious vases on tables. The child does not have the evaluation that these things are held to be otherwise valuable in the society, and so the child is denied continually its conquest of MEST. Nowhere is this denial as acute as in the denial of reality. None agrees, evidently, with the child. And thus, very early in life a large number of locks begin to build up upon the basic engrams of the case. But disagreement with one's reality is not limited to childhood. Throughout life, the individual who has agreed with himself about certain realities is continually challenged in his reality by those about him, particularly those lower on the Tone Scale than himself, who seek to gain importance by reducing that individual's reality and therefore reducing the individual on the Tone Scale to a point where he can be more easily controlled. Statements, then, which tend to invalidate a person's conclusions about reality concerning his own relationship to the culture and the environ are very aberrative.

Inhibitions of communication are very common. They most ordinarily manifest themselves in this society with spectacles, with hearing aids, with tactile anesthesia, with stutterers and people who will not write letters or pass along messages. Communication breaks, on the inhibition side, stem from the denial of a person's ability to see, to feel, to hear, to be, denial of a person's rights to talk or listen—in other words, denials of a person's right to communicate. These manifest themselves, when underlain by engrams, in terms of inhibited relations with one's fellows and a lowered position on the Tone Scale.

The hurdy-gurdy system of Straightwire takes into account all of the above data and puts into existence a method by which the auditor can exploit each person surrounding the preclear. We have already spoken of the triangle of Dianetics: affinity, reality and communication. The auditor works on the principle that a datum desired from the preclear's memory today may not be forthcoming but if requested again in a day or two may be forthcoming, and if not then, may be available two or three days after that. The auditor then makes a list of all the persons who surrounded the preclear: Father, Mother, aunts, uncles, guardians, nurses, grandparents, great-grandparents, teachers, brothers, sisters, employers and subordinates, as well as mates. Two triangles and two circuit slots exist for each of these persons. The preclear does not need to know about this. The auditor can very simply draw up a plan of questioning which then permits him in his requests for memory of certain locks to cover the ground over and over and each time with new people, repeating questions asked about people covered in sessions before. In other words, this is a tally sheet which the auditor could use in order to assay the case and blow, if possible, locks of enforced ARC, inhibited ARC and circuits. For instance, the auditor draws one triangle and a slot, a straight line, for Father and he labels these "enforced" and "dominating." Then he draws another triangle and another slot and labels these "inhibited" and "nullifying." Then he makes a similar graph for Mother and for every person intimately related to his preclear's life.

His system of questioning then is to find out when Papa enforced affinity, when Papa enforced reality, when Papa commanded higher communication and when Papa sought to dominate. He asks around the triangle and with the slot. He will discover that the preclear may or may not have certain immediate memories concerning Father's conduct and favorite phrases. The auditor then proceeds to the inhibition triangle and nullification

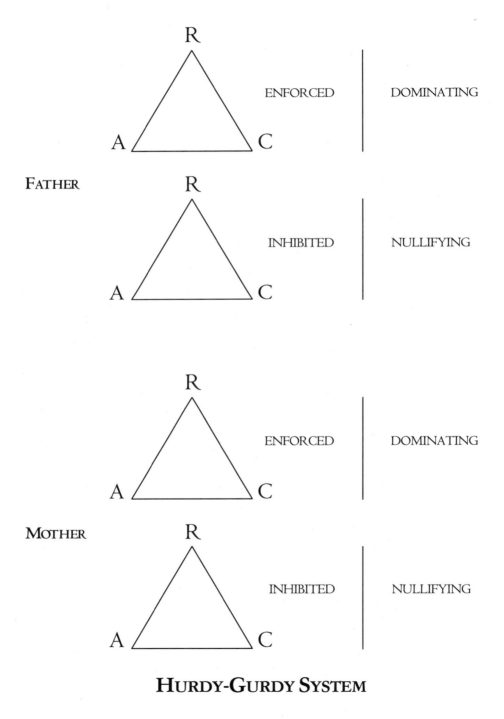
FATHER

ENFORCED | DOMINATING

INHIBITED | NULLIFYING

MOTHER

ENFORCED | DOMINATING

INHIBITED | NULLIFYING

HURDY-GURDY SYSTEM

slot. He asks when Father inhibited or refused affinity, when he inhibited or refused reality or agreement, when he inhibited or refused communication, and when and if Father attempted to nullify the preclear. In the same session the auditor goes on to Mother and to other people, with the same plan.

Because the preclear's memory can be refreshed by this procedure, the auditor does not abandon Father after one session but carries Father for three or four sessions on Straight Memory and asks a similar set of questions in the next session. When did Father enforce affinity, demand that he be loved, demand that he have affection shown to him? When did Father demand agreement? When did Father demand communication? When did Father attempt to dominate? When did Father attempt to cut off or inhibit affinity? When did Father attempt to cut off or inhibit reality? When did Father attempt to cut off or inhibit communication? When did Father attempt to nullify? The auditor then goes on to coverage of Mother or some other person.

Systematized Straightwire like this will turn up an enormous amount of material. The hurdy-gurdy system was created so that the auditor would not have to keep long sheets of questions.

This is the general plan of questioning. The questions need not be the same every time, but their general import should include this plan. In such wise, the most aberrative forms of entheta in locks can be contacted by Straight Memory, and session after session the preclear's material becomes fuller and his memory steadily improves.

The valence problem is also resolvable in terms of Straight Memory. It often occurs that the preclear is suffering some physical disorder which can be freed by Straight Memory, along the following lines. Should the preclear have dermatitis of the hands, one might discover that some person in the preclear's background had dermatitis or some ailment of or injury to the hands. This person may be located, and it may be discovered that some lock command exists which causes the preclear to be like the previously sick person. This is often found with a preclear who has lost an ally. Such a case is illustrative. The preclear's grandmother died of cancer of the hands. The preclear was suffering from dermatitis of the hands. It was discovered that many remarks had been made by relatives concerning how like his grandmother the preclear was. This likeness was so closely followed out by the preclear that he attempted to develop cancer of the hands, which manifested itself as dermatitis.

The whole problem of valences is one of allies and antipathies. The preclear very often may be in the valence of someone who is normally hated. He is forced by lock commands, people telling him things like "You're just like your father. You're growing more like him every day, and you'll grow up to be no good." Because of such commands the preclear may not be able to help hating himself, since he is forced into the valence of a person who is hated and whom he hated. Straight Memory can often resolve this problem merely by asking whom the preclear was most supposed to be like and what was the general attitude toward this person.

It is vital in Straight Memory to reach the actual context in the actual incident of every memory. The first stab of the preclear into his memory bank will be one of vague feeling that there was such an incident and that somebody said something like that. This is not good enough. The auditor must pin the preclear down to a specific incident and the words of that incident. If this is not possible in the first session, it will be possible in a succeeding session. Until it has been achieved, the lock will not be blown. A good trick to get a preclear to remember a specific incident is to ask the preclear if such an incident exists and then, when he vaguely asserts that it must, to ask him where he was sitting when he heard somebody say this or where he was standing. The preclear may quickly correct the auditor, saying that he was lying down or walking, and thus will have recovered data. There is a certain amount of challenge which the auditor can use in using Straight Memory. He puts the preclear on his mettle. If this is not carried too far it acts as a very stimulating factor to the preclear.

It is quite remarkable how many "psychosomatic" disorders and how many aberrations Straight Memory can resolve after the auditor has had a little practice. He can actually get his preclear out of some chronic valence, rid him of some aberration, bring him up to present time and generally raise him on the Tone Scale merely by asking the right questions.

The auditor should not confine himself to the hurdy-gurdy system of Straightwire. This is only provided to relieve the maximum amount of entheta in the minimum amount of auditor time. The auditor can use his imagination considerably with regard to what must have been said or done to this preclear. The auditor can profitably open any session by asking, "Well, what are you worried about today?" When the preclear tells him, the auditor wants to know who in the preclear's background might have thought that, and it sometimes results that the preclear can spot immediately what he has been told in the past which compares to the worry which he now has, and if the two are cause and effect, the preclear will immediately rid himself of the worry. It is quite remarkable how swiftly this can be done.

When the preclear recovers a lock which has considerable entheta on it he ordinarily chuckles or smiles. The preclear who does not react in this fashion may yet be getting a little bit of entheta off of the lock, but the possibility is that an earlier-similar lock exists when the preclear does not laugh. Thus, when the preclear is caused to remember some early incident, and yet does not experience any relief, although he should, from the nature of the incident and its hidden character, the auditor does well to try to discover some earlier incident than the one remembered, which is similar to it. The principle here is to discover, if possible, the key-in, the first time the underlying engram was restimulated.

Straight Memory is also used in order to discover a certain type of incident which can then be lock-scanned. The preclear who is directed to a certain type of circuit command in his case may not experience much relief through Straightwire. But now that the auditor knows this type of circuit is in existence he can cause the preclear to lock-scan the circuit, returning to the first time he can discover it and scanning up through all similar incidents to present time. Thus, Straight Memory is combined with Lock Scanning, which is actually a high-speed memory rather than a return through locks.

No auditor should feel uncomfortable about using any quantity of Straight Memory. It will happen, however, that an auditor will get relief in the preclear by Straight Memory, then return the preclear down the track to an incident which is then run, and after bringing him back up the track will find that the relief which had been achieved before is now apparently gone. This comes about because a present time lock has been laid in by returning. Merely having the preclear remember his own act of running the incident, once he is back in present time, should restore his aplomb and equilibrium.

The benefits of Straight Memory are many. The duration of these benefits is in question. By Straight Memory of pleasure moments or of the first time one had a certain illness, one can alleviate headaches, stomachaches, worries and anxieties. This does not mean that the effect is permanent, as would be the case when the basic engram is run out. But Straight Memory is the parlor trick[1] of the auditor. In any group of people he can always find at least one that he can make much happier simply by a few adroit questions. The auditor who uses Straight Memory for this purpose should also develop the technique of the marksman who when he makes a bull's-eye is clever enough immediately to lay aside the gun. Once the auditor has achieved a spectacular effect by Straight Memory he should leave the case alone for that session—unless, of

1. **parlor trick:** something that impresses or entertains. The term may have originally referred to small magic tricks performed in a parlor (a room in a house used primarily for receiving and entertaining guests).

course, he is engaged in a regular progress up the Tone Scale with his preclear.

Straight Memory is a technique which should be studied and practiced with considerable alertness as to the good it can do. No auditor should fall into the rut of believing that simply remembering the past can do very much for the preclear. Remembering specific, causative locks can, however, produce a marked change and improvement in an individual. Straight Memory is not free association and is not random maundering; it is a precision technique and should be studied and used as such.

C O L U M N A D
PLEASURE MOMENTS

THE DIANETIC DEFINITION OF pleasure is that the organism tending toward survival obtains pleasure by survival actions and the seeking of survival goals. In the organism below 2.0, tending toward death, a reactive pleasure is taken in the performance of acts which lead to succumbing on any of the dynamics. In other words, above 2.0 pleasure is survival, and below 2.0 pleasure is obtained only by succumbing or by bringing death to other entities, or by causing self or other entities to be suppressed on the Tone Scale.

True pleasure leads toward happiness. The "pleasure" which tends toward death is a reactive counterfeit, but seems intensely valid to those in the death bracket of the Tone Scale.

Happiness could be said to be the overcoming of not unknowable obstacles toward a known and desirable goal.

This postulates that the greatest happiness is the nearest approach to immortality. A good job, skilled abilities, bountiful harvests, possessions; these are goals. There are very finite goals for the happy man in every day of the week, as well as the big goals toward which he directs his efforts. His happiness does not come from the attainment of the goals but from overcoming obstacles on the way to those goals.

Pleasure and immortality are near synonyms for individuals above 2.0 on the Tone Scale. There is a gradient scale of the types of pleasure enjoyed by those above 2.0. It seems evident that the person at 2.5 actually takes pleasure in being bored, but surges up toward higher levels when interest is concentrated on some goal not outside the understanding of the 2.5.

The 3.0 takes pleasure in reaching toward very clearly observable goals. The 3.0 accepts his pleasure cautiously and tentatively, but nevertheless enjoys it. His pleasures are apt to be routine and relatively unimaginative.

The 3.5 tends toward higher goals of survival and has confidence in reaching those goals. He can embrace more bountiful levels of survival. He can realize that survival as a bare-necessity-level process is unsafe and intolerable and that if all computations demonstrate that he will require two bushels of wheat per month to eat, then he had better provide twenty bushels of wheat per month. His pleasure is wide and ambitious.

The 4.0 achieves considerable exhilaration. His concept of survival is so bountiful and he is yet so confident of his ability to reach such levels of survival that he can take in a universe of goals and, within the limits of his skills and talents, accomplish them.

Here we have a definite manifestation of attitudes toward goals, magnitudes of goals and the ability to attain and enjoy pleasure. No man is happy without a goal, and no man can be happy without faith in his own ability to reach that goal. The highest form of security is confidence in one's self, in the future, in the group and in mankind. Without such confidence and without the will to make the various dynamics survive, an individual has no security. That person who measures his security in terms of a good job purposely short-sights himself as to the actual insecurity of his position. A man who works for an organization which may endure long or may be transient, according to popular indoctrination, is secure. And yet he may work to the period of his life when he is no longer adaptable and find himself, of a sudden, without any job because of the simple sudden shift of a board of directors or because of the antagonism of a foreman. Security would consist of this man's being able to adapt himself to his environ, being prepared for any possible shift in the factors which influence his job and being confident of his ability to meet and deal with any possible shifts. Security is not a static thing. Security would only lie in a man's confidence in reaching his goals and, indeed, in his having goals to reach.

There are automatic goals inherent in the plan of life. The conquest of MEST, the survival of the theta body, faith in immortality and the Supreme Being are all high-level automatic goals. They potentially exist in anyone, but the amount of entheta inherent in the theta body and accumulated within the generation may cause the individual or the group to fall far short of any realization of its ability to attain these goals. The more entheta existing in the theta body and accumulated in the generation, the lower or less reasonable will be the goals of the individual or group.

Without goals, hopes, ambitions or dreams, the attainment of pleasure is nearly impossible. Many individuals do not realize this and, even though capable of assigning to themselves goals and pursuing those goals, they permit lower-toned people around them not only to undermine their confidence in their own ability to attain security and survival but also to deny them the right to formulate and strive toward goals of a desirable magnitude.

At the lower levels of the Tone Scale one finds individuals who purposely enturbulate, upset, destroy and with great ardor inhibit the goals, hopes and dreams of those about them. Here we have the individuals from 2.0 down. These have goals which are themselves no less definite than the survival goals above 2.0. It is a piteous and terrible thing that individuals above 2.0 expend vast amounts of coaxings and persuasions on mates, associates and fellow group members below 2.0 in an effort to get them to go toward survival goals. Individuals who engage in this activity are immediately targets for those who exist from 2.0 down, since these see in the higher individuals a method of furthering their own goals—and the goal of the 2.0 down is death.

An examination of the anatomy of death demonstrates that death can be a small or a great thing. Death is actually a gradient scale. Small mishaps and accidents can tend toward greater and greater accumulation of mishaps and accidents, until death of an ambition, death of an individual, death of a cause or death of a group is attained. Here is the story: "For want of a nail the shoe was lost, for want of a shoe the horse was lost, for want of a horse the rider was lost, for want of a rider the battle was lost, and all for the want of a horseshoe nail." Death stems from small things and proceeds toward great things.

Death is a soft-footed thing. Today a man makes a flagrant error in bookkeeping. He makes it because his wife has nagged him the night before. Tomorrow his superior finds the error and marks it down that this bookkeeper is not always accurate. In itself this is nothing. But next month, when a bookkeeper has to be discharged, it is recalled that one made an error, and all other abilities being more or less equal amongst bookkeepers, the one who made the error is discharged. Out of a job, the bookkeeper finds himself even more enturbulated at home and spends little time finding new employment. He takes a job beneath his skill in an office where everything is hectic, and he makes more mistakes because he is now worried. This is a little bit of death.

There are those who talk about "lucky breaks" and who speak of the "hand of fate" in their undertakings, but a forthright examination of the field of man's activities will show that nearly all success is most adequately deserved. The head of an imposing institute of psychology in a major American city told me recently that when he first entered upon his profession he was to some degree convinced that the capitalist, the big industrial manager, the director of the great corporation had arrived where he was because of carelessness of the feelings of others and avarice.

In the course of the many ensuing years he had, however, either with his own hand or through his staff, done industrial psychometric testing of many organizations and with this work had had an opportunity to test a great many of the capitalists, managers, directors and industrial giants of America. He had found in every case that "those who were at the top very well deserved to be there." He had discovered that the endowment of these individuals included a rich appreciation of life, a great feeling for their fellow men, an enormous persistence, an intelligence in planning and execution. He had discovered that the world is carried on the backs of a few desperate, but very big men. And he had discovered that luck was not chance.

Individuals above 2.0 on the Tone Scale are uniformly lucky. There is something more to theta than quite meets the eye. Here are the men on whom God smiles.

Below 2.0, we have the unlucky. One could with some surety give to a person high on the Tone Scale a few dollars and expect him to come out a winner at Las Vegas. And one could expect that the same few dollars given to a person low on the Tone Scale would see him coming out of the game very much the loser. Above 2.0, the individual plays to win. Below 2.0, the individual uniformly plays to lose. And not only does the individual below 2.0 play to lose for himself, he plays to lose for everyone else around him and for the future.

It is part of the mechanism of death that individuals below 2.0 talk as though they play to win, talk of the desperate need of saving and winning, talk of emergencies by which one is expected to win. This is all a part of the trap. Given every opportunity and every facility and every circumstance by which they can win, people below 2.0 will inject into every plan the germ of death, and acting ever so reasonably will permit that germ to grow until death is attained for the individual, for his associates, for the future or for his organization. A Hitler brays his anger at the world and hounds all Germany into action with the argument of glory and yet brings, through not very mysterious mistakes, the hopes of Germany to death. He makes a charnel house of Europe, slaughters thirty million human beings, brings suicide to himself and the extinction of hopes to his German nation. Yet many times in the course of Hitler's 1.5 activities he could have converted Germany into the glory of the world. As a matter of fact, before he began to manufacture nothing but munitions he had revived German science to a point where it was respected above the science of any other nation. And by the simple and direct appeal that Germany had become vital to the survival of other nations Germany could have risen and become glorious. But at no time when Germany could have risen did Hitler take the turning toward survival. He chose instead the turning toward death.

This play is not enacted always upon the stage of nations. It happens in many households. It is a pathetic and terrible thing to find a man mated with an individual below 2.0. He does everything he can to succeed, and yet at every turn of his career he finds himself balked by some strange noncompliance or some new enturbulation, and gradually, little by little, his energies decline until he himself is outward bound toward death and a new generation. A woman, mating herself to a man below 2.0, who is herself capable of a high level of survival, will find herself broken by little "misunderstandings," strange perversions and quarrels at inopportune times, until at last her ambitions for a family and a future or even for a career for herself, lie in the dust where so many dreams go. The man who takes unto himself a business partner below 2.0, who is himself well above that line, will find a strange concatenation of events building around him which bring about the destruction of that business regardless of the hopes with which it was founded and regardless of his own ability to carry it through. It would be far, far better for an individual engaging in a marriage, a business or a group action to inject himself with the most deadly poison or virulent bacteria than to ally himself with anyone below 2.0 on the Tone Scale. If this seems strong, look around you at the blasted men, the blasted dreams, the stories never written, the songs never sung because someone out of some pap of sympathy or "obligation" allied himself with an individual below 2.0 on the Tone Scale. This is death—death as certain as laying one's neck below the blade of a guillotine and tripping the trigger.

From 2.0 down, the individual takes a reactive but very definite pleasure in attaining the "goal" of death for himself, for the future and for individuals around him. Here is entheta seeking to separate theta from MEST to bring about death and to accomplish a new generation. In the vicinity of such people death may be silent and waiting but ready to influence and pervert every action in the direction of succumb.

At 2.0, the individual finds a reactive "pleasure" in sending forth antagonisms, in carping and nagging and criticizing. Left at liberty, he will not sink any further on the Tone Scale but will continue to "abreact[1] his hostilities." He is dramatizing engrams. But should these dramatizations be broken, he will descend on the Tone Scale. It is an actual fact that whatever pleasure he obtains is obtained through these dramatizations. He can, by processing or education or changed environment, be brought up the Tone Scale, but left where he is, he will certainly drag others down it, since he is a point of turbulence, as are all people below 2.0.

At 1.5, the individual finds reactive "pleasure" only in the venting of anger. He has no actual concept of pleasure, but he gains a feeling of dangerousness and therefore of "pleasure" in the dramatization of his dominating or angry engrams. If permitted to go on being angry, he will remain static, to some degree, on the Tone Scale, but if these dramatizations are balked or fought against, he will descend down the Tone Scale, since he is not permitted to experience the "pleasure" which he can "attain" by being angry. It should not be expected that reasonable causes must

---

1. **abreact:** to release or express an impulse, emotion, etc., such as one previously forgotten or repressed.

exist for this person to vent anger. This person will make his own causes, so that he can be angry. His goal is to achieve destruction of things or people. He has considerable joy in achieving that destruction. People who are only temporarily at the 1.5 level, which is to say who are being acutely 1.5, know well the satisfaction obtained in smashing something. The chronic 1.5 can rise no higher than the smashing of things. At times in the past it has been felt that the individual who threw things, who went into a rage and who talked in desperately destructive terms was at the lowest possible depth of insanity. This is very far from true. This is the very high bracket of insanity. One should beware of those who are lower on the Tone Scale and who bring about destruction only by covert means, for there is no forewarning of what they will do. Any preclear whose reactive mind (and all reactive minds are below 2.0 on the Tone Scale) is coming up toward a Release will pass through the zone of anger reactively and will be furious with people who have done things to him and may even be furious at the world at large. This is a symptom of his getting well and not a symptom of his going mad. People are not easier to handle below the zone of anger. People below the zone of anger are much more dangerous, since they will take much wider steps to bring about death. They do not bring about destruction in clean daylight as does the angry individual, but in the dark alleys and cesspools of humanity. The person who is chronically angry can be processed rather easily by Dianetics up into the higher tones, since he still retains his vitality. It is only necessary for him to discover those things about which he is really angry in order for him to centralize and focus his attention, and he still has considerable theta with which to convert entheta. But, and never neglect it, this person's pleasure is in being angry, and in running pleasure moments one had best discover moments in which the individual could be unreservedly angry at something.

The 1.1 tends even more markedly toward death than the outspokenly angry individual. The 1.1 will make small slips and errors and bring about upset and turmoil in his vicinity with considerable aplomb. These are his joys. If the 1.1 is to experience any "pleasure" it will be in an act which is deviously and hiddenly destructive to himself, to the future, to his group, or to mankind, to life itself, to theta, or even, although that is impossible, the Supreme Being. It should be understood that an individual may have a 1.1 reactive mind and yet be quite analytically alert and only drop to 1.1 when he is enturbulated. This would be an acute 1.1. But such a person is still dangerous. With the smoothest possible face, the 1.1 can deny any and every destructive or death act which he or she has engaged upon. The 1.1 hides all destructive acts and quite commonly puts a face of construction upon these activities. The 1.1 finds "pleasure" in sex only if sex is engaged upon with many people and in strange and peculiar ways. This does not contradict the fact that a man, like any male, may seek to own and impregnate as many females as possible—not a 1.1 characteristic. The 1.1 does not enjoy sex save only when it is hectic and enturbulative. Here is the satyr, the nymphomaniac. The 1.1 will injure or maim animals or men for "pleasure." And in running "pleasure" moments on the 1.1 the auditor will find such moments existing around the injury of somebody's dreams or the body of some helpless being. Here "pleasure" is obtained not in the clean daylight but clandestinely and often hideously. The 1.5 takes "pleasure" in bringing about the incapacity of a powerful enemy. The 1.1 takes "pleasure" in breaking his enemy's back while the enemy lies wounded and helpless. The 1.1 may appear appealing, he may make a great show of his powerlessness, but when the lights are dimmed the actions of this individual are directed energetically toward death, whether the death of a reputation, the death of a cause even though the cause is apparently supported or the death of himself no matter how far he seems to think his actions are from suicide. In the 1.1 band, by the way, we find the individual most blatantly insistent upon ethics and morals for others.

The 0.5, being that much further toward succumbing and dying, attempts to bring about the death of his family, associates and self by continual forthright enturbulence in terms of death. Truth is, of course, no consideration at any level below 2.0. The most flagrantly untruthful is the apathy level of 0.5. The individual at 0.5 obtains reactive "pleasure" in lying wildly but dolorously about the hopelessness and horribleness of life and what has been done to him. To run what any individual at an acceptable level of the Tone Scale would consider a pleasure moment on a person at 0.5 is, of course, all but impossible. But reactive "pleasure" can be obtained by the 0.5 in being as thoroughly 0.5 as possible.

The 0.1 can sometimes be coaxed into running a "pleasure" moment on the subject of how dead he is and how lacking in any dangerousness. If the auditor can contact him at all, it will be at this level where the "pleasure" moments can be found.

It is a general rule, then, that pleasure moments are run at the level where the individual finds himself on the Tone Scale. Do not expect the 2.5 to run moments of high exhilaration, since the entheta on his case prevents him from reaching such a level. Do not expect the 1.1 to run a moment when he was extremely angry, since his position on the Tone Scale makes overt anger a very dangerous thing to indulge in, and the fear implicit in his position may prevent him from showing it. However, if you can get him to recall a moment when he was outstandingly and admirably moral and ethical, when all around him were being dishonest and insincere, you may find that he experiences a great deal of "pleasure" in this counterfeit situation.

The general rule is that, above 2.0, the auditor discovers constructive and creative acts of greater and greater triumph and magnitude as the preclear rises up the Tone Scale. And below 2.0, he finds greater and greater efforts toward death in the "pleasure" moments chosen by his preclear. In any case, it is overcoming obstacles toward the goal which is important to pleasure. Below 2.0 of course, the individual is overcoming "obstacles" which tell him to survive as he travels toward his "goal" of death. Death, to individuals below 2.0, is the only valid and obtainable "goal"—whether for self, future, group or mankind. Anything which interrupts this course toward the "goal" of nonsurvival will be fought by people below 2.0. Such avidity for extinction is commendable only for the thoroughness with which these individuals will struggle to die. Because one deals here with eight dynamics, one should not believe that the individual below 2.0 works only toward his own death. At 2.0 he works rather mildly toward the death of a very wide periphery but does not much desire death for himself. At 1.5 he works toward the death of other beings or life forms or other dynamics. He will, of course, bring about death for self, but he does not give heed to this. One cannot reduce the other dynamics without reducing the first dynamic, of self, and bringing about one's own death. At 1.1, we get only an occasional conscious awareness that the individual is himself tending toward his own suicide. Death is intended, by devious means, for a lesser periphery. Where the 1.5 will seek the death of many, the 1.1 will seek, by covert means, the death of a few. The 0.5 seeks death in obverse ratio to the amount of attention he can give to his environ, and that attention is normally isolated in the first dynamic and may include only a few intimates in the environ. The 0.5, then, is the suicide, but before suicide, can almost be counted upon to attempt the death of at least his closest associate, whether by murder or by enturbulation via sympathy. Occasionally the 0.5 will include the murder of children as a part of personal suicide. The intimate of a 0.5 stands, actually, in the gravest peril in which an individual can possibly stand.

The general running of pleasure moments can accomplish a very great deal in a case. There is the case of an elderly woman who had no other kind of processing done on her for many weeks. She was at the beginning of this period, according to report, bedridden. An auditor with an experimental inclination spent two hours a day running pleasure moments with this person, petty triumphs, joyous meetings, moments of good health and well-being, moments of pride in accomplishment or in loved ones. At the end of this period, the elderly woman was no longer bedridden and evidenced a considerable rise on the Tone Scale. Not a single lock, secondary or engram was run on the case. This should give the auditor some idea of the value of pleasure as a target for processing.

There is also the case of a person who could run no grief until pleasure moments were scanned intensively on his case. Such contact with the fact that pleasure actually existed in his life enabled him to support, because of the free theta returned to him through the attraction of his attention to pleasure moments, the contact with moments of misemotion necessary to free his case.

Pleasure moments seem to say, first and foremost, that survival is possible. But below 2.0, "pleasure" moments give the encouragement that death is possible. In either case the tone is raised whether the preclear desires it or not.

The running of pleasure moments is done exactly as one would run an engram or a secondary engram. One requires the preclear to return to the moment when the pleasure was actually taking place and to contact all the perceptics of the incident, seeing and hearing and feeling the experience as fully as possible, over and over. The preclear can run the incident many times before tiring of it, since at each running he should discover new instants and perceptics that had been hidden before. Running pleasure in this way seems markedly to increase the amount of free theta in the case.

On lower levels of the Tone Scale, actual pleasure in a person's life, moments of survival, particularly those of triumph, are not easily obtainable. However, the auditor, by having the preclear run possible pleasure moments as concepts and then, as they are contacted more closely, as actual incidents, can possibly demonstrate to the preclear that pleasure has existed and is available.

In view of the fact that obtaining pleasure is one of the primary goals of life, the running of pleasure moments can do a very great deal for a case. There have been cases which have had sonic and visio turn on merely by the running of pleasure moments.

The case is most readily stabilized by the running of pleasure moments. In trying to bring a case up to present time one should run several pleasure moments if the case is difficult to stabilize in present time. After running such moments the preclear often comes easily to present time, having recovered attention units from secondaries and engrams somewhat restimulated in processing.

Memory itself can be refreshed just by running on the track. One can, as an experiment, choose some specific date in the preclear's lifetime. This date may be completely occluded. But the auditor insists that the preclear return to this date. The preclear may be completely in the dark as to what happened on, let us say, January 3, 1943. The auditor has the advantage over the preclear, since he knows that when he has told the preclear to go to a certain date, then the preclear has gone there whether the preclear knows it or not. The auditor then requires the recounting of the happenstances of, say, 9:30 A.M. on that date. The preclear may be able foggily to point out certain incidents in the year 1943. If the auditor is very patient and persistent in his address, he will gradually cause the "I" of the preclear to obtain the specific details of the date and moment, and he can then run this moment with its own actual perceptics. This is no less valid a technique than running pleasure moments. The mind has recorded everything, and the auditor knows that when he sends the preclear back to such and such a time, the preclear is there even though the "I" of the preclear may be barred from the perceptics of the incident by entheta on the case. With patience and persistence the auditor can always obtain the data which he requires.

Moments of triumph are, of course, pleasure moments. But one often finds preclears, particularly those below 3.0 on the Tone Scale, who run pleasure moments without experiencing any pleasure from them. The auditor may find the preclear winning a silver cup at a horse show, and the auditor may return the preclear to the incident and run him through it over and over, only to discover that the preclear felt he did not deserve to win the cup. This is the difference between the preclear's concept of reality and the auditor's concept of reality. By all reason, the preclear should have obtained pleasure in winning this silver cup at the horse show, but in accordance with the preclear's tone no pleasure was obtained from the incident, since possibly it brought about too much notice and notoriety or it conflicted badly with some specific engramic computation of the preclear about winning or about hurting the other contestants by having won. This should not discourage the auditor; it should only point out to him that he is attempting to run pleasure moments too high up the Tone Scale for his preclear. In such a case, the auditor should go down the Tone Scale and find a time, perhaps, when the preclear was able to destroy the reputation of some dear friend by some lying gossip and run this as a pleasure moment. He will obtain in such wise, despite the preclear's feeling that it is impossible, a rise in tone.

The auditor should not neglect the fact that pleasure moments may be created and that a present time pleasure moment is itself a point on the track and will tend to disenturbulate the preclear. This does not mean that the auditor should countenance the "pleasure" that would be sought by some individuals low on the Tone Scale, pleasure which might consist of the destruction of the reputation, future or health of some young woman or child. But it does mean that the auditor should encourage the preclear to provide himself with pleasure, as an assist to processing.

The auditor, if he is advising pleasure, should not fall into the old error of believing that pleasure is idleness and wastefulness. The greatest pleasure, for instance, that a composer can achieve is in composing. A genius in management achieves his greatest pleasure in overcoming obstacles to management. The best pleasure for an individual is in the attainment of happiness, the overcoming of not unknowable obstacles toward a known goal. The auditor may by adroit questioning discover for the preclear the fact that he has goals toward which he can proceed. It is a below-2.0 trick to take a creative and constructive individual and set him aside from the route of his greatest pleasure, which may be the pursuance of highly arduous goals. The auditor would not tell a mountaineer to go to the seashore for a rest but should encourage the mountaineer in the belief that he can conquer a much higher mountain than he has ever attained before, since if his mountaineer is ailing it is because some less-than-2.0 individual in his vicinity has brought him, by great and detailed discouragements, to the belief that he can climb no more mountains.

Pleasure, whether for life or death, is attainment or the overcoming of obstacles toward that attainment. When running pleasure moments or when advising his preclear to create and construct present time pleasure moments to raise his level on the Tone Scale, the auditor should not overlook the fact that happiness is the overcoming of not unknowable obstacles toward a known goal. He will find the majority of his preclears without any goals. The auditor, by questioning and without interfering with the self-determinism of his preclears, can help them to discover and clarify their goals. Or he can assist in the identification of obstacles toward any goal which the preclear already recognizes. Or the auditor can simply encourage the preclear to keep on overcoming the known obstacles toward his known goals.

The auditor will discover preclears who are not particularly low on the Tone Scale, who have yet had insufficient opportunities to experience pleasure, and so have behind them a barren life. An auditor is justified in advising the preclear to go out and create and live through a pleasure moment, so that the auditor afterwards can run it, to the enhancement of the case. The living of it, of course, is more important than the running. The primary consideration is whether or not pleasure moments exist.

It is interesting to note that any society declines in exact ratio to the contempt in which it holds pleasure and advances in ratio to the respect it has for pleasure.

Above 2.0, pleasure contains more construction than destruction, more good than evil. Below 2.0, "pleasure" contains more destruction than construction, more evil than good. Immorality comes about when a thing contains more pain than it does pleasure. Societies have existed which found their pleasure in observing or inflicting more evil than good. The Roman circus[2] is an example of this and marked a point in the decline of the Roman Empire which forecast an early death for that great political organization.

By true pleasure is meant acts which contain more good than evil.

Before one condemns pleasure, one should understand the kind of pleasure about which a person is talking. But there happens to have been, down through the centuries, such a revulsion toward what the Roman Empire called pleasure in the early Christian days, that pleasure itself became inhibited. There are individuals and groups which consider the enjoyment of life a crime. This immediately and automatically spots these individuals and groups on the Tone Scale. They are below 2.0 and are headed toward succumbing. Yet the auditor will have to cope with people who have been indoctrinated into an inhibition of pleasure and who by education are unable to experience pleasure. The auditor should have ready his definitions of pleasure and an understanding of what pleasure actually is. From those who tell him that pleasure is evil he should gain a definition of what they think is enjoyable. This is the type of incident which can be run on the case as a pleasure moment. For those who tell him that pleasure is good and then proceed to detail promiscuity and sadism the auditor should have at least an intellectual understanding.

Because of the various situations which exist in the life of any person, pleasure as survival and pleasure as death sometimes intermingle. It occasionally happens that some individual has lost,

---

2. **Roman circus:** an amphitheater in ancient Rome in which horse and chariot races, brutal athletic contests, gladiator combat and similar entertainment took place. Such activities were extremely popular and drew huge crowds. *Circus* in Latin means "oval space in which games were held," coming from the Greek word for ring, circle.

through the chicanery, treachery or betrayal of others, his woman, his business or his reputation, and his idea of pleasure is the painful extinction of those who have injured him. This does not immediately denote a low position on the Tone Scale, for the auditor may find that such an individual delves into death for only one circumstance. If the other circumstances of the individual are high on the scale, the auditor should recognize an immediate indication of where he should work in order to free considerable theta, which is tied up in plots of revenge and dreams of painful punishment for the enemy. Such an individual, however, can ordinarily run pleasure in other spheres of life. Even a low-toned individual can sometimes find some sphere of activity, if very isolated, which is constructive, and thus the auditor knows where to look for actual pleasure on the case and can use this particular incident or type of incident in order to free theta.

The whole subject of pleasure moments is allied intimately with survival, where true pleasure is concerned. The auditor, however, should not overlook the fact that it is "pleasure" for the 0.5 to contemplate the most gruesome possible suicide or the most pathetic death of the nearest "loved one."

The auditor should not be critical of the type of pleasure which his preclear selects but should work continually to select the highest possible pleasure on the Tone Scale available to his preclear. In other words, for the 1.1 he should try to find 1.5 or 2.0 or 2.5 pleasures rather than persisting along the line of 1.1. The auditor is attempting to raise the preclear up the Tone Scale and in the process of doing so he will find that higher and higher levels of pleasure can be obtained not only in present time but in the past. The amount of pleasure of the true variety which the preclear can experience or run is symptomatic not only of his chronic position on the scale but of his progressive rise toward more desirable levels.

C O L U M N   A E

IMAGINARY INCIDENTS

ONE OF THE SOCIAL ABERRATIONS of America is that imagining things is a misconduct. "Imagining things" has been made equivalent to "insanity." It is a common derogatory statement to say that one is "imagining things." It is a nullifying criticism to say that one experiences delusion. The child is particularly subject to a bombardment of criticism for being imaginative.

The condemnation of imagination signifies a fear of a departure from reality. But if imagination is so thoroughly condemned, then those who condemn it must have some basic fear that they themselves cannot hold on to a reality.

There is nothing wrong with imagination. There is a great deal wrong with the type of aberration which makes it impossible or at least difficult for the individual to differentiate between the imaginary and the actual. So long as the individual knows he is imagining when he is imagining and he knows he is dealing in fact when he is dealing in fact, imagination has a high validity.

There are three types of imagination. One is creative imagination, whereby in the field of aesthetics the urges and impulses of the various dynamics are interwoven into new scenes and ideas. The second type is the more or less practical type of imagination which comes about as a result of computation. Without this second type of imagination an individual could not forecast the future nor could he postulate a goal desirable in the future. This type of imagination is so vital to computation that the individual who lacks it can be seen to be definitely deficient analytically. The third type of imagination is delusionary or hallucinatory.

If the culture desired to make itself more sane, it would cease to apply the word *imaginary* to things which are delusionary or hallucinatory. Delusion connotes a type of imagination which is not known by the individual to be imaginary. However, in engrams one commonly runs into the phrases "It's all your imagination," "It's all in your head," "You're just imagining things" and other command phrases which short-circuit the preclear's ability to differentiate between what we should now call the imaginary and the hallucinatory. The imagination becomes hooked in to the fact bank, and "I" receives data as fact which is actually the product of imagination.

There are, one could say, four distinct sources of aberration. The first is occasioned by phrases in engrams which specifically dictate certain obsessions, compulsions, repressions, delusions, neuroses and psychoses. Such phrases, however, have command value on the analyzer, which does not know they exist below it in the reactive mind, only to the degree that the case is charged with entheta. Command phrases and action phrases become more and more obeyed by the analyzer the more the analyzer is shut down through cumulative aberration. Action phrases are effective more and more as the individual descends on the Tone Scale.

Therefore, there is a second type of aberration source which is simply the amount of charge there is on the case. This might be called mechanical aberration. It does not stem from specific commands but stems from mental inefficiency by reason of cumulative entheta. As the preclear descends down the Tone Scale, certain definite manifestations take place by reason of cumulative entheta. The whole chart around which this book is written is a result of the study of the effect of accumulating entheta on aberrated individuals. Entheta by itself can charge up a case to the point where the case will behave in certain definite ways regardless of the command content of the engrams.

The third kind of aberration is environmental and is the result of aberrated persons and situations in the individual's present time environment. This is normally temporary, but cumulative environmental entheta has a chronic effect in the case.

The fourth type of aberration is educational, being the cumulative entheta of the culture in which the preclear was raised, the irrationalities and bad data he has received as a result of his education—by parents, in schools and by experience.

There should be listed a fifth type of aberration, and even a sixth and seventh type, but these are at this time of less concern to the auditor. The fifth type would be the cumulative aberration of the theta body through its many generations, which he may or may not have to address in the clearing of the case. The sixth type would be the pattern behavior inherited on the genetic line, of which very little is known, but it can be estimated that any organism has some pattern behavior of which some small portion might be considered incorrect for the environment and so, by a stretch of definition, could be considered aberration. The seventh type would be aberration due to missing or malformed portions of the human structure, either through genetic inheritance or through accident or psychosurgery.

Thus, we see that imagination is valuable and vital both to creating tomorrow's realities in the society—the invaluable contribution of the artist, writer and composer—and in the practical computations of everyday living, and that it should not be discounted in value in the rational human being.

Then we see that imagination by engramic command, which confuses the real with the unreal without proper evaluation, can introduce falsity into the thinking and execution of the individual.

Additionally, we have imagination, by reason of charge on a case, beginning to supplant reality as the case descends down the Tone Scale. Imagination thus becomes mechanically more and more short-circuited into a supplantation of reality, as the position of the individual decreases on the scale. In the past it was thought that people imagined things willfully in order to "escape" reality. These therapies never bothered to evaluate reality, but were very glib in demanding that people face it. "Escape" and "delusion" were epithets used in order to pound the patient into obedient subjugation. (The practice of telling the patient that his incidents are imaginary rapidly reduces the individual on the Tone Scale, since it destroys the patient's sense of reality, and is a practice definitely calculated to further incapacitate the patient.) The fact of the matter seems to be that as an individual drops down the Tone Scale, the cumulative charge on the case makes existence in its actual form more and more intolerable. What theta he has left, perhaps because of reversed polarity, cannot perceive into the entheta of the reactive mind and the mostly shut-down analyzer. It is not that the person is unwilling to face reality; it is that he is incapable of facing reality. Said in another way, the individual is veered away from the things which have been done to him in life toward imaginary postulates which can serve in lieu of fact. It is true enough that the individual who cannot feel that he is a threat to the enemies in his environment, at least to some degree, is insane or becomes insane. Thus, as the individual descends on the Tone Scale he becomes, by imagination, first a threat to real things and then, by imagination, a threat to imaginary things, and finally no threat at all to anything, at which point he has reached pretended death. Thus, the individual departs further and further from reality, at first knowing that he is departing from reality, and then being unaware that he is departing from reality, at which point he could be considered to some degree insane.

A possible explanation for the short-circuiting of imagination by the mechanical means of cumulative charge on a case may be of interest to the auditor. There is no good description and, indeed, no accurate postulate or theory which accounts for the ability of the human mind to remember in the quantity that it does. The most recent attempt was made by a person who had dabbled in physical structure but who did not know his mathematics. He originated a punched protein molecule theory,[1] and stated that memory charges were stored in punched protein molecules. His theory holds up only so long as it takes one to work out by mathematics that if an individual recorded only the major perceptions of his environment day after day and stored them, by this theory of holes in molecules in which are stored memories, he would still have in storage capacity only enough, in the ten-to-the-twenty-first-power binary digits[2] of cells the mind contains, to serve for three months of memory. Therefore, this theory of punched protein molecules is not valid.*

*It was my privilege to take one of the earliest courses given at an American university in atomic and molecular phenomena. My purpose was not, however, the same as that of some of the other students in the course, who went on to make atomic fission practical and give us the atom bomb. I was trying to find life force as an energy. Studies and experiments at that time—1931—brought me to the conclusion that physical-universe energy did not account for human memory, because there was no wavelength small enough nor possible basic unit of human structure small enough to account for the vast storage of memory of which the mind is capable. While further studies in the next two decades brought about these concepts of Dianetics and some ideas and axioms concerning thought energy, this field is now but barely entered and should receive the attention it deserves. The bare entrance which has been made into this field has already given us a better understanding of man, aberration and human conduct than we have ever had before, but the surface is so faintly scratched that great benefits should accrue from a thorough and continuous penetration of this new universe. —LRH

1. **punched protein molecule theory:** a reference to a theory concerning memory storage in which it was believed certain molecules in the body were perforated and memories were stored in each hole.
2. **ten-to-the-twenty-first-power binary digits:** a reference to a very large number. The word *power* means how many times a number is multiplied by itself, thus, ten to the twenty-first power means 10 multiplied by itself 21 times or 1,000,000,000,000,000,000,000. "Binary digits" are either of the digits 0 or 1 of the binary system of numbers—that system of numbering that employs only 0s and 1s. The phrase *ten-to-the-twenty-first-power binary digits* then refers to 1,000,000,000,000,000,000,000 of the 0s and 1s strung out one after another.

A workable analogy on the subject of structure—and it should remain an analogy only, since it does not do any more than help a person understand what is happening—tells us that we may be dealing, in memory and in the human computer, with a problem not unlike physical universe electrical charges surrounded by insulation. Certain things tear down this insulation, so that memory items begin to short-circuit, one to another. This would account for the identification of one fact with another which occurs more and more as the Tone Scale is descended. Low on the Tone Scale, things are identified with other things which are actually widely different, but at the higher levels of the Tone Scale, where the mind is in good working condition and there is no great charge on the case, minute differences can be detected by the computer between one memory item and another. At the top of the scale, the mind is capable, for instance, of differentiating between two cigarettes which, though they appear identical and are of an identical brand, are different, if only to the degree that they occupy different units of space. At the bottom end of the Tone Scale, not only would these two cigarettes seem to be the same cigarette but these two cigarettes would also be tobacco, which would also be tobacco smoke, which would also be chewing tobacco, which would mean that chewing equaled a house on fire. At the top of the Tone Scale, at the highest levels of reason, one has sharp, high-level differentiation between facts, and at the lower end of the Tone Scale the most widely different facts and items are associated as equal. One could say that the equation of the reactive mind was "A equals A equals A equals A" regardless of what A stood for. In an engram, all things and remarks are equal to each other are equal to the pain are equal to the perceptics, and hearing equals vision and vision equals tactile, and a complete identification occurs. The analyzer when full on thinks in minute differences. The ability to think has to do with the ability to differentiate. Unthinkingness has to do with a lack of ability to differentiate and a compulsion to identify unlike things with each other as though they were not only like things but the same thing.

In an insane person, the administration of sedation seems to bring about a momentary recurrence of sanity. As an analogy only, then, it could be said that entheta breaks down the structural insulation separating one memory item or unit from another and so causes identification. And it could be said that the presence of any euphoria would rebuild or reestablish this insulation to some degree and make rational thinking possible. The auditor who audits a preclear who is under sedation will discover that so long as the preclear is under sedation he appears to be responding to treatment, but the moment the sedation wears off, all the auditing and most of the entheta which was thought to be turned into theta have now become short-circuited into brand-new aberration. Probably the most dangerous thing one can do to any aberrated mind is to place it under heavy sedation and try to treat it, or while it is under sedation place it in an atmosphere which is restimulative. Sedation of the insane is, shortly and abruptly, criminal, since it permits new percepics to become entangled with an already confused mind under circumstances of perception which, if the patient were not under sedation, could not take place.

It should be thoroughly understood that this analogy of insulation between memory units in the mind is, very definitely, an analogy and is used for illustration only, so that the auditor may know better what he is confronting. Entheta definitely seems to tear down and arc across any divisional and insulatory barriers in the mind.

As a further analogy, it could be postulated that as the mind breaks down in its ability to differentiate and begins more and more to identify, the various units of the analyzer begin themselves to become too closely associated and begin to replace each other, so that that portion of the mind which is used for imagination becomes undifferentiated from that portion of the mind which is doing computation on fact.

This would also be an analogy which took place regarding valences, wherein the "I," which is the real individual, becomes obliterated in favor of highly charged other sections of the analyzer. And here the analogy breaks down, since the valence walls between different personalities the individual may be grow more and more sharply defined as the individual descends on the Tone Scale, so that at last the heavily charged case goes from one valence into another so sharply that one can almost hear the click as he crosses the valence wall. Of course, one could add to this analogy and say that the theta which has become entheta at last begins to form up insulation of its own, but this does not seem very likely. Certain it is, however, that the identification of incidents which are in no way even similar is symptomatic of the insane.

The auditor should understand, then, as he confronts his preclear, that he may have before him an individual who is incapable of facing any facts in his case. This may be limited to an inability to face facts in certain spheres of his life, such as failing to face facts concerning his wife. He may have such a thoroughly charged second dynamic that he can face no facts concerning his marital existence or his children, but will turn to imaginary "facts" which are, if untrue, still very safe. The auditor, as has been said before in this book, should not under any circumstances try to slug, bang, hammer or electric shock his poor preclear into admitting that all is imagination. The auditor should be perfectly willing to accept that in certain spheres of the preclear's life the actual facts of the case are so definitely entheta that what theta exists in the preclear's mind is unable, by reason of polarity, to encounter the real facts in the case. Almost any human being, in some sphere of activity, will deal in imaginary incidents, up to the level of 3.0. This one, when he faces the idea of school, will detail imaginary incidents simply because his own school experiences contained so much entheta that the theta veers away from it and turns to the imagination to be supplied with "facts." Another individual will deal in factual material throughout his field of activity except where religion is concerned. He may have so much entheta on the subject of religion that he veers away from actuality here and talks in terms of atheism, or mad-dogism, or may go in the other direction and become completely hallucinatory. But in this case, he is veering away from his MEST universe to the point where he is constructing an imaginary sphere of activity. (The individual who simply turns to the theta universe and perceives there certain visionary things is not necessarily aberrated at all but may be simply high on theta perceptics. The aberration which is cited above is of the variety of the sadistic zealot, who has been, is and always will be so much trouble to the church.) Or the imaginary sphere, which "I" believes to be wholly factual, may be the existence of lost gold mines. Here, so much entheta exists with regard to practical and workable means of living that he must deal in imaginary means without realizing the impracticalities of those imaginary means. Or the sphere of delusion may be educational, wherein one has been brought to believe that because one has studied for twelve years and has been given a license one is capable of aiding his fellow human being. This would not be the product of individual delusion but of social delusion, based on the cumulative entheta of no knowledge whatsoever of human behavior but only superstition and authoritarianism, and the real and urgent problem that something had to be done with the insane even if it was only to give them into the hands of sadists and butchers.

Somewhere in every case you are going to find the preclear running imaginary incidents in lieu of real incidents. As an auditor you should not worry unless your case is running a majority of imaginary incidents in lieu of real incidents, for your case then is running delusion rather than fact, by reason of a very low position on the Tone Scale. Here is a problem for you. You don't dare tell this preclear that he is running delusion. This would be a break of the Auditor's Code. But somehow you must persuade him to address present time or some locks long enough to free some theta so that he will have a theta ability to face reality. On such a case you could actually blunder and run physical pain engrams, but you would only enturbulate the case further by trapping the existing free theta on the case into the existing entheta, and you would assuredly send the case down the Tone Scale rather than bring it up. Where the imaginary incident becomes generally preferred to the actual incident you can be quite sure that you are dealing with a low-tone preclear.

Now there are three ways of handling this delusion. The first way is to electric shock or prefrontal lobotomize or sedate the preclear into utter apathy and uselessness in the society and wreck him completely. This is not recommended.

The second way is to scan free or obtain in present time enough free theta to bring the individual up the Tone Scale to a point where he will run actual incidents rather than imaginary incidents. This is highly valid.

The third way is to coax the preclear into running avowedly imaginary incidents, and this is the crux of this particular technique of processing. By openly inviting the preclear to run imaginary incidents the auditor is breaking down the barrier of pretense which the preclear will unknowingly put up. The running of avowedly imaginary incidents is quite productive. Sometimes the preclear will run them, quite astonishingly, with somatics. But he is not being required to face any reality about them and the auditor is not insisting that any reality exists concerning them. In an astonishingly high percentage of times, however, he will be running actual incidents. So long as he does not have to admit that these incidents are actual he can do something about them. One might say that the auditor is thus validating the imagination mechanism of the mind and is strengthening it and is already beginning to put the general and broad segments of the mind into good working order by differentiating one from another with the preclear. Of course there is always the danger that the auditor's use of the word *imagine* will restimulate the preclear, because this preclear may have engrams which tell him that he does not know true from false and that it is all imagination anyway. But this chance should be taken.

It should be understood that no amount of imaginary incidents can supplant the running of real incidents. The first value that this technique has—the invitation to the preclear to run avowedly imaginary incidents in his past—is to build up the preclear's confidence in the auditor. The preclear begins to feel that he will not be censured for indulging in fantasy. In this great, wide and undoubtedly rational culture, almost any preclear has been cut to ribbons as a child for indulging in fantasy. The child lacks data and makes up for this lack with a wild and rugged imagination. The child quite easily sees fairies and strange animals walking about, with his imagination. If he finds life dull and elders hard to shock into taking an interest in him, he may recount these things as valid. He is, of course, inevitably censured by the hardheaded, practical and undoubtedly rational elder and so accumulates a series of locks on any engrams he may have. Left to himself and to his fantasies and imaginings, the child will eventually, of course, find out what reality is—that grim thing in our world of the twentieth century—and what is fantasy. But the elder is apt to press the child into too early a compression by this "reality." Actually, of what reality is neither you nor I have much notion, but we have agreed upon certain facts, and having agreed, we wish to remain friends, and so we continue this agreement. As a culture ages, these agreements are harder and harder to disturb, and are maintained not because they are true but because they are simple and easy and because no energy is required to maintain them. The child, fresh and new in the world, would like to see a little excitement in his reality. And the elder, worn and haggard by a combat with an environ which offers little in terms of security and much in terms of menace, fights back against these bright bubbles and dreams. Thus, any preclear you have on the couch is fairly certain to have experienced a confusion between what he wanted to think was reality and what he was told he would have to accept as reality. Thus, there was an invalidation of his reality, even though his reality was actually imagination. When the preclear on the couch discovers that he has an auditor who not only will listen to imagination but who encourages it, the affinity level rises, and actually the preclear's ability to differentiate in terms of reality will itself rise.

In the running of imaginary incidents, the auditor must never, after the incident has been run, then insist that the incident was real. This would be a break of faith. He and the preclear have entered into a contract that what is being run is pure imagination, and the auditor must not break this contract.

The running of imaginary incidents may consist of running imaginary pleasure moments, which is heightening in terms of theta, or it may consist of running imaginary moments of grief or physical pain, which makes available to the auditor more data on the case and may actually increase the theta on the case.

Here is a most interesting fact for the auditor. It may happen with an aberrated child that he has occasionally pretended injury or illness for the sake of accepting sympathy or interest from his parents, guardians or mentors. The auditor would do well to discover the times in the life of the preclear when he has *knowingly* feigned injury or illness in order to *knowingly* receive sympathy or interest from those about him. In the first place, when an individual will do this he is in fairly bad shape, for this is a form of pretended death. The environment wherein the preclear would do this must have been a highly restimulative environment which had the preclear low on the Tone Scale. (One should realize that in the course of a lifetime, environ to environ, an individual varies markedly on the Tone Scale.)

These *knowing* pretenses are of interest to the auditor because they are invariably real as to their background. The preclear may have supposed at the time, in all confidence, that he was lying, but he was actually offering a sympathy engram to those about him, and the auditor can thus discover a highly aberrative engram on the case. Whether this case is in shape to run this engram or not is up to the judgment of the auditor, but he at least knows that it exists. The preclear who continually pretended an injury to his foot, for instance, may have supposed that he was lying and may have supposed that he had never had a foot injury, but in actuality somewhere, earlier, hidden from his analytical mind, a foot injury exists for which the preclear received a great deal of sympathy.

Sympathy incidents are relatively hard to locate. The preclear will hold on to an incident in which he received sympathy for longer than one where he received only antagonism. The location of the allies of the preclear is thus rendered difficult to the auditor, but the mechanism of discovering the "imaginary" illnesses which the preclear offered to the world around him discovers the allies. (There is another method of discovering allies which is of interest. One finds an antagonistic personality in the preclear's life and runs the preclear back through incident upon incident where this antagonistic personality was attacking him, until one finds a point where the preclear was being defended by someone. The person who does the defending is an ally or a pseudoally* of the preclear and incidents with this person should be followed backwards and forwards and cleaned out of the case, as one of the most aberrative elements of the case.)

The imaginary incident serves four purposes. First and foremost, it gives the auditor data about his preclear, since the imaginary incident which the preclear will recount has some basis in actuality.

The next point is that the recounting of an imaginary incident heightens the affinity between the preclear and the auditor in that the preclear begins to find that the auditor must be somewhat compatible with him, since the auditor will accept the preclear's evaluation of existence and thus seems to be in agreement with and similar to the preclear.

---

*For a discussion of allies and pseudoallies, see the handbook, Dianetics: The Modern Science of Mental Health. A brief definition of these terms may be given here. Ally: a person recorded in one or more of the preclear's physical pain engrams who is, because of this recording, believed by the preclear to have defended him or promoted his survival. Pseudoally: a person about whom the preclear has a similar computation, not based directly on an engram recording but on a similarity to an ally. —LRH

The next value of the imaginary incident is that it increases communication between the preclear and the auditor. Here, at least, we have the preclear talking about something and the auditor listening, and the preclear discovering that the auditor will listen, without interruption or criticism, to a recounting which may be quite wild and sensational.

The fourth value of the imaginary incident is that it finds the auditor noninsistent upon a high level of fact, and so will find the preclear more willing to deliver fact.

The imaginary incident could be said to be a testing ground. The auditor asks the preclear to run an imaginary incident. This is all right with the preclear, since they have agreed that the incident is to be imaginary, and thus the preclear cannot be censured for saying anything he pleases.

It will happen, in the running of imaginary incidents, that somatics will turn on. Or it will happen that the preclear is suffering certain somatics and yet is too low on the Tone Scale with regard to this particular subject to admit the actual cause of these somatics. By running off imaginary words and phrases, imagining what Papa says, imagining what Mama says or imagining the year in which this happened or imagining the circumstances relating to this, it may come about that the somatic disappears. One has actually run off an engram or a heavy lock and the case is thereby benefited.

The auditor does not cavil with the preclear about facts, in any case. Where the auditor has to use imaginary incidents to get any information of any kind out of the preclear, he is dealing with a preclear who has been invalidated very thoroughly by the people around him most of his life. The imaginary incident is a mechanism which actually repairs past invalidations. The preclear will not admit that an incident is actual, because those around the preclear have too often challenged his ability to recount actuality or to deliver forth facts. The auditor gets around these past invalidations by himself refusing to invalidate, by inviting an incident purely on the basis of imagination. The preclear is heartened. The auditor will receive data. And free theta may be liberated in the case.

THE PRECLEAR AND AUDITOR AS A GROUP

It must be noted somewhere in this work, and may be noted here since the running of imaginary incidents is most productive of the result, that the preclear and the auditor form, actually, a group. One need not know the high level of technology which is Group Dianetics to understand that two human beings make a group. Two is the basic unit not only of theta but of human beings in group terms. The group may number millions at its largest, but in its basic size it is at least two.

Occasionally the preclear will discover in the auditor an antagonistic personality. This comes about when the auditor reminds the preclear of some personality earlier in the preclear's life who did something nonsurvival to the preclear. The auditor who permits himself to go on in this imaginary role of a past antagonist will find that his task is greatly increased.

It is of very great value to the auditor to clear himself and the preclear as a group, before he begins any serious auditing.

In the optimum group, a high level of affinity, reality and communication must exist. Between the auditor and the preclear ARC must be high.

There are various ways to clear groups. The auditor should not be as anxious to approve of the preclear as he should be to have the preclear approve of his auditor. Nevertheless, it will take considerable strain off the case and the processing if this works both ways. One auditor, in order to clear the group, himself and the preclear, habitually requests the preclear to tell him what the preclear does not like about him. The preclear at first, through propitiation or social usage, will not admit that there is anything about the auditor which he does not like, but on pressing the case, this auditor very shortly discovers for the preclear antipathetic individuals in the preclear's past of whom the auditor reminds the preclear. The first act of the auditor then is, by Straight Memory, to clear up these bad associations.

The establishment of affinity, communication and reality between the preclear and the auditor is a vital concern if processing is to follow anywhere near an optimum course.

Where a co-auditing team is being formed, and the success of Dianetics is built upon co-auditing teams, a mutual clearance is required, whereby each unburdens himself to the other, and by Straight Memory, undesirable associations are cleared out of the relationship. It is remarkable that between any two human beings bad associations by reason of past existing personalities are almost inevitable. Individuals on the normal level of this social culture associate hidden past personalities with present personalities they meet. Straightwire can easily clear up this situation. The auditor mentioned above was having some difficulty with a woman preclear until he discovered that the way he cleared his throat reminded her of the first of her husbands, of which she had had three. The point here is that the auditor did not forgo his habit of clearing his throat merely because the preclear objected to it. The auditor immediately went to work and caused her, by making her remember, to conceive a difference between himself and her first husband. The moment she did this, the auditor's habit of clearing his throat was no longer of any importance, and he could go on clearing his throat. The auditor should not change his habits and training pattern to match every preclear, but should use the effect of these upon the preclear to locate past antipathetic personalities. This in itself frees theta in the case.

The use of imaginary incidents acts to form a smoother relationship between the auditor and the preclear by establishing for the preclear the auditor's willingness to accept anything the preclear has to say. But it does more than this. It gives the auditor a valuable assessment of the preclear's position on the Tone Scale, for he can judge this rather easily by the type of incident which the preclear likes to imagine (see Pleasure Moments), and it tells the auditor what may be in highest restimulation in the present time environment.

The auditor who will scorn imagination or condemn anything the preclear says as delusion, regardless of the auditor's inability to compare it with his own concept of reality, will inevitably bring about the destruction of the auditor–preclear group. And they will not be able to work together.

The husband–wife team has been found in Dianetics to be the least compatible group—a commentary upon American marriage, the training of the male to accept marriage as part of his environment, and the lack of training of the female in how to be a wife. A few husband–wife teams are successful, but the majority are not, and husbands and wives should look outside the home for co-auditors, or the marriage may collapse.

CHAPTER TEN

COLUMN AF

LOCKS

ELSEWHERE WE HAVE THE ANATOMY of entheta. Entheta could be said to be in four forms. There are probably more than that. By entheta we mean, of course, enturbulated theta. The first form is that which is the basic cause of entheta, the engram. Here, theta in its effort to conquer MEST has come into too heavy a collision with MEST. In an organism this causes physical pain.

Theta, after it has become enturbulated with MEST, can, either by the mechanism of death or by Dianetic processing, be withdrawn from the MEST and brings with it an intelligence of the laws of MEST, which it can then use in a further conquest of MEST on a more orderly and harmonious level. All things begin with a heavy impact and enturbulence, if anything is to be learned by theta about MEST. The Foundation, for instance, in its first year of existence smashed heavily into MEST, and if this delighted those who desired to preserve the status quo or those who had no use for an end of aberration, yet much was learned, so that Group Dianetics could come into being and so that improvements could come about as a result of new data on the third dynamic, which in turn resulted in improvements along the first dynamic and in the techniques of individual processing. The engram is a moment of physical pain and unconsciousness which is recorded in the reactive mind with all perceptions during the period of unconsciousness. It can be keyed in by conscious-level experiences, it can be dramatized and it can manifest itself either as mental aberration or as physical aberrations, which were called in the past psychosomatic illnesses.

The engram consists of enMEST, which is the MEST of the organism enturbulated or disordered by impact, and entheta which is mingled with the enMEST.

Entheta can exist as temporary enturbulence in the individual's life force or reason when he is confronted by unreasonable or nonsurvival circumstances in his environment. This could be called temporarily enturbulated theta. However, in any situation in present time which is restimulative, a certain amount of entheta becomes fixedly entheta and is stored in the reactive mind and thereafter, save in those extraordinary circumstances wherein enormous quantities of free theta are in the environment of the individual, or but for Dianetic processing, this fixed entheta remains fixed.

The "permanently" fixed entheta remains in the reactive mind in the form of secondary engrams or in the form of locks.

The secondary engram will be described in its own turn, but is a low tone level experience of loss, or fear of loss, or anger because of threatened loss, or apathy because of accomplished loss.

The lock has two variations. One of them is where the individual has been prevented from carrying out the commands of the engram which is restimulated by present time environmental perceptics (broken dramatization). The other is merely where the perceptics of the engram are approximated by those of the present time environment (restimulation).

In order for a lock to be formed it is necessary for the analytical portion of the person's mind to be somewhat lowered in activity or alertness. Locks can be received only when an individual is weary, upset by reverses or is in a generally nonoptimum situation. These light approximations of engrams in the analytical present time environ pass for aberrative in themselves. Actually, they are not. The lock is only the surface manifestation of the total environmental cause of aberration. Underlying any lock must be an engram. A lock occurs also when the individual is attempting to carry out the however irrational commands of the engram and is prevented by the society's or some individual's counter "reason" from accomplishing the dramatization.

Locks are analytical-level encystments of entheta.

The average case probably has several thousand engrams. Individuals are often questioned on the subject of how often they have been unconscious. A few of them will answer that they have never been unconscious in their whole life. As soon as they are sent back down the track, they begin to discover period after period when they have been injured or operated upon, and certainly every individual has been born, and birth above all other experiences is sufficiently arduous to bring about unconsciousness. Since the reactive mind registers upon a cellular level, and also upon a theta-body level if evidently to a lesser extent, the earliest moment when an engram can be received is certainly no later than conception. Engrams do not begin to receive locks, ordinarily, until well after birth, and usually well into the speech period, although babies will react to the uncomprehended sounds in the environment which are also included in their engrams.

A lock is, then, a relatively light incident which betokens a restimulation of some engram on the case. There are in any case tens of thousands of locks. If one continued to address locks and only locks in a case, processing would be almost interminable. This is fortunately unnecessary. Locks have only to be addressed in a case until the preclear has run out engrams; the locks consequent to any one engram or chain of engrams which he has run out can be scanned off with great speed.

Locks are interesting to the auditor mainly on the low-tone cases. On many cases the auditor will discover that locks have to be run as engrams. He will find a period where some preclear has, as a young girl, been forced to eat spinach, and this will seem to be a highly aberrative incident.

The preclear, if very low on the Tone Scale, may be responding to the action phrases or commands in the lock, yet this incident contains no physical pain of any kind, and still, once sent to the incident the preclear is unable to leave it until it is run, complete with action phrases. This would betoken a very low-tone preclear. The auditor should not think that the reason his preclear is aberrated is because she was made to eat spinach when she was eight years old. The auditor should understand that underlying this incident is an engram, or many engrams, whereby the preclear is dominated. But if the auditor discovers that the lock is in itself aberrative, he should understand that this is no time to run engrams, since this preclear must be unburdened of many locks and minor engrams before she will be in shape to run engrams. Here is a very heavily charged case.

As one can read in the column on the Tone Scale chart, a Clear has all locks discharged. This is sometimes overlooked by the ambitious auditor. A Clear is, by definition, one who has had all entheta in his current life converted to theta. This means that his engrams must have been erased, that his secondaries must have been discharged and that his locks must have been scanned out.

The 3.5 will blow locks almost as fast as the engrams underlying chains of locks are reduced.

The 3.0 does not have to have locks addressed as individual incidents, but in order to clear up the case, scanning of locks is necessary, as will be seen in the next column.

The 2.5 can have locks treated with benefit as individual incidents. It will be found that moments when the 2.5 was criticized for stepping out of line at school or for being mean to sister will release some entheta. However, the auditor is to some degree wasting his time by treating, at this level of the Tone Scale, nonphysical pain and nonmisemotion incidents as individual occurrences.

Around 2.0, locks begin to become important. The auditor can go into a moment in the preclear's past life when the preclear was consciously alert and had something happen to him which was productive of entheta, and yet discover that the incident will not reduce. This nonreduction of relatively simple incidents, as it proceeds from 2.0 on down on the Tone Scale, indicates a considerably charged case. Minimal physical discomfort in an incident, if the restimulative agents in the environment are high, can produce moments when the preclear was alert and awake which then refuse to reduce when addressed by the auditor.

The 1.5 is peculiarly susceptible to the type of lock which breaks the dramatization. Let us say that the 1.5 is being angry against something, and someone criticizes him for being angry or prevents him from carrying out the full cycle of his anger. A lock results which will be remarkably effective in reducing this person on the Tone Scale. Of course, any 1.5 receives a nearly countless number of such incidents, since the society generally frowns upon people being angry and would rather have them apathetic. On a 1.5 an auditor can run these broken dramatizations with benefit as individual incidents just as though they were engrams.

At 1.1, we begin to find locks extremely effective, particularly when they concern breaks of affinity, breaks of communication and breaks of reality, or enforcements of ARC. The 1.1 lives in fear most of the time, fear of something, if only as a nebulous anxiety. The remark of a 1.1's "friend" which leads the 1.1 to believe that he will not immediately see his friend again may produce a lock, even though the 1.1 that very evening may dine with his friend. Here the entheta is beginning to pile up at a very rapid rate. The auditor can run such incidents just as though they were engrams with some benefit to the case.

At 0.5, we begin to discover that locks must be handled gingerly, for locks, in a 0.5, can be heavy enough to cause the preclear to hang up on the track, except of course in the wide-open case, which runs on the track even when completely insane. In the apathy case the loss of a glove or the mere receipt of a letter even though it is good news can cause a lock which has to be run as an engram by the auditor. A heavy lock where something really happens would be much too strong in entheta for the preclear to attack, and the auditor should avoid incidents which would be productive of aberration at the 1.5 or even the 1.1 level. The 0.5 can be aberrated by a sneeze.

The 0.1, if the auditor can contact this individual, is so low in theta that incidents which would be pleasure moments to anyone else are the strongest and heaviest encystments which can be attacked. The only past moment which can be attacked in a 0.1 is an instance of the mildest variety, such as going for a ride in a car, or eating supper. Any incident of mental stress is to be avoided and any incident of physical stress is, of course, entirely out of the question, as it has been from 1.1 down the Tone Scale.

CHAPTER ELEVEN

COLUMN AG

SCANNING LOCKS

T HE ADVENT OF LOCK SCANNING was the greatest single advance in techniques of application in Dianetics in the last six months of 1950.

Lock Scanning was developed in an effort to convert the maximum amount of entheta into theta in the least possible time. It is a remarkable technique. It was discovered that individuals who were thoroughly stuck on the time track and heavily overcharged could send a few attention units earlier and later than the point where they were stuck and could in such a fashion actually emerge from a chronically fixed spot on the time track and so come to present time.

The value of Lock Scanning can hardly be overestimated. The heavily occluded case can be lock-scanned. Auditing, bad and good, can be removed from a case by Lock Scanning. Invalidations of Dianetics, which reduce the preclear's ability to be processed, can be removed from the case. ARC locks in enormous quantity can be deintensified. It is a technique with which the preclear can be moved swiftly up the Tone Scale. Lock Scanning can produce sufficient change in a case to move the case two points on the scale in a single session.

A case which has been audited inexpertly can be set to rights and boosted up the Tone Scale by Lock Scanning. Some cases on which many engrams have been run may yet not have risen on the

Tone Scale, because the entheta of the processing enturbulated present time and created new locks. Lock Scanning remedies this. Some cases which have been book audited remain relatively static on the Tone Scale, but with two to four hours of Lock Scanning rebound swiftly and attain a new level of activity.

The technique of Lock Scanning is a very simple one. All aberrative incidents are in types in series of a similar nature. All affinity breaks by a certain person on a case could be considered a chain. All affinity breaks by anyone in any environ at any time could be considered a very broad consecutive chain in the preclear's life. All affinity enforcements by a single person on the preclear could be considered a brief chain. And all affinity enforcements by all people could be considered a broad chain. Communication, talking, listening, seeing, not seeing and all other perceptics, enforced and inhibited, make up their own chains. Reality enforcements and inhibitions make up their own chains of agreements and disagreements. The auditor can actually draw up a chart on which all possible chains of locks can be shown, in terms of affinity, reality, communication and broken dramatizations.

Engrams also exist in chains, as will be covered later. The engram or chain of engrams provides the basic upon which locks can be accumulated. Hundreds and hundreds of incidents may be derived from an engram or chain of engrams. To run each one of these incidents as itself would require far too much time on the part of the auditor. But the preclear can readily be brought by the auditor to scan, slowly or rapidly, similar types of incidents, from the earliest to the latest, either with regard to one person or with regard to all persons or with regard to a period of time.

The commands necessary to permit the preclear to lock-scan are very simple. These can be made far more complex, since speeds of scanning can be demanded of the preclear. It is discovered, however, that the preclear will normally scan at his own speed. The auditor asks the file clerk if there is a type of incident which can be scanned in the case. The file clerk, at a snap of the auditor's finger, answers yes or no. The auditor requests the name of the type of incident. The file clerk gives the name of the type of incident. The auditor then tells the preclear to go to the earliest available moment on this chain of locks and again asks the file clerk a question, as to whether or not this chain can be scanned without running through any engrams. Assured that it can be, and only if assured that it can be, the auditor tells the preclear to scan from this earliest moment to present time through all incidents of the type named. The auditor makes a drill of this and never varies his procedure. He sends the preclear back to his starting line, the earliest available lock of this type. He makes certain the preclear is there by asking, "Are you there?" When the preclear assents, the auditor then says, "Through this chain of incidents, avoiding all physical pain, begin scanning." *(snap!)* The final command, telling the preclear to begin scanning, is like the starter's gun. Slowly or rapidly, the preclear goes up through these various similar incidents. These incidents may consist of all the times when anybody stopped or interrupted him when he wanted to talk. Or they may consist of the times that a certain person, such as the preclear's mother or wife, demanded affection. But whatever the type of incident, the auditor must adopt a routine and not vary this routine. The auditor should always tell the preclear when to begin scanning. The preclear should not be encouraged to go to the earliest moment he can discover and then start forward without any further signal. The preclear should report to the auditor when he has reached the earliest available moment, if he is able to know this. And the auditor should instruct the preclear to report when he arrives at present time, so that no time will be wasted.

Scanning can be done either vocally or nonvocally. The preclear can give the auditor, each time he touches a new incident, the most aberrative phrase of that incident. This would be vocal scanning. Or the preclear can simply go through the incidents recognizing each one as he passes it, or racing through them so fast that they are merely a blur, without telling the auditor what he is contacting.

It will be discovered that the preclear ordinarily finds the most recent locks in his case the first which can be scanned. As he begins to scan chains of locks off his case, he will begin to find earlier and earlier chains of locks and portions of chains which he can scan. He should be encouraged to discover earlier and earlier moments in his life.

Any time a preclear starts to scan a chain of locks, he can be expected on the second or third time through to find earlier incidents of the same type which he previously missed. This is symptomatic of more and more theta being available to the case, so that earlier and earlier moments can be reached. The auditor should not bully the preclear, however. If the preclear cannot discover an earlier incident after the auditor has requested one, the auditor should not be insistent.

Any chain is scanned many times. It will be discovered that at first there are only one or two incidents on the chain. Further scanning brings forward five or ten incidents on the chain. Then the old incidents begin to drop out as unimportant and new incidents, hitherto unrecalled, begin to appear. The chain is, ordinarily, short during the first scan, then it appears to lengthen, and finally the preclear either becomes interested in his outside environment or in another chain or the chain becomes so short that it takes him only a moment to scan through many years of his life.

The mechanism of scanning is this: one contacts an incident and recognizes it as a concept of an incident. Perhaps one has a phrase in the first incident. The auditor may ask the preclear to repeat that phrase or not, as the auditor desires. The preclear then goes forward from this incident to the next one of a similar type that he can recognize. The mind is intensely selective of types of incidents it can scan. It seems that there is a filing system in the mind which files according to types of topic. This is what is used in lock scanning.

If one wishes to be precise about lock scanning, there is vocal rate in which the preclear scans, pausing at each new lock up the chain only long enough to give the most aberrative phrase out of it. There is nonvocal scanning, in which the preclear recognizes the phrases as he goes by them, incident to incident, from early to late, but does not tell the auditor what phrases he is contacting. There is accelerated rate, which is merely a rapid glance at the incident, before the preclear goes on to the next, and in which the auditor is not told what the individual incidents are. And then there is maximum speed. Maximum speed can be so fast that the incidents are simply a blur. The preclear has no analytical recognition of what is happening beyond differences of position, flashes of faces and flashes of words.

Lock Scanning frees theta from innumerable incidents and is highly instrumental in raising the tone of the preclear. It should not be confused with the chain scanning of engrams. Chain scanning through moments of physical pain is not desirable in cases below 3.5 on the Tone Scale, since the engrams, by their physical pain, will snatch more free theta back into enturbulence than will be freed.

Theoretically, a case can be lock-scanned to a point where practically no aberration is manifested, but this is only theoretical, since only one of four types of entheta is being converted. The four types, of course, are entheta received because of the present time environment, entheta encysted in the form of locks, entheta existing as charge in engrams and entheta existing as engrams themselves.

The type of entheta which exists as charge in locks (and in secondaries) frees from late to early. Engrams run from early to late. Thus, one begins Lock Scanning very late in the case. One may find it necessary to scan out a marriage or a business relationship which exists near to present time before one can continue with anything else in the case.

It does not much matter to the auditor whether or not the preclear is in valence—inside himself—when he scans through these chains of locks. Lock Scanning is a broad, sloppy technique.

The preclear can be out of valence; he can scan imaginary incidents; he can scan concepts; he can scan even his own conclusions about life. He can scan anything from which entheta can be freed.

In order to get rid of the entheta on an education there is nothing that compares with Lock Scanning. One can also do this trick with Lock Scanning: he can refresh an education. An individual can be given an examination in, let us say, history, eighth grade. He can then be lock-scanned through the actual study of history in the eighth grade and given another examination. It will ordinarily be found that he will receive a higher grade after he has been lock-scanned through that educational period. And yet the Lock Scanning may not have required more than fifteen or twenty minutes. In this wise, Lock Scanning is an excellent trick for those about to take an examination on academic subjects.

People can lock-scan themselves with considerable ease, unless they are too low on the Tone Scale. They merely start at the earliest incident they can remember of a certain kind which may be troubling them and come forward through all similar incidents to present time. They do this over and over until they become interested in their present time environment.

The time to stop lock-scanning of any particular chain of locks is when the preclear is extroverted, which is to say interested in his present time environment, or when the chain requires only an instant or two to scan. It can happen that a preclear is scanned through a chain of locks beyond the point when scanning this particular chain of locks should be stopped. The auditor will then find himself with a preclear who is running another set of locks. There is nothing particularly bad in this, but the auditor has lost control of the case for a moment. The auditor should, then, be alert as to how long it takes the preclear to scan each chain and as to how the preclear feels each time he finishes scanning the chain, and he should ask questions about these points.

Lock Scanning is a highly unrestimulative type of technique to the auditor. The preclear, unless he is running at vocal rate, is not uttering restimulative phrases, and he can go from early to late and pass through the most amazing array of incidents without the auditor being aware of what is going on. Therefore, the auditor does not become restimulated. It happens that an auditor running locks in chains on a preclear can, however, become somewhat bored. He should not, no matter how much he would like to relieve his tedium, interrupt the preclear in any way until the preclear has finished scanning the chain. Each time, the auditor should let the preclear sweep forward to present time. As in any other case, the auditor should always check the preclear to find out if he is in present time at the end of each scan, unless the preclear is scanning a period of time which does not include present time.

One can scan locks in terms of time, let us say from the fifth to the tenth year of the preclear's life, or from the twentieth to the twenty-fifth year, or from the thirtieth to the forty-first year. Or he can scan between specific dates. Or scanning can be done on one person on one subject. Or scanning can be done on one type of activity. Or scanning can be done on education or early training. Or scanning can be done on the immediate environment of the preclear.

Lock Scanning of auditing is a highly valuable procedure. The auditor, in every session, if his preclear can scan at all, should scan off all of the auditing. This is to say, send the preclear back to the moment when the session began and have him scan forward to present time. It does not, then, much matter how many engrams the preclear has restimulated or what has happened during the session; the preclear by scanning can destimulate the incidents which rise. The failure to reduce an engram was much more serious in the past than it is at this time. Lock Scanning makes it possible to run the session in which the engram was restimulated. Of course, the restimulation of an engram without reducing it is merely the creation of a new lock. Lock Scanning reduces this new lock.

The auditor should never be critical of how carelessly the preclear may be scanning. Lock Scanning is broad enough to include such proclivities.

Looking over the Tone Scale one discovers, first, that any 3.5, when he has had his engrams run out in their entirety, has to be lock-scanned through all activities of life in order to qualify as a Clear. This frees up all locks. Locks, of course, at this level of the Tone Scale are very easy to free, since they have few engrams underlying them. In the near Clear, they have no engrams underlying them, but locks can still exist on a case which has been cleared of engrams. Although these locks may work out in the next many months after the last engram is run, it is far easier to sit down to a systematic scanning of all the persons and circumstances of the preclear's past life.

The 3.0 can be lock-scanned with great profit and will scan through locks without hanging up in any of them. In this way, new series of engrams can be bared to view. The only reason engrams cannot be run is because too many locks exist on top of them, and Lock Scanning is the best method of getting off this entheta in order to make the engram itself available.

The 2.5 has to be lock-scanned in order to get engrams to show up clearly. After Lock Scanning has taken place, an engram can be expected to come into view with all of the necessary perceptics. Lock Scanning tunes up the 2.5 to a point where engrams can be cleanly run. In order to discover new engrams in the 2.5, new chains of locks should be scanned.

The 2.0 can be lock-scanned, but the auditor should work with chains of locks given by the file clerk. Every chain which is contacted by the auditor on the 2.0 should be reduced, just as one would reduce engrams that were contacted. No chain should be left in restimulation at this level but should be run completely. If the session is too short for this, scanning of the session will probably cause the restimulation to fade out.

From 2.0 on down, Lock Scanning begins to develop a brief liability, but not a lessened workability. The preclear is apt, after he scans a certain chain of locks a few times, to hang up in one of the locks or to hang up in some minor secondary. It is then necessary to run whatever incident the preclear finds himself hung up in as an engram in itself, although it may contain no physical pain.

The 1.5 will, as a common result of Lock Scanning, hang up in a lock. The auditor starts scanning locks and after a short time finds that the 1.5 is not moving on the track. He should always admonish the 1.5 to inform him when he stops on the track or when he appears to cease moving on the track. Otherwise, the 1.5 is likely to flounder around and wonder why he is not going forward to present time and not say anything about it, and so many minutes of auditing are wasted, until the auditor recognizes that something is wrong and does something about it. If the 1.5 hangs up in a lock and the auditor by running this lock as an engram cannot reduce it, then it is only necessary to start the 1.5 scanning another set of locks (gotten from the file clerk, of course). By scanning the new set, he drops out of the engram or lock in which he was stuck. This is the peculiar virtue of Lock Scanning. If one cannot reduce the engram or secondary or lock in which the preclear may hang up, it is only necessary to cause the preclear to scan a new chain of locks in order to release the preclear on the track. This is a mechanism which must be stressed, for it is very important. Whenever a preclear hangs up in a lock, and by running the lock just as though it were an engram the auditor finds that it will not immediately reduce, all the auditor need do is consult the file clerk to discover another chain of locks which the preclear can scan or to discover an earlier incident of the same type in which the preclear is locked up. Scanning the new set of incidents or contacting the earlier incident by Straight Memory will cause the preclear to become free on the track.

Below 1.5, a new mechanism is introduced into Lock Scanning. Actually, this is a combination mechanism. At 1.1, or for that matter from 2.0 down, Lock Scanning can be combined with Straight Memory. By Straight Memory, a certain type of incident which is found to be aberrative in the preclear may be contacted. When this type of incident is contacted, the auditor need not necessarily leave it at that, but may direct the preclear to go back to that incident which was discovered and scan through all similar incidents. Very shortly, earlier incidents of the same type will show up, and so an enormous number of such incidents can be taken off the case. Lock Scanning can actually be called a high-speed Straightwire rather than anything else. Straight Memory combined with Lock Scanning can isolate certain circuit commands or domination commands or "control yourself" commands which would remain hidden under ordinary lock-scanning procedures.

The 1.1 can be expected to hang up in some lock after the auditor has started him scanning. The auditor, then, scans locks on the 1.1 in the full expectation that he will shortly find the 1.1 not moving on the track. Indeed, that 1.1, unless a wide-open case, will commonly or chronically be stuck on the track, as will be also a 1.5. Lock Scanning brings into view, however, heavier locks. Entheta is converted to theta until the heavier lock will show up. The heavier lock, of course, was no less effective when hidden. Lock Scanning bares it to view. The auditor then runs this new incident in which the preclear has stuck in order to free him, or failing to free him, finds another chain which can be scanned in order to free him. The scanning of a new chain to free the preclear from a point on the track where he is stuck can be overcomplicated by the auditor. Actually, it is only necessary to direct the preclear's attention to a new subject or to ask his file clerk for a new subject. The preclear might get so thoroughly involved with the lock in which he sticks that it would not occur to him that he could scan any other subject at the moment. It is up to the auditor to realize this and to direct the preclear's attention to another type of incident. Scanning the new type of incident, the preclear may free up from the incident in which he was stuck but hang up in a new lock. The auditor tries to reduce this lock as though it were an engram and failing that he goes on to a third type of chain.

The 0.5 cannot be lock-scanned, with profit, since the 0.5 will inevitably hang up too thoroughly. But if the auditor does make the mistake of scanning a 0.5 through locks, he must remember that it is only necessary to scan a new type of lock in order to free the 0.5, or to use Straight Memory.

The 0.1 should never be scanned through any locks.

One of the ways of freeing an individual who is being lock-scanned out of an engram or lock in which he has suddenly hung up is to give him Straight Memory. Straight Memory acts as stilts by which he can be brought up again to present time.

The scanning of locks can be combined with the running of single locks and with Straight Memory, with great facility. An individual who is stuck somewhere on the time track can be given Straight Memory or new chains of locks to scan.

The scanning of pleasure moments should not be overlooked as a valid technique for raising the tone of a preclear. When a preclear is particularly low, at the beginning of a session, or at the end of one if the auditor has made some mistake, it is necessary to raise his tone. Scanning of pleasure moments will very often permit enough free theta to come into existence either to make new incidents available or to successfully end the session.

It should be admonished again that when one scans locks he should work as closely as possible with the file clerk, consulting the file clerk as to what chain of locks should be next scanned on the case and then following as nearly as possible the file clerk's directions. In the absence of file clerk directions the auditor should use his own judgment or talk the subject over with the preclear.

It will very often happen in the process of Lock Scanning that the preclear goes into a boil-off. It should be remembered that boil-offs are highly beneficial and should not be interrupted for any cause whatsoever. When the preclear comes out of the boil-off, the auditor should ask him for the phrase which put him into the boil-off and should ask the preclear to repeat that phrase again. The preclear, repeating this phrase out loud or to himself several times, will ordinarily then go back into the boil-off. Boil-offs should be exhausted completely. They are a condition of somnolence which is sometimes indistinguishable from sleep, and a preclear should not be disturbed while he is in one. The removal of boil-off from a case is the removal of accumulated anaten, and is highly beneficial. Some cases can do nothing but boil off.

The individual can lock-scan himself, if he keeps in mind the fact that when he hangs up in a lock somewhere out of present time he must nudge himself into scanning another type of lock rather than trying to fuddle through the place where he is stuck.

It will also happen that the preclear will run into grief charges as a result of scanning locks. It may be that he gets grief on a single phrase. He may not know from what incident this phrase comes. If he is fairly low on the Tone Scale, he may have no conception whatsoever of what he is crying about, but the release of grief in any event is beneficial. It may occur that the only way the auditor can get grief off a case is by scanning certain chains of locks and then getting grief off a single phrase.

An individual who has a chronically restimulated somatic which is giving him sinus trouble or a headache can be scanned out of it without any recognition of what was the source, in engramic terms, of the headache or other malcondition. In such an instance it is mainly beneficial to scan pleasure moments. This will almost always raise the preclear's tone.

The value of Lock Scanning, it may be repeated, is difficult to overestimate. The auditor will do a great deal of it on any case. Any case, except the 0.5 and the 0.1, will benefit from Lock Scanning. The auditor may make the serious mistake of believing that because the engram is the basic cause of aberration it is therefore the only thing or the main thing that he should contact. He should disabuse himself of this idea. With the high-speed technique of Lock Scanning he can bring a case up to the point where running engrams will permit the case to proceed to Clear. Without taking this charge off the case, he could run engrams for a thousand years and not bring his preclear up to Clear. The auditor should use Straight Memory and Lock Scanning and the running of secondaries until the case has enough theta to run engrams.

It is possible to run actual engrams on a low-toned preclear session after session without raising his tone. This is because the running of engrams on such a case lays in auditing locks. The theta which is freed from the engram is immediately re-enturbulated and the preclear's tone remains the same or sinks because of the enturbulation of more and more free theta in numerous auditing locks. Such a case should be lock-scanned.

The auditor should develop his technique of Lock Scanning and should be very patient in his use of it. He will find himself at times sitting for twenty or thirty minutes while the preclear scans one chain. The auditor should be content to sit there and let the preclear scan, until it becomes apparent to him that the preclear is not moving on the track or is in some difficulty. He should have a complete understanding with the preclear about what they are doing. The preclear should understand that the auditor, working with the preclear's file clerk, is the one who selects the chains of locks to be scanned. The preclear should understand that it is the auditor who starts him scanning and that the auditor is still in control of the case.

By Lock Scanning, the auditor will get the maximum amount of entheta on the case converted back to free theta, where it belongs.

C O L U M N   A H

SECONDARY ENGRAMS

P ROBABLY THE MAJORITY OF ENTHETA which accumulates in an individual becomes tied up in secondary engrams.

A secondary engram can be defined as a period of anguish brought about by a major loss or a threat of loss to the individual. The secondary engram depends for its strength and force upon physical pain engrams which underlie it. Without a physical pain engram it is apparently impossible for a secondary engram to be formed.

The type of entheta which becomes trapped in a secondary engram is evidently a heavy reverse of polarity of theta. Emotion becomes misemotion. Affinity, reality and communication components of theta, by the loss or threat of loss to the individual, convert and thereafter repel the affinity, reality and communication components which yet remain in a state of theta.

An engram is a moment of physical pain, such as an anesthetic operation, an accident, an illness or any condition producing unconsciousness. An engram can occur, however, and remain inactive. No engram is active until it is "keyed in," which is to say until a moment when the environment around the awake individual is itself similar to the dormant engram. At that moment the engram becomes active. It is keyed in and can thereafter be dramatized. It will affect, by virtue of its commands, the processes of thought of the individual, creating obsessions, compulsions, neuroses and psychoses below his conscious level. Or the physical pain component can create "psychosomatic illnesses," which are in Dianetics more accurately called the "chronic somatics" of engrams.

Physical pain engrams can exist in large numbers on a case without being keyed in and without being active. The key-in may be only a lock. The key-in and additional locks begin to give the engram more and more entheta, and it becomes more and more powerful in its effect upon the individual. It has to be, in short, "charged up" in order to affect the individual.

The heaviest and most abrupt charge which an engram can receive is a secondary engram. The physical pain in the physical pain engram makes it possible for large amounts of theta to be trapped when that theta is enturbulated by a present time shock such as the loss or threatened loss of survival factors in the person's life. If the physical pain engram were not there to entrap the temporarily enturbulated theta, the theta, apparently, would simply unenturbulate and the individual would return to a fully rational state. With the physical engram present, which has some approximation of the loss or threatened loss, when a severe shock of loss or threatened loss occurs, the turbulence of the individual is, apparently, to a large degree trapped and a heavy charge enters the physical pain engram and remains there until Dianetic processing removes it or until the theta and MEST of the individual are separated by death.*

A physical pain engram, once it has charged up with secondary engrams, becomes inaccessible to the analyzer to such an extent that the individual trying to address this engram or series of engrams cannot, with the free theta available to him, penetrate the core of the physical pain. Hallucinatory impressions of the engram may occur. The engram may be run almost as a dream sequence. The somatics

*The theta body has been discovered to contain amounts of entheta as secondary engrams, but the charges are not as heavy as those of the current life, according to observation. —LRH

are light or nonexistent. Content is markedly altered. The position of the engram on the time track may be seriously occluded. In short, the existence of secondary engrams above primary engrams makes it impossible for an individual to run physical pain off of his case. A few minor secondary engrams on a case may only cut off the sharpness of the perceptics, but the usual case has many heavy secondary engrams on it. The seriously occluded case is occluded because of the existence of secondary engrams.

The demarcation line between theta and entheta is 2.0 on the Tone Scale. The present time environment of the individual varies on the Tone Scale, just as the individual, from period to period in his life, may vary, although in the absence of processing the individual's course is a gradual decline. One could take any environment and judge its position on the Tone Scale. In other words, the individual can be located on the Tone Scale for his chronic position, or for a momentary position. A group can be located on the Tone Scale, for its chronic or temporary state. And the present time environment can be located on the Tone Scale.

Today one's environment might be happy. This environment would assist one's tone, pulling one slightly up the Tone Scale. Or when the environment is very happy it has the occasional result of making the individual's activities and conduct momentarily those of a Clear, even if he is ordinarily considerably aberrated. But where a Clear would have a resilience and would respond only partially to a present time environment, a thoroughly aberrated person is almost a slave to the environment, and the lower the individual is on the Tone Scale the more seriously he is affected by low tone environments. Thus the 1.1 might act like a 2.0 in a very happy and secure environment, but in an even slightly enturbulated environment the 1.1 might act momentarily like a 0.8.

Good news, sudden successes, the envisionment or attainment of new components of survival make for a pleasant and happy environment. This would be an environment above 2.0 on the Tone Scale, the tone of the environment rising in direct ratio to the potentiality of the environment for the survival of those in it.

When an idea, a datum, a circumstance, a person or the general environment is conducive to the survival of the person in question, it can be said to be on a Tone Scale level above 2.0.

Environmental circumstances which lie below 2.0 on the Tone Scale are entheta circumstances and are enturbulative to the individual. Ideas, news, associations, persons or the general environment in the band from anger down to pretended death restimulate the individual's existing entheta and enturbulate more of the free theta of the individual and so bring about a reduction of the individual on the Tone Scale. These are nonsurvival factors, factors which tend toward the death of the individual or the group, even though the tendency may not be in terms of actual death.

It should also be recognized in viewing this and in understanding secondary engrams that when one looks at the Tone Scale one is looking at both pitch and volume. In music, a note may be anywhere on the musical scale and yet not be loud. This would be a note of a certain pitch but small volume. A note can be of a certain pitch with a great deal of volume. Further, the note, by harmonics and overtones, may have quality.

It is much the same on the Tone Scale of human reaction and behavior. The position on the Tone Scale of a momentary circumstance or of a chronic state tells us only the "pitch" of the individual's or the group's or the environment's tone. Volume is the second factor which must be studied in considering the Tone Scale. An individual may be bored but not, as the saying is, "to a degree." He is bored only a minor amount. He may at another time be bored a major amount. In the lower tones, he may be afraid, but only slightly afraid. Or he may be so greatly afraid that the fear is terror. The amount or volume of enturbulence might be read in a third dimension, extending from the face of the chart out toward its peruser. There might be a little bit of grief or a great deal of grief, but the position on the Tone Scale would be the same.

There is also the matter of quality of enturbulence. The quality of the fear or the anger or the quality of the happiness is important.

But this would be a factor which would be different from pitch or volume on the Tone Scale.

The amount of free theta with which an individual is endowed is enormously important. The amount of free theta has a great deal to do with the persistence or reasoning force of the individual along any course. This would be the volume of a person. The quality of a person would be more a structural thing. To make this clearer, a person may have an enormous volume of endowed theta and yet not have the structure with which to be intelligent. Or he may have a quality index which is very high and yet not have sufficient endowment of theta to execute the plans which he can conceive. We have all known the individual who received A's in every course and yet who was never able to do anything with his education. And we have known the individual who received nothing in the way of grades and who indeed never seemed even to comprehend elementary subjects and yet who by power of personality forged ahead to a high position in life. A study of this matter gives a useful evaluation of human potentiality and behavior. More importantly, it gives some understanding of what happens to the individual in the process of becoming aberrated. Aberration, considered as pitch or tone, is theoretically independent of quality (structure, probably) and volume (theta endowment). The factors of quality and volume would account in part for the individual differences which may be found in aberrated persons at similar levels of the Tone Scale. (The analogy with music should not be overworked, of course, since a low tone in music may be delightful, but a low tone in aberration is not.)

Physical pain engrams are a major ARC break between theta and MEST. By our Dianetic theory, theta and MEST have a certain native affinity for each other, but when the collision or impact of one against the other is too great or too sudden, a reversal of polarity takes place, and this affinity is changed to a lower-level manifestation. Theta and MEST coming together at 4.0 would be in complete harmony with each other. A working organism would result wherein the chemicals and compounds in space and time, running on MEST energy, would be motivated and animated by the ideas and experience of theta energy, and a high level of survival would be postulated. Given a little physical pain, however, a slight drop on the Tone Scale occurs, since the theta and MEST have lost some affinity for each other, are not in such good communication with each other, and thus cannot attain such harmonious agreement, or reality, as to their purposes. It is a mission of MEST to survive or succumb. It is a mission of theta to survive or succumb. The purposes have parallels between theta and MEST. When theta and MEST are in union on a harmonious level, one could say that the ARC of theta forms a nearly perfect and resonant chord with MEST. When physical pain occurs a slight amount of dissonance results. This dissonance is insufficient to cause a separation of theta and MEST, until 2.0 on the Tone Scale is reached. After this, the dissonance is so great that theta is antagonistic to MEST but still operating. At 1.5, an active and violent discord exists to separate the theta from the MEST. Lower, the dissonance grows wider. By the time 0.5 is reached a near null of dissonance has been descended to, which makes the theta almost inactive with MEST. At 0.1, this null has become so wide that the two are not existing together at all. And at 0.0, death is reached for the organism.

There is the overall life of the organism, which could be said to be the theta body. Then there is somatic life, or the life of cells. The life of cells persists below organism death, but as the basic organism life and the MEST have mutually rejected each other, somatic life, unless assisted by other organisms, as in the experiments of Alexis Carrel,[1] dies away within the next few minutes or a year, thus producing complete organism death and leaving in its place the MEST compounds which have been

1. **Alexis Carrel:** (1873–1944) French biologist and surgeon known for his experiments on keeping organs and tissues alive while they were outside the body. In the early 1930s Carrel, along with American aviator Charles Lindbergh (1902–1974), created a device, known as a mechanical or artificial heart, that made it possible to support the life of an organ once it was taken out of a body.

organized by the theta and which are themselves a sort of evolution of MEST.

It is at 2.0 (and the Tone Scale is somewhat arbitrary, though based on observation and workable) that loss of life has set in. Separation of theta from MEST is necessary, in the absence of processing, for the chronically enturbulated individual or group, from 2.0 down. Momentary enturbulation because of environmental circumstances brings about the same intention. This intention, when manifested at anger, is not immediately observable. But anger is destruction and death. From there on down, loss becomes more and more likely.

There is a distinct parallel on the Tone Scale between the position of the individual, the condition of the theta and the way MEST is handled by theta. At 4.0, theta is handling MEST with great adequacy. At 3.5, there is a little less certainty on theta's part in handling MEST. At 3.0, theta has, through learning it can lose MEST, become conservative in its handling of MEST. At 2.5, theta is handling MEST in a relatively lackadaisical fashion, since it is not well convinced that it can continue to do so. At 2.0, theta is unable to handle MEST adequately enough and so begins to reject MEST and to attempt to eject itself from MEST. At 1.5, theta is determined to reject MEST and to eject itself from MEST. But its determination is still directed at all the MEST surrounding it, not so much at the organism in which it is contained. It is attempting at this level to eject the organism from the environment by destroying the environment. At 1.1, the stratum of fear has been entered. The theta in the organism has to be very careful how it destroys the area around it for the organism, but the ejection of itself from the organism and the rejection of the environment is nonetheless certain. Here the organism is still functioning but is under threat of loss. At 0.5, the organism has accepted the fact that the theta and MEST will separate and that the environment contains no survival factors but only nonsurvival factors. At 0.1, death has been accepted by the organism as a condition of a death environment.

A study of this demonstrates an evident third factor in the theta–MEST theory. The organism itself has an intention of survival, possibly, even when the theta and MEST composing the organism have determined to separate. Much theory can be postulated concerning this. That which is interesting to us in processing is that below 2.0 the theta intention is toward separation from MEST, either the separation of the organism from MEST by the destruction of the environment, or the destruction of the organism itself. Theta has many choices in the way this can be accomplished.

Survival is often obtained by an organism through the agency of another organism. As the mistletoe lives upon the life of an oak, so may an individual exist by virtue of a powerful ally. Any child has, in his parents, allies which assist his survival. The child, if these parents materially assist the survival of the child and yet deny the child his self-determinism, begins to live almost as though he were the parents. The theta of the child becomes invested, one might say, in the theta of the parents.

It might be said that the theta of an individual, when it is suppressed from the control of its own organism, can commingle with the theta of other organisms. This is an unexplored observation. But this much is certain, that the theta of any individual may identify itself with the theta of the individuals around to such a degree that the death, or even the illness, of the surrounding individuals, one or more, may cause the same reduction on the Tone Scale of the dependent individual. This could be worked out on the basis of restimulation in the environment, but it seems to have deeper significance than that. The auditor will often find his preclear so thoroughly associated with another individual who is dead that his preclear upon going into a session may cross his hands upon his chest as though he were a corpse. Investigation of the situation demonstrates that this preclear has lost a powerful ally, such as his mother, grandmother, father, grandfather or guardian, and that the preclear is stopped on the time track at the moment of death of this ally. This preclear's theta has become so thoroughly associated with the theta of another that when the other person died, the preclear to all intents and purposes died himself but continued to live as an organism, though thoroughly interrupted as an identity.

This confusion of identities between one person and another is severely aberrative. By Straight Memory technique an auditor can begin to separate identities out of his preclear, discovering in the preclear habits* and patterns of thought and action and finding who in the past had these patterns of thought and action. The preclear may identify the person to whom these habits and actions really belonged and thus to that degree regains his own personal identity.

Personal identity is very important. It is a parallel to self-determinism. When the individual's identity has been absorbed to a great degree in the personality of another person, another way of saying the commingling of theta, a loss of personality ensues with a consequent reduction of analytical dynamic and ability to reason. It is very important for the auditor to cause this separation.

The secondary engram may consist of any misemotion from 2.0 down the scale. First, there is antagonism because of a threat of loss of survival components to the individual. Then there is anger toward the sources that threaten loss. Then there is fear that loss will occur, either loss of one's own life or loss of one's allies. Then there is the level of the accomplished fact of loss, whether of position, of persons or of things. This is the level of grief. Next, there is the level where loss is not only accomplished but the individual thinks because of this loss that he himself and all around him is lost. This is apathy. Finally, the loss is so thoroughly accepted that the environment and everything in it are renounced and life itself is renounced as lost. This is pretended death, only a decimal above actual death.

Here we have the dwindling spiral. All locks actually lie below 2.0 on the Tone Scale if they are themselves aberrative. These are

----

*HABIT: *a stimulus-response mechanism similar to the training pattern but set up by the reactive mind out of the content of engrams. It cannot be changed at will by the analytical mind.* —LRH

383

the minor threats to survival, the introduction of minor components into the life of the individual which threaten his existence. There are many of these. They are of small volume, such as momentary incidents of fear and losses of small possessions. Other persons' losses may form locks, where engrams exist earlier in the case which contain the physical pain which makes possible the entrapment of the entheta.

The secondary engram is a large volume affair. In the secondary engram one has, at 2.0, antagonisms felt because of major losses which are threatened. At 1.5, one has the anger because of a threatened major loss. At 1.1, one has the fear that a major loss will occur. At 0.5, one has the grief because a major loss has occurred, and an apathy resulting because of the apparent inability to recover what has been lost. At 0.1, we have such a magnitude of losses that life is unsupportable and the entire environment seems to the individual to have collapsed and become dead itself.

The secondary engram can then consist of a major antagonism, a major anger, a major fear amounting to terror, a major grief or a major apathy or a major concept of nothing but death. Here we have a gradient scale of major threats of losses, losses and results of losses.

A child has many momentary or fleeting moments of fear or grief because of lack of data. Very little of this enturbulence is of lasting consequence, which is to say that it does not become trapped because the child has few engrams in restimulation, ordinarily. However, in the processing of children, one can run off many fear and grief incidents, since there is some residual lag in the enturbulence. The very major secondaries in an adult are normally quite few, but these consist of such violent impacts from the environment in terms of threats of loss or loss that, engrams being already restimulated, great quantities of theta are enturbulated and encysted in the form of secondary engrams.

The running of a secondary and its complete exhaustion from the case is of enormous importance. There are those who, knowing that every secondary engram exists only by virtue of the physical pain engram which underlies it and who themselves are afraid of grief, hopefully attempt to audit individuals by avoiding secondary engrams and attempting to run the physical pain engrams instead. The physical pain engrams, bluntly, will not exhaust unless the grief is run first.

The secondary engram is reduced by the physiological discharge of tears or, possibly, some other bodily fluids. Grief seems to be reducible only in terms of tears. Fear or terror, inelegantly, seems to be reducible in terms of urine, sweat and other bodily excretion. Anger seems to be reducible by certain physical excretion. Apathy is reducible simply by running the feeling of apathy, and this is accomplished by certain physiological symptoms.*

A secondary engram is run exactly as one would run an engram. One starts at the earliest moment of the engram that one can discover and proceeds, picking up all perceptics, to the end of the engram. One then goes back to the beginning and

---

It is worthy of notice that another column could have been added to this chart, which already contains so many columns. This would be the column of body odor. The body is normally sweet-smelling down to 2.0 but begins to exude chronically certain unpleasant effluvia from 2.0 down. Individuals from 2.0 down commonly have bad breath. Their feet may have a considerable odor. The musk glands are very active. The sweat has a peculiar smell. Sexual organs emit a repelling odor. And various bodily exhaust functions are not under very good control. The person may have to urinate or defecate under slight stresses or may weep easily for no apparent cause. This column has not been added to this chart because it has not been thoroughly explored but is only known in a general way. Any slightly or greatly repulsive physical odor from an individual does, however, indicate a Tone Scale position below 2.0. It is amusing to note that in the Orient wives are commonly selected by the sweetness of their perspiration. This is apparently a very reliable test for position on the Tone Scale. People who have bad breath as they are processed lose it when they are above 2.0 on the Tone Scale. People who are even temporarily suppressed below 2.0 commonly have bad breath. —LRH

reexperiences it again. The auditor continues to have the preclear reexperience the incident until the preclear, with regard to this secondary engram, is at a high position on the Tone Scale. If the secondary engram is one of anger, the preclear will readily come up through boredom and commonly to false four. If it is fear, the preclear will come up through anger, boredom and again to false four. If the secondary engram begins with grief, it will proceed, commonly, through grief, up through fear, up through anger, up through boredom and to false four. If the secondary is an apathy secondary, it will proceed first through apathy, which is very hard going, then through grief, then through fear, then through anger, then through boredom and to false four. A pretended death engram is a much deeper apathy and much more difficult to run. Much theta must be accumulated from other portions of the case before a pretended death engram can be run.

The auditor should never make the error of thinking that the concept is the engram. He should do his best to coax the preclear into every single perceptic, as a secondary or any other engram is run off. However, at the beginning of running a secondary only the vaguest concept of it or only some small phrase out of it may be available. The auditor by causing the preclear to repeat this many times may be able to get more of the engram and so work it out until it lies there in its entirety and can be reexperienced, at which time the preclear will come up the Tone Scale.

Getting any misemotion off a case is beneficial to the case. It may be possible only to work out a secondary engram partly. But the auditor should never make the mistake of permitting a preclear to leave a secondary engram before it is exhausted of all possible misemotion. Every secondary should be brought as high up the Tone Scale as possible. The auditor, further, should not make the mistake of abandoning the engram at the point of antagonism. Occasionally the preclear, on recounting this experience all the way through with all possible perceptics, will get to the point where he is flippant about the circumstance. This flippancy is nearly always rendered in phrases which still remain in the secondary or the engram. The auditor may find a bit of resistance from the preclear at the antagonism level, but he will do well to continue running the engram. It will then come up to boredom. The preclear has to be persuaded to go through it again. He will ordinarily state that he is bored with it. This is not good enough. Further recounting is necessary to bring it up to the desirable tone level.

It must be remembered, as it will not be remarked again, that misemotion is part of every physical pain engram. The misemotion will rise up the scale out of an engram just as it will rise up the scale out of a secondary.

Do not neglect the secondary engram's importance in the case. For example, the newly made widow of a very successful man one week after his burial had become physically ill, wore weeds, looked some ten years older, and could not face any portion of existence. An auditor worked with her for nine hours and ran out her husband's death completely. At the end of this time she looked younger than she had looked for some years, was able to dress and to meet life with considerable aplomb. The change was so remarkable after this nine hours of processing that one would not have been able to recognize her after processing as the same woman who had entered the session under the duress of this secondary.

A Minnesota Multiphasic test given to some individuals before and after the running only of secondary engrams showed these individuals, before the secondaries were run and discharged, to lie above the severely aberrated line, and after the secondaries had been run and discharged, to be well within the normal range. There is nothing more spectacular in the rise of a case on the Tone Scale than that which takes place after the discharging of one or more secondary engrams. This is particularly true of grief engrams, but others also produce beneficial effects. The reason for this seems to be that the physical pain engram makes possible secondary engrams and locks, but the secondaries entrap the majority of the theta on the case and keep it as entheta in an encysted condition.

The auditor should pay very particular attention to his own attitude when he is attempting to run a secondary engram on the preclear. The present social order has a considerable compunction against crying or showing fear and a general inhibition of displays of misemotion and emotion. When these inhibitions lie in the form of circuits, as will be covered later, it is difficult to get the secondary engram to exhaust. However, if the auditor is demonstrating a high level of ARC, if he seems sympathetic, his work will be made much easier. The preclear cannot run secondary engrams in the presence of an auditor for whom he has antagonisms. The auditor, thus, must be compatible with the preclear and must have been cleared with the preclear as a group of two, if he expects to run any secondary engrams on this preclear.

The file clerk and somatic strip, as will be covered in the running of engrams, are not particularly reliable in the presence of secondary engrams. Here we have enormous quantities of entheta, and so theta entities such as the somatic strip and file clerk have difficulty approaching such areas. However, the recovery and conversion of considerable entheta from locks will bring the case up the Tone Scale to a point where the analytical mind will have enough free theta to attack the secondaries.

The primary reason why an individual is severely aberrated is, of course, secondary engrams. If the individual is well down the Tone Scale, one can assume as a matter of course that he has a large number of heavy secondary engrams, whether the individual is able to run these secondaries or not, for here we have the main deposits of entheta on a case.

Certain auditors, because of their sympathy and their ability to develop a high ARC with the preclear, become experts in the running of secondary engrams. Anyone to whom people will tell their troubles will be able to run secondary engrams. The process of running a secondary engram does not differ from running a physical pain engram. This is very important. The secondary engram is called secondary because it depends upon an earlier physical pain engram to exist, being itself occasioned by a conscious moment of loss. It is called an engram in order to focus the attention of the auditor on the fact that it must be run as an engram and that all perceptics possible must be exhausted from it. It occasionally will occur that after lock-scanning a preclear over a certain chain of locks, the auditor will suddenly find that the preclear is in a secondary engram. Perhaps some phrase will suggest itself, and the individual will cry or show fear. The auditor should cause this phrase to be repeated over and over. Perhaps neither the auditor nor the preclear knows the source of this phrase, but the exhaustion of it by itself may, in a heavily occluded case, bring about a considerable rise, if momentary, on the Tone Scale. It may occur that after lock-scanning a whole secondary will lie ready to be run. The auditor should then run it.

The existence of circuits on a case, which is to say the existence of suppressors to secondary engrams or to any other entheta, should not be exaggerated in importance. Scanning of locks and Straight Memory can either locate the locks of the circuit, or the circuit to some extent may be ignored. The circuit is a favorite alibi of the auditor. Nearly everyone who is low on the Tone Scale has been suppressed by the dominations or nullifications of persons or the environment. It must be remembered that the circuit derives from the engram and is charged up by entheta. The entheta can be to some degree converted into theta, thus nullifying the circuit without discovering the engram in which this particular circuit is contained.

Secondary engrams, or at least phrases from them, can be discharged from any case, no matter how occluded. It is simply a matter of recovering enough free theta so that the individual has a sufficient quantity of free theta to make the exhaustion of secondaries possible. It should be remembered that when a case is overburdened with entheta, light and catfooted methods can still bring to the preclear enough theta so that the entheta can be attacked. A secondary engram, being a very heavy deposit of entheta, will repel theta.

The auditor will occasionally discover a preclear who will run imaginary secondaries, with enormous effect in terms of terror, grief or apathy. He is dealing here with circuits (which will be covered later) which will furnish physical manifestations but which will not exhaust engrams. An individual can have a portion of the analyzer segmented off by charge and under the command of an engram statement to the effect that he must run grief. As a result the individual will manufacture grief incidents. An engramic command such as, "You are always afraid and you imagine things to be afraid of," or any of a multitude of approximations, may cause the individual to manufacture and run fear incidents. The reality of such incidents is very low, but the individual will run them and manifest fear. Unfortunately, these incidents do not produce any alleviation of aberration in the case. This is a manifestation of dub-in. It is very easily distinguished from real incidents, since the preclear hardly ever is able to repeat the same incident in the same way a second time, and since the preclear is anxious to sell the auditor on the idea that the incident is very real, although the auditor has made no suggestion that it might be unreal. The auditor uses as his yardstick the probability of the incident, but he is not particularly worried about one incident. A circuit has the habit of manufacturing the same type of incident over and over and over again but locating it at various points on the time track. The preclear, if he is very low on the Tone Scale, may himself be unaware of the reality of this incident. But the auditor, knowing the preclear to be low on the Tone Scale, suspects the possibility of dub-in when the preclear runs five or ten incidents in which he is tied to a railroad track by his mother and is rescued at the last moment by his aunt. Here is delusion rampant. The preclear will manifest considerable relief after running the incident, but here is a circuit at work, and no matter how many times this incident is run, the condition of the preclear will not be bettered. The auditor, by giving credence to this incident and by continuing to run it, is actually validating the incident and strengthening the circuit. Such incidents are usually bizarre and sensational. Very often, however, the auditor actually has on his hands incidents which are quite true and are bizarre and sensational, since the things done to human beings in this twentieth century are not always tame and routine. The test of any secondary is whether or not it runs the individual up the Tone Scale. When the auditor discovers that he is running fear or apathy charges on the account of some circuit, he should immediately be aware of the fact that he is trying to address much too heavy a form of entheta. He should not be running secondaries but should be running locks. A preclear who will run such dub-in misemotion is very, very low on the Tone Scale. An estimate of this preclear on the chart would have told the auditor in the first place that the preclear was low on the scale. The auditor should, thus, be alert for dub-in. Dub-in misemotion is best handled not by running thirty consecutive incidents in which the preclear is placed in the washing machine by his father, or hoisted up a flagpole by his elder brother, but by addressing the locks in the case, the nearer present time, the better. Very shortly the auditor will discover that the environment of this preclear is normally very restimulative and that individuals exist in the environment of this preclear who habitually lay in heavy locks. Further, the auditor will discover in Lock Scanning that this preclear will commonly hang up in locks after the chain has been scanned and that the locks themselves have to be run as incidents. Such a preclear should not be subjected to the mishandling of being run through heavy secondary engrams. Of course, in a wide-open case, on which few occlusions exist, actual secondaries might be run fairly early in the case, with an enormous rebound up the Tone Scale. It is in the occluded case that the auditor should expect to find circuits which produce misemotion at will.

The auditor who is handling a preclear above 1.5 should not much worry about dubbed-in misemotion.

On the subject of secondary engrams, the auditor, regardless of his own personal feelings about fear, grief or apathy, should keep firmly in mind the relief which is obtainable for the preclear and the rise which is possible on the Tone Scale by running secondary engrams. It is a theoretical truth that a case would become a Release if the auditor could run off of the case only the secondary engrams in their entirety. This is impossible in practice, since after a secondary has been run the auditor quite commonly finds that he is running a physical pain engram which underlies it. The auditor should not be surprised when he is running a secondary engram to find, after the exhaustion of a few tears, physical pain turning on as a consequence. Clears are produced by running all the physical pain engrams, secondaries and locks off a case. But engrams quite ordinarily cannot be contacted until locks have been scanned and secondaries have been run off of a case.

It is an adroit auditor who can elicit from some "hard-boiled and emotionless" denizen of our culture the tears or fear necessary to resolve his case. But the scanning of lock chains or the running of available physical pain engrams off of a case will place in the auditor's hands, willy-nilly, discharge of secondary engrams. The auditor can convert the entheta of locks to theta to such a degree that secondary engrams will begin to discharge almost automatically. At such time as this happens the auditor must be careful to minimize his own conversation or comment, to minimize his auditing, simply sympathetically persuading the preclear to run the incident again, and then again, and then again, until it is exhausted. The auditor, by attacking secondary engrams as though they were game on which the state pays a bounty, such as jackals or crows, and using an approach too exhilarated or enthusiastic toward the preclear's secondaries, can actually cut off the discharge of misemotion.

Some experiments have been carried out on the use of sad music or other dolorous perceptics in the environ of the preclear to encourage the discharge of secondary engrams. Much work can be done on this. The work which has been done demonstrates, however, that individuals who are chronically very low on the Tone Scale respond to sad and mournful perceptics by simply running dub-in incidents, which do them no good, and that individuals above this level can commonly discharge secondaries whenever the proper amount of theta has been recovered for the case. This does not discount the possible use of aesthetic perceptics in the encouragement of secondaries.

In inventorying a preclear one should be careful to establish all the major losses and major threats of loss that have happened to the preclear in his lifetime. On each one of the losses or threats of loss, either of position or possessions or people, by departure or death, one will find an encystment of entheta. Where the child has been raised by nurses in the vicinity of relatively antagonistic parents, one may expect to find a secondary engram every time a nurse is discharged. In the "coffin case," who lies with arms folded, never assuming the fetal position when running prenatal engrams but always lying as though laid out for burial, one will certainly find the death of a major ally somewhere back on the track. Where the entheta surrounding such an incident is strong enough to paralyze the individual at this point of his life, the secondary engram responsible for the coffin case is ordinarily not contactable early in the case. The auditor should merely continue, alert to the fact that sooner or later he is going to encounter a very heavy charge on the death of an ally. In such a case, the amount of entheta in relation to the existing theta on the case is very heavy. Lock Scanning, Straight Memory, and the running of locks, and even merely perception of present time may be the only processing which can be delivered to the case in its early stages. Sooner or later some secondaries will be discharged. No physical pain engram should ever be run on such a case. Imaginary incidents are peculiarly useful to the processing of such a case, as limited by the chart.

The best skill an auditor can develop is the running of secondaries. Their discharge produces the most effective rise up the Tone Scale.

🪶

BOOK TWO
CHAPTER THIRTEEN

COLUMN A I
ENGRAMS

THE BASIC CAUSE OF ALL HUMAN aberration is apparently the engram. There may be other causes more fundamental than the engram, but certainly to date they have not been discovered. Psychotherapy found out about locks, but did not know they were locks, and did not know to what the lock owed its power. But psychotherapists did know that when an individual was able to remember certain mentally painful incidents in his life, he became to some minute degree better.

Sigmund Freud discovered the lightest type of entheta, and although he placed his probes no deeper, an entrance was made into the field of human behavior. The secondary was discovered, but not identified in any way. By sheer observation of numberless cases it was found that once in a while, when a patient could be made to cry, the patient got better. But the therapist did not know what the patient was crying about and neither did the patient, but the strange title of "release of affect" was assigned to this crying and much extraneous technology was developed around it. Psychodrama and other techniques were developed in order to make the individual "release affect." This was the second slight incursion into the field of human thought. If the results were not all that could be desired it was because they overlooked the important, Dianetic fact that secondaries were restimulated more often than they were relieved. Secondaries have to be run as engrams, with the preclear returned on the time track.

The leap which was made between psychotherapy and Dianetics did not gather force in psychotherapy but in an independent study of epistemology and thought as an energy. However, the basic teachings of Sigmund Freud, as relayed to me in the twenties by Commander Thompson, Medical Corps, US Navy, who had studied with Sigmund Freud, considerably enhanced my desire for reexamination of thought in human behavior.

The existence of the engram was predicted, by derived computation, from other observations of thought. Investigation showed this existence to be actual. Anyone can discover an engram with great ease once he knows that it exists. Take an individual, tell him to close his eyes and *go back* to the last time he received some minor injury (do not ask for a major injury) and request that he reexperience the moment of injury. Cause him to recount and reexperience this moment of minor injury several times. If he cannot do so, he is fairly low on the Tone Scale and his somatics are shut off. Most normal people can reexperience these moments of injury. In causing an individual to do this, the experimenter will find that the injury is again felt and that the sights, sounds, smells and other perceptics at the moment the injury was received again recur to the experimental subject. Another phenomenon will be discovered by the alert investigator. It will be found that the individual, on the first return to and recounting of this moment of minor injury, will conceive it to be shorter than it actually was. On recounting, he will discover during the instant of impact of the injury new perceptics showing up, things he did not notice at the time he was injured. Here is a moment when the analytical mind, even though the injury was slight, went out of circuit, and here is a moment of "unconsciousness" wherein the reactive mind was recording all the perceptics which were available in the environment. As these hidden perceptics are recovered, the additional perceptic of physical injury, which is called in Dianetics a somatic, will reduce in force and, unless the experimental subject is extremely aberrated, he will finally no longer be able to feel it, but all other perceptics which were recorded during that moment of physical pain and "unconsciousness" will be restored to the analytical mind as standard memory data.

In effect, this is a Dianetic "assist." The auditor may take an individual who has been injured and run the injury as an engram even though it contains extensive unconsciousness. The last engram on the case has had relatively little chance to become charged up by locks and secondaries, and so is available for auditing regardless of the preexisting engrams on the case. The auditor can walk into a maternity ward and take over the case of some young mother who through an arduous birth has developed a postpartum psychosis[1] and can audit out the birth in its entirety. Unless this young mother was extremely low on the Tone Scale in the first place, so that she cannot reexperience somatics, the discharge of the actual delivery, perceptic by perceptic, including the "unconsciousness" induced by anesthesia, everything the surgeon (and let it be hoped that surgeons of tomorrow's America learn to keep their mouths shut) said to the nurse and remarked in general. In the analytical mind's interpretation of the remarks made during this delivery the source of the postpartum psychosis will be discovered. Any late or recent injury can be run in such a fashion. The individual who is receiving this auditing will, according to observation, recover much more rapidly from the illness or accident, the healing will be cleaner, the incidence of infection will be less, and the seriousness of the injury and the shock contained in it will be greatly reduced by the reduction of the moment of injury itself. It is hoped that sooner or later an auditor will stand at the emergency entrance of some hospital simply to audit all accident victims who come in, and that the statistics of infection rate and mortality rate of this hospital's patients will be compared with those of other hospitals. Evidence indicates that the mortality rate will be much lower on those who

---

1. **postpartum psychosis:** any psychosis occurring in a mother after childbirth. *Postpartum* means after childbirth.

have had the last injury audited out, that the incidence of infection will be less, and that the time of recovery of the patient will be greatly shortened by this Dianetic Assist.

The making of this experiment, on a slight scale, regardless of the Dianetic Assist, should demonstrate to the experimenter that physical pain at once inhibits consciousness, and that in the presence of physical pain all the perceptics of the environ, sight, smell, hearing, tactile, etc., are recorded elsewhere than in the analytical mind, but that the running of the incident removes from the case the mental loginess caused by the unconsciousness itself, that all aberrative effects of remarks made during the incident are removed, and that the physical pain is no longer stored, being a highly perishable quantity.

This is the anatomy of an engram. It contains physical pain. It contains a greater or lesser shutdown of the analytical mind (conscious mind). It contains all the perceptics of the environment in which the physical pain was received. It contains the physiological condition of the body, including endocrine balance at the time. It includes the age of the individual. It includes the misemotion or emotion contained in the incident, as manifested by persons around the injured person. It contains unconsciousness, in the form of anaten (analytical attenuation). And it contains the interruption of the computations the person was making at the time, which is the interruption of the theta creative cycle and is slightly aberrative. And it contains, additionally, all the locks and secondaries which, by contagion during the restimulation of the engram, it caused the person to receive while analytically awake, or conscious, at later times. These are the things which an engram contains. And these are the things which exhaust from an engram which is thoroughly erased.

When the engram is approximated in the environment, during a time when the individual, by reason of weariness or illness or stress of other kinds, is less analytically aware, various manifestations may occur by reason of the above-mentioned contents of the engram.

The individual who is under the stress of a restimulated engram will attempt to dramatize the engram. That is to say, he will say the things contained in the engram, and he will do the things dictated by the engram, or he will make the analytical computations demanded by the engram, and he will, generally, try to comply with the dictates of this moment of physical pain. If his environment makes it impossible for him to carry out this dramatization as dictated by the charged-up engram, then he is subjected to further charge by reason of not being able to do what the entheta of the engram commands him to do. An individual who has had his dramatizations broken time after time gradually descends down the Tone Scale. Engrams are based on the nonsurvival circumstance of theta and MEST colliding too sharply together, with the attendant reversal of polarity. All engrams, even those which are highly complimentary to the ability of the individual (such as hypnotic suggestions, which are a light form of engram and depend on early physical pain engrams), are nonsurvival. There is no such thing as an engram which assists an individual in his business of living. The engram merely uses some natural ability of the individual and may feverishly but inefficiently reenforce it. This would be a manic engram. Engrams dictate unalterable courses of action, without any regard to reason. Such a circumstance is, to a greater or lesser degree in every case, nonsurvival, since the survival of the individual depends upon his ability to adjust his action to the environment or to adjust the environment to him according to the circumstances. The engram is as stet as a phonograph record.[2] It dictates that a person do certain things in the presence of certain perceptions. In an unthinking organism, such as the lower forms of life, the engram does provide a certain method of thinking and acting, but in man, who depends upon reason as his chief weapon, the engram is nonsurvival in the extreme. The accumulation of engrams and their secondaries and locks brings the individual

---

2. **stet as a phonograph record:** a coined phrase meaning fixed or permanent. The word *stet* is a printer's term, meaning "let it stand": used to show that something, such as a word or grammatical symbol, at one time deleted or marked for omission is to remain in a manuscript or the like.

eventually to the point of death. Although his theta may, by continual enturbulation with MEST, be highly informed at the period of death with regard to MEST and may, according to some observations, be able in the next generation to accomplish a much better course of survival, in the existing generation the entheta never frees itself except by Dianetic processing. Yet, the auditor will continually discover preclears low on the Tone Scale who, by education or by the content of the engrams themselves, will seek to hold on to the engrams in the belief that they are an aid in the business of living. The auditor should thoroughly ignore this situation. In a very short time he will by his own experience see very clearly that the relief of engrams vastly increases the preclear's ability to meet life and to advance in the business of living. There are cases which contain engrams such as attempted abortions and which seek to retain the engram because it says, "If I lose it I'll die!" Many engrams contain phrases which seem to make the engram valuable. The engram is never valuable. Here is nonsurvival in the most basically known package.

The engram is the basic source of human aberration. There are usually hundreds, or even two or three thousand, engrams in the lifetime of any individual. Each and every one of these may have its own locks. The whole language of the individual may be contained basically in his engrams. Compulsive and obsessive phrases, circuit phrases which set up computive sections in the analyzer, "psychosomatic illnesses" (which are now known as chronic somatics) and aberrative forms of thought, to say nothing of reduced physical state and disabilities, as represented on the Tone Scale chart, result basically from engrams.

It should be understood by the auditor, however, that although the basic source of human aberration is the engram, according to accumulated evidences, he should not therefore consider that the only thing he should touch in a case is an engram. Locks and secondaries, in low-tone cases, must be addressed long before he touches engrams. The moment of physical pain and unconsciousness is basic, but it is not the principal point of address in very aberrated cases.

Cases fairly well up the Tone Scale, however, have engrams available for running, and when these engrams are run, remarkable improvements in the habits, welfare, behavior and physical health of the individual ensue.

Before the auditor runs engrams off a case, there are certain definite things he should know. He need not be nearly as skilled to run locks as he need be to run engrams. A very inexperienced auditor can successfully scan locks or even run minor secondaries, but an auditor should definitely know his tools and have confidence in them before he attacks engrams. In the first place, it is possible to enter a deceptively open but really heavily charged case and attempt to run engrams, when the preclear is completely unable to perceive enough of the perceptics in the engram to bring about a reduction. Thus, the auditor leaves an engram in restimulation and does not much assist the preclear but on the contrary may turn some of the preclear's theta back into entheta by causing the engram to have a new lock by reason of auditing. While all auditing can be scanned off and this theta can be recovered, it does not improve the case.

Further, engrams in the hands of an inexperienced auditor are sometimes improperly evaluated, which is to say the auditor may attack one which is very late in life or very late on a chain of engrams and work and worry on the thing until it merely goes into recession. Two or three days later this engram will reappear. This is because it has not been really reduced or erased, because the auditor did not know enough to go earlier in the case in order to find the basic engram on the chain. Thus certain cautions must be observed in running engrams, but they can be run successfully if these cautions are observed.

To run engrams, the auditor must be aware of and have confidence in the tools of his trade. These consist of the somatic strip, the file clerk, the time track and the perceptics. The file clerk is an extremely useful mechanism, not only for the running of engrams, but for the scanning of locks, the discovery of locks, and for obtaining data from the standard memory banks which would otherwise be occluded. The file clerk is a response mechanism which is instantaneous. One could postulate that the file clerk is a group of attention units with ready access to the reactive mind and to the standard memory banks and which in common mental operation forwards data through to "I" as memory. However, the charge on a case—the amount of entheta—may be so very heavy that the file clerk is unable to force through the data desired by "I" and so "I," working all alone with the file clerk, sometimes finds it difficult to receive answers to his questions.

The auditor adds, with his demands and signals, what might be considered the additional power necessary to bring the file clerk answers through to "I." This process is extremely simple. The auditor asks questions, normally, which can be answered in terms of yes or no or numbers or dates. Then, at a sharp snap of the auditor's fingers, a sudden thought, a yes or a no, occurs to the preclear, who tells the auditor what response he has received.

For example, the auditor may desire to know the place where the preclear is stuck on the time track, or whether or not the preclear is in present time. The auditor says, "Give me the first number that flashes into your mind. How old are you?" *(snap!)* An age flashes and the preclear tells the auditor. It may be that the preclear has developed a circuit which gives his chronological age in answer to the question, "How old are you?" A double-check for the auditor, then, is to ask the question, "What is your age?" *(snap!)* He may or may not get the same answer as before, since the circuit may not be educated to the second question. Another method of establishing where the preclear is on the time track is to ask for the year, the month and date. In addition to the location of the preclear on the time track or discovering the point in the preclear's life where a certain incident occurred, the flash answer mechanism will tell the auditor at the end of the session whether or not the preclear is in present time. The preclear should always be brought to present time, if possible, either by simply being told to "Come to present time," or by being scanned up to present time through pleasure moments.

The auditor works *with* the file clerk. The auditor does not order the file clerk around. The auditor consults the file clerk. The file clerk will tell the auditor the name of the chain of locks which is to be scanned. The file clerk, questioned by flash answers, will tell the auditor whether or not a chain can be scanned. The file clerk will, questioned by flash answers, identify types of incidents which are interrupting the case. In short, the file clerk is a consultant who answers with specific data any question asked with the flash answer mechanism. It is interesting that material completely unknown to the analyzer of the preclear can be discovered by questioning the file clerk.

The somatic strip is so called because it seems to be a physical indicator mechanism which has to do with time. The auditor orders the somatic strip. There is this difference between the file clerk and the somatic strip: he works with the file clerk but commands the somatic strip. On command, the somatic strip will go to any point of the preclear's life, unless the entheta on the case is so heavy that the somatic strip is frozen in one place. This might be called, as well, the concentration of attention of "I." The somatic strip goes to the point of return, but it is not the same as completely returning, since the preclear's "I" can stay in present time and the somatic strip can be sent back to earlier periods of his life. This is a very useful mechanism. The somatic strip can be sent back to the beginning of an engram and will go there. The somatic strip will advance through an engram in terms of minutes counted off by the auditor, so that the auditor can say that the somatic strip will go to the beginning of the engram, then to the point five minutes after the engram began, and so forth. In such a way, observing the behavior of the preclear (who may be oblivious of what is taking place except by observing his own physical symptoms change), the auditor can send the preclear through an operation minute by minute, or in larger increments, and the auditor can tell with certainty exactly how long that operation required.

The somatic strip can be sent to a certain date, hour and minute in the preclear's life, and will go there. "I" in the preclear does not necessarily follow the somatic strip. Unless a case is very heavy with entheta, the somatic strip, for instance, can be sent by the auditor's command back to the moment when the preclear, as a baby, was being burped. Much to his own astonishment, the preclear might then burp. The auditor can send the somatic strip to a moment when the preclear was sunburned, and the sunburn somatic will turn on. The somatic strip, in short, can be sent all up and down the time track, both to pleasant moments and unpleasant ones, by the auditor, even though the preclear may be relatively unwilling to cooperate. This is definitely not power of suggestion, since the preclear is wide awake and alert. Further, the auditor in commanding the somatic strip can discover data, such as how long an operation took, which is evidently completely unknown to the preclear, although this use of the somatic strip is neither usual nor general, but is more of a stunt.

The main thing the auditor should do in using the somatic strip is to credit the somatic strip with obedience to the auditor's commands. The auditor does not send the somatic strip to the beginning of the engram and then wonder whether or not the somatic strip went there and ask questions as to whether or not it did and how the preclear feels. The auditor, with considerable confidence, should assume that the somatic strip has gone exactly where he said. If the preclear is unable to detect any difference, this is not the fault of the somatic strip, but is occasioned by the amount of entheta on the case. The somatic strip moves about the track at the auditor's commands regardless of the quantity of entheta on the case, unless the somatic strip is itself thoroughly stuck in some engram.

The somatic strip and the file clerk are two of many mechanisms and entities discovered by Dianetics. There are many other phenomena in the mind, which are not at this time used by the auditor but which, nevertheless, exist. There are, possibly, such things as theta perceptics, which respond to auditor consultation. Very little is known about them, and it is felt that incorrect use of them or invalidation of them after they have been used is harmful to a case; so experimentation with them should be very carefully done. A book could be written which covered additional entities and phenomena of the human mind, but until these can be intimately associated with processing in such a way as to aid the auditor, a discussion of them in a book of processing is extraneous. Exactly to what extent these additional perceptics and entities influence human behavior has been far from thoroughly established.

The time track, as covered elsewhere, is simply the consecutive moments of now which proceed in one lifetime, from conception, or a few days before conception on the sperm and ovum sequence, up to present time. The time track is actually a cable, or bundle of perceptics, since all twenty-six perceptic channels register, when there is anything for them to perceive and are in phase in a case which does not have an extremely heavy burden of entheta. The individual can be sent by the auditor back from present time simply by being told to close his eyes and go to a certain moment in the past. He can be sent to a very precise moment on the track, since every instant of the preclear's past life is recorded on this track. Some of the recording, of course, is done in the reactive mind, when unconsciousness and physical pain are present. It is interesting that a preclear can be sent to January 3, 1936, a very random and obscure date, to the hour of eight-fifteen in the morning, and although the preclear may not realize he is there, requesting him to contact even hazy data about it will shortly place him at the instant, which if run several times just as though it were an engram, will begin to show up in considerable detail in most cases. For instance, if at eight-fifteen in the morning on January 3 the preclear entered his office and began to open mail, he may not know at the beginning even if he had an office at that date, but after he has run the incident several times he will be able to read you the names and addresses off the envelopes as he opens them and sorts his morning mail. Because sense of time and ability to return are thoroughly discounted by social aberrations in this culture, these skills have remained hidden. When the preclear's sense of reality is very low, when he himself is very low on the Tone Scale, the preclear may have no confidence at all in any data which he brings up about his past. Knowing that the somatic strip, the file clerk and the ability of "I" to return are accurate, the auditor has the responsibility to encourage the preclear to credit his own senses.

Thus, we see that we have three things at work in the operation of going back from present time to an earlier incident. First, we have the file clerk. Next, we have the somatic strip. And third, we have "I" or a large percentage of the attention units of the mind. And these three together are used by the auditor to work the preclear on his time track and discover and reduce or erase past moments of physical pain and unconsciousness or encysted areas of entheta.

The auditor consults with the file clerk as to the "incident necessary to resolve this case" or the "chain of locks necessary to be run at this time" or "Yes or no, should we run engrams at this time?" or "Is there a grief charge available at this time?" and after this consultation, asking, "Can we scan this chain of locks at this time?" or "Is this engram susceptible to being run?"

One might say that the auditor and the file clerk are consultants over the case of the preclear as to the best method of raising the preclear on the Tone Scale. The file clerk's interest and participation in this is very large. The file clerk's ability to answer questions sometimes extends to suggestions as to how to run the case when these are requested by the auditor. Now it is a strange thing that the file clerk always knows the type of entheta which can be run on the case. The file clerk also knows the next engram which can be reduced or erased. All the auditor has to do is request the file clerk to present the engram necessary to resolve the case, and the file clerk will do so, no matter where that engram lies on the track.

Engrams follow the general law that they must be reduced or erased from early to late, which is to say that the earliest engram on the chain must be the one first contacted. Engrams in the basic area are surprisingly early. The auditor will have to get used to the idea that physical pain and perceptics are recorded, if not understood, long before there is anything like an analytical mind in the organism. The file clerk is slightly sketchy on how early he must look for the engram to resolve the case, and unless the auditor is occasionally insistent on the file clerk's presenting very, very, very early engrams, the file clerk may not look earlier than two or three or five years of age (late life, in Dianetics). With this single limitation, the choice of the file clerk as to the engram to be run should be considered primary above the auditor's or preclear's idea of what engram it is now necessary to address and reduce. The auditor cannot know this too thoroughly: that the file clerk's choice of engrams takes precedence over the desires of the preclear or the wishes of the auditor, and the file clerk will present the engram necessary to be run next in order to resolve the case.

Although engrams normally run from early to late, it sometimes happens that a relatively late life engram is so tenuously connected to the remainder of the bank that it can be run off and erased, almost as an independent entity. Although birth should always be approached by the auditor with caution, the file clerk may present birth, and if the file clerk does so, then birth should be run.

The auditor should be very careful of forcing his preclear into any engram which is not presented by the file clerk. Running late life engrams early in the case will, as a general rule, merely enturbulate the case, since these engrams will not reduce until earlier physical pain moments have been reduced or until a great deal of entheta is taken off of the case by other means.

Once the file clerk has presented an engram—and the auditor simply assumes that his request for the file clerk to do so has been complied with—the auditor then directs the somatic strip to go to the beginning of the engram. The somatic strip does this immediately and needs no further coaxing, and indeed, a failure to take this for granted has a tendency to invalidate the somatic strip and to render its response uncertain and the preclear confused as to what is taking place.

With the somatic strip at the beginning of the engram which the file clerk has presented, there may still be no awareness of somatic or change so far as the preclear's "I" is concerned. It is now necessary for the auditor to get "I" in contact with the stage which has been set by the file clerk and the somatic strip. The auditor does this with an additional request for a flash answer. Although it does not always happen that engrams contain conversation, it is a fairly safe assumption that any given engram contains conversation. In order to get "I" in contact with the engram and to turn the somatic on full so that the engram can be run, the auditor now asks for the first phrase in the engram, and snaps his fingers. A phrase occurs to the preclear, which at the first moment that it occurs may seem completely irrelevant. The preclear repeats this phrase two or three times and "I" is in contact with the beginning of the engram. The preclear becomes aware of the somatic and of other perceptics and, phrase by phrase, runs off the engram, reexperiencing it, feeling the generally modified version of the pain the instant once contained, recounting all the conversation which he perceives to have taken place in the incident, getting rid of the "boil-off" which smothered the incident or yawning away the remaining anaten in the incident or experiencing the misemotion of the incident and, in short, reducing or erasing the engram.

The auditor must be aware of the existence and importance of action phrases in engrams. These phrases are actually commands in the engrams which take over as a sort of inner auditor, and before the auditor knows it these phrases are sending the somatic strip elsewhere up or down the track or mixing up the file clerk as to the next phrases. The auditor, if he notices any peculiarity in the running of this engram—that the somatic turned on once but will not turn on again, that sonic was nearly on but now doesn't exist—and yet knows the engram is not yet reduced, suspects an action phrase and asks the file clerk whether or not a bouncer, denyer, grouper, valence-shifter or holder is acting. He does this by saying, "Is there an action phrase present?" *(snap!)* With a yes answer, the auditor then asks, "What type?" *(snap!)* The file clerk then says (through "I") that it is a bouncer, holder, grouper, misdirector, denyer or whatever. The auditor then says, "The phrase will now flash!" *(snap!)* The phrase flashes, the preclear repeats it and gets back into the engram from which he has been bounced, if it was a bouncer. Actually, a case is in very bad shape which has positive responses to action phrases and probably should not have engrams run on it at all. Cases further up the Tone Scale do not respond at all to action phrases, which is to say the file clerk and somatic strip have sufficient theta behind them to override even strong and energetic commands to do something other than work with the auditor in reducing or erasing the engram. The response value of the action phrases is, indeed, an index of where the preclear is located on the Tone Scale. Very noticeable response to action phrases indicates that some other type of entheta than engrams should be run off the case before engrams are reduced. If the auditor finds his preclear bouncing badly every time the phrase "get out" occurs in an engram, he should reduce if possible the engram on which he is working and then address his attention to other types of entheta, such as chains of locks and secondaries, rather than continuing to run engrams.

The auditor should understand that an engram does not always begin with a phrase and that the phrase he gets first may not begin the engram. He should further understand that the heaviest entheta in the engram, if the engram were occasioned by a blow, occurs at the beginning of the engram. Thus, the file clerk may present this beginning, and the somatic strip may try to go all the way to the beginning, but the entheta is heaviest right at the start. Thus the auditor should always check to find out whether there is an earlier phrase or an earlier somatic on the engram, before he works very hard to reduce the whole engram, since it is the earliest part of the engram which suppresses the remainder of the engram. Once you get the entheta out of the very beginning of an engram of the blow variety the rest may reduce as easily as a lock. Always get the earliest part.

There is another type of engram, in which unconsciousness sets in slowly and perhaps physical pain does not develop until after unconsciousness has begun to set in. This would happen in the case of loss of blood, or during an anesthetic operation, where the anesthesia is administered before the physical pain of the operation itself begins.

Then there is the combination of these types of engrams, where a blow or shock begins the engram, unconsciousness sets in and deepens, and then further blows and shocks occur during the course of the unconsciousness, again deepening it. The lightest phrases of unconsciousness will lift off an engram first. The deepest part of the unconsciousness or the deepest point of physical pain will lift last. Thus, an auditor can run through an engram several times and consider that he has almost reduced it, only to discover that several new phrases have appeared in the engram. This happens because some portions of the engram contain deeper unconsciousness and more severe pain than other portions, and these lift last.

The engram can do three things: it can erase, it can reduce or it can recess.

The erasure of an engram takes place when it is either one of the first few engrams existing on the time track or when the engram is relatively independent of the remainder of the reactive mind. The phrases and other perceptics appear. The engram is recounted from the first moment of physical pain and unconsciousness to the last. And after a few recountings, the engram vanishes in yawns. The auditor can be fooled at times, by having the preclear bounce out of an engram, into believing that the engram has been erased or reduced, but in this case yawns do not come off. Yawns always mark the end of an erasure, since this is the last of the anaten (the physiological byproduct of unconsciousness) which has pinned down the rest of the engram. The entire case, which is to say all the content of the reactive mind, will eventually erase. An erasure thoroughly done, simply by recounting all perceptics of the engram over and over with the preclear returned to that instant on the track, does not reappear again. An erasure is final and complete. The engram is gone. The physical pain will not reoccur. The phrases are no longer aberrative in any way and are quite often gone so thoroughly that the preclear cannot even remember what the engram contained.

In view of the fact that the engram is the basic source of human aberration, these phrases which are enforced as hidden commands upon the analytical mind are the most productive of aberration, if the engram is charged up by later entheta on the case. If these commands cannot be obeyed or dramatized by the analyzer, then the engram attempts to force compliance by turning on physical pain which it contains. That portion of the body which was injured when this engram was received will become painful again, or will manifest some discomfort. This has been called psychosomatic illness. It is actually the somatic of some past moment of physical pain turning on again because of the overcharge of the engram by later entheta and the inability of the person to dramatize the verbal content of the engram. All these things are gone, the anaten which shuts down the analytical mechanism and power of the mind, the aberrative force of the commands of the engram which are accepted literally by the analyzer and the physical pain of the engram which can become a chronic somatic, disappear and do not return when the engram is erased.

To be erased, an engram has to be early on its own chain of engrams, there must not be too many secondaries or other types of entheta charging up this engram, and the bulk of the perceptics must have been present while the engram was being run. The unobservant auditor who knows little of his subject may occasionally think he has erased engrams, only to discover a few days later that the engram, in some part, has returned. In order for this to happen, the engram must have been fairly late on a chain or there must have been considerable entheta above it. The earlier engram must be discovered, or entheta must be removed from the case in some other way.*

A reduction is done exactly as an erasure, but the engram will not completely erase, remaining, after a few recountings, in a more or less static condition of low aberrative power and with no physical pain remaining in it. Early in the case the auditor obtains more reductions than he does erasures. When an erasure of the case begins the auditor feels very confident, for an erasure carries the preclear up the track to present time, and although another pass may be made to discover missed engrams, the auditor knows he is bringing the preclear through to Clear. In the matter of a reduction, entheta is recovered from the incident, the preclear is made considerably more comfortable, but the engram remains there in a quiet state. Ordinarily, erasures and reductions require only seven to ten recountings or reexperiencings of the engram. The reduction is

---

*One auditor, who was in Dianetics very early but who left it through his inability and lack of courage in handling psychotic cases, had so much grief on his own case that he was afraid to run grief on any preclear. Thus, in any case below 2.0 on the Tone Scale, he was unable to secure any erasures, for he simply could not bring himself to face the sight of a preclear crying and would quickly and sharply stop any preclear who sought to discharge a secondary engram. Rather than face his own inability and unburden cases of their secondary engrams, this individual went to the extraordinary lengths of laboriously trying to change the basic tenets of Dianetics until they agreed with his own engrams. This rather pathetic case is cited to demonstrate to the auditor that he must not permit his own shortcomings to reduce his skill in auditing, but must raise his necessity level and personal courage up to a point where he can run a preclear through anything. Before he tries to alter the axioms and practices of Dianetics, which have produced results, the person who would audit should begin by using these axioms and practices as they are described in this volume. —LRH

recognizable because the somatic in the engram, recounting by recounting, reduces a little further, and continues to reduce until the somatic is gone. A reduced engram does not build up again but remains in this quiet state and permits the auditor to go on to other engrams.

The recession is the third thing that will happen to an engram which is being processed. The recession is not desirable. A recession occurs only in engrams which are not early enough in the chain of engrams to be reduced or which are too charged. The file clerk will never present an engram which can only be recessed. A recession takes place when the auditor "knowing better" than the file clerk forces the preclear back down the track, uses repeater technique on some phrase the auditor has selected as being aberrative, and generally mishandles the case. A recession is evidenced by the failure of the somatic to reduce beyond a certain point. The engram will drop down to a certain volume of intensity, but no matter if it is recounted thirty, fifty or a hundred times, a somatic will still remain. In contrast with a reduction, during a recession the somatic of the engram first reduces slightly and then continues constant. In the reduction, the somatic, little by little each recounting, reduces. In a recession, the somatic remains steady. If a recession takes place, it means simply that an engram similar to the one which is being reexperienced is earlier on the case, or that a tremendous quantity of entheta in secondaries and locks exists above the engram that is being recessed. Recessions occur only where the auditor has not taken off enough entheta from the case in the form of locks and secondaries to permit engrams to be run. It is a premature address to engrams. Or it is caused by auditing in violation of the file clerk's data.

One would ordinarily suppose, for instance, that conception would be the earliest engram on the case. It sometimes happens that the auditor contacts conception and finds it will not reduce. Obviously, conception is very early. There may be some engrams before conception, on either the sperm or the ovum side. But unless one understands that a great deal of charge can exist which suppresses any engram, one may recount, for instance, a conception engram only into a recession. It should not surprise an auditor, if he demands that conception be run before conception is ready to be run, to have a recession take place. Perhaps no engram exists in current life before conception, but enough entheta in secondaries and locks above conception will cause its charge to be highly resistive.

There is a trick of reaching conception in a case. This trick should be used with caution, because of the entheta which may have charged up this early engram. The auditor asks the preclear to run a moment of sexual pleasure, and then when his preclear, who does not have to recount this moment aloud, appears to be settled into that moment, the auditor demands that the preclear go immediately to conception. The preclear will normally do so and conception can thus be found and run. But, as has been said, it may have too much charge to reduce or erase. This trick can be applied to any engram in the basic area. The auditor can require the preclear to run a moment when the preclear was angry, and when the preclear seems to be well settled into recounting his own near present time dramatization of being angry, the auditor merely tells him to go to the earliest engram in the bank which contains anger. The preclear ordinarily will go there. This applies as well to fear, and to grief, but it is far better to discharge the case well and have the file clerk in good working condition before one uses such a trick.

Conception is definitely an engram, in the majority of cases. Now and then, conception will be found to contain only a moment of unconsciousness in the sperm line and another in the ovum line and be otherwise unaberrative. But the usual conception contains considerable perceptics and physical pain. Great care should be used not to try to contact and run conception prematurely on a case. An individual who is fairly low on the Tone Scale, below 2.5, will usually have enough charge on conception so that it cannot be reduced. Running conception on an individual below 2.5 intensifies his aberrative manifestations. A borderline psychotic can actually be placed in a psychotic break if an auditor authoritarianly slams him into conception and insists that he run it, on the theory that conception, being an early engram, should erase.

Possibly the mistaken emphasis of outmoded therapies upon the second dynamic occurs because the basic engrams of the case are sexual. This would bring about an incorrect conclusion on the part of those who did not understand the mechanics of aberration. Because Dianetics has not at this time much explored structure, no slightest effort is made here to justify the existence of preconception sperm engrams or preconception ovum engrams or conception engrams or birth engrams. Actually, these have been found time and again in some advanced modes of psychotherapy and abandoned only because they did not agree with the reality of the practitioner. Recent experiments at Rutgers University validate the ability of the embryo to react to sounds and other stimuli. Books written as early as 1912 and 1914 mention these early recordings, labeling them "cellular experiences," which in Dianetics we do not now know to be a correct label. The work of biologists in the field of embryology adequately validates the reaction capabilities of the embryo to stimuli. In Dianetics, engrams from the earliest periods have been checked with reality and have been found to have taken place. Many a parent watching his child or teenager being processed has been startled to hear from engrams the names of maids fired long before the child was born, or circumstances surrounding the marriage which were not particularly complimentary to the devotion of the parents to the letter of morality, and other matters which would not be otherwise known to the preclear. Some mothers who may not have been as careful in their fidelity as their husbands expected may even sacrifice the health of the child, who could otherwise be processed into better mental and physical condition, rather than have their husbands learn of these infidelities which are unfortunately recorded word for word in the engrams of the child.

Knowledge that these recordings exist and are valid and actual will discourage a below-2.0 individual from permitting her children to be processed. The auditor should always be wary of a mother who is actively trying to invalidate Dianetics to the husband or children. Case after case has been accumulated in which this invalidation process took place for no other reason than to hide data which the parent did not wish to be known. The only other reason an invalidation of Dianetics takes place, after an individual sees it operate and understands it, is that the aberrated condition of the mate or employee permits the invalidator to continue in control of that individual. This is highly discreditable, but will be found many more times than the auditor will like and will be a considerable problem to him. Those who oppose processing either have something to hide or suppose they gain in some way by continuing authoritarian control of the preclear in question.

Because he is running moments when the preclear was sick, distressed, injured or otherwise disturbed, the auditor can expect to find himself viewing almost any state of health, neurosis or psychosis at one or another stage of the preclear's advance to Clear. These states will be very transitory, taking place only when the preclear is returned to an engram and during the period, usually a few minutes or an hour, required to run that engram. Unless one understands that reexperiencing engrams is the reexperiencing of the very stuff of which insanity is made, one can become alarmed about this. The only really dangerous thing about the running of engrams is simply becoming alarmed. The preclear, sent back into the basic area, will roll into a fetal ball. The girl sent back to birth may get into Mama's valence and scream loud enough time after time to disturb the neighbors a block away. The individual returned to when he had the mumps may be seen to have a very puffy face. The boy sent back to a severe sunburn may manifest redness and considerable discomfort, until the engram is reduced. The temperature of the preclear will rise markedly when he is sent back down the track to a moment when he had a high fever.

Reduction of the engram reduces the fever and reduces the aberrative effects which the preclear felt for years after that illness.

A medical doctor, observing Dianetic processing for the first time, watches the preclear cheerfully lie down on the couch, listens to the auditor utter certain phrases, then sees the preclear become flushed and red or otherwise apparently ill for a brief time. A medical doctor observing this is alerted by his impulse to heal by his own methods to a point where he will sometimes request that the session be stopped because this preclear may be running a temperature or seems to have severe cramps or is generally uncomfortable. The preclear will be the first one to try to reassure the doctor, for the somatic that the preclear is experiencing is highly transitory, and the preclear learning why, and getting rid of the reason why he has had, for instance, migraine headaches most of his life, will not mind these manifestations but indeed will rather welcome them, since they will shortly reduce. If the preclear is brought to present time before such an engram is reduced, the somatic and other manifestations, which were mild at the place on the track where they first occurred, will usually intensify. And if brought to present time by a poorly informed or cowardly auditor before the engram is reduced or erased, the preclear may experience some aftereffects which are far less pleasant than running the engram. There is a motto governing this: "The only way out of an engram is through it many times."

If the file clerk presented an engram, it will reduce or erase, or the basic on its chain will reduce or erase. Thus, it is up to the auditor to have confidence in his tools and to address his skill to the case, as detailed in this chapter. There is nothing very dangerous in running engrams except in failing to reduce them or to reduce the earliest engram on the chain—or in invalidating them to the preclear, branding them delusion or some such thing. Anything which in a few moments can take a human being who is healthy and cheerful, run his temperature up three points, roll him up into a ball or cause him to turn red all over is not something caused by delusion. You could even hypnotize a preclear (but don't ever let me catch you doing it!) and tell him that he is going to manifest the very same things, and he will not manifest them. Thus, these are not by power of suggestion and there is no delusion mixed up in it. If you run a preclear back down the track into an engram, reduce the engram. Or if it starts to recess, demand the earliest engram on that chain and reduce that. If this earlier engram begins to recess, get an even earlier engram. Sooner or later you should get to the bottom of the chain, even when you have foolishly driven the preclear hard into a part of the bank the file clerk did not present.

Don't go in for the processing of engrams halfheartedly. You can be careless about running locks, without any casualty. You can even be somewhat careless about running secondaries without producing any serious condition in the preclear. But don't run the basic source, the engram, unless you mean to reduce it, or to reduce the basic on its chain, by recounting it, perceptic for perceptic, until it no longer bothers the preclear. Any new thing collects experimenters about itself. But one should not experiment with the running of an engram; one should continue on, by rote, until the engram is reduced. It is actually very easy to process an engram if you really mean to process it, and are trying not just to find out whether or not engrams exist. One gentleman was curious about engrams, and without any study of the subject of processing them, much less a course at the Foundation, told his wife to shut her eyes and go back to the time when she had measles. Unthinkingly, because this sort of thing simply did not happen before 1950, the wife closed her eyes and very shortly felt the warmth of measles. She was quite surprised. So was her husband. But they were even more surprised one day later when she broke out with a rash. Her husband promptly took her to the doctor, who said, "I would swear she had measles, except that she hasn't any respiratory symptoms and she hasn't any temperature." Two days later her rash disappeared of its own accord, as engrams placed into restimulation in such wise normally will settle out. What this husband should have done in the first place was inquire from the file clerk if there was an engram ready to be run, and then ask for the identification of the engram, and then run it by rote until it was reduced.

There is nothing that validates Dianetics to the preclear like being sent into a mass of somatics he did not suspect he had ever experienced. It is the person who is so heavily charged with entheta that he cannot experience somatics who most seriously questions the validity of Dianetics. But even these individuals, seeing the effect of Dianetics on people who are higher up the Tone Scale and can experience somatics, will eventually concede. The person who does get somatics is most forcefully struck by the fact that this new thing, Dianetics, can do a thing which was never done before, namely, to change radically and at will the physical being of an individual. Not even in the days when witchcraft was rampant was one able to utter a chant and have immediate results follow. In Dianetics words which are simply the words of one ordinary human being addressed to another can roll the other individual up into a ball and turn on a fever or turn on a sunburn or blur his vision and create many other manifestations in the case which is fairly well up the Tone Scale. This is so marked, and the validity of Dianetics, if only in the terms of manifestation, is so strong that a physics professor at Columbia[3] once came to the Foundation just to remark on the "diabolical accuracy of Hubbard's predictions of human behavior."

"Be surprised at nothing," "Always ask the file clerk," and "Always reduce every engram you contact, or the basic on the chain" are the three rules of processing engrams. Follow these, and you can't get your preclear into very serious trouble.

Further, there now exists Lock Scanning, a technique developed in the fall of 1950 after observations made by two Foundation auditors, which takes off the auditing that has thus been done. Theoretically, this permits the auditor to make almost any kind of blunder he wishes. After he has made some mistake, placed some

---

3. **Columbia:** a reference to Columbia University in New York City, New York, USA, founded in 1754.

engram into serious restimulation, wound his preclear up in a ball, found no way out of the situation, the auditor, theoretically, can lock-scan off the auditing and relieve the restimulation which he has occasioned. The word *theoretically* is used here advisedly, since in cases which are below 2.0 on the Tone Scale, the auditor could place a preclear so thoroughly into an engram that no free theta would exist with which to scan off this auditing. This would be a very extreme case and would apply only when the preclear under treatment was a borderline or actual psychotic rather than a person with a great deal of free theta who is yet below 2.0 on the Tone Scale. Always finish any session by scanning off the auditing anyway, but don't encourage yourself to make mistakes just because you can remedy them with Lock Scanning.

In order to lock-scan off auditing, one merely says, "Can we now scan off the auditing?" *(snap!)* If the preclear's file clerk says no, the auditor should discover if some other chain has to be scanned before the auditing can be scanned off, and if this is the case he proceeds to have it scanned. Ordinarily, the file clerk will say yes, and the auditor then directs the preclear to go back to the first moment of the session and to scan through the session to present time. He does this by requiring the preclear to tell him when he is at the beginning of the session and not permitting the preclear to start scanning until the auditor has said, "Begin scanning." *(snap!)* The preclear scans through the session at any speed he desires, contacting the consecutive events of the auditing, moment by moment, with his attention mainly directed to the exterior stimuli of the auditing session rather than to the engrams through which he has been run. This extroverts the preclear. Lock Scanning of the session should be continued time after time, but only provided the auditor asks the file clerk after each sweep, "Should we scan the auditing again?" *(snap!)* The file clerk will usually reply yes to this two or three times, and will finally reply no! Then the auditor should ask the file clerk, "Can we end the session?" *(snap!)* Usually, the file clerk will reply yes. If the file clerk replies no! some earlier chain may have been accidentally thrown into restimulation which will have to be lock-scanned before the session can be ended in order for the preclear to be comfortable after the session, but this is rare. This ritual, when followed, undoes any errors in the session, unless, as has been said above, the auditor is dealing with a borderline or actual psychotic, in which case he should have identified the preclear as such on the Tone Scale chart in the first place and should have audited the preclear as directed by the chart. On such individuals, engrams must *never* be run, until they are advanced up the Tone Scale by establishment of affinity, communication and reality with the auditor, the establishment of contact with the environment, Straight Memory, light Lock Scanning, and the occasional running of a secondary.

It should be remembered by the auditor that phrases in engrams are always literal. A phrase in an engram means exactly what it says, just as Simple Simon[4] would have interpreted it the day he was so careful to step in every pie. For instance, the phrase contained in an engram, "I can't make it out," does not mean to the preclear on his first contacts that he cannot understand it or see it—it means simply that the preclear is unable to get out of the engram. The engram which has the phrase "Beat it" is not interpreted by the analytical mind at first glimpse as meaning "Get out" and is not a bouncer but merely an aberrative phrase which might cause the preclear to repeat the phrase several times. The auditor, particularly when he is running engrams, should make a considerable study of the literalness of language. This is the main trouble with an engram, that it has command value which is literally interpreted. "I see what you mean" will cause the preclear to get a picture rather than to understand. This is true of both ordinary aberrative phrases and action phrases. The difference between an action phrase and an aberrative phrase is

---

4. **Simple Simon:** a reference to the children's story *Epaminondas*, which tells of a young boy, Epaminondas, whose mother instructs him to, "Watch out when you go outside to play. I've got six mince pies cooling on the doorstep and you be careful how you step on those pies." Taking his mother's directions literally, Epaminondas goes out onto the porch and steps, very carefully, right in the middle of each pie.

that the action phrase causes the preclear to go somewhere or stay somewhere or not get in touch with something, in terms of space and time. The aberrative phrase merely dictates conduct and is not nearly as serious to the auditor as the action phrase. The aberrative phrase has been inhibitive to the abilities of the preclear, but the action phrase is inhibitive to the auditor's ability to keep the preclear in this engram and run it. When action phrases are very active in engrams, causing the preclear to bounce or to come back to an engram, or to go later in the engram, or to become mixed up, or to find that the time track has collapsed around the engram, as would happen in the case of any grouper on a heavily charged case, the auditor should not be running engrams in the first place and is doing so only because he has failed to evaluate his preclear properly on the Tone Scale and to follow its directions about the case.

Theoretically, one could strip a case of locks and secondaries without touching any engrams; however, there are such things as circuits, as will be covered later, and sometimes it will be necessary to run engrams on a heavily charged case in order to attack a circuit, but this would be an extraordinary proceeding, and should only be done by a skilled auditor, as trained at the Foundation.

The engram is suppressed and out of sight of the analyzer. This is a primary characteristic. At the shock of physical pain or at the beginning of unconsciousness, the analyzer goes out of circuit and ceases to regulate bodily functions or record or think, to a greater or lesser degree. The analyzer can be partly on or nearly off or entirely off during an engram. In any case, the perceptions are recorded in the reactive mind. The reactive mind was once known as the "unconscious mind," but this terminology is highly misleading, because the reactive mind is the mind which is always conscious, and the conscious mind is the mind which shuts off or goes unconscious. The total content of the reactive mind, then, is entheta held down by physical pain engrams which form the basis that causes later enturbulated theta to be "permanently" trapped. Into the reactive mind, in the course of a lifetime, because of physical pain engrams, the bulk of a person's free theta disappears from conscious view and is no longer available for computation but reacts against the analyzer and "I" to disturb and enter hidden and arbitrary data and values into thinking. The physical pain in the reactive mind acts against the physical body of the preclear, and when the analyzer does not obey the engram commands, this pain turns on and aberrates the physical body.

The task of the auditor, it is repeated here, is to exhaust from the reactive mind the accumulated entheta by whatever means are indicated or possible and to convert that entheta into theta, by the simple expedient of bringing the entheta into memory or separating it from the physical pain which traps it. The task of the auditor is not simply to run engrams off a case. An auditor can make this mistake very easily because of his ambitiousness to create a Clear. A Clear, technically, is simply an individual from whom all physical pain engrams, all secondaries and all aberrative locks have been erased. *The Clear can receive new engrams,* but these must be of a very severe nature to be highly aberrative, because it is the early engrams on a case which produce the greatest aberration and effect on the individual. However, do not mistake the fact that heavy intentional engrams hammered by ferocious physical pain into a Clear, should that Clear have been basically low on endowment of free theta, may produce a psychotic break. But do not expect that engrams once erased and the entheta exhausted from the reactive mind will then return in some strange fashion. They will not, once they are properly addressed and converted. It takes new physical pain to produce more engrams in a Clear. A Clear will, however, become enturbulated by the environment, but will enturbulate temporarily only and will suffer no aftereffect from the enturbulence, since there is nothing to trap the entheta.

Taking the locks and secondaries off a case, and perhaps a few engrams in the course of accomplishing this, produces a Dianetic Release.

Thus, the auditor can understand his point of concentration on the case. The progress of any preclear is measured by the preclear's rise on the Tone Scale, not by the number of engrams which are reduced or erased in the preclear. Authoritarian auditing on a low-tone case can reduce engrams, and erase them, hour after hour for scores and scores and scores of hours, but can leave the case in such turbulence that the rise on the Tone Scale is relatively slight. The physical pain brings about the "permanence" of entrapment, but the auditor will find his greatest store of entheta, which he can convert into theta, in secondaries and locks.

An engram which has many locks and secondaries above it is completely buried and out of sight and unavailable to auditing. An engram which has almost no secondaries and locks has in it all its perceptics, which is to say that the preclear, in recounting it, returned to that point on the time track, can see, hear, feel and experience motion, moisture and temperature, much as he did when he lived through the moment at the time it occurred. After the engram is keyed in thoroughly and accumulates secondaries and locks, the sharpness of the perceptics begins to disappear out of it, so far as the returned preclear is concerned, in direct ratio to the amount of entheta which has charged this engram up. A very heavily charged engram, then, is not seen, heard or felt by the preclear. An extremely heavily charged engram doesn't even exist so far as the preclear is concerned, but its presence is indicated by the fact that heavy secondaries and locks occur along a certain line. After these have been run and their entheta converted to theta by the standard processing techniques delineated herein, the engram itself will emerge, and it or its chain, since engrams exist in chains, may only then be available for the auditor's address. But it should be understood that once this engram is thus available the bulk of the entheta which it contained has already been turned into free theta by Lock Scanning or the exhaustion of secondaries, and so the engram is relatively harmless save that it will accumulate new secondaries and new locks. Further, it still retains the physical pain, and its commands are still aberrative, and so it must be run. But the auditor should expect more change in the case from running locks and secondaries than from running physical pain engrams, even though engrams are the basic source of human aberration. The engram is pinned down and hidden from view, of course, by entheta. Entheta has many forms. It could be said to exist on the case by the virtue of enMEST, which is to say that for the entheta released on the case there will be a physiological reaction, whereby the physical side of the organism undergoes some chemical alteration or gives off some chemical product. Oxygenation apparently has a great deal to do with the release of entheta. Tears and urine, sweat, body odors, glandular products come off of a case as the enMEST accompaniment to the entheta released, and physical energy as well. The auditor should not expect to find these enMEST manifestations only in engrams. They are most marked in the discharge of secondaries and locks. This subject will be further covered under another column.

Case accessibility is measured by the Tone Scale and is very important to the auditor. A case may be very low on the Tone Scale apparently and still may be accessible, which is to say, the preclear wants to get better. This denotes the existence of considerable endowment of free theta in the first place and of enough free theta, regardless of its low percentage in ratio to the amount of entheta on the case, for the preclear to desire a return in the direction of survival. Of course, the entheta on this case is descending in the direction of succumbing. This case could be considered an accessible case even though it lies below 2.0 on the Tone Scale. In processing it, the auditor should particularly respect the survival ambition of the remaining free theta and should be gentle with the case, removing entheta and converting it to free theta as lightly as possible. Such a case should never be run into engrams, since the restimulated engram will form a new lock and absorb some of the existing free theta. Above 2.0, cases are normally accessible, but occasionally due to education or environmental stigmata with regard to getting better or because of a peculiar type of engram command which prohibits contact, these cases will be inaccessible.

Accessibility, then, could be considered, generally, the desire of the individual to attain new and higher levels of survival and the betterment of mind and body. Accessibility is roughly proportional to the amount of free theta existing on a case, but this ratio may be interrupted by inhibitions, educational or engramic.

The wide-open case is peculiarly deceptive to the auditor. This case is a weathercock in the environment, and in the presence of high-level people and in a high-level environment may seem quite normal, but given an average environment this case is considerably below normal, and given a small amount of enturbulence this case begins to obey engramic commands whichever way they drive. Yet this case apparently has all perceptics available. Such a case, around 1.1, will even run engrams, but the somatic will probably be light even if the other perceptics are apparently sharp. Here is the case which lacks, structurally probably, a mechanism by which to occlude charge. This case, below 2.0, is quite ordinarily inaccessible, unless assisted by manic engrams or a general feeling in the environment that being processed is the thing to do, for this case is often quite impressionable and follows the fashion of the environment easily. The inexperienced auditor may find such a case, may discover that sonic, visio, tactile exist and so decide, without beginning to look at his Tone Scale chart, that the case can run engrams. Somehow or other he persuades the case to begin processing and plunges the case down the track into moments of physical pain and unconsciousness. He will find this case resistive, quite ordinarily, or easily distracted in processing, but he may persist and discover only after he has done considerable processing that the case is not rising very markedly on the Tone Scale.

Should the auditor be shortsighted enough to start running engrams on such a case, additional manifestations will tell him that he is doing wrong. The wide-open case will have, usually, some of the perceptics markedly missing. One of these is physical position. This case does not roll into a ball or otherwise change position even when apparently strenuous engrams are being run with full sonic and some other perceptics in the basic area. The reverse is occasionally true. This case may always roll into a ball and have sonic and visio but will lack many of the other perceptics. The constant of this wide-open case low on the Tone Scale is that it has sonic and visio, that the somatics are light ordinarily, that the case does not progress rapidly up the Tone Scale despite the fact that engrams are evidently being reduced and, most importantly, the case rarely manifests any relief while engrams are being erased or reduced. This is to say that the incidents never come up to laughter, but the case will run very soberly. This last denotes that the analyzer is not comparing conduct in the usual environment with what has been commanded by the engrams. Now and then one will find a low-tone wide-open case which laughs long and uproariously over everything which is contacted. The auditor should not be alarmed by or censure this but should be aware of the fact that he is running a great deal of what is called "line charge" off a very heavily charged case.

Engrams can be reduced and erased in these low-tone wide-open cases, but the sense of reality about the incidents is commonly low and, as has been said, the rise up the Tone Scale is not very apparent. There are some of these wide-open cases which seem to have all their real somatics converted into physical distortion and without getting pain will go into various contortions. They will apparently reduce engrams by doing this.

Any wide-open case which is low on the Tone Scale should not have engrams run on it until a very great deal of entheta is converted to free theta by the discharge of secondary engrams and the scanning of locks, for this case will probably become less and less accessible to the auditor and will protest against being processed and will complain of no relief. This case is not being contrary. It is an actual fact that the case is experiencing no relief, although the auditor, knowing engrams when he sees them, and seeing them erase, has another idea about how this case should be behaving.

A low-tone wide-open case, then, should be handled like an occluded low-tone case, which is to say that the address of the auditor should be toward secondaries and locks, as directed on the chart.

Accessibility is a considerable problem to the auditor. He must always work in the direction of increasing it. Of course, by accessibility is meant the willingness of the preclear to accept auditing and the ability of the auditor and the preclear to work as a team to increase the position of the preclear on the Tone Scale.

A case is as accessible as it is willing to cooperate and be audited. Some cases are completely inaccessible, and this inaccessibility is not confined to the sanitarium or should-be-sanitarium case. Indeed, the only cases which arrive at sanitariums are those which seem flagrantly to be a threat to their own lives, to the lives of others or to property, although those who are a threat to property normally wind up in a penitentiary, though they are usually no less psychotic. The low-tone case that is not obviously a suicide but is apparently able to cope in some routine fashion with the environment passes the notice of the heavily burdened state, which just now tries to cope with the problem of 19,000,000 obviously insane persons.

Unwillingness to improve in ability to think or act is overcome with considerable ease in persons above 2.5 merely by the auditor's demonstration of the workability and effects of Dianetics. Here is a problem the auditor solves by education. No one above 2.5 who sees some validation of Dianetics in terms of psychometry or who through a little Lock Scanning or Straight Memory picks up some material he thought he had long forgotten and which has been troubling him, will refuse processing, unless there is a question of finance involved which he cannot resolve, but this is solved by the formation of co-auditing teams. This is not just an optimistic remark; it is borne out by considerable experience. Of course, individuals above 2.5 can still be possessed of a very low theta endowment or may be to some degree structurally deficient in intelligence. But even these, if the auditor takes care with them, gather some understanding of the subject. Some of these are incompetent co-auditors, and thus must be assisted by others whom they will not assist in turn.

From 2.5 down, inaccessibility is a problem, but even here, individuals who have a high theta endowment or who are only temporarily at this level will cooperate. There are two types of cases which will baffle the auditor. The first is one who is passing for normal in the society because of some routine ability to cope with the environment, who is yet low on the Tone Scale, who is very trying to the people about him or her, yet who is confirmed in resistance to any aid or assistance. This type of case is not normally recognized as insane in view of the enormous numbers of insane who are dramatically so. Yet this inaccessible case, just as bacteria crawl through the society, is injuring and enturbulating mates, children and friends, down the dwindling spiral. Such people are so "reasonable" as to why they are doing what they are doing and are usually so set in their enturbulative ways and have been so nonclassifiable to one and all that they—like the lepers who once begged through the streets of Paris, their threat to the social health misunderstood—continue to plague the society with the justification of their engrams and their destruction of the dreams, minds and health of this and the next generation. Here is the real problem for the auditor. The husband of such a woman may be a desperately driven man by the neglect he finds in his home, by the scoffing which meets his dreams, by the nagging or nullification or domination of his just as thoroughly driven children. He may come to the auditor or may himself undertake a study of Dianetics in an effort to remedy his situation. Dianetics can remedy that situation, but he will not be able to process his wife, for such husband-wife teams do not work, and if he tries to coax her to process him he is placing into her hands a further weapon for his own destruction. In the hands of another auditor, she will be capricious or sullen or angry. And even if the auditor does achieve success with this case to the degree of recovering and converting some entheta, he and the husband may discover this woman possessed of just enough more self-determinism to run off with another man. The wife who has this same type of situation with her husband may have an even more difficult time. Dianetics is a remedy which will apply and achieve results, but the auditor is quite commonly baffled when he encounters these "rational" inaccessible cases. He should lay aside his bafflement and treat these cases as he would treat the most inaccessible, obvious psychotic. Because such people can keep a flow of "reason" running along accepted or normal channels, the auditor need not be deceived into thinking them genuinely rational. Here is a case where affinity, reality and communication must be built, where the preclear's perceptics must be directed to present time objectives and where the most gentle entrance into the entheta must be made. The fact that such cases do not wear a large sign which says "INSANE!" and the fact that the death they deal to those around them is not sudden, swift and spectacular, but slow and creeping (and equally fatal) are not reasons to audit them as though they were nearly Clear. Methods of processing for these people should be those which the Tone Scale chart indicates. If an evaluation of them shows them to be at 0.5 or 1.1, then the appropriate methods should be used, no matter how "rational" the preclear is.

It should be remarked that individuals may be low on the Tone Scale and still have enough theta endowment to desire processing and receive it and make use of it. These are accessible cases but, of course, should have light methods used on them and should not be allowed to run engrams any more than the inaccessible person at this level.

The next type of case which will give trouble to the auditor is the obviously inaccessible psychotic. A psychotic is that person, according to Dianetic definition, whose theta has become entheta completely, and who is either entirely locked up in an engram or chain of engrams and does nothing but dramatize them, or who is under the command of a control circuit and does limited if unreasonable computation. The psychotic varies in manifestation, but the reason he is psychotic does not vary. There are psychotics who are completely entheta all of the time, psychotics who are only acutely so, under certain circumstances, and psychotics who become completely enturbulated during certain periods of the day or of the week or of the month. (The last type, which is restimulated cyclically, is generally running on a time factor contained in the engram. The incident may have occurred on the twenty-fifth of the month and continued to the thirtieth, so this person becomes psychotic from the twenty-fifth to the thirtieth of every month. Or the incident may have occurred at ten o'clock at night and the psychotic is only insane at ten o'clock every night. The cyclic psychotic is processed by the auditor only during periods when a small amount of free theta is available.)

No engrams must be run on individuals who are below 2.0 on the Tone Scale whether they are accessible or inaccessible save in those rare instances when the file clerk insists on presenting an engram, and they must be run then only with the gravest caution, and they must not be run even then if the auditor considers himself inexperienced.

With the inaccessible psychotic whose "reason" is so evasive and aberrated as to appear so even to the casual observer, and with the psychotic who is caught in some engram, the auditor should give his whole effort to establishing contact, even by mimicking the psychotic or by discovering some small interest the psychotic may have in his environ and directing his attention. Perceptics may be encouraged and recovered by as mild a thing as additional contact with some object in the environ. This, after it has brought some recovery of affinity, communication and reality, may be followed by Straight Memory.

All this is included here because auditors, knowing the basic cause of aberration, are ambitious to treat cause. The basic cause of human aberration, however, is a deeper one than a physical pain engram. It is, by Dianetic theory, an enturbulence and entrapment of theta. Free the theta. When the engrams are to be run, they will present themselves.

The patter of the auditor in running engrams is a very simple one. It is easy to overcomplicate the simplicity of processing.

People have written demanding to know how reverie is obtained, saying that after twenty tries they still have not been able to accomplish reverie in their preclear. They evidently have reverie mixed up with hypnotism and consider it unusual merely because it has a name. One induces reverie simply by asking the preclear to close his eyes. One brings a preclear out of reverie simply by telling him to open his eyes.

The patter of running an engram is as follows:

"The file clerk will present the engram necessary to resolve the case. The somatic strip will go to the beginning of the engram. When I count from one to five and snap my fingers the first phrase in the engram will flash. One, two, three, four, five." (snap!)

The first phrase of the engram presents itself. The auditor causes the preclear to repeat it until a somatic turns on. Then the auditor tells the preclear to go to the next phrase in the engram and repeat that, and so on, phrase by phrase, until the engram is run, then to go back to the beginning. Above 2.5, the action phrases in the case may not be very forceful, and the preclear may without much auditor assistance, after the above patter of repeating the first phrase is done, run the engram consecutively, repeating each phrase only once. If the preclear begins to come out of the engram suddenly and move on up the track into locks or if he suddenly starts telling the auditor about locks, the preclear has bounced and is no longer in the engram but has struck a phrase which has caused him to move out of the engram. If the preclear suddenly moves down into a lower engram, he has hit a down-bouncer. In each case, the auditor working with the file clerk should procure the data necessary, asking if there is an action phrase, obtaining the action phrase, and causing the preclear to repeat that phrase until he is back in the engram he should be running. However, when action phrases are this active the auditor has no business running very many engrams on the case, regardless of his hurry to get his preclear Clear. He will do it faster by addressing secondaries and locks. The command value of phrases in engrams upon the preclear is shown by how well bouncers bounce the preclear out of the engrams, how well misdirectors misdirect him, how well denyers deny further content in the engram. This is a very important fact. When the auditor has discovered how active action phrases are, he will know better whether he should run further engrams on the case or not. When the entheta in locks and secondaries is unburdened, the command value of action phrases and all phrases in engrams will reduce markedly. An engram phrase depends for its strength upon secondaries and locks. You can run out of almost any preclear an engram which has just occurred and which therefore contains no locks, but even this has its exceptions. The fact that has no exceptions is that a phrase in an engram loses its potency when the entheta in secondaries and locks is removed from above the engram by Lock Scanning or running secondaries or by Straight Memory. Get rid of the charge, and the ability of the engram to aberrate the preclear is slight.

This does not gainsay the fact that after you have run a few secondaries or scanned locks or done some Straight Memory on a preclear and regained some free theta, even though the preclear remains fairly low on the Tone Scale, an engram may come into view which will have to be run by the auditor.

The engram is basic, evidently, because it is the basic collision between theta and MEST. It is important because it is a trap for future enturbulences. Any case may possess from hundreds to thousands of physical pain engrams. It is a dull, inexperienced, and skill-less auditor who will run engrams on a case without assigning the case to its proper position on the Tone Scale and being governed thereby.

CHAPTER FOURTEEN

COLUMN A J
CHAINS OF ENGRAMS

E NGRAMS EXIST IN CHAINS. PHRASES exist in chains. Somatics exist in chains. Perceptics exist in chains. The mind files in terms of time and topic. It is an elaborate filing system which, though simple in concept, would stagger anyone who would attempt to duplicate it in purely mechanical ways.

All the injuries, for instance, to the right thumb lie in the reactive mind in a chain of injuries to the right thumb. The phrase "I love you" lies in a chain, wherever it appears, in the reactive mind and in another chain in the analytical mind, and in times of restimulation the two may become one chain. A smash on the right thumb which was accompanied by the words "I love you" would be a crossing of the right-thumb somatic chain and the I-love-you phrase chain. Thus, somatics and words can crisscross each other up the bank. A time track exists, then, for every topic which can be indexed. This filing system is a highly complex interweaving, possible to compute mathematically but rather impossible to draw, so varied may it be.

When one speaks of a chain of incidents, one means usually a chain of locks or a chain of engrams or a chain of secondaries which have some similar content. These incidents in chains may contain the same dramatic personnel, such as all secondaries which contain Mother and Father or all engrams which contain Grandmother, or maybe all locks which depend upon a certain unknown engram or chain of engrams for their existence but which can be identified by the file clerk as a chain of locks, or may be any incident or perceptic lying on the time track which is interrelated with other incidents or perceptics.

A single engram is a consecutive series of perceptics, which may or may not include consecutive phrases, having to do with one injury at one period on the time track. Because an aberree can be expected to say the same things at any time when a certain same set of circumstances is approximated in his environment, one can expect the engrams of any person who was many times unconscious in the vicinity of that aberree to contain this same dramatization over and over again.

Any of these things cause a chain. The single engram could be considered to lie across the time track in one place, but a chain of engrams is a series running on up the time track. Or a chain could be considered a series of recurrences of a certain phrase, each time perhaps with a different somatic, which ran up the time track.

It is possible to collapse the time track. In a very heavily charged case a grouper, a phrase which pulls everything in toward it such as the phrase "Everything happens at once" or "You're all against me" (the sure central engram phrase of the paranoid or paranoiac), can, when too thoroughly restimulated, crunch the time track together. This occasionally occurs simply in the business of living. An individual has an engram restimulated which contains a grouper and the case is so heavily charged that the entire time track collapses. The auditor will enter such a case and find everything mixed and scrambled, no time track in existence, the preclear befuddled, low on the Tone Scale, ordinarily physiologically malformed, and certainly in a highly aberrated mental condition. It would be very nice if this preclear could simply have this one grouper run out of him, but all the elements of the case (entheta) act to smother this grouper. Thus, lighter methods of processing than running the engram itself have to be utilized.

The grouper is the chief danger in any scanning of physical pain engrams. A grouper can be hit on a highly charged case which will collapse the time track. The auditor, if this happened, by acting quickly might get a flash on what the grouper was and get it repeated soon enough to keep it from being closed in upon. But if the time track will collapse on a grouper, it means the action phrases on this case are extremely active and the auditor has no business whatsoever scanning engrams.

The scanning of engrams was originally developed and used on any and all cases, and while it produced alleviation in some cases (if not the erasure of engrams), in others it produced marked deterioration. Here is a technique of limited use, which can be used only when the amount of charge on the case has been accurately estimated by the auditor.

As will be seen on the Tone Scale chart, the scanning of engrams can never be undertaken with any safety below the level of 3.5. An individual can be scanned from 3.5 up to Clear, but he can only be scanned when bouncers do not bounce, misdirectors do not misdirect, when the majority of the perceptics are very clear and when the bulk of the secondaries are gone from the case.

The scanning of engrams, then, offers a quick way to finish up a case which has already been raised to 3.5 by other auditing skills. Below the level of 3.5, chain scanning of engrams should not be adventured upon, since sooner or later the auditor will strike a grouper or some other action phrase and enturbulate the case enormously. This is a dangerous technique and should be used only when the auditor is absolutely certain that he is dealing with a 3.5.

The scanning of secondary engrams can sometimes be done, but again, only if the individual is at 3.5 on the Tone Scale, since all the grief on the case may enturbulate into a ball.

The scanning of locks can be done from 1.1 on up the Tone Scale, and cautions relating to the scanning of engrams do not apply to the scanning of locks. However, in the process of scanning locks one will occasionally find his preclear dropping into an engram. This is because entheta in being freed exposes an engram which is not suspected. In a case which is too low on the Tone Scale to have an engram run comfortably the preclear may be set to boiling off and then may be scanned on some other chain until he is out of this engram, but ordinarily, physical pain should be avoided. In Lock Scanning, the file clerk should be consulted as follows: "Can this chain be scanned without contacting physical pain?" *(snap!)* If the answer is yes, then the chain is scanned. But if the answer is no, then another chain is requested. In short, one should not scan through physical pain on any case below 3.5 on the Tone Scale.

There are many ramifications to this technique of chain scanning. At first glance, chain scanning appears to be an excellent way to sweep all the engrams out of a case hastily and have a Clear, but this is not what happens. Even at the 3.5 level, chain scanning leaves on the case many somatics which then have to be cleared up. It might be said that the top comes off the engrams during chain scanning of engrams. Engrams which are scanned lower than 3.5 on the Tone Scale reduce but little, and below 2.5 entrap more theta than is freed, according to observation.

One scans chains of engrams, when he is sure that his preclear is a 3.5, by consulting with the file clerk as to whether or not a chain of engrams can be scanned. On an affirmative response from the file clerk, the auditor tells the preclear to go to the first engram on the chain. When he is sure that the preclear is there, the auditor signals him to begin scanning, and the preclear scans to present time through all such engrams. The preclear can scan at a speed slow enough to permit him to vocalize the most aberrative phrases which he crosses, or he can scan slowly enough to recognize the phrases but not to vocalize them, or he can scan at a medium speed, getting concepts of the incidents he is passing on the time track, or he can scan at maximum speed, knowing that he is passing through incidents only by the flicking on and off of somatics.

Lock Scanning can remedy damage which has been done by chain scanning. In other words, if the auditor makes an error and chain scans, let us say, a 2.5 level preclear only to discover that action phrases are sufficiently strong to cause the preclear to hang up on the track, the auditor can then lock-scan off the last few minutes of auditing and lock-scan it off very thoroughly so that the damage to that degree can be remedied. However, one should not always count upon this as possible.

CHAPTER FIFTEEN

COLUMN AK

CIRCUITS

THE CIRCUIT IS CAUSED BY A SPECIAL type of engram command which, sufficiently charged up by locks and secondaries, evidently compartments off some section of the analytical mind which thereafter, to a limited degree, acts as a separate entity or another personality. "You" phrases such as "I have to do all your thinking for you," "I'm going to tell you what to do and you've got to do it," which are said to the individual or near him when he is unconscious and in physical pain, bring about this phenomenon, according to theory and observation. In practice, these circuits resolve when the case is unburdened of charge or when the engram containing the circuit is erased or reduced.

Distinct from circuits is the valence compartmentation which takes place in the mind. As has been elsewhere discussed, the individual's survival may become so intricately concerned with that of another human being, particularly during the unconsciousness or illness of the individual, that the dramatizations, personal habits and even factors of personal appearance of the imitated person seem to become set up as a segment of the analytical mind. The individual may have several valences by reason of this kind of association. A child quite commonly has the valence of his father and the valence of his mother and the valences of other people around him.

Valence is an exaggeration of that basic of education, mimicry. A human being learns his first lessons, and most of his basic lessons thereafter, in habits, mannerisms and skills, by mimicry. Anything which can be aberrated in the mind has a specific use toward survival when unaberrated. A child learns how to talk by imitating sounds. It learns how to walk by imitating the steps of its elders. During moments of physical pain, unconsciousness and illness, this ability enters into the reactive mind, which thereafter forces or can force the analytical mind to pattern itself, without any self-determinism in thinking or acting, after another human being. The valence is a representation of a whole individual. When a case becomes fairly well charged a person can or does get into a valence and thereafter demonstrates the mannerisms, habits and patterns of thought of that valence. A person has his own valence and, potentially, the valences of the people around him. A case which is very heavily charged goes into valences so completely that the person sharply and distinctly changes personality and appearance when shifted from one valence to another. The original definition of *schizophrenic* or "scissors personality" was in observation of this shift of identity. A case must be very highly charged indeed and, of course, well below 2.0 for these valence walls to become so well defined that they are actual compartments in the mind and have such distinct memory banks that when the individual shifts from one valence to another he may have no recollection of what he did when he was in another valence, or even that he was ever in another valence. An individual can have two, six, ten or any number of valences, potentially. A psychotic may be, to an intensified degree, two or more people, changing from one to another without any recognition that another has existed.

Nearly everyone has some valence trouble, in that when he is confronted by different people he feels he is himself a different personality. A man may feel like a lion when playing golf with his friends and like a mouse when he is talking to his wife. With his friends he may possibly be in his own valence (the happiest condition) or in the valence of some jovial individual he has known, but confronted by his wife, whom he married because she reminded him, unknowingly, of his mother, he is forced into his father's valence, and his father may have been a badly intimidated man.

These valence compartments of the mind operate in an individual above 2.0 under the very close attention of "I." The "I" of persons above 2.0 could be said to be actually in control of each valence, but as the charge on the case increases, "I" is less and less able to control these valences. And below 2.0, the charge is quite commonly such that the valence compartments of the mind develop their own "I" or awareness of awareness center. Here the real "I" of the individual is relegated to the few remaining attention units which compose basic personality.

Self-control is an actual thing exerted by "I." So long as "I" has enough attention units to control or command the analyzer, self-determinism exists, and exists to that degree to which "I" is able to exercise this command or control.

In the matter of valences, the submergence of "I" into these valence compartments brings about a condition, as the individual descends the Tone Scale, wherein when he is in Father's valence he controls himself as Father would have, and when he is in Mother's valence he controls himself as Mother would have.

Valences could be said to have bouncers, groupers, denyers and holders, just as does an engram. This is to say that the phrase known as the "valence-shifter" may force the person to be in one particular valence (holder), or may force the person to be in any or every valence (grouper), or may force him to be barred out of a valence (bouncer) so that he cannot imitate some human being such as Father, who may have had very good qualities well worth imitating. Typical valence-shifters are such phrases as "You're just like your father," "I'll have to pretend I'm somebody else," "You're just like your mother, and you grow more like her every day, and I hate you for it" (which would make a person be like his mother and hate his mother and thus hate himself). There is also the synthetic valence, which is an artificial person. Or the valence command which makes a person like every stage actor he sees. Valences commonly exist for household pets, and it is not uncommon for a little girl to be in the valence of her dog or her cat and express herself with imitated mannerisms. When this happens to a marked degree, this child has a valence-shifter which shifts her into the valence of the pet, such as, "You're just like Bonzo!" Whenever Mother is angry, the child becomes "like Bonzo."

The most obvious place to observe valences is during the running of an engram. An engram has a valence potential for every individual surrounding the unconscious person. If a doctor, a nurse and a parent are present, for instance, around a tonsillectomy, and if they talk during the operation (something which should never be done!) there is then a potential valence set up for the doctor, for the nurse and for that parent. Of course, such an engram requires very heavy charge before these valences can take over any section of the analyzer. In running a heavily charged engram the preclear will be found, quite commonly, to go into the valences of people around him in the incident. He will not get his own somatics but he will get somatics which are commanded by phrases in the incident. If he is in a prenatal and running in Mother's valence, he will have Mother's stomach upset rather than the pressure which was on him at the time. He is, thus, out of valence. After the particular valence is discharged or the valence-shifter is located, the preclear can then run in his own valence, and only in such wise does he experience much relief. The auditor should not be running engrams continually on a case so heavily charged that it gets command somatics and goes easily out of valence.

The circuit is different from the valence. The valence mechanism produces whole people for the preclear to be and will include habits and mannerisms that are not mentioned in engrams but are the results of the preclear's compulsion to copy certain people. The circuit is a mechanism which becomes an identity in itself, with its own "I" which takes a piece of the analyzer, walls it off with charge and thereafter dictates to the preclear. In olden times, these were called demons. Socrates, for instance, had a demon which dictated to him, although the Socratic demon might not have been the result of an engram but, instead, a theta perceptic.

People commonly have various types of circuits and are unaware of the fact that they do have circuits. The "stream of consciousness" of an individual, his vocal maunderings over his problems, is actually a circuit at work which "tells him how to think" or "tells him how to act." Thinking is so rapid and complicated that one would never have a chance to vocalize it. When thinking becomes vocalized, it is usually at the dictation of a circuit. A preclear may have one circuit that criticizes him, one circuit that seems to order him around, another circuit that mocks or derides him when he does something wrong, and yet another which gives him imaginary pictures.

The preclear who has active circuits has a relatively highly charged case, and the case should be unburdened of charge before the auditor attempts to locate these circuits in engrams. It can happen when a circuit results from some dramatization of the parent, such as "You stay there and listen to me!" that Straightwire can locate an awake incident in the life of the preclear when the parent was saying this to someone. The simple location of the actual dramatization and the identification of it, by Straightwire, may nullify this circuit. Similarly, when the preclear commonly acts like his father and is ill with the same chronic somatics his father had (or approximations of them), it occasionally happens that the identification of the basic valence-shifter, by Straight Memory, will cause the preclear to shift into his own valence. It also may happen that by Straight

Memory one can locate a time when Father was complaining about his stomach, with the result that the preclear, who has been having trouble with his stomach, suddenly ceases to have that trouble.

Ordinarily, however, cases have to be unburdened of entheta to a considerable extent before circuits and valences become inoperative, at which time the preclear's "I" regains its self-determinism and control of the organism which had been contested by artificial "I's" resident in the engrams.

All circuits could be said to be control circuits, in that they are attempting to do something to the preclear in contest with the preclear's own "I." These control circuits are artificial controls and should not to any degree be confused with the desirable self-control of the individual. No control circuit is actually able to control the individual toward survival. Admonitions to a human being to control himself, if he is awake, may perhaps stimulate "I" to assert "I's" right to handle the body, but this may as easily restimulate a circuit and put the individual under the control of some command in an engram.

There is a specific type of control circuit which is quite remarkable for giving the auditor trouble. When an engram contains a very forceful phrase such as "Control yourself," the auditor, running that engram even though it is heavily charged, may suddenly find the preclear running "auto" and going here and there on the track without any further commands. Here an auditing circuit has suddenly taken over. It is necessary for the auditor to discover the identity of this phrase and then have it repeated. The file clerk is sometimes unable to deliver up a control circuit, and when the file clerk becomes suddenly inoperative, although he has been working well before, the auditor should suspect that a control circuit phrase has shown up.

Similar trouble is encountered in the valence-shifter, but here sonic and the somatic may go off while the preclear is yet in the engram. The valence-shifter asserts its control only to the point of changing the preclear into another identity rather than changing his position on the time track. This is not true of a control circuit. The control circuit may conduct itself as an interior entity which takes the preclear out of the auditor's hands.

When preclears are very hard to handle, take the bit in their teeth and try to run their own cases despite anything the auditor may do, providing the auditor has been doing a fairly good job of it (for "I" will sometimes pull the case out of the auditor's hands if the auditor is doing a very bad job), they are running on control circuits, recorded commands which make the preclear misbehave under auditing. The case which will do this is very heavily charged, and one should not be running engrams on it.

Control circuits not only dominate and order the preclear about, but they also nullify him. The preclear may have a circuit of a defeatist variety which makes him believe that he is unable to do what is asked of him and decreases his tone by telling him continually that he will fail. Such a circuit might be worded "I'm here to tell you that you'll never amount to anything. You're nothing. You're nobody. You'll never succeed. You'll never be a success, and it's time someone told you the truth." This circuit, with a heavy charge on it, commands the preclear continually down into the lower ranges of the Tone Scale by discouraging him. But to be operative at all this circuit would have to be very heavily charged and, probably, restimulated by some other person in the environment who is from day to day echoing this same attitude toward the preclear.

There are such things as sonic-disturbance circuits and visio-disturbance circuits. Sonic circuits are very easily recognized, for they speak audibly inside the head of the preclear or give him faint sonic impressions. This sonic circuit may occasionally try to manufacture engrams for the preclear, but there is one characteristic about circuits which always permits the auditor to differentiate. Circuits are ordinarily stupid. They are also discourteous.* The auditor should pay no attention to them once he detects them, for to pay attention to them is to validate them to some degree. Where he discovers a circuit of this character he should not try to hammer toward the circuit; he should take enough charge off the case so that the circuit will be inoperative. These sonic and visio manufacturing circuits are very limited in repertoire, and the auditor should not be upset when he encounters them, nor should he then think that what the preclear is running is always a result of such circuits. To have these circuits, the case must be well below 2.0 on the Tone Scale, and the data at this level is rarely properly interpreted by "I" anyway. The auditor is not interested in data in this area. Thus, the visio and sonic circuits should not worry him, since they will not impede getting charge off of a case. The auditor is not trying to run engrams.

*Some further comment should be made on the case who begins to audit himself. Evidently a few isolated cases have been able to do self-auditing without any damage and, indeed, in one case with considerable benefit. A case may begin to self-audit when there are factors in the case and in the environment which are unsolved by the preclear or the auditor. The moment the proper computation is struck on the case, the self-auditing ceases. While anyone can straightwire himself, and this is a very useful procedure, and while almost anyone can do Lock Scanning by himself, the heavier forms of entheta are more and more difficult to attack unassisted. The person who feels the need to run grief over some specific incident should, of course, run it whether there is an auditor present or not. But the individual who deliberately forces himself into an engram and attempts to reduce it will, in ninety-nine cases out of a hundred, merely restimulate the engram and enturbulate himself into helplessness and discomfort before he has gotten beyond the first phrase. Self-auditing is really "doing it the hard way," when carried beyond Straight Memory or light Lock Scanning. In almost every case, heavy self-auditing can be put down infallibly to the engrams' defending themselves from real auditing by deceiving the befuddled preclear into running himself through irreducible or dub-in incidents. —LRH

There is also the occlusion type of circuit, the circuit which drops curtains across certain pieces of information or may mask "I" from contact with the standard bank or the reactive bank. This circuit might be worded, "For your own good I have to protect you from yourself." This may be very sympathetically uttered in some engram and may be uttered enough times thereafter by the same person in the preclear's environ to give a thoroughly charged-up occlusion. This individual, because he is "protecting himself from himself," cannot get into any portion of his mind for anything like optimum operation. But, again, to be effective, any of these occlusions circuits require a great deal of charge. Lock Scanning and Straight Memory will do much to alleviate these circuits, but the occlusion circuit can persist, worded a thousand different ways, to such a degree that all entheta becomes more or less occluded.

Circuits are peculiarly vicious in inhibiting the release of emotion. Here the auditor has a real problem in the heavily charged case which is yet running on circuits which tell him not to cry, not to feel anything, to forget it, and so forth. The auditor may find his initial entrance into the case seriously impeded. The circuit makes it impossible for the preclear to discharge a secondary engram. But by Straight Memory and Lock Scanning the auditor, ordinarily, can bring the preclear up to an ability to run secondary engrams, even without discharging these inhibition circuits.

Circuits exist which either enforce or inhibit affinity, reality and communication. "You never love anybody" inhibits affinity. "You have to love me" enforces affinity. "Nothing is real to you" and "You've got to believe everything you hear" inhibit and enforce reality. "You've got to listen to me" or "You never hear what I'm saying" enforces or inhibits communication.

Valence shifts also give the auditor trouble when he is trying to unburden a case of secondaries. A preclear can be in the valence of Father, who was not an emotional man, and so be unable to shed tears. A person may be in the valence of Mother, who wept all the time, and may be in that valence so thoroughly that he appears to be running secondaries but is in reality obeying commands or responding to an imitative urge to cry. The case is not unburdened in such wise of any secondary. The simple fact of being out of valence places him out of contact not only with his own pain but also with his own emotional charge. The pain and emotional charge are on the case very heavily but the preclear, shifted into another valence, is feeling command somatics or the pains of the other person and is weeping the tears and feeling the fears of that other person. An individual could go on doing this for some time without much improvement in the case. It should be understood that only below 2.2 can a case be heavily enough charged to shift the preclear out of his own valence to the point where he cannot feel his own pain and emotion on at least part of the track. When a preclear is out of valence this way, Straight Memory, Lock Scanning (in which the auditor never worries about whether the preclear is in valence or not) and the running of locks are alternated until enough charge is off the case so that the case comes naturally into its own valence and naturally runs its own physical pain.

Fortunately, a case, no matter how badly out of valence it is, and no matter how heavy the circuits are, releases its own anaten in the form of yawns or boil-offs, even though it may not release its own fear or tears.

The valence sometimes has a relatively imperfect but nonetheless existing time track, and one can send a preclear who is in Father's valence down Father's time track, which will exist wherever Father was in contact with the preclear. This track can actually be lock-scanned, but this is a mechanism the auditor need not worry too much about.

The auditor should understand the mechanisms of valence and circuits to understand what may be holding up his case and to understand and evaluate human behavior, but a study of this chapter should impress upon the auditor that a valence or a circuit has to be heavily charged in order to be highly operative, and thus the resolution of cases which are chronically out of valence (such as the coffin case) or cases which are heavily control-circuited depends upon the resolution of charge. Charge can be gotten off of a case in the form of locks and even secondaries by Straight Memory and Lock Scanning as well as by high affinity, reality and communication as a result of the association with the auditor or of strong present time survival factors or pleasure or even of education, as will be witnessed in group discussions, where the tone of a person quite often rises.

Early in Dianetics, a tremendous amount of knowledge and skill was necessary in order to handle circuits and valences. This was because engrams were being run before the case was sufficiently discharged to have engrams run upon it. Now that a better understanding can be communicated to the auditor of what he is doing, now that the auditor can understand better what is meant by charge and how to get rid of it, this enormous technology is not so necessary to the auditor. However, he should have an understanding of it, since there will be those cases which would resolve much more rapidly if the auditor understood that all the preclear was doing was crying Mama's tears or obeying a circuit.

One of the most blunt manifestations of circuits and charge in a case is what is called "prenatal visio." There actually is a prenatal visio, but it is black. The blackness of the prenatal, when the individual is stuck in a prenatal engram, will actually blot out his visio. Because he is stuck in an engram, his sonic will be blotted out. But here in the matter of visio it should be understood that while cells and the theta body probably record light, there is no mechanism save that of the imagination which is known to produce the pictures that come about with "prenatal visio."

"Prenatal visio" may consist of whole colored scenes, outside of Mama. Or it may consist simply in seeing sudden pictures go and come.

A control circuit will produce "prenatal visio." "Prenatal visio" is false and has no bearing upon reality and means simply that the case is heavily charged. It quite often happens that "prenatal visio" will turn on for a moment while a preclear is running an engram in the prenatal period. The auditor should immediately ask for a control phrase when this momentary manifestation of visio occurs. He will find some phrase such as "I see what you mean" or simply "Control yourself," which somehow crosses the imagination into the factual bank.

"Prenatal ESP" is another manifestation of charge and circuits. A circuit may exist which says, "I know what you're thinking about," and when returned to its vicinity the preclear seems to get the thoughts of Mother and Father by ESP. Actually these "thoughts" are composites of phrases which occur in the reactive and standard banks of the preclear. There may well be extrasensory perception, but "prenatal ESP" is false.

There is an additional type of visio which the preclear gets that the auditor should know about, and this is not unlike the mirage which appears on the hot desert. A heavy boil-off, or heavy areas of anaten, may cause the preclear to drift off out of contact with reality and see scenes and even hear voices. These scenes and voices are quite disconnected, ordinarily. The preclear should never be interrupted when doing this. This is a sure symptom of a boil-off. Shortly (usually) this phase will pass and other perceptics of the engram will turn on. The preclear must always be permitted to go through such boil-off uninterruptedly, without being jogged or shaken or spoken to, because things which happen while he is in this condition become recorded, since he is close to being unconscious.

Dreams seem to stem from this type of circumstance. The dream is usually an engram which reflects through the haze of anaten up to "I" by some bypass route and is considerably distorted on the way. The dream makes a great deal of sense when one has the engram. It even may enable one to find an engram which he would not otherwise suspect. But ordinarily, this type of guesswork is unnecessary, since a case that dreams heavily is either low on vitamin B_1 or heavy with charge.

CHAPTER SIXTEEN

COLUMN AL

CONDITION
OF FILE CLERK

A S ELSEWHERE MENTIONED, THERE are apparently several entities or response mechanisms in the human mind. Chief among these for the auditor, if not of the highest rank, is the file clerk.

It is evident, upon examination, that the manifestations of aberration in general—valences, circuits, abilities of the mind and their distortions—depend upon the fact that the construction of the analytical mind contains, basically, the mechanisms which are subject to aberration by engrams. The reactive mind does not have the operating mechanisms necessary to put engrams into effect beyond their contents of entheta and physical pain. A person suffering from a manic engram which tells him he is the greatest streetcar conductor in the world may very well perform as a great streetcar conductor. It is the analytical mind which could be said to contain the only potentiality for being a streetcar conductor. This potentiality is not increased by the engram, but only enforced by it, to the exclusion of other abilities of the individual. Relief of the engram makes it even more possible for the individual to be a great streetcar conductor, since the engram contains the factors of physical pain and unconsciousness, which reduce analytical ability and thus make a person less able to perform.

The control circuit can exist as a manifestation of engram command only because the analytical mind possesses natively the mechanism of control circuits. The "I," as a part of its usual thought procedures, sets up and knocks down these control circuits at will. A whole series of circuits are set up by any new learning pattern, and these in turn compute independently of "I," to drive an automobile, for example. "I" gives little or no attention to many of the routine acts of the body but provides, through learning, circuits to handle these. Furthermore, "I," in full control of the analyzer, subdivides and makes up or breaks down compartments of the analyzer to care for various reasoning processes. The salesman, for instance, sets up a circuit to sell his product. The "I" of the salesman may be paying very little attention to what the selling circuit is saying or doing while carrying out the routine sales talk. Thinking is so complex that circuits are very necessary to care for various things about thinking. The cook ordinarily has many circuits which tell her what to do with various dishes, while her "I" goes on planning on higher-echelon policy or being amused by the radio.

In the preceding chapter, the reason for valences was discussed.

The imagination can be exaggerated or inhibited by engrams or charge and can actually be crossed into computive circuits by engrams or charge, but the imagination has to exist as an analytical if sometimes independently self-controlled and apparently automatic function and a native portion of the analytical mind, before an engram and entheta can aberrate it.

Apparently, the main function of the file clerk is taking perceptic data, old conclusions and imaginations, and other data from the standard memory banks and forwarding them to the lower-echelon computers or to "I." There are probably many attention units back along the standard banks performing this function, since there are obviously many subcomputers operating in any well-functioning mind.

The analytical mind that is in very good working order, which is to say, not misinformed by the arbitrary data in engrams or suppressed by the entheta in the reactive mind, gets most of its answers on a flash response basis. The "stream of consciousness" of the fiction writer or the useless maundering of the individual who has a circuit which tells him he has to "think things over very carefully" and who verbalizes endless conclusions to himself are usually the result of engrams and entheta. The file clerk, or his minions, still hand through to "I" that data which is valid and accurate. The transaction is done, ordinarily, in milliseconds.

As the analytical mind becomes more and more shut down by entheta and engrams, more and more attention units are tied up or smothered. As this condition progressively worsens, the file clerk has more and more difficulty passing data through to "I," since he is beginning to have to send it through circuits, through valence walls, and on unlikely routes. Under such conditions the milliseconds stretch out not just to seconds or minutes but to as much as three days. In a mediumly aberrated person the file clerk has to receive the order and return the answer through so much entheta and over so many circuitous routes that one "has to think" to remember something and may, indeed, suddenly receive the data requested yesterday at ten o'clock this morning, completely unrelated to anything one is doing at the time.

As a case becomes even more suppressed by entheta and the analyzer even more compartmented from the same cause, the file clerk becomes only a faint echo. Memory is considered to be "very bad," the individual reaches his conclusions very slowly.

When the individual has dropped below 2.0, not only does the file clerk, as such, cease to exist for the individual, but the data begins to be passed back and forth by substitute entheta file clerks. The real file clerk is still there, but he is so suppressed that his functions are usurped. Thus, the receipt of data and the conclusions of an individual below 2.0 on the Tone Scale may be astonishing, to say the least. Not only is his analyzer cut down to a point where it computes instinctively in the direction of succumbing even though that direction may be masked, but the data on which the computation is done is misselected and distorted by entheta engramic selectors and storers. One might even go so far as to say that the individual below 2.0 fished most of his data from his engram bank rather than from his standard memory bank.

It is remarkable that in even a heavily aberrated individual who is amnesia tranced[1] or heavily sedated (and don't try these things in processing, since they would result in a much further enturbulence and aberration of the preclear) the calm and serene basic personality may be discovered, and the file clerk, deeply buried but now revealed, may be found to be still in good working condition. But so few attention units remain in basic personality, even though it contains the fundamentals of what this person would be if cleared, that this should be considered only as a comment and not as anything useful in processing. It is stated merely to bring home the fact to the auditor that the file clerk does not die or vanish even in the psychotic, even though the auditor may feel this when he is working with the severely aberrated.

The file clerk normally gives answers which contain specific data rather than answers which require computation. For instance, one can ask the file clerk any question which can be answered by yes or no with fair confidence, above 1.5, and receive the reply. Further, the file clerk will give data on time, in terms of days of the week, dates of the month, months or years, to locate the preclear or an incident on the time track. Furthermore, the file clerk will offer up the names of things or of people or of chains when they are asked for. Or the file clerk, if the conclusion exists elsewhere in the mind, will forward through to the auditor the worded conclusion as to what should be done with the case.

----

1. **amnesia trance:** a coined phrase used to refer to a condition where a person is in a state of unconsciousness and insensibility and has no conscious memory of what has occurred during such. *Amnesia* is a partial or complete loss of memory. A *trance* is a condition marked by a more or less prolonged suspension of consciousness, inability to function and an inertness to stimuli.

The ordinary use of the file clerk is very simple. The auditor merely asks, "Yes or no: are you stuck in birth?" *(snap!)* The reply will be yes or no. The terms in which the auditor desires his reply should be stated first. Thus the auditor says "yes or no" *before* he asks the question. He would also say "date" before he names the occurrence. And each time he would follow the question with a snap. Common, careless mistakes consist of reversing this procedure, so that the file clerk receives the "yes or no" after the question. In an ordinarily aberrated person the file clerk may simply echo "yes or no." Another but ridiculous error is to snap before the question is fully asked. The snap is the sound impulse which drives the answers through the circuits. To snap before the question is complete is to have no data to drive through the circuits.

The file clerk must be handled with complete regard to the Auditor's Code. It actually occurs that the file clerk in a relatively heavily charged case may work perfectly for one auditor who has high ARC with the preclear but may not work at all with an auditor who has slightly lower ARC with the preclear. This applies, of course, only to those cases which are below 2.0.

The snap impulse seems necessary in most cases. There are cases which object seriously to the auditor snapping his fingers. These cases are restimulated by the sound of the snap, and a little Straightwire usually finds the source of the objection. However, the auditor should not throw his hand toward the preclear when he snaps his fingers, as this is very restimulative to any preclear who has been slapped. The motion of the hand toward an individual, if done suddenly, is uniformly evaluated as a hostile gesture. Just as the auditor should keep his feet off the couch or bed or its baseboards, should refrain from touching the preclear save when the preclear in distress wishes to hold his hand, so should the auditor use all courtesy with regard to the file clerk.

The file clerk should never under any circumstances be invalidated. He should not be asked questions one way and then another, as though the auditor doubted the first reply. The exception to this is the low-tone case which has a built-in circuit that responds to age questions. This the file clerk can evidently appreciate. But a very questioning attitude on the part of an auditor may well silence the file clerk.

There is a great deal to be said on both sides of reality. The file clerk may be validated by an overly interested and satisfied reception of his data by the auditor, and can be invalidated by raised eyebrows or shrugs on the auditor's part. The preclear, in the middle bands, quite commonly distrusts his file clerk and will do enough invalidating himself. But when the preclear discovers that the auditor is accepting these answers, the preclear ceases this practice.

Just as a general observation in the field of working with the file clerk and the preclear, an auditor can rush a case which is in the middle or low bands of the Tone Scale and begin to audit with such energy that the preclear is enturbulated and sometimes sinks considerably in tone. Similarly, the file clerk and the preclear become annoyed and restless in the presence of an apathetic or uninterested auditor, one who will doze when a long chain of locks is being scanned, or one who will ask questions of the file clerk only when the preclear himself demands it. Too furious an interest, then, and too small an interest affect not only the file clerk but the general working of the case. The auditor must learn to adjust himself and his mood not only to the type of incident the preclear is running and to the personality of the preclear but also to the position on the Tone Scale of the preclear. The lower on the Tone Scale the preclear is, the more gentle, patient and understanding must be the auditor. Even low on the Tone Scale, a preclear may have a file clerk that occasionally works, and this occasionalness can be, by validation of the file clerk, coaxed forth to a steady response. But if the auditor is less gentle and efficient than he should be, then the occasional workability of the file clerk will cease.

Nothing shuts off a file clerk or a preclear faster than ineptness. A few errors can be condoned, but continual fumbling and uncertainty can cause a file clerk to give up and can produce a similar reaction in the preclear.

Rather amusingly, in the Foundation there was a spell of deification of the file clerk and other entities that had been discovered in the mind. The overall result was that auditors started talking to these entities rather than to the preclear. This tended to invalidate the preclear as an individual. The preclear is entitled to his opinions and is the focus of attention. The file clerk and other entities are simply, one supposes, portions of the analytical function of the mind. At one time, the auditor form of address became "Mr. File Clerk," and the file clerk was thanked for every flash answer. This kind of courtesy is evidently not particularly needed by the file clerk, but now and then the auditor will find himself working with a response mechanism in the mind which is very insistent upon courtesy and protocol. The auditor is not in this instance working with the file clerk, since the file clerk is a rugged mechanism with little to say and a brief way of saying it. But this does not mean that another entity should not be accepted.

Now and then the auditor will become concerned as to whether he is talking to the file clerk or to a demon circuit. His preclear would have to be fairly low on the Tone Scale in order to make this confusion possible. Demon circuits will actually respond, but they do not respond with the quick flash and simplicity of the file clerk. Now and then one will run into a real audio demon circuit which is highly insulting to the auditor, for demon circuits are both stupid and unmannerly. The moment the auditor finds himself addressing such a circuit he does well to pay it no further attention and accept no further replies from it, because additional attention to this entheta form serves to validate it for the preclear, if not to strengthen the form itself. Even though these demon circuits are amusing, the auditor should limit his attention to them, since all address in this direction is wasted effort. The auditor should merely know that such a thing can happen so that he will not be surprised if, as it rarely occurs, a demon circuit gets in his way.

The sharpness and accuracy of a file clerk declines as the case descends down the Tone Scale. Generally, the more entheta there is on a case, the less reliable is the file clerk. This normally does not become serious until the case is down to 2.0. After that, the condition of the file clerk not only becomes poor, but manifestations of the file clerk around 1.1 and 0.5 are such that no credence can be placed in them by the auditor.

One will now and then encounter a preclear who gives "file clerk" answers, according to the preclear. The auditor should already recognize where his preclear lies on the Tone Scale before he begins processing, but even so the auditor may now and then be surprised by a "file clerk" who gives very extraordinary responses. "File clerks" have been reported by preclears which gave their yes-and-no answers as visible traffic signals. On the flash response, the signal arm would rise with a yes or a no, sometimes complete with red or green light. Or a "file clerk" may be reported by the preclear as a pair of hands that deal playing cards on which are written yes and no. Or, as in one case, the "file clerk" may be a toy railroad train which comes swinging by, stops and turns up a dump car with yes or no painted on the bottom. These "file clerks" are not file clerks at all but circuit mechanisms customarily found in very heavily charged cases which have a great deal of control circuitry.

There is something about this control circuitry that turns on visio. Possibly it is because the imagination runs on a relatively self-controlled basis and because a control circuit can switch on imagination. However that may be, these mechanical devices and other manifestations when the auditor wants an answer from the true file clerk are symptomatic of cases low on the Tone Scale. The answers of these mechanisms should not be trusted.

There are heavily enthetaed cases in which the file clerk always responds "yes-no" or "no-yes." Here again, too much charge inhibits the auditor's use of the file clerk.

Unless the auditor can get a clear and authentic, even if occasional, response from the file clerk, he should not attempt to work with the file clerk. Here is the most certain and automatic division of types of processing to be used which the auditor can have: Does the preclear have a working file clerk? If the preclear does, then Straight Memory, Lock Scanning and secondaries are usually workable.

If the file clerk does not respond, or responds unreliably or with some strange mechanism, the auditor should limit his processing as a general rule to Straight Memory, very light Lock Scanning and possibly fear secondaries, but avoid grief or apathy.

If the file clerk's response is strong and accurate, engrams can probably be run on the case.

These comments will give the auditor a quick, jackleg diagnosis, if for some reason he wishes to work with a case for a short time as a demonstration or an assist and yet does not have a chart at hand or the time to locate his preclear on the chart. The auditor should always locate his preclear on the chart as accurately as possible if he is taking on a case for any term of processing more than a short session.

C O L U M N   A M
HYPNOTIC LEVEL

IT IS PERTINENT TO DIAGNOSIS whether or not the preclear is highly suggestible or can be hypnotized.

Hypnotism is an address to the reactive mind. Bluntly, it reduces self-determinism by interposing the commands of another below the analytical level of an individual's mind; it enturbulates a case, markedly and materially aberrates human beings by keying in engrams which would otherwise lie dormant, and is the sort of control mechanism in which an authoritarian individual, cult or ideology delights. People who indulge in hypnotism may, only very occasionally, be interested in experimentation on the human mind to learn more about the mind. Genuine experimental hypnotism, strictly in the laboratory and never in the parlor, and done wholly in the knowledge that one is reducing the efficiency of the human being on whom he is experimenting and may do him permanent damage, and the use of hypnotism by a surgeon but not in company with any other anesthetic should end the extension of hypnotism into the society.

Submission to being hypnotized is analogous to being raped, with the exception that the individual can, generally, recover from being raped. To any clear thinking human being who believes in the value of people as human beings, there is something gruesomely obscene about hypnotism. The interjection of unseen controls below the level of consciousness cannot benefit but can only pervert the mind. It does not matter if the hypnotist tells his subject that he is going to be better at his job or that he will be healthier. Whatever the apparent attempted beneficence may be, the individual who would permit himself to be hypnotized is, frankly, a fool.

Hypnotism, in common use, is simply a dramatization of some individual desiring covert control over his fellow human beings.

Hypnotism, by an investigation of it and its uses in the society, has been demonstrated to be much more widespread than was ever before suspected, since prior to Dianetic processing there was no method known to man by which the damage of hypnotism could be undone. It was thought by hypnotists that the mere remembering of these suggestions would relieve them, and that the power of the suggestion died out with time. These two ideas do not happen to be true. The hypnotic suggestion has to be run as a very heavy deposit of entheta, nearly as heavy as a secondary engram, and it is thoroughly permanent until relieved by Dianetic processing and is subject to restimulation just like any engram or secondary.

Of course, the surgeon or dentist who permits any unnecessary conversation or perceptics to exist in the anesthetized patient's environ is practicing a brand of hypnotism much more serious, long-lasting and savage than ordinary hypnotism, even though the latter does not include physical pain or hypnotic drugs. In having Dianetic processing demonstrated to them, surgeons who *knew* their patients were unconscious and *knew* that no recording was taking place are astonished when these same patients, under auditing, play back the same conversation the surgeon well remembers having used, and describe in tremendous detail operations of which, lacking technical training, they could have had no knowledge. The medical doctor and dentist forget that anesthetics came into general use only late in the last century and are definitely newcomers in the medical field and that not very much is known, or *was* known, about anesthetics. Considered in this light, it should be less astonishing that they did not know what was happening to a patient under anesthesia, since neither has man had much data about anesthesia itself.

The obstetrician whose patient after delivery suffered from a postpartum psychosis cringes when he discovers that it was his words, spoken over the *obviously unconscious* girl, which laid into her mind the command that causes her to abhor the child and to attempt to kill it ten days after delivery. It is difficult to get a human being to accept responsibility of this magnitude, since it is so appalling what can be done in the operating room. Obscene jokes and crass, derogatory personal remarks about the patient are the common conversation in the operating theaters of America today. Surgery should not be censured for this, since Dianetic processing and the knowledge of the consequences of noise and talking and even music around the anesthetized patient were not released until last year (1950). More and more hospitals in the United States, now cognizant of the harm which can be done, are training their surgeons into silence around anesthetized patients and offering severe penalties for any conversation in operating rooms. So medicine at least is trying. However, the individual who knows Dianetics should not be shy or fall back from invalidation by the doctor when a friend or loved one is going to lie on an operating table. For one can afford a few setbacks, invalidations or rebukes from some behind-the-times doctor if it means that one's friend or loved one will get well much more swiftly and will show no greatly increased level of aberration or descent on the Tone Scale because of the operation or exodontistry. You will yet live to see the time, not many years off, when a criminal charge will be placed against anyone speaking in the vicinity of an unconscious person.

The regular intake of sedatives such as phenobarbital causes the individual to walk around in a light hypnotic trance. The drug itself may not be very harmful to the nervous system, but this light trance makes it possible for the person to be keyed in by anything and everything around him despite the fact that under sedation he does not apparently notice it. Sedation of the neurotic or psychotic is a very dangerous practice. If one must do something by way of drugs for these people, better effects, according to medical observation, can be achieved by the administration of stimulants such as Benzedrine. For some reason or other, probably because in a low-tone society individuals under thorough control excite less fear, sedation is considered less harmful. The stimulant is somehow considered to be too energizing, and medical doctors seem to prescribe sedatives much more rapidly than they will prescribe stimulants. Investigation of literature and consultation with accurate medical observation demonstrate that the individual shows less active aberration under mild stimulants. Below a certain point on the Tone Scale, of course, sedatives are administered in the hope that the patient will then cause the doctor, nurse or others around him much less trouble, and are not administered in any hope or belief that they will in any way aid the patient. Actually, a few hours of Lock Scanning on any case will do more for his "nervousness" than a barrel of phenobarbital.

There is another form of hypnotism which falls between the surgical operation and straight hypnotism without physical pain. This form of hypnotism has been a carefully guarded secret of certain military and intelligence organizations. It is a vicious war weapon and may be of considerable more use in conquering a society than the atom bomb. This is no exaggeration. The extensiveness of the use of this form of hypnotism in espionage work is so wide today that it is long past the time when people should have become alarmed about it. It required Dianetic processing to uncover pain-drug-hypnosis. Otherwise, pain-drug-hypnosis was out of sight, unsuspected and unknown.

Pain-drug-hypnosis is simply an extension of narcosynthesis, the drug hypnosis used in America only during and since the last war.

Hypnotism has the virtue, at first at least, of requiring the consent of the hypnotic subject before the hypnotism is done. Further, hypnotism has an additional virtue over drug hypnosis and over pain-drug-hypnosis in that an individual in a hypnotic trance will rarely perform an immoral act even though commanded to do so by the hypnotist, unless that individual would normally perform such acts.

Drug hypnotism does not have to be done with the individual's consent. An individual who is drugged can receive and will obey hypnotic commands given to him by the doctor or operator and will continue to obey these commands after waking from the drugged sleep. By using the method of dropping a heavy sedative such as chloral hydrate into an individual's drink, by suddenly muzzling him with a silk scarf from behind and injecting morphine into his arm, or by discovering the individual when he is drunk or shortly after he has been operated upon or during an operation, or during the administration of electric shock or sedation in an insane asylum, drug hypnosis can be induced. Thereafter, the operator works much as in ordinary hypnotism. Drug hypnosis can be administered with such wording that the patient will not only forget what he has been told and yet perform it, but will also forget that he has ever been given drug hypnosis, if that command is included, and he may even be given data to account for the time during which he was given narcosynthesis. Drug hypnotism, then, can be done without the consent of the subject and is commonly so done even by doctors in the normal course of practice. There is nothing new or strange about drug hypnosis. It occasionally fails to work as the operator intends, and it does not usually strike against the individual's normal moral tone save that, of course, it inevitably lowers him on the Tone Scale, thus bringing about a tendency to generally lowered morals.

It has been discovered that a drugged individual when beaten and given orders would almost invariably obey these orders regardless of the degree to which they flouted his moral tone or his position or his best interests in life.

Until Dianetics, the widespread use of this practice was unsuspected, simply because there was no means by which one could even detect the existence of pain-drug-hypnosis. An individual might be given pain-drug-hypnosis on Tuesday night and wake up Wednesday morning without any knowledge of the fact that he had been slugged when he stepped out of his car, given an injection, painfully beaten but not so as to leave any marks and put quietly into his own bed. This individual does not know that anything unusual has occurred to him, nor will he suspect it even when he is confronted with the fact that his conduct is extremely changed along certain lines from former conduct. This individual, if the criminal operator desired it, would actually obey the command to the point of striking up a friendship with some person the operator indicated, thereafter conducting his business along lines suggested by this "friend."

The Foundation undertook some tests with regard to the effectiveness of pain-drug-hypnosis and found it so appallingly destructive to the personality and so unfailing in its action, save in cases of individuals with theta endowment far beyond that of the normal man, that a wider investigation was undertaken to discover just how many people one could find within easy reach who had been given pain-drug-hypnosis. Pain-drug-hypnosis is so effectively destructive that the Foundation has ceased experimentation along this line, having already learned enough and refusing to endanger the sanity of individuals. Psychotherapists with whom the Foundation has dealt have been eager to plant an engram in a patient and have the Foundation recover it, to see how many of the perceptics are recoverable. The Foundation will accept no further experiments in this line and informs experimenters that they do this at their own grave risk. A much more natural and valid validation of engrams can be done without the use of drugs.

A knowledge of engrams and the fact that people can be aberrated into becoming insane or criminal by the existence of engrams should be validation enough for the fact that pain-drug-hypnosis can be done without the knowledge of the individual and can command him to do things which are not only counter to his own survival but highly immoral or destructive.

The hypnotic level of the individual is directly proportional to the ratio of entheta on the case. Hypnotism deals in entheta, not in reason. The implantation is made directly into the reactive mind.

The more entheta or charge the reactive mind contains the more easily implantations may be made to work and the more easily the person may be hypnotized.

Each hypnosis enturbulates to a slightly greater degree and entraps and encysts more theta into entheta in the mind of the hypnotic subject. Continual and repeated hypnotism, simply by continuing to convert more and more free theta into entheta, causes the individual to descend on the Tone Scale. The manic effect of a manic hypnotic command has a limited duration, but the lowering of tone it produces is permanent, but for Dianetic processing.

Hypnotism, further, acts as a key-in of many engrams and a restimulation of locks and secondaries, and thus increases the aberration of the hypnotic subject by approximating the words in engrams and secondaries, at a time of lowered or absent analytical awareness.

The auditor should realize, then, what hypnotism does to a case (1) so that he will not use hypnotism and (2) so that he will pick up out of the case all hypnotic commands as one of his first orders of business.

The patter of hypnotism goes somewhat as follows: "You are relaxing. You are sinking down, down, down (which sends the subject down the time track, although the hypnotist didn't know it). You are getting sleepier and sleepier. All you can hear now is the sound of my voice telling you to go to sleep (which installs a circuit). You want to believe everything I am telling you (which cuts down the ability of the subject to evaluate data). Everything I say to you will make a deep and lasting impression on you. When you wake up you will discover that you feel very light and airy. You will want to be kind to people. Any time in the future that I say the word 'Abracadabra' you will go into a hypnotic trance, no matter where you are or what you are doing. You want to do exactly as I tell you to do. I am your friend. I am the best friend you have. When you wake up and I touch my necktie, you will take off your left shoe. When I put my hands in my pockets, you will put your left shoe back on and explain your actions (the subject would, anyway; this is a posthypnotic suggestion, and the subject when he wakens will perform this act at the operator's signal). You will now forget everything I have said to you during this session. You do not want to remember. The harder you try to remember, the more you will forget. As I count from one to seven, your memory of this incident will grow less and less and finally will vanish. One, you are beginning to forget. Two, you are forgetting a little more. Three, you are forgetting more. Four, you are forgetting even more. Five, it is becoming very dim. Six, it is just a dim, dim dream. Seven, now shake your head and the facts will all fall out."

This is rather typical patter. It varies somewhat and the phrases are often repeated many times. The auditor who knows that hypnotic patter is more or less like this can, when he is reaching for it, cause the preclear to repeat these phrases, or phrases like them, or get the phrases from the file clerk—which is the reliable way to do it—and so, by knocking out the forgetter mechanism at the end, or knocking out an idiotic (but not uncommon) statement like "shake your head and all the facts will fall out," he may restore to the preclear considerable memory not only of the incident but of his life in general.*

*The auditor can make the mistake of thinking, because his preclear was hypnotized at the age of eleven by her cousin Freddie and not by some professional stage or "clinical" hypnotist, that the hypnosis is nothing to worry about. Experience, however, demonstrates that frightened, guilty amateur hypnotists tend to use even more forgetter and reality-breaker mechanisms than the confident professional or criminal hypnotist, and these incidents may be expected to be a morass of "Can't remember," "Forget," "Don't believe it ever happened," "Can't tell anyone about it, they wouldn't believe you if you did," etc., etc., etc. On an already occluded case, this kind of thing can easily blank out five or ten years of the preclear's life almost by itself. Straight Memory and Lock Scanning on these periods will have the effect of bringing the preclear in contact with the hypnosis, which the auditor may then be able to run. —LRH

When drugs are added to hypnotism the amount of entheta is considerably increased, but the drug effect will come off in processing in the form of boil-off (which is covered under "Relative Entheta on Case").

When an auditor finds his preclear unusually suggestible, he should be very careful what he says to the preclear. He may notice that a preclear after he closes his eyes will begin to flutter his eyelids. This is a symptom of the very lightest level of hypnotic trance. The auditor cannot avoid processing the case, but he should be careful to use language quite unlike hypnotic suggestions and be certain at the end of the processing session to scan off the auditing.

There is very little the auditor can do to a case which goes into a hypnotic trance each time a command is given to close the eyes. Returning back down the track slightly increases the suggestibility of any person. There is no harm in this except during boil-offs. During a boil-off, remarks which are made to the preclear may be forgotten and lost, thus becoming hypnotic suggestions. All sessions, therefore, should be scanned out with particular attention to any period when the preclear was boiling off.

The auditor may find a preclear who insists on being drugged or hypnotized in order to be audited, as a dramatization of some past command. If this preclear insists on being hypnotized, the auditor can be certain that hypnotism exists in this case, whether or not the preclear has any recollection of it. Hypnotism is general in our society, and a request for hypnotism is a dramatization of hypnotism. Further, the percentage of people who remember that they have been hypnotized or how many times is very slight.

Hypnotism has been a parlor game, the tool of the pervert, the command assertion of the authoritarian, and is more general than one would immediately suspect, as the auditor will discover after he has processed a few cases. He should not be surprised at what he finds in a hypnotic incident, since the facts may differ entirely from what the hypnotist told the subject had taken place. A motto one could use is "Never believe a hypnotist."

In Dianetic processing we used to use what was called a "canceller." At the beginning of the session, the preclear was told that anything which had been said to him during the session would be cancelled when the word "cancelled" was uttered at the end of the session. This canceller is no longer employed, not because it was not useful but because Lock Scanning provides the means of scanning off all the auditing. This is a far more effective and positive mechanism than the canceller. In scanning old auditing off cases, the auditor will occasionally find that the preclear cannot recover what the auditor said. The reason for this is that the canceller has acted as a forgetter mechanism and has closed off the auditor. Merely using repeater technique, which is to say the standard words of the canceller said over a few times, will bring the preclear into contact with the first canceller in the case, and the consequent cancellers will then have no great aberrative effect.

It should be remarked about hypnotism that an early hypnotic session is the more valid one, even if it is cancelled by a later hypnotic session. The mere command in a later hypnosis that the early hypnosis does not exist will do nothing to render the early hypnosis less effective, but it will make the subject forget it more thoroughly. And the commands of the earlier incident will still be accepted over those of the later. This is the way all engrams work. However, in unburdening hypnotic sessions from a case, sometimes one has to start with the latest session and work back, because of the amount of entheta entrapped in the last sessions, which, being the latest of a long line, will be found to be very aberrative to the case.

C O L U M N A N
LEVEL OF
MIND ALERT

IT COULD BE POSTULATED THAT there are actually several levels of mind function. For purposes of analogy and the communication of the technology of processing, we use, generally, simply the reactive mind and the analytical mind. The analytical mind would be that part of the being which perceives when the individual is awake or in normal sleep (for sleep is not unconsciousness, and anything the individual has perceived while he was asleep is relatively easy for the auditor to recover) is recorded in the standard memory banks. The standard memory banks, then, would be recordings of everything perceived throughout the lifetime up to present time by the individual except physical pain, which is not recorded in the analytical mind but is recorded in the reactive mind. The analytical mind would have, additionally, recordings of its conclusions at the time it perceived certain things in the environment. Conclusions in the analytical mind are taken from observation and experiences and education adjusted to the environment of present time and the future. Conclusions and perceptics are filed by time and topic. The computive mechanism of the analytical mind works, evidently, on the basis of comparison of data and evaluation in terms of differences. The brightness of the analytical mind consists first of its ability to record perceptions in the environment; next, of its ability to recall them either to review memory or to bring about new computations; third, to compare and evaluate data for purposes of optimum survival along any or all of the dynamics; fourth, its ability to refile the conclusions so reached; fifth, its ability to summate and compare those conclusions as needed in further computation. The analytical mind would also contain the imagination, which either creates new realities out of whole cloth[1] or patches them together out of old bits and pieces of experience. The function of the imagination is to postulate goals, foresee obstacles toward them and give definite shape to present and future environments. The analytical mind also records, in company with conclusions, all imaginings and compares and reimagines these as an aid to optimum survival.

Uninfluenced by arbitrary data, the analytical mind theoretically is capable of perfect computation at all times. The data on which it computes may be erroneous, but the computer itself is *right*.

An adding machine gets right answers so long as it is used, unless there is something wrong with the operator or with the machine itself. As the analytical mind is its own operator, in looking for errors, then, one must examine the sources of data. The standard memory banks have erroneous data in them only on an educational basis. Consider an adding machine which added an extra five into every column without the knowledge of the operator. Each time the operator added five to five he would get fifteen. When he added twenty to ten he would get thirty-five. In the case of a multiplying machine, if the machine multiplied by an additional five each time a product was required of it, the operator when he multiplied two times ten would get one hundred, when he multiplied one times five he would get twenty-five. In each case, the error in the machine is the addition of a hidden arbitrary. If one were doing subtraction, and the machine always subtracted five more than the operator called

---

1. **out of whole cloth:** created entirely and completely fresh.

for, when five was subtracted from ten, the operator would get zero. When ten was subtracted from twenty, the operator would get five. In the case of division, if a machine divided by one more than the operator desired, when the operator punched out five into thirty, he would get a quotient of five. When he punched out three into twelve, he would get a quotient of three. Here, unseen and hidden errors, lying below the observable mechanical level of the machine and out of the operator's knowledge, would, by injecting hidden numbers into sums and multiplications, subtractions and divisions, produce wrong answers.

The analytical mind is continually subjected, in an aberrated individual, to these arbitrary data. The individual is unaware of the existence of these data since these data arrive into the reactive mind at a time when the analytical mind is unconscious. The analytical mind did not perceive or record the fact that the data came in and it is, then, not aware of the fact that the data exists. Thus, the analytical mind can be subjected to hidden arbitraries, which obsess or compel it or inhibit it from making correct conclusions.

The purpose of the analytical mind is to be *right* and never to be wrong. A person who is generally more right than wrong survives. A person who is more wrong than right succumbs. It is not until the analytical mind is almost completely shut down, as at 2.0 and below, that the direction toward succumbing is taken, since the analytical mind is not present in sufficient force to take the course of survival in the face of the arbitrary data forced upon it by the reactive mind.

The reactive mind is the composite of entheta on the case. The analytical mind would be the sum of reasoning theta. The total content of the reactive mind consists of locks, secondaries and engrams. These contain phrases which are capable of considerable deranging computation and imagination. Enforced by the physical pain portion of the engram, these arbitrary data have command power on the analytical mind. The analytical mind, resisting this command power, will force the pain to turn against the body, producing chronic somatics, which compare to rheumatism, bad hearts, migraine headaches, malfunction of the endocrine system and other undesirable, characteristic chronic somatics.

Theoretically, the analytical mind has as part of its ability, when it is working freely, command over any part of the organism. This is true at least when the analytical mind works via the somatic mind. The somatic mind would be that mind which takes care of the automatic mechanisms of the body, the regulation of the minutiae which keep the organism running. Here is a vast system of valves and meterings. However, the reactive mind can work against the analytical and somatic minds to enforce and inhibit all these regulative functions and throw them out of adjustment, bringing about various nonoptimum physical conditions.

As has been stated, other levels of mind can be postulated. One could consider as many as eight or ten mind levels. The somatic mind level would be that which concerned body cells. These seem to run on a theta–MEST union which gives to each cell an organism life of its own. Science for many years believed that the life of the whole organism was only the composite life of the cells. This is extremely unworkable, and the discovery of the point field[2] of energy of the body by recent scientific workers gave the most precise kind of evidence as to the existence of an overall organism life. A body composed simply of cells, each one with a life of its own, would not have a point field. The overall organism, however, does have a point field. Here is a measurable aura which evidently is in addition to and, according to work in Dianetics, independent of the cellular life of the body. In other words, there is evidently a theta body, capable of its own independent survival, superimposed on the organism. The departure of this theta body marks the point of organism death. The organism, however, still contains life. The cellular organism survives, as concerns the least independent cells,

---

2. **point field:** an area or region within which an energy exerts some kind of influence and which influence emanates from a single source-point.

eight to ten minutes, or, as in the case of highly independent cells, upwards of a year. In other words, there is a separation of the organism body and the theta body, according to these postulates and observations, and then ensuing death to the cellular life of the organism body.

The somatic level could, then, be considered a low mind form, for these cells have certain responsive actions and habit patterns of their own, and their overall network of organization is below the level of rational thought. Next would be the reactive mind, that type of mind which predominates in most lower forms of life. The reactive mind learns by physical pain, and thinks in identities, and reacts by absolute authoritarian command. It carries the organism up to 2.0 on the Tone Scale.

From 2.0 down on the Tone Scale, nearly all thinking is stimulus-response, the type of thinking which some authoritarians would have liked us to believe was all the thinking of which man was capable.

The analytical mind comes more and more into command of the organism as the Tone Scale is ascended. Of course, it occurs in all human beings, even those below 2.0, that some analytical activity remains. But from 2.0 down, this analytical activity is normally used for justification of the organism's reactive actions. From 2.0 up, the analytical mind is more and more in control of its own organism and computes more and more along optimum levels of thinking, which is to say it becomes more and more reasonable. By the time 4.0 is reached, the free theta with which the person is endowed is able to circulate freely through the thought structure possessed by the person (and by thought structure is not meant, necessarily, physical structure).

Many more mind levels apparently exist above the analytical level. There is, for instance, clear evidence that there is an aesthetic mind level, which is probably immediately above the analytical mind level. The aesthetic mind would be that mind which, by an interplay of the dynamics, deals with the nebulous field of art and creation. It is a strange thing that the shutdown of the analytical mind and the aberration of the reactive mind may still leave in fairly good working order the aesthetic mind. The aesthetic mind is not much influenced by the position on the Tone Scale, but as it evidently has to employ the analytical, reactive and somatic minds in the creation of art and art forms, the amount of aberration of the individual greatly inhibits the ability of the aesthetic mind to execute. A person with a great deal of theta as an initial endowment may be potentially a powerful musician by reason of his aesthetic mind. The aesthetic mind, evidently, attempts to execute music through the existing media of the analytical and reactive minds, and both the analytical power of the individual and the aberrations of the individual, because of heavy theta endowment, will be manifested. The more theta, whether in terms of free theta or entheta, an individual has, the more forceful will be his demonstration of *all* factors, both analytical and reactive. Because individuals who are very heavily endowed with theta seek to control enormous quantities of MEST and other organisms, they are fought hard by organisms exercising their own self-determinism. Thus, a person of great theta endowment picks up more numerous and heavier locks and secondaries than persons of smaller endowment. This is not because more theta is there to enturbulate, but because there is more counterattack against the individual. The aesthetic mind, according to theory, attempting to bring about art forms, uses *all* the theta.

It was once thought that it was absolutely necessary for an artist to be neurotic. Lacking the ability to do anything about neurosis, like Aesop's fox[3] who had no tail and tried to persuade the other foxes to cut theirs off, old schools of mental healing glorified what

---

3. **Aesop's fox:** a reference to the fox in the fable *The Fox Without a Tail,* written by legendary Greek author, Aesop. The fable tells of a fox who gets caught in a trap. Unable to get out, he resolves to bite off his tail to free himself. Shortly thereafter, realizing how odd he looks without a tail, he decides to convince the other foxes of the virtues of being tailless and persuade them to get rid of their own. The other foxes see through this and his plan fails.

they could not prevent or cure. Silly little books on the subject of how fortunate was the crazy person were offered in this justification of this defeatism and helplessness.

Aesthetics and the postulate that there exists an aesthetic mind are both highly nebulous so far as our present understanding of them is concerned. But this is known, that any creative artist, as he descends down the Tone Scale, becomes less and less able to execute creative impulses and at last becomes unable to contact his creative impulses. By Dianetic processing, we take a currently successful but heavily aberrated artist and we bring him up the Tone Scale. We can observe that his ability to execute what he conceives and the clarity with which he conceives it both increase very markedly. His aesthetic ideas do not become more conservative or humdrum but may become wider and more complex. He becomes more himself and better able to do what he can do in the field of aesthetics. The only modification of this is that as he rises up the Tone Scale he adopts greater scope and robustness in his work. The art form with which he is working and his method of handling it might have demonstrated considerable aberration, as measured by the casual observer. His paintings might have been strange and creepy, or his music hauntingly morbid. His art form, as he rises up the Tone Scale, evidently alters little except to increase in force of execution and deftness of communication. The morbidity in his music, if it did not depend on how sad he was personally with life, does not disappear. But as he rises on the Tone Scale, he is no longer fixed at a position where he *must* paint strange and creepy paintings or write morbid music. His versatility increases. The author who can write only one book of one kind with one tone is not, frankly, much of an author.

Almost any artist laughs himself into a very short breath over the fumblings and mumblings of the various split schools of mental healing when they confront aesthetics. Some of them even dare to assume that they can judge the mental state of an author by reviewing his writings. This is somewhat on the order of a snail giving his opinion of the Parthenon by crawling through its reliefs. As an illustration, any able composer or author can write in many aesthetic forms and can approximate with their work any level of the Tone Scale. No artist attempting to interpret life is worthy of being called an artist unless he can view almost in the same sweep both apathy and exhilaration. A good poet can cheerfully write a poem gruesome enough to make strong men cringe, or he can write verses happy enough to make the weeping laugh. Any able composer can write music either covert enough to make the sadist wriggle with delight or open enough to rejoice the greatest souls. The artist works with life and with universes. He can deal with any level of communication. He can create any reality. He can enhance or inhibit any affinity. The aesthetics have very much to do with the Tone Scale and with the interweaving of the various dynamics and urges along these dynamics into harmonious patterns random enough and artful enough to accomplish what the artist intends to accomplish. The artist has an enormous role in the enhancement of today's and the creation of tomorrow's reality. He operates in a rank in advance of science as to the necessities and requirements of man. The elevation of a culture can be measured directly by the numbers of its people working in the field of aesthetics. A society which in any way inhibits, suppresses or regiments its artists is a society not only low on the Tone Scale but most certainly doomed. A totalitarian state, following its usual line of perversion of truth, talks endlessly and raucously about its subsidization of the artist. But it subsidizes only those artists who are willing to work for the state exactly as the state dictates. It regiments the artist and prescribes what he will do and what he will write and what he will think. This is in direct controversion to the function of the artist in a society. Because the artist deals in future realities, he always seeks improvements or changes in the existing reality. This makes the artist, inevitably and invariably, a rebel against the status quo. The artist, day by day, by postulating the new realities of the future, accomplishes peaceful revolution.

It happens, however, that democracies and other forms of government are prone to overlook the role of the artist in the society. In the United States, for instance, the artist may write one great book or make a great motion picture or compose one great symphony and may achieve, all in a moment, the bulk of the gains of his lifetime. His whole dedication, from childhood, might have been toward the creation of this one great work, and yet democracy, avidly taxing its powerfully creative individuals into nonproduction, snatches from the artist any such fruits of victory and exacts an enormous penalty for the creation of any work of art. One of the greatest single moves which could be made to advance and vitalize a culture such as America would be to free, completely, the artist from all taxes and similar oppressions, and thus attract into the arts the most ambitious and able and invite them to pursue unchecked the creation of all the beauty and glory on which any culture depends if it would have material wealth. The artist injects the theta into the culture, and without that theta the culture becomes reactive.

This dissertation on the function of the artist is given at this place partly because it should be said and partly because the auditor should understand that the impulse to create and construct surmounts the merely rational and reactive fields of reason. Further, the auditor may occasionally have to defend Dianetics against the strange neurosis to the effect that when an artist becomes less neurotic he becomes less able. Some artists, regrettably, have been educated to this belief and so, by this very education, seek to act in their private and public lives in an intensely aberrated fashion in order to prove that they are artists. The education to this effect is such that the auditor can commonly discover some young girl in the field of the arts living like a prostitute in order to convince herself and her friends that she is truly artistic. In the early days of Rome, art was fairly good. The Christian revolted against Roman disregard for human life and slaves. When the Christian revolted he did the reactive computation that he was revolting against Romans. He condemned everything that was Roman as bad, and for fifteen hundred years it was an evil thing to take a bath, because the Romans had bathed. Unfortunately, although the Catholic church recovered early and began to appreciate the artist, this was not true of some of the early religions which came to America. These were still in full revolt against anything that was Roman. They revolted against pleasure, against beauty, against cleanliness and against many other desirable things which are in themselves the glory of man. The artist then revolted against this declared unreasonableness and went on a course as thoroughly reactive as had been the course of Puritanism and Calvinism. Being artistic was commonly identified with being loose-moraled, wicked, idle and drunken, and the artist, to be recognized, tried to live up to this role. This feeling persists to this day and low-tone people often embrace the arts solely as an excuse to be promiscuous, unconventional and loose in morals.

One finds, hanging around the easel of the painter, women who are "artistic" but who are, so far as their actual conduct is concerned, seeking not to create anything but to escape the name which is rightly theirs. One finds some poor young fellow who could have been a fine architect educated into the Great-Art-Can-Only-Be-Done-By-Moral-Lepers school. These observations are brought to the attention of the auditor for just one reason: The individuals of greatest potential worth that he will process will probably be artists. He will do well to address thoroughly all the "education" and "artistic environment" of the artists and would-be artists, whether writers, composers, poets or painters, because here he will find the track strewn with entheta.

If the auditor wishes to rehabilitate an aesthetic mind, he must address all the entheta which has accumulated around the subject of aesthetics. No more authoritarian field exists, since none of the principles of aesthetics have been accurately formulated, and it is an axiom of Dianetics that the less accurately known about a field of the humanities the more authoritarian will be that field. Any field which has critics galore, wherein a thousand different schools of divergent opinion can exist, where opinion is listened to with open mouths in lieu of reason by which any man can reach a conclusion, is an authoritarian field. Aesthetics, unfortunately, abounds in these critics and opinions.

The whole field of arts is thus enturbulated, and the artistry of a culture is thereby greatly reduced. The rehabilitation of that art-ability of a culture is a tremendously valid undertaking, and will repay a culture a thousand times over for any effort made in that direction. A culture is only as great as its dreams, and its dreams are dreamed by artists. When the level of existence of the artist becomes impure, so becomes impure the art itself, to the deterioration of the society.

It is a dying society indeed into which can penetrate totalitarianism. The group aesthetic mind of that society must be almost wholly unable to operate. No society in which art was elevated and supported, in which the writer, the musician, the poet or the architect had any stability or position, would tolerate the work-dog[4] theory of man's highest destination. For if the industry and commerce and material projects of a nation are carried on the backs of a few able, desperate men, then the honor and the glory of that society is carried and enhanced by the artist.

There may be many levels of mind above the aesthetic mind. It would be presumptuous to classify them if one did not understand but had only observed the possibility of existence. Classification of or assignment of names to things which one does not encompass with his understanding is an authoritarian procedure and leads to nothing but confusion. A mental illness, for instance, should be classified with a designation which would lead to its alleviation. Simply classifying one introduces complexity without advancing understanding. It is quite common in authoritarian fields to advance a great many descriptive names for things based on partial

---

4. **work-dog:** characterized by menial, lowly work—suitable for a dog only.

or obscure observations or uninformed and unskilled observers. This makes for a vast amount of "technology" and gives a certain "dignity" (actually, a pomposity) to an "authority" in an authoritarian field. One would not in any sense consider a professor of English literature a creator of literature simply because the professor knows the names of the writers and all their works and the multitude of opinions critics have expressed about them. This cataloging can very easily pass for "appreciation." In a low-tone society, which will admit authoritarianism without much rebuke and bend before the thundering witless manifestoes of some critic or practitioner who knows nothing more of his subject than an enormously complex vocabulary, one can expect the definition of a "cultured person" to be that person who can recite and give the standard opinion about numerous artistic works and humanitarian "ologies." This makes it very simple for an individual to obtain "culture." He must only memorize, without thinking about, the names of the great operas, the great books, the great paintings and the humanitarian projects of the past. In a low-tone society, the universities perform this function ably, if nauseously. In a very low-tone society, institutions of "learning" are commonly deserted after a year or two by most persons who, through reason, wish to be of worth to their fellow men. In other words, in a low-tone society, education is denied, because it is education by classification, to most of the individuals who would actually help that society.

Thus, no attempt to classify any level of mind alertness above the level of the aesthetic mind will be made beyond stating that these mind levels more and more seem to approach an omniscient status. Somewhere, possibly on the fifth level, lies the functioning mind of the spiritual or religious man who has passed over the border of a consideration of MEST or of organisms and is turned toward an understanding of and a cooperation with both the theta universe and the Supreme Being.

What vast frontiers are opened by the scientific evidence which continues to accumulate in Dianetics, what these frontiers and the knowledge they embrace will do to alter or enhance man's culture cannot at this time be estimated. For example, even at this time in Dianetics one can prove, as science demands proof in terms of sensing, measuring and experiencing, the immortality or near immortality of the individual. Oddly enough, or perhaps not so oddly, hardly any reinterpretation of scripture is necessary, save that the boldness and scope of past considerations about the human soul, God and the Devil, and Heaven and Hell are stabilized and made contactable. The importance and value of organism death is enormously reduced, should Dianetic investigations and conclusions continue to be corollary to or concordant with man's great religions. Religions, fighting uphill against the oppressions of godless ideologies, may gain new strength and meaning. The level of behavior of the individual, whether good or evil, would appear to have new significance. For those people who overcome the suppressors to their goodness, ethics and honor, an upward surge toward spiritual immortality seems to be indicated. Those who succumb to the forces of evil and are unable to live more than evil and destructive lives would seem, should these conclusions be borne out on further investigation of a scientific nature, to be entered not only upon a dwindling spiral in one generation but upon a decline toward a final end of pain or nonsurvival as personal identities. Some of these partially observed and explored possibilities (or probabilities) would seem to give new meaning to the cycles of societies and groups and their survival or death.

As one examines these upper levels of mind, when one examines the evidence of the theta body, and when one himself experiences, incidental to processing, the evidence of his own continuation into yesterdays and an evident guarantee of his tomorrows past his death in the current generation, one's orientation with regard to goals and purposes may undergo a considerable alteration. The biologist, revolting against churches which may or may not have considerably suppressed scientific research in the past, has sought to dream for man an origin out of mud[5] and ammonia seas[6] and a source for him independent of God, but springing only from material things. This reactive overreaching gave us no method of alleviating the unhappinesses of man, even in the restricted fields of chronic somatics and mental aberration, and gave to us instead tremendous weapons of destruction without providing as well any sanity with which to use them. Under the guidance of the material-blinkered scientist, whose greatest goal was a work-animal adjustment of man to a physical environment, whose end for the individual was six feet of ground and a coffin sometimes proof against worms, and whose goal for the group was an ant society wherein the smallest unit of life worthy of notice was ten thousand individuals, we have been led down dark and evil byways of destruction not only of the dreams, hopes and ethics of men but of the MEST planet as well. Materialistic science, operating on the premise that man came from mud only, that the mind is a queerly erroneous stimulus-response mechanism, that the human soul is a delusion, that God was a myth of some aberrated Mesopotamian, has presented us at last with the immediate and real threat of man's extinction as a species. In view of the fact that this materialistic science led only, then, in the direction of death, even the unthinking should see the fact that something must be desperately wrong with the teachings of the

5. **origin out of mud:** a reference to the theory that man arose from mud. Per this theory, it is alleged that chemicals formed in mud and through certain combinations and accidental patterns a primitive single cell was formed. This primitive cell then collided with other such cells and through accident formed a more complex structure of single cells which made itself into a unit organism. Purportedly, from this combination of cells, man was eventually formed.

6. **origin out of ammonia seas:** a reference to one of the theories of the origin of "life" on this planet. Per this theory, life arose through a series of spontaneous chemical reactions involving various substances including ammonia. The theory surmises these compounds fell from the atmosphere into the sea creating a kind of prebiological soup, interacted and grew larger and larger. Somehow, cells were formed which eventually led to the life forms that inhabit Earth today, including man.

Lysenkos, the Darwins, and my learned schoolmates, the atomic scientists who have given man at last for his grave-spade the atomic bomb. However, it was natural for man, as an organism heavily enturbulated with MEST, to bring to perfection something like the understanding of the laws of MEST before he looked about to see whether anything else might exist. The materialist scientist has enormously advanced man's control of MEST, even if he has by his doctrines considerably inhibited man's understanding of what in Dianetics we call theta. Francis Bacon, Newton and the rest developed ways of thinking about thinking and ways of reasoning about reason which have been of considerable value to Dianetics and without which, indeed, Dianetics could not have been formulated. But Bacon and Newton did not espouse the materialist cause. Their disciples developed the doctrine that man came from mud and that man's destiny was mud.

If Dianetics does not come too late upon the scene, its investigation of higher mind levels, even at this low and undeveloped point, may be of assistance to a resurgence in man of something of his belief in a Divine Being and in himself as an entity partially divine. The basic principles of Dianetics demand that a fact, to be proven, must be sensed, measured or experienced. When science thrust this onto the scene of thinking, man's willingness to accept a fact merely upon faith was in itself reduced. Caught unprepared before this new doctrine without which, so its espousers claim, nothing could be valid, the religions still attempted to hold at high value what was actually a vitally necessary part of man's social existence. But generation after generation of young men and (why, we certainly cannot tell) young women came off the assembly lines marked "educational courses" filled full of doctrine that they must believe only what they could experience and ground very fine in the mills of the materialist. These generations, actually, regardless of their ability to "quote Bach or play Hamlet on the piano," to look into microscopes, to serve as executives in steamship offices, to shift and command and generally alter MEST, were, nevertheless, socially lost generations which had no concept of the value of themselves as individuals, which had no workable social order worth mentioning if the value of a social order is to be measured in terms of happiness. These generations were wracked by divorce, inhibitions, purposelessness, sophistication, insincerity and general hopelessness. Representative of their feeling in the field of humanity were schools of thought which taught them that a man's highest goal was to become "adjusted to his environment" without once realizing that man's only advance depended on man's ability to *adjust the environment to him as a species,* which taught that genetic heredity alone was responsible for neurosis and insanity, and that filth and muck alone covered the entire problem of the human mind from top to bottom. This is a sad and piteous thing. No empire one has studied in any former day had ever become so depraved and godless in its senility as the overall average of the societies of man in the world today. It is no wonder that an ideology which holds that man, generation after generation, can be molded into mindless machine parts, that there is no destiny for the individual beyond his place as an emotionless, rigidly held cog in a dully, hopelessly grinding social wheel, commands of its minions the destruction and eradication from any society of the producer, the individualist, the thinker or any noble man.

The progress upward toward survival on higher levels is a progress as well toward God. The auditor will notice this in case after case. He will probably be struck first by the fact that those atheists he processes soon cease to be atheistic in their inclinations and attain at least a tolerance for the idea that religion can exist and have a valid function in a social order. Scanning out some of the education of the individual simply as a step toward converting entheta along a very likely line, the auditor may be interested to note that the preclear begins to speculate on the possibility of a spiritual existence. Although he may embrace no doctrine, the preclear, when he is well up the Tone Scale, is apparently instinctively aware of some higher level of existence. He normally

"Although he may embrace no doctrine, the preclear, when he is well up the Tone Scale, is apparently instinctively aware of some higher level of existence."

abandons a materialistic stand as he advances up the Tone Scale, since this stand happens to be compatible with individuals from 2.0 down.

One could postulate that from 2.0 down there is more MEST in an individual than there is theta, for individuals along these levels prefer to use MEST force, foot-pounds of energy, in order to accomplish their desires, rather than reason. Individuals on this level normally do not improve MEST but will make existing structures into enMEST. When individuals are enturbulated below the level of 2.0, they tend, as a general rule, to consider all life, all organisms as MEST and will in their handling of life and organisms reduce them down toward MEST. Oddly enough, this happens to compare with past ideas of missions of minions of the Devil. The forces of evil reduced life down into materialism and death.

Above 2.0, the tendency of the individual is to enhance life and organisms in their existence and to assist them to a harmonious control over MEST. This is strangely similar to what in the past have been considered good and godly actions.

It should not be considered strange that the organism can go so much higher above 2.0 than it can go down below 2.0. 4.0 is so far short of the altitude evidently obtainable by whatever means, according to tentative observations, that one cannot but feel that man so far in his evolution of existence has been but slightly graduated from his animal cousins in comparison to the distance he has yet to travel to attain anything like an ultimate. To observe that an entire social order such as America can drift around 2.5 and that the normal individual probably falls below 3.0 is to compare man's current state with that of the ugly duckling who will grow up to be a swan. But the comparison is not complete. There is something like an inevitability in an ugly duckling's growing up. It has to *live* to become a swan. Faced with the insanities of the world today, man's chances of reaching God are not that good.

CHAPTER NINETEEN

COLUMN AO
RELATIVE
ENTHETA ON CASE

AS NOTED IN THE ACCOMPANYING graph, an organism, by Dianetic postulate and observation, is composed of theta and MEST and their altered form, entheta and enMEST.

By theta is meant, of course, thought energy, possibly existing as thought matter in thought space. By MEST is meant the physical universe of matter, energy, space and time, as we know them in the physical sciences. It is postulated that these two energies combine, and through the harmonious control of MEST by theta a life organism is formed. Theta plus MEST could be said, then, to compose life.

The formation of organisms and their development evidently comes about through four evolutionary tracks. First, there is the evolution of the theta body, of which we know little beyond the fact that it appears to exist, at least for human organisms, and to move forward in time, developing from generation to generation independent of the genetic line. The second evolution is, apparently, the evolution of organisms themselves, continuing along a protoplasmic line from generation to generation, each generation altering somewhat by virtue of the environment, by natural selection which weeds out the least fit or least adaptable, and by what appears to be planned construction based on computation for the future. The third evolution is the evolution in MEST. This may not be readily seen, but MEST is changed, ordered, disordered and made more complex by the advancing generations of life forms: the intricate complexity of bacterial byproducts and the formation or destruction of mountains or machines is no less an evolution than that along the organism line.

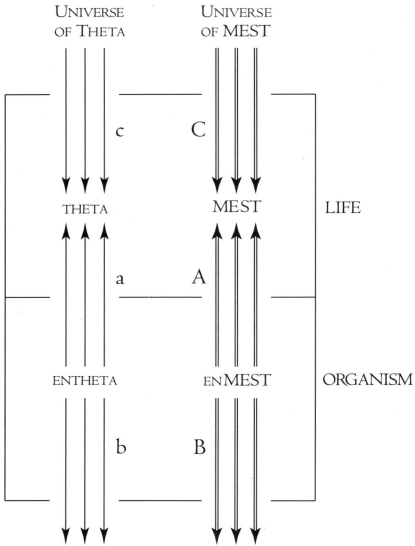

During processing, entheta is converted into theta, and enMEST is converted into MEST. It is postulated that this happens in the following way. ENMEST becomes MEST, part of which (A) is retained for use by the organism, and part of which (B) leaves the organism, to be replaced later (C) by new MEST. Entheta (a) becomes theta. It may also be postulated that entheta leaves the organism (b) and is replaced by new theta (c).

There is a fourth evolution which has been but slightly considered. This is the gradient scale in present time of growing complexity of life forms as they support themselves, in now, on MEST. The basic on this scale of complexity is, of course, those minute life forms which live on sunlight and inorganic chemicals alone and which convert rock and sand into soil, or in the sea, which provide food for the next highest vegetable form. The soil then supports a slightly higher plant form. This, in turn, makes better or more soil or, in the sea, better or more food, and an evolution of complexity then is observed in the higher and higher levels of the vegetable kingdom, then in the more simple animal and fish forms, and finally forms as complex as man. This last evolution is taking place continuously in present time and is a ladder of support, since man and other mobile animals depend upon lower and lower forms to do more and more basic work in providing MEST and its fuels for the construction. This present time evolution is in continuous existence, and here with us at this moment the lowliest forms are actively converting sunlight and minerals for the support of higher forms. The more MEST the form handles external to itself, the more complex are its requirements in terms of preprocessed MEST. This processing of MEST, then, for higher and higher form consumption is necessary as a staff of life.[1] Theta could be said, then, to exist across the MEST line of parade in time as a "now" band, just as the MEST universe probably lies in the continuous present time of the theta universe.

It seems to be a rule of theta and MEST that they form union only at a moment of heavy collision with each other. Although theta has a natural attraction for MEST and MEST has a natural attraction for theta, if MEST has any intention, this does not mean that the first union to any advance is a harmonious one. The first moment of impact is a collision in which a considerable portion of the theta becomes tangled with the MEST, leaving some free theta and some useful MEST. The remainder changes wavelength or

---

1. **staff of life:** something which serves as a basic support or essential element of life.

polarity and becomes what we call enturbulated theta and enturbulated MEST, which in Dianetics we shorten to entheta and enMEST.

While some organization may be made in this first union, it seems that the entheta and enMEST must separate in order for the theta to extract with it knowledge of the physical laws of MEST. Then a second collision is made, and a greater advance comes about, since theta has more knowledge of MEST and can make a more harmonious conquest. Continual repetitions of this bring theta more and more information, and more and more ability in the handling of MEST brings about more complex forms and organizations. This is as true of the group as it is of the individual, and all group activities which will eventually result in learning begin with considerable turbulence. After the turbulence is over, greater advances are then made possible through a much greater understanding of the physical universe by theta. An illustration of this would be the scientific advances obtained in wars, which in the afterpeace serve men constructively. There is a limiting factor on this, however, in that all the theta must not become enturbulated, thus carrying the organism evolution downward.

Death is a name assigned to what is apparently the mechanism by which theta recovers itself and the bulk of its volume from the MEST, so as to be able to accomplish a more harmonious conquest of the MEST in a next generation. Species advance so long as the theta and the MEST can still separate, leaving free theta, but at last the theta apparently begins to enter the genetic line on a dwindling spiral, the species decays and dies out.

The Tone Scale does not represent the idea that everything above 2.0 is theta in pure form and everything below 2.0 is entheta in pure form, nor that in the organism everything above 2.0 is MEST well organized by theta, and that, sharply, everything below 2.0 is enMEST, or disorganized matter. In older ways of thinking, which permitted only two-valued logic, which is to say black and white or right and wrong with no in-between values, the Tone Scale and its usefulness would have been greatly decreased. In Dianetics, there is a new way of thinking about things which underlies a great deal of its technology. Instead of two-valued logic or three-valued logic we have infinity-valued logic. Here is a gradient scale which permits no absolute at either end. In other words, there is not an absolute right and an absolute wrong, just as there is no absolute stillness and no absolute motion. Of course, it is one of the tenets of Dianetics that absolutes are not attainable but only approachable. Thus, we have gradient scales. Death is approached by degrees, in terms of failures, being wrong, accumulated sicknesses and accidents. An ascendancy upward toward life is an accumulation of minor successes which lead to higher and higher levels of survival, successes in organism growth and perfection and in education and in attaining goals.

Actually, 2.0 on the Tone Scale is the place where the ARC of theta and the organism order in terms of MEST have each and intermingledly become sufficiently dissonant so that a slight discomfort exists. The enMEST is not very enMEST, and the entheta is not very entheta, but as the scale is descended this dissonance grows stronger and wider until it is finally so wide that it is almost a null, which is to say that very little interactivity between entheta and enMEST exists and that the components of enMEST are becoming so poorly organized as not even to be in conflict with one another, and so that the ARC of theta is practically out of contact with themselves. The complete null point for the organism life is 0.0, where theta and MEST, so far as the organism is concerned, have so little in common with each other that they separate. This separation of the theta body from the MEST body ejects into being for further use in new organisms the MEST of the old body and releases into freedom for future conquest of organisms, according to present theory, the theta body.

If the auditor finds this too vastly technical, he should at least understand that in order to bring an organism up the Tone Scale he has to separate the enturbulations of theta and MEST, which exist as entheta and enMEST in the organism. Every moment of hard collision between the theta portion and the MEST portion of the body or between the organism and other organisms or MEST has formed a point of such intensity of entheta and enMEST that this point will thereafter enturbulate the theta and the MEST with which it comes into contact.

This is the engram, a moment of physical pain with its resultant unconsciousness and the perceptics entrapped therein. Entheta and enMEST from 0.1 up to 2.0 are seeking to separate and in so seeking enturbulate the existing theta and MEST. Any instant or area of physical pain, then, is trying itself to die, so that the entrapped entheta and enMEST can become free enough for new conquest to form less enturbulated entheta.

In Dianetic processing, something new, in that it can be done thoroughly, in the evolutions of organisms, the theta body and MEST, has been introduced. Processing separates entheta and enMEST without bringing about the death of the organism. These points of contagion, if unprocessed, sum up finally to organism death.

Just as, apparently, the MEST body of the organism is replenished by other MEST, processes it and gives off MEST, so is the theta body, possibly, replenished and so does it, evidently, give off theta. Beyond the fact of existence of and basic descriptions of theta, which are useful to the auditor, very little is known about theta at this time, although the recognition of its probable existence has enormously widened the scope of knowledge on the subject of the humanities, and the discovery of the theta body in terms that can be sensed, measured and experienced according to good scientific usage means a considerable advance, if it continues to be borne out by accumulating evidence.

Entheta, either over some bypass route or directly, converts into organism theta or makes it possible for more theta to be attracted to the organism simply by, according to present theory, the address of theta itself to the vicinity of the entheta and enMEST. The mere proximity of a considerable quantity of theta, apparently, to an area of entheta causes the entheta to change wavelength, vibration rate or polarity and either to become theta or to discharge and leave an area into which fresh theta can penetrate. Just as enough smoothly flowing water overcomes the turbulence of a disturbed area of flow, so does theta introduced into an entheta area convert or smooth out the entheta. It happens that the conversion effect of theta on entheta can occur when the theta to be applied to the entheta, or brought to bear upon it, exists in another organism or in a group of organisms. There is something everywhere-coexistent about theta, and perhaps there are various forms and types of it, all having more or less the same basic components, just as there is a great difference in quality amongst ideas, which seem to be the matter of theta.

From 2.0 up on the Tone Scale, the theta is less and less dissonant, or more and more compatible in its three components of affinity, reality and communication, but this does not mean that 4.0 is perfection of theta. Theta contained in organisms, from one organism to another, seems to have at least some of its factors more refined, and theta appears to assume other qualities above 4.0. Exactly how high these qualities go, whether or not the 2.0 to 4.0 range is highly personalized, where the band of true free theta is, if there is increasing power above these levels, are all questions subject at this time to considerable speculation. Only enough data exists to make it fairly certain that with the theta theory we are dealing with something much closer to natural law than man has widely accepted before in his attempts to understand life, human behavior and the humanities in general. Thus, it may be that as one proceeds on up the Tone Scale one discovers progressive advances in theta.

MEST is considerably easier to understand, being an old idea which has been worked over by several generations, to say the least, of physical-universe-minded individuals. Yet here again, with Dianetics, there was a great deal more to learn, particularly where MEST was concerned as a component part of the organism.

However lightly the auditor wishes to study or regard the above data on the theta–MEST theory, this following data concerning MEST and enMEST is vital to processing, and the auditor who does not know this data will not be able to achieve very good results on a case. Much of this data is new and has not before been released, but it has resolved, by theory and application of the techniques, cases which hitherto were considered extremely difficult, such as the heavily occluded case, which not only "could not get out of present time" but did not even seem to benefit very greatly from processing. Any auditor who has difficulty with his preclear would do well to read this section over again.

During processing, the individual can be observed to have what may be considered to be increased theta as fast as entheta is recovered and converted. There may be other manifestations of the release of entheta which have not yet been observed. If they exist and are observed, possibly processing may increase in technology.

The enMEST portion of conversion or exhaustion of charge on a case is considerably more obvious to the observer, possibly because at this time our knowledge of the material universe is so much greater and because we are trained to observe organism behavior.

We have already covered descriptions of locks, secondaries and engrams. What we are covering here is the mechanical process of removing areas of turbulence and, by theory, converting entheta to theta and enMEST to MEST.

The largest deposits of entheta and enMEST exist in secondaries, not in physical pain engrams. A physical pain engram acts as a sort of trap. It is the basic enturbulator. By contagion it can, in moments of loss or threatened loss, contain various misemotions. The secondary, primarily, charges up the physical pain engram to a point where it can assert its entheta side strongly against the analytical processes, or its enMEST side strongly against the physical part of the organism, creating chronic somatics, to which Dianetics attributes psychosomatic illnesses. A great deal of entheta, but not as much as can be trapped in secondaries, is contained in lock chains. Here gradually, day by day, little by little, theta is caught and converted into entheta, and the MEST at its level on the time track is converted into enMEST, to a slight degree. One should not ignore any deposit of entheta and enMEST. The whole task of processing confines itself to this conversion.

Contact with present time, if any part of that time can be demonstrably present to the preclear, has some tendency to disenturbulate some entheta. Straight Memory, by bringing to bear the theta of the analytical mind on the past, particularly in areas which are occluded, since all those occlusions are entheta areas, brings into being some theta. The running of a lock through and through as though it were an engram can, in a low-tone case particularly, bring into being more theta. Lock Scanning is a particularly efficacious technique in converting entheta. Secondaries, during moments of severe present time enturbulence, can greatly charge up engrams which have been keyed in, and are heavy, extensive deposits. Engrams themselves have the basic entheta and enMEST and are able to enturbulate and hold to themselves considerable entheta, but it is interesting to note that the engram could be taken down to a level of entheta content approximating that which it had originally without running the engram. This is easily understood as soon as one tries to run out a near present time injury. This near present time injury has not been charged up. The last moment of physical pain and unconsciousness on a case can usually be run. After a time, which may extend from a few days even to years, this engram is keyed in, at which time it begins to link up and index itself with the reactive mind, in direct ratio to the amount of restimulation that it receives, which is to say in direct ratio to the number of times words and other perceptics contained in this engram are approximated in an enturbulated environment.

The skill and ability of the auditor is, then, addressed to removing entheta by converting it, and anything which will do this is valid processing.

There are certain definite components in enMEST which manifest themselves during their release. Whenever entheta is converted to theta it is always done with an accompanying physiological manifestation. It is very easy for the auditor to aim for and achieve this physiological manifestation, for enMEST has certain definite components.

In other words, when entheta is being converted to theta, the organism manifests certain signs. These can be divided into the four general classifications of gases, liquids, solids and physical energy. One should understand that the enMEST portion of charge is the physical suppressor of aberration and chronic somatics.

One of the main manifestations in the organism, on the release of entheta and its conversion to theta as in the running of locks, secondaries or engrams, or occasionally even doing Straightwire, is gas. There is something about oxygenation which is not yet understood but which again might speed up processing. When one erases an engram, for instance, the erasure is accompanied by yawns. This is a gaseous and energy manifestation. Something is coming off of the case. In running locks, the preclear occasionally yawns. Flatulence also occasionally accompanies the release of entheta.

Liquids are released by the body in several forms during the release of enMEST. The most obvious form is tears. When a secondary engram is reduced, on the grief level, it is reduced in tears. When tears occur, the secondary should be run until it is completely exhausted, or the phrase, if that is all that can be recovered, should be repeated by the preclear until it no longer occasions tears, since the exhaustion of tears seems to be the primary manifestation of the exhaustion of the most harmful secondaries, those of grief. But tears are not the only manifestation. Fear seems to be released with accompanying sweat, sometimes of a peculiar odor. There are individuals who are chronically in such a state of fear that each present time perceptic discharges itself through sweat. Apathy commonly discharges itself as panting or urine, but more work must be done to establish the discharge of apathy in physiological terms.

Solids are discharged on the level of fear as vomiting, and there also, and on lower levels, as excreta.

There is a peculiar manifestation in Dianetics known as boil-off. Boil-off has assumed tremendously important proportions in processing, since the case that is very heavily enthetaed has its charge held down by such quantities of anaten that the induction of boil-off seems to be the most efficacious way to unburden the case. In a boil-off, a preclear will go into an apparent sleep. This is not sleep, no matter how much it may appear to be, but is actually a release of unconsciousness which is extremely concentrated and heavy. The release of this permits the case to go forward much more rapidly, because under it will lie quantities of specific incidents which otherwise are masked by this heavy layer. It is possible that a preclear may boil off for twenty-five to fifty hours, if he is extremely heavily burdened with entheta. The boil-off has certain strange manifestations. The preclear may, when running an incident, suddenly begin to maunder and trail off, giving muttered accounts of strange pictures and disrelated events. This is a mirage effect, through boil-off, and peculiarly disrelated things will clutter up his attention at this time, but he does all this in a very sleepy, dazed condition and shortly after may go into an even deeper boil-off.

Early in Dianetics, it was thought necessary to keep the preclear more or less alert in a boil-off. This was an error. The preclear should never be disturbed in a boil-off, but should be permitted to continue in this state until the boil-off is exhausted. Further, it was once thought that the preclear could be brought up to present time during the boil-off and that the boil-off would continue automatically. This does not appear to be the case. A boil-off must be continued on the point of the track where it began to occur.

A boil-off may be boring for the auditor, for the preclear lies in a dazed state and may do so for many minutes or even one or two hours. Even so, the auditor should not interrupt the preclear. The efficacy of boil-off is demonstrated by the fact that when one is finished the preclear is alert and can run other forms of entheta, but that when one is interrupted the preclear will be in an unsatisfactory condition. When boil-offs are not permitted or induced, the case will not progress rapidly, and in an occluded case may progress with remarkable slowness. Perhaps the boil-off's importance was minimized in the past because insufficient patience was devoted by the auditor to watching one continue through its full extent, which can be very long.

A boil-off can be induced, and fade away, and be reinduced, by a single phrase. The file clerk should be depended on by the auditor to give the phrase which will induce a boil-off. It has been commented upon that the boil-off occurs on circuit phrases and that it is actually the exhaustion of enormous quantities of anaten in a very concentrated form from the reactive mind from areas which have formerly been valence compartments or the location of demon circuits. This has not been adequately observed at this time for confirmation, for boil-off has been noted on phrases which were not circuit phrases. The auditor may ask the preclear's file clerk whether or not a boil-off can now be obtained and then request the phrase. The preclear repeats this phrase a few times and suddenly goes into a boil-off. He may emerge from this boil-off very shortly, at which time the auditor requests him to repeat the phrase, and he goes back into the boil-off. This phrase is repeated by the preclear, to himself or to the auditor, each time the boil-off recedes, until there is no longer any boil-off on the repeating of this phrase. Then the auditor may procure from the preclear's file clerk another phrase on which boil-off can occur, and so on until a considerable amount of this apparently concentrated anaten has been exhausted. The case will show a very marked improvement.

Physical pain should not be overlooked as one of the factors which holds entheta in place. It may occur that the auditor has a case which cannot run engrams but which can occasionally get physical pain on the repetition of a single phrase. If the preclear has a new, not a chronic, somatic, the auditor may request him for the phrase which will reduce this somatic, but only after he has ascertained from the file clerk whether or not the somatic will reduce. Such somatics, normally, are best reduced merely by scanning pleasure incidents, if they are bothering the preclear at the beginning of the session or at the end of it.

The perceptics are contacted when the case is lock-scanned. The perceptics themselves seem to have an entrapment of entheta. Thus, running all the perceptics out of an engram releases considerable entheta.

Additionally, there is body movement. The preclear may twist and turn while running fear, or may beat the bed with his fist while running anger, but in any event, by physical motion he exhausts energy. This is apparently beneficial, and the phrases and circumstances which cause the preclear to do this should be repeated. However, the auditor should not be deluded into wasting his time on simply a dramatization. The preclear must be in processing and, ordinarily, returned to a specific incident before any physical motion is of benefit.

There are probably numerous other manifestations of entheta and enMEST, and future observation should be devoted to their determination and their use in processing.

It is known that a good protein ration and certain vitamins assist the exhaustion and conversion of enMEST, and that a fairly stable present time, including a high theta auditor, assists the exhaustion and conversion of entheta, and it is known that certain physiological manifestations accompany the conversion of enMEST, and possibly theta manifestations accompany the conversion of entheta, but these have not been determined or observed to the extent that they would assist processing.

In an occluded case, an auditor may very well find himself on this routine, and he should know this very well. At the beginning of the case he attempts a little Straight Memory or perhaps some Lock Scanning. He may discover that the preclear is induced to weep on a certain phrase or to be frightened by a certain phrase. The auditor should cause that phrase to be repeated and the incident with which it is connected, as nearly as possible, be given some further attention. Conversion has already begun when this occurs. Next, the auditor may find, while lock-scanning or when asking specifically for a phrase which will induce it, that the preclear is going into a boil-off. The auditor, as the boil-off recedes, should discover the phrase on which the preclear is boiling off, so that the boil-off can be continued until it is exhausted. More entheta has been converted and more incident has been made available. Additional Lock Scanning may then recover moments of physical tension or mental duress of the lock variety. These should then be scanned until thoroughly exhausted. At this time it may happen that an entire secondary engram will show up, and when this is run the case will rebound remarkably up the Tone Scale. But in the next day or two it may be discovered that another boil-off is ready or that another series of locks containing duress should be scanned. Thus, from boil-off to Lock Scanning to the running of secondaries with as many of the perceptics as are available, the auditor may find himself with a case coming swiftly up the Tone Scale.

In any event, the auditor should discover this to be taking place, and if it is not taking place, then the auditor is doing something wrong. By Straightwire he stabilizes his case, and may by Straightwire get the case out of some incident which cannot be run. Here, he is converting entheta into theta. More theta is then available to attack more entheta, and so he may be able to scan locks or run a secondary engram or even an engram on a high-level case, or he may be able to get a boil-off. But each time, the auditor should be achieving some result. And each time he gains more theta for the preclear he should reinvest in a further and perhaps heavier attack upon entheta and enMEST. If he does this his case will continue on up the Tone Scale, not in a steady rise along an even line but along an uneven course in which the highs become always a little higher and lows not quite so low. Running engrams or slugging hard into the case may simply take the existing theta, place it in proximity with too large an amount of entheta, and enturbulate and entrap more of it, thus lowering the preclear on the Tone Scale instead of raising him.

With some preclears, the auditor can be quite nondirective, which is to say he can permit the preclear to run phrases and choose the next type of entheta to be attacked. The auditor, in any event, should consult with the file clerk as much as possible.

The auditor should not permit his preclear, however, to chain-scan engrams or go around running himself automatically on various phrases, as this results in the enturbulation of the existing theta. The only time engrams can be chain-scanned is when the preclear is up to about 3.5, constantly and unmistakably, and has so much free theta and so little entheta that the effect of the theta on the entheta is overpowering, even to the point of blowing out physical pain.

The auditor, if he wishes, may even put his preclear on freewheeling with a ration of *Guk,* between sessions. He will find that this has the efficacy of occasionally knocking out whole somatics and making the future job of processing easier. In any event, the *Guk* seems to promote the case. In freewheeling, where the somatic strip and file clerk are put into unison in the running of incidents but "I" is left in present time, the preclear may hang up in a holder or hit a bouncer and the freewheeling may stop. It so happens, however, that repeating the action phrase while freewheeling does not free the preclear but acts as repeater technique and takes "I" down the bank to join the somatic strip.

This may considerably enturbulate the case. The auditor, when the preclear is hung up while freewheeling, should ask the file clerk for the phrase and then cause the preclear to remember, by Straight Memory, when he has heard that phrase uttered. When the preclear recovers such an incident, any incident containing that phrase, the freewheeling seems then to continue. Apparently, the only danger in freewheeling is the use of repeater technique in connection with it. However, one should never believe a "file clerk" when the auditor asks, "Are you Clear?" and the "file clerk" says yes! For some reason or other "file clerks" are entirely too optimistic on this subject. The "file clerk Clear" and the use of repeater technique threw freewheeling into disrepute. However, a person who has been freewheeling can and should have it scanned out by Lock Scanning, just as any session would be, and the freewheeling occasionally seems to benefit a case. To put a preclear into freewheeling it is only necessary to tell him to close his eyes and for the auditor to say, "The file clerk will furnish moments of physical pain or discomfort and the somatic strip will run them out, and this process will continue until I say 'cancelled' " (or "until I tell the somatic strip to come to present time").

It should be remembered by the auditor that the circuit phrase is both recalcitrant and resistant to auditing. One of the main troubles with chain scanning is that the individual chain-scans out all manner of phrases but merely puts the circuit phrases into restimulation. Thus, the circuits seem to be activated, and we get a condition in chain scanning where the individual apparently has no more engrams, and yet by close processing, numbers of circuit phrases complete with somatics may be discovered on the case. Lock Scanning also has this difficulty to a slight degree, but this can be remedied by finding all types of circuit phrases by Straight Memory. Circuit phrases sometimes will not even flash, even when the action phrases in the case are relatively low in power, but the auditor, by guessing and talking with the preclear may eventually discover types of phrases which are circuit phrases and which would more or less take over control of auditing from the auditor and from the "I" of the preclear. Straight Memory recovers a specific moment when a phrase was uttered and the preclear can usually be lock-scanned through all similar moments, thus taking some of the charge off of the basic engram which contains the circuit phrase and weakening or getting rid of the demon control circuit, which may have been giving the auditor considerable trouble.

There are probably numberless ways of converting entheta to theta and of relieving the deposits of enMEST in the organism. These are simply the best ways known to date. These ways are proven and reliable. The auditor can discover on the Tone Scale chart the levels at which he can run various types of entheta. This is a safeguard and will keep the auditor out of a great deal of trouble. There are several freak techniques around, such as setting a person automatically on chain scanning, which are almost certain to increase the enturbulation on the case. I tested one some time ago in which the individual was sent home at night to run out chains of secondaries in his sleep. This was rather unsatisfactory, but it was interesting to note that one who was set to running a chain of grief secondaries in his sleep woke up in the morning to find his pillow saturated with tears and yet had no knowledge of what he had been crying about. This is added here to demonstrate that there are not only many combinations of the known existing mechanisms of the mind, but that there are probably a great number of mechanisms not yet known.

Possibly a very fruitful field is the exploration of theta perceptics, for theoretically it might be possible for new resurgences of theta to be entered into a case, with excellent results. Possibly this is what is happening when a person reaches toward a spiritual resurgence. This is very well worth investigating.

The auditor should keep in mind that cases, one to another, have different amounts of free theta endowment. He will find cases which are low on the Tone Scale and very occluded, which yet have great reasoning and constructive power, despite their tendencies toward succumbing. He will find these cases rising rather rapidly, but because the individual is here and there through the columns higher than the level assigned, the auditor should not therefore abandon the types of processing assigned for the general level where his preclear is located.

Likewise, it is a great temptation for the auditor when he finds a case which apparently has sonic and visio and some perception of pain to dive for the bottom of the case and start running engrams. After he has done this for a while he may find that his case is not making a very good rise on the Tone Scale and may only then check the chart, to discover that he has been working with a 0.8, much to his dismay. These low-level cases enturbulate rapidly, and the running of engrams on them, no matter how wide-open they are, may be done for hundreds of hours without any apparent marked increase in the tone level of the case. This is because the auditor is too enthusiastically investing free theta into the running of physical pain engrams which are not yet exhausted of their secondary and lock entheta. The goal in any case is the freeing of theta, and by this the auditor should be guided.

C O L U M N   A Q

TONE LEVEL OF AUDITOR NECESSARY TO HANDLE CASE

THIS COLUMN IS INCLUDED AS AN estimate of optimum performance.

The auditor should be aware of the fact that the engrams of the preclear, his secondaries and locks, respond only in the presence of all available free theta. The theta of the auditor plus the remaining theta of the preclear are a sum which is directed at the entheta in the reactive mind of the preclear. It is a strange fact that the mere presence of an auditor makes it possible for the preclear to run incidents which he could not touch if no auditor were present, although there have been preclears who have successfully run out locks and some secondaries. But self-auditing, normally, gets a case confused, and the presence of an auditor is very desirable.

Auditors who are below 2.0 on the Tone Scale tend unconsciously, and even consciously, in the direction of succumbing. They have a ratio in themselves of more entheta than theta. Auditors below 2.0 on the Tone Scale have accomplished something with cases from time to time, because the mechanics of Dianetics can be, in part, mechanically applied. But the preclear who places himself in the hands of an auditor below 2.0 is asking for unsuccessful processing, since Auditor's Code breaks will inevitably ensue and the case will be unwittingly mishandled, regardless of the obvious intention of the auditor.

One can say, then, that 2.5 is the lowest level the preclear should accept in an auditor. And even this has some slight risk, since the interest of the 2.5 auditor in the preclear is apt to be lackadaisical and will not encourage any great or rapid advances in the case.

3.0 would be the lowest level of the auditor, for any truly successful auditing. At this level, the auditor will be interested, sympathetic, able to follow the Auditor's Code with no strain, will be quick to understand any trouble which the preclear encounters, and can, ordinarily, in the presence of education, be expected to carry out a good and responsible role as an auditor. Furthermore, any discreditable data on a case which an auditor at this level uncovers in the life of the preclear will not be used as conversational material by the auditor. This is certainly not the case of the low-tone auditors.

When one is handling preclears from 1.5 down, he will normally discover that the preclear is very highly restimulative to the auditor, is apt to become angry or recalcitrant or insulting, has a great deal of trouble contacting some of the entheta, and is in general so highly charged that great patience and tolerance is required of the auditor. This means, simply, that the auditor must not be easily restimulated by his preclear. Those cases from 1.5 down are highly restimulative, on the average. Cases from this level down, which are chronically psychotic or psychotic at the time of processing, which is to say cases which have all of their free theta enturbulated, particularly require auditors on a high tone level, for auditors at lower levels are apt to consider the psychotic too critically, and a critical or restrictive attitude toward the psychotic denies him his recovery.

Further, the psychotic demands of the auditor a high courage level, a level certainly not found below 3.0, and guaranteed (given a good endowment of free theta and an education not contrary to courage) only at the 3.5 level. The psychotic, or persons who are on the tone band below 2.0 but who are easily enturbulated, has such a highly charged background in most cases that he may scream or express misemotion or dramatize to a frightening extent. A fully enturbulated paranoid may very well attempt to kill an auditor during the processing session, if the auditor suddenly reminds the paranoid of an enemy. Below 3.0, the reaction of the processor toward the psychotic may be irrational to the point of hastily giving the psychotic sedation or putting him in restraint or giving him electric shock or ordering a prefrontal lobotomy or doing any of those things, in short, which express crawling fear of another human being whose rationality cannot be trusted. A 1.5 trying to treat psychotics can think only in terms of punishment and nullification of the psychotic, and cannot possibly produce, simply by his presence and the quality of his reasoning, any alleviation in the case, but by his own fear further enturbulates the psychotic. Additionally, living in an environment filled with psychotics, such as an institution with individuals dramatizing, screaming, being irrational or dully stupid, is intensely restimulating, so much so that a considerable portion of the attendants and attending doctors of institutions themselves eventually find their way into the wards as patients.

In short, it takes life and energy in an individual to bring into being life and energy in others. And conversely, that person low on the Tone Scale, in order to climb up the scale or even to exist at his level, pulls heavily upon the life and energy of those around him. The legends of vampires probably originated from an observation that some persons seem to have no life of their own but only express themselves in the vicinity of and at the expense of other individuals. Low-tone people commonly yearn to marry, out of no other reason than that they can obtain from a mate the energy and life necessary to continued existence, or perhaps because here they have free theta to attack and desire to pull it down.

The auditor should be very cognizant of the fact that addressing entheta in a preclear is restimulative to the auditor. A certain amount of the auditor's free theta is going to become enturbulated when he processes preclears. New locks, at the very least, will be formed on his own chains. Thus, the enturbulation is not wholly temporary, but a certain amount of the enturbulation will become "permanent," which is to say that it must be processed out. Auditors who are not themselves being processed are unsuccessful. A group of auditors processing preclears but not being processed themselves will become, in a relatively short time, a veritable snake pit of entheta and, willy-nilly, will go down the Tone Scale.

The very least an auditor should do for himself if he is processing people is to keep the processing sessions he has done on other people scanned out of himself. He should consider that this is as necessary to him as eating and getting proper rest, for his own descent down the Tone Scale as a result of auditing will be so unobserved by himself that he will not know how low he has descended until he suddenly realizes that not only is he no longer taking any pleasure in auditing but he faces the next session with considerable distaste. When this happens the auditor can be sure that through failure to observe the necessity of having these sessions lock-scanned he now needs processing fully as badly as his preclears. He should take, then, every possible measure to bring himself up the scale, and the most immediately indicated of these is having processing sessions scanned out. As the auditor descends lower and lower on the Tone Scale he tends more and more toward succumbing, and he will reach a point where he does not think he needs any processing. When this happens, he has become very enturbulated.

Dianetics provides effective means of bringing people into a higher level of reason, energy and happiness and into a better state of physical well-being. If Dianetics is to succeed widely, and it will whether it takes two years or the next twenty, that success depends upon the co-auditing team, where two people audit each other alternately. It has been publicized that Dianetics is simply a low-cost therapy. Aside from the fact that Dianetics is not a therapy, Dianetics provides a means for any two people who are intelligent and fairly well up the Tone Scale to lift themselves by their bootstraps into much more desirable levels of human existence. It has never before

"Dianetics provides a means for any two people who are intelligent and fairly well up the Tone Scale to lift themselves by their bootstraps into much more desirable levels of human existence."

happened that people could do this. The formation of a co-auditing team should be done with some care. The two individuals should be somewhere near parity on the Tone Scale and should be, certainly, above 2.0 on the Tone Scale. A disparity will bring about the condition that one of them is doing all the auditing and one of them is receiving all the auditing, and there is no mutual exchange.

Husband–wife teams do not, ordinarily, make good co-auditing teams. Whereas a few such teams have been successful, the bulk of them have after a short time broken up as unworkable, and the husband and the wife have had to look outside the home for other processors. Thus, at the very start it would probably be wise to obtain co-auditors outside the home. There are many reasons for this. In the first place, marital relations have a certain delicacy, and the introduction of Dianetic processing between two individuals brings about another type of affinity. In a co-auditing team between husband and wife many Auditor's Code breaks may, indeed, break up the marriage. Looking outside the home, one can find co-auditors, if the original co-auditing team proved to be unsuccessful. Additionally, there are certain information barriers between husbands and wives in most marriages. And where the wife cannot tell the husband all she knows, and where the husband cannot tell the wife all he knows, enough of a brake is put on communication to inhibit processing. At the recent level of teenage morals, there is usually much in any marital partner's background which he does not wish to communicate to his spouse. With a co-auditing partner outside the home one can freely communicate, and thus the affinity required for co-auditing can be established, which it rarely can between husbands and wives.

There is also the three-way team, in which three people co-audit. This has the advantage of keeping altitude for each auditor, since in the triangle, none is being processed by anyone he is auditing.

When the preclear has come up the Tone Scale to 3.0 he can be processed by nearly anyone educated in Dianetics who is not below 2.0, for he can stand up to considerable Auditor's Code breaking or ineptness, but he should be aware of the fact that he will proceed faster, the higher the level of his auditor.

Any double or triangular co-auditing team should be careful to keep parity. No member of the team should be permitted to lag back so that a disparity in tone level can result. This is quite important, since by permitting the disparity to occur, the auditor who is higher on the scale will himself be brought back down the Tone Scale.

According to theory, the best auditors would be Clears, but people who have lost their own aberrations are quite likely to be interested in the activity dictated by their basic purpose.* If their basic purpose happens to be to make individual fellow human beings happier, healthier and more reasonable, then they will remain in Dianetics, but ordinarily, they go very far afield.

---

*BASIC PURPOSE: *even at the age of two or three years an individual seems to know what his basic purpose is in life. Later this becomes corrupted by individual and social aberrations but is recovered in Dianetic processing. Possibly past lives have something to do with forming basic purpose.* —LRH

CHAPTER TWENTY-ONE

COLUMN AR

HOW TO AUDIT THE CASE

I<small>N THIS CHAPTER WE WILL TAKE UP</small> particular tone level cases. It should be remembered that an individual can exist at any one of these tone levels and still be considered "rational" by the current society.

There are two things an auditor should observe in starting a case. Either he evaluates the case on the chart with thoroughness and so knows the type of case he is addressing, or he uses, in the absence of chart evaluation, very light methods of processing such as Straight Memory or the scanning of minor lock chains. Unless the auditor is very experienced, he will not be able to determine immediately where his preclear lies on the Tone Scale, unless he has the chart before him and has made a test of the somatics and general responses of his preclear.

Learning to use the chart and to locate the preclear on it may take the auditor some time, for the chart is complicated in that it contains several elements. There are at least five different ways that tone may be said to vary. The auditor is looking, mainly, for the chronic reactive tone of the preclear, in order to know at what level it will be safe to process him. Some high-theta auditors can successfully use methods on preclears which are above their chronic reactive tone level. They do this by bringing the preclear temporarily up the Tone Scale with very high ARC. But this is, unfortunately, an unusual ability, and the auditor who wishes to make sure that he will not enturbulate the preclear should be very careful not to use methods which are above the preclear's level on the Tone Scale. Five things which affect the tone manifestations which the preclear is showing are (1) the theta–entheta ratio on the case, the relative amount of "frozen" entheta in locks, secondaries and engrams, (2) the present time environment of the preclear, its tone and volume, (3) the tone of the particular engram in which the preclear happens to be stuck, if he is stuck, (4) the tone commanded by a particular engram command phrase or series of phrases which are in restimulation, either acute or chronic, (5) the general environmental background of the preclear, the tone of his education, family, group and so on. It may be a somewhat difficult job for the auditor to separate these various elements in the preclear's manifested tone, in order to discover the one thing which is most important to the level of processing to be used on the preclear, namely the theta–entheta ratio on the case.

Straightwire on the present time environment of the preclear, the events of the last two or three days or even hours, will give the auditor some idea of what effect present time is having on the manifested tone.

Straightwire on the preclear's general background, during the taking of the inventory and after, will give the auditor a somewhat less clear estimate of the effect of this element on the preclear's manifested tone, since much of the material may be occluded or purposely hidden.

An attempt at running a pleasure moment and a few flash answers will tell the auditor whether or not this preclear is badly stuck on the track and, therefore, whether this is an important factor in his manifested tone.

The effect of a chronically or acutely restimulated engram or chain of engrams will be, perhaps, the most difficult to track down and allow for. It is here that the manic case enters the picture, and this is the greatest danger that the auditor will encounter of rating his preclear too high on the scale: a wide-open case with a high manic in full restimulation.

Because all these things complicate the problem, the auditor will find that his most reliable test of the theta–entheta ratio on the case will be the behavior columns on the Tone Scale chart—after he learns to use them, and not to be deceived by the preclear's idea of what his own tone is. Subtle, patient questioning, perhaps over many hours, will be necessary before the auditor will be justified in feeling that he has truly discovered the chronic tone level of the preclear in each of these columns. For this reason, it might be said that every case, almost without exception, should be started with many hours of Straightwire. To ask the preclear, for instance, what his attitude is about children will gain for the auditor information on what the preclear thinks his attitude is, or what he wants the auditor to think it is, or, perhaps, what it really is. The preclear's gestures and voice tones in answering the question will tell the auditor much, and the questioning is in itself of benefit to the case. But the auditor will be sure of the preclear's attitude towards children only when he has straightwired the preclear on several incidents with children. There may be cases in which direct questions on these things will only serve to alert the preclear's secrecy computations and in which the auditor would be wise to use the chart thoroughly and exhaustively but not obviously, with direct questions. A direct question such as, "Do you like children?" may easily seem like probing or criticism to the preclear, if unconsciously so. A request to relate an incident with children may provide the auditor with invaluable data which he could not get with direct questions.

"The Tone Scale chart is a delicate and somewhat complex tool. The auditor who, by practice and alert observation of results, learns to use it well will find both his abilities and his understanding immeasurably increased."

The Tone Scale chart is a delicate and somewhat complex tool. The auditor who, by practice and alert observation of results, learns to use it well will find both his abilities and his understanding immeasurably increased.

A case at 4.0, the Dianetic MEST Clear—which is to say the current-life-organism Clear until we know more areas which can be processed—can be considered to need no further processing.

The 3.5 case is very easy to process, but a case is almost never at this level when first addressed. When a case has reached this level through processing, it is relatively easy to bring the case up to Clear. Almost anything can be done with this case in the way of running entheta, and it is merely a question of how fast this individual can be brought to the state of Clear rather than whether or not he will reach it, for he can almost audit himself to that point if he has attained 3.5. Here, engrams can be scanned, a process which is done much like Lock Scanning except that physical pain incidents, secondaries and word chains which are surrounded by physical pain can be scanned. On the 3.5, however, just as on any other case, one should keep the auditing sessions scanned off the case.

The 3.0 case should not be scanned through engrams. Scanning is a very attractive mechanism. It seems to be such a simple thing to start the individual at basic-basic and tell him to scan out all the engrams on up the track to present time. But considerable entheta exists on the 3.0 and the scanning mechanism will enturbulate him and bring him down the Tone Scale. Here, circuits are still active enough so that they will be activated by chain scanning and a "false Clear" will result, which is to say the auditor will have a preclear whose circuits have been charged to the point where the auditor cannot find an engram and so assumes that he has a Clear, when he does not. However, the 3.0 has nearly all of his engrams ready to be run by Standard Procedure. The auditor sends the 3.0 back to the earliest moment of pain or discomfort, picks up the earliest phrase and runs the engram on through. Usually it is not necessary for the auditor to have the preclear repeat the phrases, each one time after time, but the auditor can let the preclear run straight on through the engram from beginning to end and then run it through from beginning to end again. On an erasure, of course, the auditor has located the first moment of pain or discomfort and has reduced a great many of the secondaries, the earliest physical pain engram has been run out, and it is necessary then only to proceed up the bank, on the ladder of time, erasing each consecutive engram as contacted, from the first inception of the pain or unconsciousness in the engram to the last. In the 3.0, it will be found that engrams erase rather rapidly. One or two passes will result in yawns, and the next engram can then be reached. It must not be overlooked by the auditor, however, that in the progress of going up the bank from engram to engram, each time taking the earliest one that can be found, secondary engrams may come to light which have to be discharged. An auditor can actually start up the bank and complete an erasure nearly to present time, and find then a new chain of secondary engrams which have to be released in terms of tears or other manifestations, and after this the auditor may discover that any new moment of physical pain or discomfort exists as early as conception. He must then return to this earliest engram. It is not difficult for the auditor to discover this, if he asks each time for the earliest moment of pain or discomfort existing on the case. The auditor remains very alert to the fact that the release of anaten, misemotion or physical pain brings into view new areas of anaten, misemotion or physical pain. By asking for the earliest moment of pain or discomfort and staying alert to the fact that new secondaries may appear, the auditor continues with his erasure of the content of the reactive mind. But at 3.0 it is necessary for the auditor to keep the case thoroughly scanned off, not only as to auditing but as to near present time incidents which may be enturbulative to the preclear. At 3.0 and below, the auditor must at all times remember that he is bringing the case up the Tone Scale and that the simple erasure of engrams is not enough to cause the case to progress satisfactorily, but that the erasure of engrams all by itself can actually, if no other form of entheta is addressed, bring this case back down the Tone Scale again, particularly in the presence of a present time restimulative situation which considerably enturbulates the preclear. The 3.0 level is definitely the area where an erasure is begun. Engrams do not reduce at this level, but erase.

The 2.5-level case offers a little more concern to the auditor than the 3.0. This is so all the way down the bank, since the lower one goes on the Tone Scale, the more entheta one finds on the case and the greater care he must take in order to keep up the present time tone of the preclear and to keep the preclear progressing up the Tone Scale. The 2.5 scans locks very easily; however, he cannot, like the 3.5, scan secondaries. It is not advisable to scan a 2.5 through any moments of heavy misemotion, because the case will become restimulated and more theta will be absorbed into the turbulent areas than will be freed out of those areas by auditing. However, the 2.5 will run engrams as a routine matter, when they are addressed as single engrams, not as chains of engrams as in chain scanning. Moments of great sorrow, loss, anger, apathy are run out as incidents, perceptic by perceptic, until they are reduced. New secondaries and new engram chains are recovered in the 2.5 by Lock Scanning. The only time the 2.5 requires Straight Memory as a processing technique is when the auditor desires to discover more about his case or to discover circuits. In the 2.5, the auditor locates circuits by Straight Memory, finding who in the preclear's environ tried to dominate or nullify him and finding moments during the awake life of the preclear when these people made statements which were circuit-type statements, such as "Control yourself" or "Keep a good grip on yourself." At this level, the circuit is important. Here, considerable address should be made to circuits. The phrases should be located by Straight Memory and should then be lock-scanned out as phrases so as to discharge and deintensify all circuit phrases contained in engrams; for here, and on down, a circuit can more or less take over from an auditor, so that the preclear will occasionally insist on running his own case. Or a circuit can bar off large quantities of entheta. The biggest trouble the 2.5 gives the auditor is the fact that the 2.5 normally considers himself to be in a fine state of health and is rather bored with processing. When a preclear has reached the level of 2.5 from a lower level, he would quite commonly just as soon forgo further processing. It is at this point that the auditor must apply his own personality to the situation and coax his preclear through this rather stagnant area on the Tone Scale.

The 2.0 who is willing to work does not offer any particular problem to the auditor. Here the auditor can scan locks, he can run secondaries as individual moments of misemotion, but here the auditor may very well overestimate his preclear and decide to run, as routine, physical pain engrams. Here, the auditor can run physical pain engrams one after another, but he will tie up more free theta by creating new locks on the case through the running of these engrams than he gains out of the engrams. Any auditor is very ambitious for his preclear and is likely to begin running engrams long before the preclear is able to benefit from or even support running them. Nevertheless, particularly in the case where the preclear has received a drug-hypnosis or has had a recent operation, some physical pain engram may present itself at this level and insist on being run. The file clerk is usually working at 2.0, and the file clerk should be very carefully consulted before any physical pain engrams are addressed. If physical pain engrams are run on the 2.0, the auditor should be very careful to thoroughly scan off the session of auditing, in order to knock apart the locks which are formed by the auditing itself.

The 1.5 responds to the scanning of locks, but the auditor will find that the 1.5 will sometimes hang up in individual locks. When this happens, the lock may have to be run like an engram, perceptic by perceptic, until it is reduced. After this, Lock Scanning can continue. This is of benefit to the case, since the scanning of locks brings the preclear closer to the most severe locks, which can then be contacted and run. These heavy locks remain out of sight until scanning brings to the preclear enough free theta to permit an address to heavy locks which are holding up the progress of the case. On a 1.5, secondaries can be located best which are at the anger level. The auditor can discover a moment when the preclear was dramatizing anger and can ask the preclear to run through this moment or ask him to go back to an earlier moment when somebody was that angry with him. The preclear will discover an earlier lock where he himself was the recipient of the anger he later dramatized, and ordinarily, he will run this early lock. The auditor should be very careful of any physical pain he runs on the 1.5. Here is a level where any physical pain is a thoroughly greedy trap. The engram in the 1.5 has so much authority that when free theta approaches it, that theta is itself enturbulated. Thus, the auditor should avoid running engrams at 1.5. The use of Straight Memory becomes very important at 1.5. Here a trick of Straight Memory becomes very important. The auditor should try to find an incident of an ARC break or enforcement variety which the preclear can credit with thorough and full reality. Actually, from this point on down the reality of the preclear can be confirmed and should be confirmed at every opportunity by Straight Memory contact with locks which the preclear himself and without any assistance from the auditor fully credits as actually having happened. This boosts the preclear up the Tone Scale more swiftly than any other method of processing which can be used from 1.5 on down. Here, the auditor should be particularly careful to keep the auditing scanned off and should use any and every means to keep the free theta which he finds in the case as free as possible. Bad auditing and Auditor's Code breaks at this level can cost the preclear in one session more theta than can be won in several sessions. The preclear at 1.5 commonly becomes angry with the auditor. He is still at a level where he seeks to dominate, and his method of domination is to express anger. This does not mean that the 1.5 is only angry or that he will not work smoothly for the auditor. Usually, only bad auditing will cause anger. There are 1.5s which are wide open and which deceptively seem to invite the running of engrams. There are 1.5s which are thoroughly occluded. In either case exactly the same type of entheta is addressed and the same methods of handling it are used.

When one comes down to the 1.1, a great deal of care must be used because of the tremendous amount of entheta which exists on the case in proportion to the free theta. A 1.1 may have enough theta endowment originally to want to be processed. His desire to be processed, however, is very tentative and he is intensely critical of his auditor. He is afraid, and with good reason, for he has so little free theta left in comparison to the entheta on his case that bad auditing can bring about a much worsened condition. The 1.1 may not, however, be interested in processing and may consider himself in good condition, despite a very bad record in dealing with life. He is, quite commonly, chronically ill from one somatic or another. He may be diffident about his food. What free theta he has left is in such combat with the entheta, that he is continually on a borderline. The auditor must recognize this. The auditor must recognize as well that a 1.1 can be insulting, can be sullen, can be thoroughly unwilling to be processed, and can be extremely trying. The patience of an auditor is easily exhausted when dealing with a 1.1, for the 1.1 may lie down on the couch and knowingly run completely imaginary incidents, reporting somatics and perceptics which he does not have. He may manufacture for the auditor an entire past life. Further, he may unknowingly advance data which is wrong. He may consider, for instance, and believe that he is telling the truth, that he was beaten a thousand times by his father, whereas his father laid hands on him but twice in his whole life. Or he may believe that he was treated royally by his parents, when actually they were extremely nonsurvival in their attitude toward him. The auditor must remember that in both the 1.5 and the 1.1, truth is not regarded as a very valuable commodity and is hard for the preclear to contact. Although the 1.1 may continually advance protests and evidences as to his honesty and openheartedness, the auditor is dealing with a level where trickery is automatic. The auditor may actually succeed at this level in turning off chronic somatics, such as a migraine headache or ulcers, without decreasing the turbulence of the case. He has, evidently, merely turned an enMEST manifestation into an entheta manifestation, so that although the chronic somatic no longer troubles the 1.1 as physical pain, it troubles him exceedingly as mental aberrations. Transfer of one somatic to another, or transfer of physical aberration to mental aberration can be expected to result if the auditor mistakes the preclear's level on the Tone Scale and attempts to use methods of processing that are above the 1.1's level. In a wide-open case, the auditor can be completely fooled, and can go on running the case with heavy methods ad infinitum (until the preclear tires of processing and refuses it), more and more enturbulating the case, unless he pays careful attention to the preclear's behavior in locating the preclear on the Tone Scale chart.

Probably the chief characteristic of the 0.5 as far as the auditor–preclear relationship is concerned is the 0.5's complete helplessness. Even if the 0.5 wants to be audited, the auditor cannot depend upon his preclear for any responsibility about processing, or about anything else. This case requires an auditor of great patience and endurance. The auditor is faced with an individual to whom black is white, good is bad, and all is lost. His preclear may run hours of dub-in incidents if permitted, but the auditor has to be very careful how he steers the preclear toward real incidents, which should never be heavier than locks, preferably of the apathy variety, because the slightest disapproval or lack of acceptance of what the preclear is saying may enturbulate all of the preclear's meager remaining theta. The 0.5 is only half a point above death. Any auditor who uses methods heavier than Straight Memory and the running of individual light locks on a 0.5 runs a risk of causing some death manifestation in the preclear, either suicide or (occasionally) murder, and most certainly will depress the 0.5 down toward pretended death. However, if the auditor keeps his own case well processed, so that he can persevere in processing the 0.5 with the gentlest methods and so that he can preserve a very high ARC (which will depend entirely on the auditor) with the preclear, he will sooner or later have a preclear who is beginning to come up into the 1.1 band. This rise on the scale may not bring the auditor any relief, since 1.1 is a very unpleasant level, but it will be a great relief to the preclear, although the auditor should not expect any thanks from the new 1.1.

The average auditor will not be working with a 0.1 in the very near future, since most pretended death cases are in hospitals, sanitariums or institutions where they are out of contact with the society. However, the circumstances of the 0.1 in the society at this time have no bearing upon the methods used to process a 0.1, and no auditor should think that the principles of mind operation change in any way in the case of the 0.1. The auditor who is invited to some private sanitarium by an alert but baffled medical doctor, as some auditors have been, may find that he has just such a case to deal with. There are various methods of approaching the problem of the 0.1 case, but all of them add up to one thing: cause the preclear to be aware of present time perceptics, or at least of the idea that there is such a thing as present time. In all other levels it is necessary to establish and maintain high ARC between the auditor and the preclear, but here the main problem is to establish ARC between the preclear and anything in present time, including, of course, the auditor. How this may be done will depend upon the auditor's thorough understanding of the principles outlined in this book, for here is a case in which the theta might be considered to be 98 percent enturbulated. It has been seen that as the Tone Scale was descended, gentler and gentler methods of processing had to be used. The auditor may feel, then, that there is no method of processing gentle enough for a 0.1, but the auditor should not overlook the fact that the mere presence of an auditor in the room with the preclear is, to some degree, processing. Starting from there, the auditor can begin to work to make present time interesting and attractive to the preclear. The auditor's presence for a few hours may build up enough affinity to make it possible for the auditor to call the preclear's attention to some object. When the preclear communicates with this object, by looking at it, the fact that the auditor is holding it, or also looking at it, will tend to establish an agreement about this object, and some one thing in the world will then have a little reality for this preclear.

Future publications will deal more thoroughly with the processing of inaccessible psychotics, including the 0.1. But the principles which you have encountered while reading this book are the principles upon which future and more refined techniques will be based, and any auditor who has the opportunity and the perseverance to process such a case will find that, simple as these basics are, they are more powerful than any means man has had before to bring light where there is darkness, to bring order out of disorder, and to convert unreason into reason—or entheta into theta.

UNBURDENING ENGRAMS

Recently I developed a technique called "Unburdening" which seems to have considerable possibilities. I have not had sufficient opportunity to test thoroughly its potentialities or to properly locate it on the Tone Scale. I give it here for your information and would greatly appreciate hearing about whatever results you achieve with it.

Ordinarily the last engram on a case can be run providing it has not acquired too many locks. Further, any engram seems to depend, for its inaccessibility, on the locks it has accumulated.

The auditor occasionally finds it necessary to run an engram even though he cannot get all the perceptics which are contained in that engram. It would be valuable if he could obtain all the perceptics and reduce or erase them. Unburdening would be a technique designed to assist the auditor in running out all the perceptics.

The engram, in this technique, is run until everything in it which can be contacted is reduced. Then the auditor lock-scans the preclear from the moment of the engram up to present time through all the locks of that engram. The auditor has the locks scanned one or more times, working with the file clerk. Then the auditor, using again Standard Procedure for engrams, runs that engram once more or twice more or until any additional material has been reduced. Then he again has the preclear scan all the locks of that engram again. Then he once more runs the engram.

It is the charge in the locks which seals in the engram. By discharging the locks, through the technique of Lock Scanning, more and more perceptics should show up in the engram.

Unburdening, then, would be the technique of thoroughly bringing to view everything contained in an engram by scanning its locks. Alternate running of the engram and scanning its locks should bring about a maximal release of entheta.

The practicality of this technique is certain. The extent of its usefulness has not been thoroughly explored.

It is completely assured that a physical pain engram underlies all misemotion and that when misemotion is run from a secondary, a physical pain engram is commonly exposed to view. Indeed, the preclear may dive into the physical pain engram and start running it while the auditor is still attempting to get a discharge from the secondary. It also happens that when an auditor is trying to run an engram his preclear may suddenly run into the misemotion of a secondary (which should then be run).

It also occurs commonly that the preclear, when the auditor is trying to run an engram, will soar up into the locks of that engram. This is the result, usually, of a bouncer in the engram. But bouncer or no bouncer, the locks are there and they are important. Thus, when an engram is reduced, the locks may be run, after which more perceptics may be found.

POSITIVE PROCESSING

A variation of technique which is of value to the auditor is "Positive Processing." This consists of addressing the theta on the case and bringing it to view. The auditor may become so engrossed in addressing entheta directly that he may overlook the fact that theta may be buried under the entheta. By looking for and bringing to view the theta, a preclear may be considerably improved in tone.

Below many areas of entheta on a track there may be what we could call deposits of theta. The theta of the auditor and preclear addressed to such deposits of theta will disenturbulate the entheta which may overlay such a moment.

Pleasure moments are, one could say, deposits of theta. Such deposits assist the conversion of entheta to theta. The running of pleasure moments then materially assists the raising of tone. One can use this in many ways and all these ways could be grouped under "Positive Processing." There are probably innumerable variations of Positive Processing. The running of a pleasure moment just as though it were an engram, until all perceptics are recovered, is just one instance of Positive Processing. The scanning of chains of pleasure moments is another variation. The running of "future pleasure moments" ties in the imagination but is just another variation of Positive Processing.

Affinity, reality and communication can be used to excellent advantage in Positive Processing. The auditor, in this instance, is not looking for ARC locks when ARC was enforced or inhibited. He is looking for moments when they existed. By Straight Memory the auditor causes the preclear to recall moments when he *actually* felt he was receiving or giving affinity or communication, or actually experiencing reality. The preclear fairly well down the scale may have to search for some time before he can recall an instance when he actually felt affinity for something or some person or actually felt he was receiving affinity. Similarly, the preclear may have difficulty finding a moment of actual communication—he may be in an audience or talking with a friend or even simply talking to a dog. Further, the auditor should remember that communication extends to perception and that actually seeing something or recalling that something was heard or felt may discover a theta deposit. Causing the preclear to recall something he knew was truly real or even recall somebody agreeing thoroughly with him is another instance of Positive Processing.

Straight Memory on ARC positives is very valuable on low-tone cases. Further it is valuable in any case as a means of ending a session.

The auditor will find sometimes that when he gives Positive Processing he will get yawns from the preclear. This is particularly true of scanning pleasure moments. These yawns indicate that the preclear has pleasure suppressors—that something makes him feel guilty for experiencing pleasure. By some standards, not survival ones, pleasure is seen to be wicked and the engrams of the preclear will be found to contain admonitions against pleasure.

Occasionally the auditor will find a preclear breaking into tears under Positive Processing. Here, evidently (though several opinions could be advanced) the suppression of pleasure is such that the overlying entheta is of the same value as that in a secondary engram. The tears of relief signify the progress of the preclear up from apathy through grief in certain incidents. For any incident, irrespective of the preclear's tone, has its own position on the Tone Scale and, as it is reduced, comes up the scale in stages.

There was once a whole philosophy devoted to pleasure —hedonism. Survival is pleasure, but idle satisfaction of the senses without plan or progress toward any goal is itself (like Aesop's grasshopper)[1] destructive in the long run. It was this idle and purposeless gratification of the senses at which the moralist

1. **Aesop's grasshopper:** a reference to the grasshopper in the fable *The Ant and the Grasshopper* by the Greek author, Aesop. The fable tells of a grasshopper who only thinks of the good time in the present and does not work and prepare for the winter. It therefore finds itself starving of hunger, while the busy ant had lots of food.

raged—and with considerable justification. But better terminology should have been used. Pleasure is something neither man nor a civilization can do without—its omission results in succumb. In that happiness can be found to be the overcoming of not unknowable obstacles toward a known goal or the contemplation of goals, one can see that *idle* pleasure would have to be static or destructive sensual gratification. Pleasure is seldom idle in that sense, but it is as often lazy and relaxing as it is dynamic and constructive. Man cannot live without it. And the auditor, using Positive Processing will find it a helpful ally.

The goal of processing is to raise the individual on the Tone Scale. Part of this procedure is the running out of all engrams in order to make the rise permanent. But the important thing is the rise itself. The behavior of a 4.0 or even a 3.5 is so far superior to normal human behavior, the ability of these higher levels to provide happiness, accomplishment, creation and joy in living is so great, that we tend to think of them as distant goals simply because they are so high. But they are not so distant. Even as this book is completed, new methods, new approaches to a case are developing which make the higher ranges of the Tone Scale easier to reach for more and more cases. The validation or positive approach to the case, the advent of Dynamic Straightwire (in which the effect of each dynamic on every other discovers all possible locks), the discovery of the fundamental nature of MEST locks* and the development of MEST technique,** are but some of the new things that are coming off the "drawing boards." Dianetics does not rest or stay, it does not flag or halt. As the auditor and preclear continue

---

*MEST LOCKS: *locks which come about through the inhibition or enforcement of the individual's experience or control of matter or energy or space or time. It is postulated that the reduction of the MEST locks in which the individual was made to go up or not permitted to come down will make any bouncer phrases in the case inactive, and so on with all types of action phrases.* —LRH
**MEST TECHNIQUE: *Straightwire, Repetitive Straightwire (slow, auditor-managed Lock Scanning), and Lock Scanning on MEST locks. Language locks are found by Straightwire only as a clue to the underlying MEST locks. MEST technique and validation technique may be combined and should be.* —LRH

their progress up the Tone Scale, they may be encouraged not only by their own successes but also by the fact that as they approach the goal, it is approaching them. A fact which has been forgotten in this time of war and spiritual pestilence is that there have been times in man's history and prehistory when he has *succeeded*. It has not all been gloom and hopelessness, else we would not be here today—even as poorly as we are. Men have lived to conquer all other forms of life, from the mastodon to the microbe. Men have lived to build walls and roads and pyramids which have defied the elements for thousands of years. Men have lived to write music which has pleased the gods and lines which have made the angels sigh and the Devil weep. This is a time for man to succeed again. Here is the word, the technology, the goal. The job is cut out: and its name is *Survive!*

APPENDIX

DEFINITIONS
AND AXIOMS

SURVIVE   The dynamic principle of existence is *Survive.* At the opposite end of the spectrum of existence is *Succumb.*

DYNAMICS   The dynamics are the urge to survive, expressed through a spectrum, which is here given with eight divisions. (1) self, (2) sex, the family, and the future generation, (3) the group, (4) mankind, (5) life, all organisms, (6) MEST, (7) theta, (8) the Supreme Being.

IMMORTALITY

Infinite survival, the absolute goal of survival. The individual seeks this on the first dynamic as an organism and as a theta entity and in the perpetuation of his name by his group. On the second dynamic he seeks it through his children, and so on through the eight dynamics. Life survives through the persistence of theta. A species survives through the persistence of the life in it. A culture survives through the persistence of the species using it. There is evidence that the theta of an individual may survive as a personal entity from life to life, through many lives on Earth.

PLEASURE Pleasure is the reward of survival activity along any of the dynamics. Successes bring pleasure and survival.

SUCCUMB Succumbing is the ultimate penalty of nonsurvival activity. This is pain. Failures bring pain and death.

HUMAN THOUGHT

A process of perceiving and storing data, computing conclusions, posing and resolving problems. The purpose of this is survival along all of the dynamics.

INTELLIGENCE

The ability to perceive, pose and resolve problems. Intelligence and the urge to survive (the dynamic) are both necessary to continued existence. The quantity of each varies from individual to individual and group to group. The dynamics are inhibited by engrams which block their flow of theta, or life force, and disperse it. Intelligence is also inhibited by engrams, which enter false or improperly graded data into the analytical mind.

HAPPINESS The overcoming of not unknowable obstacles toward a known goal.

ANALYTICAL MIND

That portion of the mind which perceives and retains experience data to compose and resolve problems and direct the organism along the eight dynamics. It thinks in differences and similarities.

REACTIVE MIND

That portion of the mind which files and retains physical pain and misemotion and seeks to direct the organism solely on a stimulus-response basis. It thinks only in identities.

SOMATIC MIND

That portion of the mind which, at the direction of either the reactive or analytical mind, puts solutions into effect physically.

TRAINING PATTERN

A stimulus-response mechanism set up by the analytical mind to carry out activity of either a routine or an emergency nature. The training pattern may be said to be held in the somatic mind, but it can be changed at will by the analytical mind.

HABIT

A stimulus-response mechanism similar to the training pattern but set up by the reactive mind out of the content of engrams. It cannot be changed at will by the analytical mind.

ABERRATIONS

Irrational behavior or computation (thinking). They are stimulus-response in nature and may be prosurvival or contrasurvival. The engram is the basic source of aberrations.

$PV=ID^x$

This formula expresses the Potential Value of an individual. "I" represents intelligence, and "D" represents dynamic.

WORTH

If an individual's PV is high and is aligned with the dynamics toward survival, his worth may be said to be very high. A person with a high PV, however, may be aberrated so that his PV is reversed in the direction of succumbing and his worth is low. This may be computed for any one of the eight dynamics or for all.

THETA (θ)

Thought, potentially independent of a material vessel or medium. Life force. *Élan vital.*

THETA UNIVERSE

Thought matter (ideas), thought energy, thought space, and thought time, combining in an independent universe analogous to the material universe. One of the purposes of theta is postulated as the conquest, change and ordering of MEST.

MEST (φ) — Matter, Energy, Space, and Time. The physical universe.

LIFE (λ) — The harmonious conquest of MEST by theta in which a self-perpetuating organism is formed. Death is the withdrawal of theta from the organism.

ENTHETA — Theta which is enturbulated with MEST (enMEST) in an inharmonious combination. Irrational thought.

ENMEST — MEST which has been enturbulated by entheta or crushed too hard into theta and rendered less usable.

PAIN — The alarm reaction to theta which has been crushed too severely into MEST. The penalty of nonsurvival activity.

ENGRAM — An encystment containing entheta and enMEST. A recording (possibly cellular) of a period of pain and unconsciousness (or anaten). Not available to the analytical mind as experience. The sole source of aberrations and "psychosomatic illnesses."

LOCK — An analytical incident of greater or lesser enturbulence of theta which approximates the perceptics of an engram or chain of engrams and therefore becomes trapped due to the physical pain recorded in the engram and remains as an encystment of entheta.

SECONDARY **E**NGRAM

A lock of such magnitude that it must be run as an engram in processing. A lock with great magnitude of entheta.

CHARGE — The accumulation of entheta in locks and secondaries which charges up the engrams and gives them their force to aberrate.

DEATH — The withdrawal of theta from an organism, leaving only MEST, in order to conquer new MEST and form another organism which can better survive.

LIFE CYCLE The periodic conquest of, withdrawal from, and reconquest of MEST by theta. It is postulated that a given segment or entity of theta (in human beings, at least) undergoes birth, growth, death, birth, growth, death, etc., each time learning more about the business of making MEST into successful organisms which can better survive.

EVOLUTION There are four evolutionary tracks, evidently. Organism evolution, through natural selection, accident and (evidence suggests) outright planning. MEST evolution, brought about through the agency of life organisms. Theta evolution, a postulated process of learning in theta as a whole or as entities. And present time ladder-of-support evolution, in which less complicated organisms support more complicated organisms.

THETA BODY

The personal theta entity. The soul. Evidence suggests that the theta body may, through many low tone lives, become an entheta body, but that such an entheta body might be cleared by Dianetic processing. It is probable that the theta body can, in part at least, leave the organism temporarily without causing death to the organism.

MEST BODY

The physical body. The organism in all its MEST aspects. The MEST body is animate or inanimate, alive or dead, depending on the presence of or absence of the theta body.

PERSONALITY

A complex of inherited (MEST, organic, theta) and environmental (aberration, education, present time environment, nutrition, etc.) factors.

GENETIC PERSONALITY

Personal characteristics and tendencies derived from the three inheritance sources (MEST, organic line, the theta body). This might be said to be basic personality, or the core of basic personality.

ABERRATED PERSONALITY

The personality resultant from superimposition, on the genetic personality, of personal characteristics and tendencies brought about by all environmental factors, prosurvival and aberrational.

ENVIRONMENT

All conditions surrounding the organism from the first moment of present-life existence to death, including physical, emotional, spiritual, social, educational and nutritional.

EDUCATION

All perceived data stored in the standard memory banks. This might also be extended to include all data stored in the banks, including conclusions and imaginings.

NUTRITION

Support of the organism by organic and inorganic means (food, water, air, sunlight) during all of the present life, from conception or thereabouts to death. The nutrition of a genetic line, of course, would pass from parents to children in the forms of organic inheritance and gestation environment.

CULTURE

The pattern (if any) of life in the society. All factors of the society, social, educational, economic, etc., whether creative or destructive. The culture might be said to be the theta body of the society.

TIME TRACK

A representation of the fact that a person exists during a period of MEST time. The present-life time track begins at the first moment of recording and ends at present time, or at death, and it includes all consecutive moments of "now" and the perceptics of those moments. The theta body evidently has a MEST time track of its own.

ACTION PHRASES

Words or phrases in engrams or locks (or at 0.1, in present time) which cause the individual to perform involuntary actions on the time track. Action phrases are effective in the low tone ranges and not effective in the high ranges. As a case progresses up the scale, they lose their power. Types of action phrases are bouncer, down-bouncer, grouper, denyer, holder, misdirector, scrambler and the valence-shifters corresponding to these.

BOUNCER   Sends the preclear up the track toward present time. (Get up, get out, don't touch me, leave me alone, I've got to get ahead.)

DOWN-BOUNCER

Sends the preclear earlier on the track. (Sit down, get down, it's underneath, you're early, he's down, slide Kelly slide!)

GROUPER   Collapses time track, brings many incidents together. (I have no time, put them all together, it's all up to me all the time, I have to do everything around here, you're all alike, I'll get even with you, solidarity forever!)

DENYER   Denies existence of phrase or incident. (No, don't, I won't, I can't tell, you mustn't, it's not here, never, impossible, unknown, unthinkable, you know [no] everything.)

HOLDER   Holds preclear at a point on the track. (Stay here, don't leave me, hold on to this, don't let go, keep quiet, take this it'll make you feel better.)

MISDIRECTOR
> Sends preclear in the wrong direction. (Not that way, the other way, that's wrong, I don't know whether I'm coming or going, you don't know up from down.)

SCRAMBLER Scrambles incidents and phrases. (I'm confused, I'll take mine scrambled, stir it up, it's all mixed up and I'm in the middle.)

VALENCE-SHIFTER
> (You're just like your father, don't be like Uncle Rudy, you're just like everybody else, you're exactly like Rover, you're nobody, you're not human, you're out of this world, you can't ever be yourself, I'll just have to pretend I'm somebody else or I'll never be happy again.)

ARC Affinity-Reality-Communication, the triagonal manifestation of theta, each aspect affecting the other two.

AFFINITY The attraction which exists between two human beings, or between a human being and another life organism, or between a human being and MEST or theta or the Supreme Being. It has a rough parallel in the physical universe in magnetic and gravitic attraction. The affinity or lack of affinity between an organism and the environment or between the theta and MEST of an organism and within the theta (including entheta) of the organism brings about what we have referred to as emotions, in the past. The affinity scale includes most of the common emotions, apathy, grief, fear, anger, hostility, boredom, relief, contentment, enthusiasm, exhilaration, inspiration.

COMMUNICATION
> Communication with the recorded past (through recall and memory), the present (through perception) and the future (through imagination and/or other

mechanisms), communication between people by writing, talking, touching, seeing, etc. Also, communication as in groups and the technology thereof (Group Dianetics). There are emotions on the communication scale, but they have not commonly been named in our society.

REALITY   Reality of the past ("I"'s reception of the past agrees with the recorded data, and "I" agrees that it does). Reality of the present ("I"'s reception of the present agrees with the data impinging upon the organism from the environment, and "I" agrees that it does). Reality of the future ("I"'s concept of the future agrees with past and present data, and "I" agrees that it does). Reality between two people (they agree on something). Reality in a group (the majority in agreement). Physical, "actual" reality — the only kind considered by many people — is merely agreement between MEST conditions or life conditions and some person's perceptions of those conditions. If these do not agree, we say that he does not know the reality (ours, that is, for we have only our own perceptions by which to judge the MEST conditions). There are emotions on the reality scale. One of them is shame.

EMOTION   This word is redefined in Dianetics and is given an opposite for comparison, "misemotion." Previously the word *emotion* was never satisfactorily defined. Now it is defined as an organism manifestation of position on the Tone Scale which is rationally appropriate to the present time environment and which truly represents the present time position on the Tone Scale. Rational affect.

MISEMOTION

An organism manifestation which pretends to be emotion (as defined above) but which is irrational, inappropriate to the present time environment, or not representative of the true present time position on the Tone Scale. Irrational affect. Misemotion is also entheta in the reactive mind, emotion which has been suppressed and which remains in the case in locks and secondaries.

ARC LOCKS "Permanent" encystments of entheta resulting from the enturbulation of theta by enforcements or inhibitions of affinity, reality or communication and the trapping of this enturbulated theta by the physical pain of some engram or chain of engrams whose perceptics are approximated in the present time enturbulation. Locks are analytical experiences. If there were no physical pain to trap the enturbulated theta, it would disenturbulate, with a greater or lesser display of emotion.

ARC SECONDARIES

ARC locks of such magnitude that they must be run as engrams in processing. Or, since locks are often run as engrams, ARC locks of great magnitude.

RESTIMULATION LOCKS

Locks in which the chief noticeable factor is the approximation of engram perceptics in present time, rather than any particular break of ARC. These require a low level of analytical alertness, as in fatigue, to take place.

BROKEN-DRAMATIZATION LOCKS

Locks in which the chief factor is that the individual has been prevented from completing the dramatization of a restimulated engram. These are most abundant at the 1.5 level.

PRESENT TIME

The point on anyone's time track where his physical body (if alive) may be found. "Now." The intersection of the MEST time track with the (postulated) theta time track.

FUTURE On the time track, that area later than present time. Perception of the future is postulated as a possibility. The creation of future realities through imagination is a recognized function.

PAST On the time track, everything which is earlier than present time.

OCCLUSION A hidden area or incident on the time track. The existence of a curtain between "I" and some datum in the standard memory banks. Occlusions are caused by entheta.

ALLY A person recorded in the reactive mind of the preclear about whom the preclear makes the reactive computation that this person is necessary to the preclear's survival.

PERCEPTICS Specialized data from the standard memory or reactive banks which represent and reproduce the sense messages of a moment in the past. The sense messages of present time, also. (Formerly, the word *percepts* was used to mean the sense messages of present time, but usage has dropped this distinction.)

THETA PERCEPTICS

Communication with the theta universe. Such perceptics may include hunches, predictions, ESP at greater and lesser distances, communication with the "dead," perception of the Supreme Being, etc.

MEST PERCEPTICS

Common garden-variety sense data-perceptions, new and recorded, of matter, energy, space and time, and combinations of these. There are twenty-six postulated channels of MEST perception.

SONIC The recall of something heard, so that it is heard again in the mind in full tone and strength.

VISIO The recall of something seen, so that it is seen again in the mind in full color, scale, dimension, brightness and detail.

TACTILE The recall of touch perceptics.

OLFACTORY The recall of perceptics of smell.

KINESTHESIA
The recall of movement.

THERMAL The recall of temperature.

JOINT POSITION
The recall of bodily attitudes.

MOISTURE A recalled perceptic usually associated with the prenatal period.

ORGANIC PERCEPTIONS
The perceptions of the states of various organs, pressures, well-being, afflictions, etc.

GRADIENT SCALES
The tool of infinity-valued logic. It is a tenet of Dianetics that absolutes are unobtainable. Terms like good and bad, alive and dead, right and wrong are used only in conjunction with gradient scales. On the scale of right and wrong, everything above zero or center would be more and more right, approaching an infinite rightness, and everything below zero or center would be more and more wrong, approaching an infinite wrongness. The gradient scale is a way of thinking about the universe which approximates the actual conditions of the universe more closely than any other existing logical method.

EVOLUTION OF LOGIC

	Right Wrong	Right Maybe Wrong
Single Valued Logic	**Two Valued Logic**	**Three Valued Logic**
Will of God Neither Right nor Wrong	Absolute Values of Right & Wrong Aristotelian	Absolute Right & Wrong + Maybe Engineering Logic

GRADIENT SCALE OF THE RELATIVE VALUE OF DATA

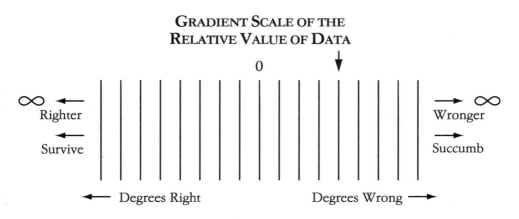

Infinity Valued Logic

Absolute Right or Wrong Unobtainable

Dianetics

INTRODUCTION OF AN ARBITRARY

An arbitrary may be considered as a factor introduced into a problem's solution when that factor does not derive from a known natural law but only from an opinion or authoritarian command. A problem resolved by data derived from known natural laws resolves well and smoothly and has a useful solution. When a problem is resolved by introducing arbitraries (factors based on opinion or command but not natural law) then that solution, when used, will ordinarily require more arbitraries to make the solution applicable. The harder one tries to apply the solution corrupted by arbitraries to any situation, the more arbitraries have to be introduced. Thus in government, laws passed which contain arbitraries create new problems which cannot be solved without more new arbitraries and thus, rapidly, a top-heavy and unworkable structure of government comes into being which would be workable only if wholly redesigned in the light of known natural laws about government.

EVALUATION OF DATA

A datum is as understood as it can be related to other data.

VALUE OF DATUM

A datum is as important or valuable as it relates to survival.

COMPARABLE MAGNITUDE

A datum can only be evaluated by comparison with another datum of comparable magnitude. This means that the basic unit must, therefore, be two.

ACCESSIBILITY

The desire of the preclear to be raised on the Tone Scale by processing. (In a past publication, the word *accessibility* was used to mean not only the above but also the accessibility of entheta on the case to various methods of processing. This last meaning is not used in the present work.) A case is considered accessible when it will work willingly with the auditor, no matter how occluded the case may be.

"I" The awareness of awareness center. Organisms are aware of their environment. Higher organisms are aware, also, of this very awareness. The "I" of the human being may be said to be the center or monitor of this awareness of awareness.

ALTITUDE A prestige which the auditor has in the eyes of the preclear. A somewhat artificial position of the auditor which gives the preclear greater confidence and therefore greater ability to run than he would otherwise have. In the society in general, there are four kinds of altitude an individual may have.

DATA ALTITUDE

Signifying that the individual has a fund of knowledge gathered from books and records, or sometimes from experience, with which others are not familiar. The college professor has data altitude.

COMPUTATIONAL ALTITUDE

Signifying that the individual has an outstanding ability to think, to compute upon data. Albert Einstein had computational altitude.

POSITIONAL ALTITUDE

Deriving from an arbitrarily assigned position. Military officers and bureaucrats often depend heavily upon positional altitude.

PERSONAL PRESENCE ALTITUDE

The individual who leads or makes an impression upon others merely by his presence, by his example and the fact of his existence, has personal presence altitude. Gandhi had this to a very high degree.

COMMAND SOMATIC

A somatic brought from a different part of the time track by some command phrase, such as "My arm hurts." The preclear may have this somatic while running a prenatal engram although he was only three days conceived in the incident. Command somatics occur where the preclear is out of valence.

FALSE FOUR

The laughter and gaiety which the preclear exhibits when he has thoroughly exhausted an incident of charge. There is nothing really "false" about false four, except that it is often of very short duration.

BASIC PURPOSE

Even at the age of two or three years an individual seems to know what his basic purpose is in life. Later this becomes corrupted by individual and social aberrations but is recovered in Dianetic processing. Possibly past lives have something to do with forming basic purpose.

BASIC ENGRAM

The first engram on a given chain of engrams.

BASIC AREA

The time track from the first recording on the sperm or ovum track to the first missed menstrual period of the mother.

BASIC-BASIC

The first moment of pain, anaten or discomfort in the current life of the individual.

LANGUAGE LOCKS

Locks in which the main aberrative content is in terms of language. These may be considered symbolic restimulators of MEST locks, which are more fundamental.

MEST LOCKS

Locks which come about through the inhibition or enforcement of the individual's experience or control of matter or energy or space or time. It is postulated that the reduction of the MEST locks in which the individual was made to go up or not permitted to come down will make any bouncer phrases in the case inactive, and so on with all types of action phrases.

VALIDATION TECHNIQUE

Processing in which the auditor, at least for one session, concentrates exclusively on the theta side of lock chains, not allowing the preclear to run any but analytical moments on any given subject. When the preclear encounters too much entheta on a given chain, the auditor takes him to analytical moments on another subject (which moments constitute, of course, a parallel chain to the locks on that subject) obtained from the file clerk. During this type of processing somatics will turn on and off, sometimes severely, but the auditor ignores them, and keeps bringing the preclear back to analytical (not necessarily pleasure) moments. Validation technique should not be mixed with entheta technique.

MEST TECHNIQUE

Straightwire, Repetitive Straightwire (slow, auditor-managed Lock Scanning), and Lock Scanning on MEST locks. Language locks are found by Straightwire only as a clue to the underlying MEST locks. MEST technique and validation technique may be combined and should be.

(Other needed definitions may be found by referring to the glossary and index.)

GLOSSARY,
INDEX AND
BIBLIOGRAPHY

GLOSSARY

AS AN AID TO THE READER, WORDS
most likely to be misunderstood have been defined in this glossary.
Words often have several meanings. The definitions used in this glossary
only give the meaning that the word has as it is used in this book. This
glossary is not meant to take the place of standard language or Dianetics
and Scientology dictionaries, which should be referred to for any words
that do not appear below.

aberrations: irrational behavior or computation (thinking). They are
stimulus-response in nature and may be prosurvival or contrasurvival.
The engram is the basic source of aberrations. (See *Definitions and
Axioms* at pages 539 to 555 for a full listing of the definitions and
axioms of *Science of Survival*.) BOOK ONE, CHAPTER 1

abreact: to release or express an impulse, emotion, etc., such as one
previously forgotten or repressed. BOOK TWO, CHAPTER 8, # 1

accessibility: the desire of the preclear to be raised on the Tone Scale by
processing. (In a past publication, the word *accessibility* was used to mean
not only the above but also the accessibility of entheta on the case to
various methods of processing. This last meaning is not used in the
present work.) A case is considered accessible when it will work
willingly with the auditor, no matter how occluded the case may be.
(See *Definitions and Axioms* at pages 539 to 555 for a full listing of the
definitions and axioms of *Science of Survival*.)

action phrases: words or phrases in engrams or locks (or at 0.1, in present
time) which cause the individual to perform involuntary actions on the
time track. Action phrases are effective in the low tone ranges and not

effective in the high ranges. As a case progresses up the scale, they lose their power. Types of action phrases are bouncer, down-bouncer, grouper, denyer, holder, misdirector, scrambler and the valence-shifters corresponding to these. (See *Definitions and Axioms* at pages 539 to 555 for a full listing of the definitions and axioms of *Science of Survival*.) BOOK ONE, CHAPTER 16

Aesop's fox: a reference to the fox in the fable *The Fox Without a Tail*, written by legendary Greek author, Aesop. The fable tells of a fox who gets caught in a trap. Unable to get out, he resolves to bite off his tail to free himself. Shortly thereafter, realizing how odd he looks without a tail, he decides to convince the other foxes of the virtues of being tailless and persuade them to get rid of their own. The other foxes see through this and his plan fails. BOOK TWO, CHAPTER 18, # 3

Aesop's grasshopper: a reference to the grasshopper in the fable *The Ant and the Grasshopper* by the Greek author, Aesop. The fable tells of a grasshopper who only thinks of the good time in the present and does not work and prepare for the winter. It therefore finds itself starving of hunger, while the busy ant had lots of food. BOOK TWO, CHAPTER 21, # 1

affinity: the attraction which exists between two human beings, or between a human being and another life organism, or between a human being and MEST or theta or the Supreme Being. It has a rough parallel in the physical universe in magnetic and gravitic attraction. The affinity or lack of affinity between an organism and the environment or between the theta and MEST of an organism and within the theta (including entheta) of the organism brings about what we have referred to as emotions, in the past. The affinity scale includes most of the common emotions, apathy, grief, fear, anger, hostility, boredom, relief, contentment, enthusiasm, exhilaration, inspiration. (See *Definitions and Axioms* at pages 539 to 555 for a full listing of the definitions and axioms of *Science of Survival*.)

ally: a person recorded in the reactive mind of the preclear about whom the preclear makes the reactive computation that this person is necessary to the preclear's survival. (See *Definitions and Axioms* at pages 539 to 555 for a full listing of the definitions and axioms of *Science of Survival*.) BOOK ONE, CHAPTER 27

altitude: a prestige which the auditor has in the eyes of the preclear. A somewhat artificial position of the auditor which gives the preclear greater confidence and therefore greater ability to run than he would otherwise have. In the society in general, there are four kinds of altitude an individual may have. (See *Definitions and Axioms* at pages 539 to 555 for a full listing of the definitions and axioms of *Science of Survival*.)

ammonia seas, origin out of: a reference to one of the theories of the origin of "life" on this planet. Per this theory, life arose through a series of spontaneous chemical reactions involving various substances including ammonia. The theory surmises these compounds fell from the atmosphere into the sea creating a kind of prebiological soup, interacted and grew larger and larger. Somehow, cells were formed which eventually led to the life forms that inhabit Earth today, including man. See also **mud, origin out of** in this glossary. BOOK TWO, CHAPTER 18, # 6

amnesia trance: a coined phrase used to refer to a condition where a person is in a state of unconsciousness and insensibility and has no conscious memory of what has occurred during such. *Amnesia* is a partial or complete loss of memory. A *trance* is a condition marked by a more or less prolonged suspension of consciousness, inability to function and an inertness to stimuli. BOOK TWO, CHAPTER 16, # 1

analytical mind: that portion of the mind which perceives and retains experience data to compose and resolve problems and direct the organism along the eight dynamics. It thinks in differences and similarities. (See *Definitions and Axioms* at pages 539 to 555 for a full listing of the definitions and axioms of *Science of Survival*.)

ARC: affinity-reality-communication, the triagonal manifestation of theta, each aspect affecting the other two. (See *Definitions and Axioms* at pages 539 to 555 for a full listing of the definitions and axioms of *Science of Survival*.)

ARC locks: "permanent" encystments of entheta resulting from the enturbulation of theta by enforcements or inhibitions of affinity, reality or communication and the trapping of this enturbulated theta by the physical pain of some engram or chain of engrams whose perceptics are approximated in the present time enturbulation. Locks are analytical experiences. If there were no physical pain to trap the enturbulated theta, it would disenturbulate, with a greater or lesser display of emotion. (See *Definitions and Axioms* at pages 539 to 555 for a full listing of the definitions and axioms of *Science of Survival*.)

basic area: the time track from the first recording on the sperm or ovum track to the first missed menstrual period of the mother. (See *Definitions* *and Axioms* at pages 539 to 555 for a full listing of the definitions and axioms of *Science of Survival*.) BOOK TWO, CHAPTER 5

basic-basic: the first moment of pain, anaten or discomfort in the current life of the individual. (See *Definitions and Axioms* at pages 539 to 555 for a full listing of the definitions and axioms of *Science of Survival*.) BOOK ONE, CHAPTER 16

basic engram: the first engram on a given chain of engrams. (See *Definitions and Axioms* at pages 539 to 555 for a full listing of the definitions and axioms of *Science of Survival*.)

basic purpose: even at the age of two or three years an individual seems to know what his basic purpose is in life. Later this becomes corrupted by individual and social aberrations but is recovered in Dianetic processing. Possibly past lives have something to do with forming basic purpose. (See *Definitions and Axioms* at pages 539 to 555 for a full listing of the definitions and axioms of *Science of Survival*.) BOOK TWO, CHAPTER 20

Bethesda Naval Hospital: a reference to the National Naval Medical Center, a large governmental hospital founded in 1942 in Bethesda, Maryland, USA. It is run by the US Navy and services navy personnel. BOOK ONE, CHAPTER 27, # 8

bouncer: sends the preclear up the track toward present time. (Get up, get out, don't touch me, leave me alone, I've got to get ahead.) (See *Definitions and Axioms* at pages 539 to 555 for a full listing of the definitions and axioms of *Science of Survival*.)

broken-dramatization locks: locks in which the chief factor is that the individual has been prevented from completing the dramatization of a restimulated engram. These are most abundant at the 1.5 level. (See *Definitions and Axioms* at pages 539 to 555 for a full listing of the definitions and axioms of *Science of Survival*.)

Carrel, Alexis: (1873–1944) French biologist and surgeon known for his experiments on keeping organs and tissues alive while they were outside the body. In the early 1930s Carrel, along with American aviator Charles Lindbergh (1902–1974), created a device, known as a mechanical or artificial heart, that made it possible to support the life of an organ once it was taken out of a body. BOOK TWO, CHAPTER 12, # 1

charge: the accumulation of entheta in locks and secondaries which charges up the engrams and gives them their force to aberrate. (See *Definitions and Axioms* at pages 539 to 555 for a full listing of the definitions and axioms of *Science of Survival*.) BOOK ONE, CHAPTER 7

Coal Hill: a man-made mound more than a mile in circumference, approximately 210 feet high (64 m), in Peking, China, covered with trees and temples and which was also the sight of a burial ground. BOOK ONE, CHAPTER 27, # 9

Columbia: a reference to Columbia University in New York City, New York, USA, founded in 1754. BOOK TWO, CHAPTER 13, # 3

command somatic: a somatic brought from a different part of the time track by some command phrase, such as "My arm hurts." The preclear may have this somatic while running a prenatal engram although he was only three days conceived in the incident. Command somatics occur where the preclear is out of valence. (See *Definitions and Axioms* at pages 539 to 555 for a full listing of the definitions and axioms of *Science of Survival*.)

communication: communication with the recorded past (through recall and memory), the present (through perception) and the future (through imagination and/or other mechanisms), communication between people by writing, talking, touching, seeing, etc. Also, communication as in groups and the technology thereof (Group Dianetics). There are emotions on the communication scale, but they have not commonly been named in our society. (See *Definitions and Axioms* at pages 539 to 555 for a full listing of the definitions and axioms of *Science of Survival*.)

comparable magnitude: a datum can only be evaluated by comparison with another datum of comparable magnitude. This means that the basic unit must, therefore, be two. (See *Definitions and Axioms* at pages 539 to 555 for a full listing of the definitions and axioms of *Science of Survival*.)

culture: the pattern (if any) of life in the society. All factors of the society, social, educational, economic, etc., whether creative or destructive. The culture might be said to be the theta body of the society. (See *Definitions and Axioms* at pages 539 to 555 for a full listing of the definitions and axioms of *Science of Survival*.) BOOK ONE, CHAPTER 2

death: the withdrawal of theta from an organism, leaving only MEST, in order to conquer new MEST and form another organism which can better survive. (See *Definitions and Axioms* at pages 539 to 555 for a full listing of the definitions and axioms of *Science of Survival*.)

denyer: denies existence of phrase or incident. (No, don't, I won't, I can't tell, you mustn't, it's not here, never, impossible, unknown, unthinkable, you know [no] everything.) (See *Definitions and Axioms* at pages 539 to 555 for a full listing of the definitions and axioms of *Science of Survival*.)

Devil and his dark angels: a reference to Satan and the fallen or rebellious angels that work for him. Throughout history the Devil has been portrayed as an evil angel who was banished from heaven and became the archenemy of God. Other corrupt, wicked and evil angels who were cast down from heaven joined the Devil and he became their prince. Used here the *Devil and his dark angels* refers to those individuals with such characteristics. BOOK ONE, CHAPTER 24, # 1

directive therapy: a form of supposed "treatment" used in psychotherapy where the therapist takes an active, often authoritarian approach towards the patient, giving advice, suggestions, interpretations and demands for the patient to follow. BOOK ONE, CHAPTER 27, # 3

down-bouncer: sends the preclear earlier on the track. (Sit down, get down, it's underneath, you're early, he's down, slide Kelly slide!) (See *Definitions and Axioms* at pages 539 to 555 for a full listing of the definitions and axioms of *Science of Survival*.)

dymaxion geometry: a reference to a philosophy of construction and design developed by American engineer and inventor Buckminster Fuller (1895–1983). Fuller devised a system of architecture, based on specific geometrical units, resulting in the invention of large domes which had no supporting members except a frame made of these units. Fuller's dome encloses a greater volume with less material than any alternative form. BOOK TWO, CHAPTER 4, # 1

dynamics: the dynamics are the urge to survive, expressed through a spectrum, which is here given with eight divisions. (1) self, (2) sex, the family, and the future generation, (3) the group, (4) mankind, (5) life, all organisms, (6) MEST, (7) theta, (8) the Supreme Being. (See *Definitions and Axioms* at pages 539 to 555 for a full listing of the definitions and axioms of *Science of Survival*.)

dyne: a dyne is a unit of force and it's simply the amount of force necessary to move one gram of weight into a speed of one centimeter per second. —LRH

education: all perceived data stored in the standard memory banks. This might also be extended to include all data stored in the banks, including conclusions and imaginings. (See *Definitions and Axioms* at pages 539 to 555 for a full listing of the definitions and axioms of *Science of Survival*.)

electromagnetic-gravitic laws: a reference to the major laws manifested by the physical universe involving the interrelation between electricity, magnetism and gravity. BOOK ONE, CHAPTER 1, # 2

emotion: this word is redefined in Dianetics and is given an opposite for comparison, "misemotion." Previously the word *emotion* was never satisfactorily defined. Now it is defined as an organism manifestation of position on the Tone Scale which is rationally appropriate to the present time environment and which truly represents the present time position on the Tone Scale. Rational affect. (See *Definitions and Axioms* at pages 539 to 555 for a full listing of the definitions and axioms of *Science of Survival.*)

engram: an encystment containing entheta and enMEST. A recording (possibly cellular) of a period of pain and unconsciousness (or anaten). Not available to the analytical mind as experience. The sole source of aberrations and "psychosomatic illnesses." (See *Definitions and Axioms* at pages 539 to 555 for a full listing of the definitions and axioms of *Science of Survival.*)

enMEST: MEST which has been enturbulated by entheta or crushed too hard into theta and rendered less usable. (See *Definitions and Axioms* at pages 539 to 555 for a full listing of the definitions and axioms of *Science of Survival.*)

entheta: theta which is enturbulated with MEST (enMEST) in an inharmonious combination. Irrational thought. (See *Definitions and Axioms* at pages 539 to 555 for a full listing of the definitions and axioms of *Science of Survival.*)

environment: all conditions surrounding the organism from the first moment of present-life existence to death, including physical, emotional, spiritual, social, educational and nutritional. (See *Definitions and Axioms* at pages 539 to 555 for a full listing of the definitions and axioms of *Science of Survival.*) BOOK ONE, CHAPTER 1

evolution: there are four evolutionary tracks, evidently. Organism evolution, through natural selection, accident and (evidence suggests) outright planning. MEST evolution, brought about through the agency of life organisms. Theta evolution, a postulated process of learning in theta as a whole or as entities. And present time ladder-of-support evolution, in which less complicated organisms support more complicated organisms. (See *Definitions and Axioms* at pages 539 to 555 for a full listing of the definitions and axioms of *Science of Survival.*)

false four: the laughter and gaiety which the preclear exhibits when he has thoroughly exhausted an incident of charge. There is nothing really "false" about false four, except that it is often of very short duration. (See *Definitions and Axioms* at pages 539 to 555 for a full listing of the definitions and axioms of *Science of Survival*.) BOOK ONE, CHAPTER 7

flank speed: the maximum speed of which a ship is capable. INTRODUCTION, # 1

Forrestal, James Vincent: (1892–1949) American banker and government official who, in 1940, became the undersecretary of the United States Navy. During World War II (1939–1945) he directed huge naval expansion and procurement programs and was responsible for readying a peacetime navy to meet the enormous demands of global war. BOOK ONE, CHAPTER 27, # 7

future: on the time track, that area later than present time. Perception of the future is postulated as a possibility. The creation of future realities through imagination is a recognized function. (See *Definitions and Axioms* at pages 539 to 555 for a full listing of the definitions and axioms of *Science of Survival*.)

ghost dancers: members of an American Indian religious movement in the western United States, called Ghost Dance. The religion, based on the belief that the white man would disappear and dead ancestors and buffalo would return to life, centered on the ghost dance. The dancers chanted and wore special shirts, called ghost shirts, decorated with sacred symbols, such as stars, eagles and moons, believing they were protected from enemy bullets. BOOK ONE, CHAPTER 27, # 6

gradient scales: the tool of infinity-valued logic. It is a tenet of Dianetics that absolutes are unobtainable. Terms like good and bad, alive and dead, right and wrong are used only in conjunction with gradient scales. On the scale of right and wrong, everything above zero or center would be more and more right, approaching an infinite rightness, and everything below zero or center would be more and more wrong, approaching an infinite wrongness. The gradient scale is a way of thinking about the universe which approximates the actual conditions of the universe more closely than any other existing logical method. (See *Definitions and Axioms* at pages 539 to 555 for a full listing of the definitions and axioms of *Science of Survival*.)

grouper: collapses time track, brings many incidents together. (I have no time, put them all together, it's all up to me all the time, I have to do everything around here, you're all alike, I'll get even with you, solidarity forever!) (See *Definitions and Axioms* at pages 539 to 555 for a full listing of the definitions and axioms of *Science of Survival*.)

habit: a stimulus-response mechanism similar to the training pattern but set up by the reactive mind out of the content of engrams. It cannot be changed at will by the analytical mind. (See *Definitions and Axioms* at pages 539 to 555 for a full listing of the definitions and axioms of *Science of Survival*.) BOOK TWO, CHAPTER 12

handbook: a reference to *Dianetics: The Modern Science of Mental Health*. BOOK ONE, CHAPTER 20, # 1

happiness: the overcoming of not unknowable obstacles toward a known goal. (See *Definitions and Axioms* at pages 539 to 555 for a full listing of the definitions and axioms of *Science of Survival*.) BOOK ONE, CHAPTER 2

holder: holds preclear at a point on the track. (Stay here, don't leave me, hold on to this, don't let go, keep quiet, take this it'll make you feel better.) (See *Definitions and Axioms* at pages 539 to 555 for a full listing of the definitions and axioms of *Science of Survival*.)

human thought: a process of perceiving and storing data, computing conclusions, posing and resolving problems. The purpose of this is survival along all of the dynamics. (See *Definitions and Axioms* at pages 539 to 555 for a full listing of the definitions and axioms of *Science of Survival*.)

"I": the awareness of awareness center. Organisms are aware of their environment. Higher organisms are aware, also, of this very awareness. The "I" of the human being may be said to be the center or monitor of this awareness of awareness. (See *Definitions and Axioms* at pages 539 to 555 for a full listing of the definitions and axioms of *Science of Survival*.) BOOK ONE, CHAPTER 10

immortality: infinite survival, the absolute goal of survival. The individual seeks this on the first dynamic as an organism and as a theta entity and in the perpetuation of his name by his group. On the second dynamic he seeks it through his children, and so on through the eight dynamics. Life survives through the persistence of theta. A species survives through the persistence of the life in it. A culture survives through the persistence of the species using it. There is evidence that the theta of an individual may survive as a personal entity from life to life, through many lives on Earth. (See *Definitions and Axioms* at pages 539 to 555 for a full listing of the definitions and axioms of *Science of Survival*.) BOOK TWO, CHAPTER 3

Indian Swamp Root Oil: a coined variation of *snake(root) oil* which refers to any of various preparations sold by peddlers posing as scientists, doctors or the like as an all-purpose cure-all, but with little, if any, medical value. THE GOAL OF DIANETICS, # 1

insulin shock: a form of shock treatment commonly used by psychiatrists. The purported treatment consists of a series of shots, injecting an excessive amount of insulin into the body, thereby inducing a coma. BOOK ONE, CHAPTER 27, # 2

intelligence: the ability to perceive, pose and resolve problems. Intelligence and the urge to survive (the dynamic) are both necessary to continued existence. The quantity of each varies from individual to individual and group to group. The dynamics are inhibited by engrams which block their flow of theta, or life force, and disperse it. Intelligence is also inhibited by engrams, which enter false or improperly graded data into the analytical mind. (See *Definitions and Axioms* at pages 539 to 555 for a full listing of the definitions and axioms of *Science of Survival*.) BOOK ONE, CHAPTER 1

introduction of an arbitrary: an arbitrary may be considered as a factor introduced into a problem's solution when that factor does not derive from a known natural law but only from an opinion or authoritarian command. A problem resolved by data derived from known natural laws resolves well and smoothly and has a useful solution. When a problem is resolved by introducing arbitraries (factors based on opinion or command but not natural law) then that solution, when used, will ordinarily require more arbitraries to make the solution applicable. The harder one tries to apply the solution corrupted by arbitraries to any situation, the more arbitraries have to be introduced. Thus in government, laws passed which contain arbitraries create new problems which cannot be solved without more new arbitraries and thus, rapidly, a top-heavy and unworkable structure of government comes into being which would be workable only if wholly redesigned in the light of known natural laws about government. (See *Definitions and Axioms* at pages 539 to 555 for a full listing of the definitions and axioms of *Science of Survival*.)

joint position: the recall of bodily attitudes. (See *Definitions and Axioms* at pages 539 to 555 for a full listing of the definitions and axioms of *Science of Survival*.)

kilowatt: a unit of electric power. The word *kilo* means 1000 and a kilowatt is 1000 watts. A *watt* is a measurement of the rate of flow of energy, that is, how much electrical energy is flowing per unit of time. BOOK ONE, CHAPTER 2, # 1

kinesthesia: the recall of movement. (See *Definitions and Axioms* at pages 539 to 555 for a full listing of the definitions and axioms of *Science of Survival.*)

language locks: locks in which the main aberrative content is in terms of language. These may be considered symbolic restimulators of MEST locks, which are more fundamental. (See *Definitions and Axioms* at pages 539 to 555 for a full listing of the definitions and axioms of *Science of Survival.*)

life (λ): the harmonious conquest of MEST by theta in which a self-perpetuating organism is formed. Death is the withdrawal of theta from the organism. (See *Definitions and Axioms* at pages 539 to 555 for a full listing of the definitions and axioms of *Science of Survival.*)

lock: an analytical incident of greater or lesser enturbulence of theta which approximates the perceptics of an engram or chain of engrams and therefore becomes trapped due to the physical pain recorded in the engram and remains as an encystment of entheta. (See *Definitions and Axioms* at pages 539 to 555 for a full listing of the definitions and axioms of *Science of Survival.*)

logarithmic decree: by mathematical or scientific decree. *Logarithm* is a mathematical term and a *decree* is an authoritative decision or order having the force of law. BOOK ONE, CHAPTER 1, # 4

MEST (φ): matter, energy, space, and time. The physical universe. (See *Definitions and Axioms* at pages 539 to 555 for a full listing of the definitions and axioms of *Science of Survival.*)

MEST body: the physical body. The organism in all its MEST aspects. The MEST body is animate or inanimate, alive or dead, depending on the presence of or absence of the theta body. (See *Definitions and Axioms* at pages 539 to 555 for a full listing of the definitions and axioms of *Science of Survival.*) BOOK ONE, CHAPTER 1

MEST locks: locks which come about through the inhibition or enforcement of the individual's experience or control of matter or energy or space or time. It is postulated that the reduction of the MEST locks in which the individual was made to go up or not permitted to come down will make any bouncer phrases in the case inactive, and so on with all types of action phrases. (See *Definitions and Axioms* at pages 539 to 555 for a full listing of the definitions and axioms of *Science of Survival.*) BOOK TWO, CHAPTER 21

MEST **technique:** Straightwire, Repetitive Straightwire (slow, auditor-managed Lock Scanning), and Lock Scanning on MEST locks. Language locks are found by Straightwire only as a clue to the underlying MEST locks. MEST technique and validation technique may be combined and should be. (See *Definitions and Axioms* at pages 539 to 555 for a full listing of the definitions and axioms of *Science of Survival*.) BOOK TWO, CHAPTER 21

metaphysician: a person who is familiar with metaphysics or who creates or develops metaphysical theories. Metaphysics generally means that branch of philosophy that is concerned with the ultimate nature of existence or the nature of ultimate reality. Metaphysical expressions such as "Everything is part of one all-encompassing spirit," "Nothing exists except material particles," "Everything is a dream and nothing really exists outside our minds," have occupied various schools of metaphysics for centuries. BOOK ONE, CHAPTER 6, # 1

misdirector: sends preclear in the wrong direction. (Not that way, the other way, that's wrong, I don't know whether I'm coming or going, you don't know up from down.) (See *Definitions and Axioms* at pages 539 to 555 for a full listing of the definitions and axioms of *Science of Survival*.)

misemotion: an organism manifestation which pretends to be emotion (as defined above) but which is irrational, inappropriate to the present time environment, or not representative of the true present time position on the Tone Scale. Irrational affect. Misemotion is also entheta in the reactive mind, emotion which has been suppressed and which remains in the case in locks and secondaries. (See *Definitions and Axioms* at pages 539 to 555 for a full listing of the definitions and axioms of *Science of Survival*.)

moisture: a recalled perceptic usually associated with the prenatal period. (See *Definitions and Axioms* at pages 539 to 555 for a full listing of the definitions and axioms of *Science of Survival*.)

mud, origin out of: a reference to the theory that man arose from mud. Per this theory, it is alleged that chemicals formed in mud and through certain combinations and accidental patterns a primitive single cell was formed. This primitive cell then collided with other such cells and through accident formed a more complex structure of single cells which made itself into a unit organism. Purportedly, from this combination of cells, man was eventually formed. See also **ammonia seas, origin out of** in this glossary. BOOK TWO, CHAPTER 18, # 5

muster, stand: to undergo a formal military inspection. BOOK ONE, CHAPTER 17, # 1

narcosynthesis: a complicated name for a very ancient process quite well known in Greece and India. It is drug hypnotism. And it is generally employed either by those practitioners who do not know hypnosis or on those patients who will not succumb to ordinary hypnotism. A shot of sodium pentothal is given intravenously to the patient and he is asked to count backwards. Shortly he stops counting at which the injection is also stopped. The patient is now in a state of "deep sleep." That this is not sleep seems to have missed both narcosynthesists and hypnotists. It is actually a depressant on the awareness of an individual so that those attention units which remain behind the curtain of his reactive bank can be reached directly. —LRH, BOOK ONE, CHAPTER 27

nutrition: support of the organism by organic and inorganic means (food, water, air, sunlight) during all of the present life, from conception or thereabouts to death. The nutrition of a genetic line, of course, would pass from parents to children in the forms of organic inheritance and gestation environment. (See *Definitions and Axioms* at pages 539 to 555 for a full listing of the definitions and axioms of *Science of Survival*.)

occlusion: a hidden area or incident on the time track. The existence of a curtain between "I" and some datum in the standard memory banks. Occlusions are caused by entheta. (See *Definitions and Axioms* at pages 539 to 555 for a full listing of the definitions and axioms of *Science of Survival*.) BOOK ONE, CHAPTER 11

olfactory: the recall of perceptics of smell. (See *Definitions and Axioms* at pages 539 to 555 for a full listing of the definitions and axioms of *Science of Survival*.)

organic perceptions: the perceptions of the states of various organs, pressures, well-being, afflictions, etc. (See *Definitions and Axioms* at pages 539 to 555 for a full listing of the definitions and axioms of *Science of Survival*.)

pain: the alarm reaction to theta which has been crushed too severely into MEST. The penalty of nonsurvival activity. (See *Definitions and Axioms* at pages 539 to 555 for a full listing of the definitions and axioms of *Science of Survival*.)

parlor trick: something that impresses or entertains. The term may have originally referred to small magic tricks performed in a parlor (a room in a house used primarily for receiving and entertaining guests). BOOK TWO, CHAPTER 7, # 1

past: on the time track, everything which is earlier than present time. (See *Definitions and Axioms* at pages 539 to 555 for a full listing of the definitions and axioms of *Science of Survival*.)

perceptics: specialized data from the standard memory or reactive banks which represent and reproduce the sense messages of a moment in the past. The sense messages of present time, also. (Formerly, the word *percepts* was used to mean the sense messages of present time, but usage has dropped this distinction.) (See *Definitions and Axioms* at pages 539 to 555 for a full listing of the definitions and axioms of *Science of Survival*.)

peripheral vascular system: a reference to the peripheral blood vessels of the body. *Peripheral* as used here means located at or near the surface of the body; away from the central part. *Vascular* means pertaining to vessels that convey bodily fluid such as blood around the body, and *system* refers to a related body of organs that cooperate in performing vital fundamental functions. BOOK ONE, CHAPTER 3, # 1

personality: a complex of inherited (MEST, organic, theta) and environmental (aberration, education, present time environment, nutrition, etc.) factors. (See *Definitions and Axioms* at pages 539 to 555 for a full listing of the definitions and axioms of *Science of Survival*.)

pleasure: pleasure is the reward of survival activity along any of the dynamics. Successes bring pleasure and survival. (See *Definitions and Axioms* at pages 539 to 555 for a full listing of the definitions and axioms of *Science of Survival*.)

point field: an area or region within which an energy exerts some kind of influence and which influence emanates from a single source point. BOOK TWO, CHAPTER 18, # 2

postpartum psychosis: any psychosis occurring in a mother after childbirth. *Postpartum* means after childbirth. BOOK TWO, CHAPTER 13, # 1

prefrontal lobotomy: a psychiatric procedure in which the frontal lobes of the brain are separated from the rest of the brain by cutting the connecting nerve fibers. *Prefrontal* means situated at the front or forepart of the brain, *lobotomy* comes from *lobe*, a roundish projection or division, as of an organ and *-tomy*, a combining form, used here to mean an incision or cutting of an organ, as designated by the initial element of the term. BOOK ONE, CHAPTER 1, # 1

present time: the point on anyone's time track where his physical body (if alive) may be found. "Now." The intersection of the MEST time track with the (postulated) theta time track. (See *Definitions and Axioms* at pages 539 to 555 for a full listing of the definitions and axioms of *Science of Survival.*) BOOK ONE, CHAPTER 1

punched protein molecule theory: a reference to a theory concerning memory storage in which it was believed certain molecules in the body were perforated and memories were stored in each hole. BOOK TWO, CHAPTER 9, # 1

PV=ID^x: this formula expresses the Potential Value of an individual. "I" represents intelligence, and "D" represents dynamic. (See *Definitions and Axioms* at pages 539 to 555 for a full listing of the definitions and axioms of *Science of Survival.*)

reactive mind: that portion of the mind which files and retains physical pain and misemotion and seeks to direct the organism solely on a stimulus-response basis. It thinks only in identities. (See *Definitions and Axioms* at pages 539 to 555 for a full listing of the definitions and axioms of *Science of Survival.*)

reality: reality of the past ("I"'s reception of the past agrees with the recorded data, and "I" agrees that it does). Reality of the present ("I"'s reception of the present agrees with the data impinging upon the organism from the environment, and "I" agrees that it does). Reality of the future ("I"'s concept of the future agrees with past and present data, and "I" agrees that it does). Reality between two people (they agree on something). Reality in a group (the majority in agreement). Physical, "actual" reality—the only kind considered by many people—is merely agreement between MEST conditions or life conditions and some person's perceptions of those conditions. If these do not agree, we say that he does not know the reality (ours, that is, for we have only our own perceptions by which to judge the MEST conditions). There are emotions on the reality scale. One of them is shame. (See *Definitions and Axioms* at pages 539 to 555 for a full listing of the definitions and axioms of *Science of Survival.*)

restimulation locks: locks in which the chief noticeable factor is the approximation of engram perceptics in present time, rather than any particular break of ARC. These require a low level of analytical alertness, as in fatigue, to take place. (See *Definitions and Axioms* at pages 539 to 555 for a full listing of the definitions and axioms of *Science of Survival*.)

Roman circus: an amphitheater in ancient Rome in which horse and chariot races, brutal athletic contests, gladiator combat and similar entertainment took place. Such activities were extremely popular and drew huge crowds. *Circus* in Latin means "oval space in which games were held," coming from the Greek word for ring, circle. BOOK TWO, CHAPTER 8, # 2

Rutgers University: the State University of New Jersey, founded in 1766 and named in honor of a local benefactor, Henry Rutgers. BOOK TWO, CHAPTER 6, # 1

scrambler: scrambles incidents and phrases. (I'm confused, I'll take mine scrambled, stir it up, it's all mixed up and I'm in the middle.) (See *Definitions and Axioms* at pages 539 to 555 for a full listing of the definitions and axioms of *Science of Survival*.)

secondary engram: a lock of such magnitude that it must be run as an engram in processing. A lock with great magnitude of entheta. (See *Definitions and Axioms* at pages 539 to 555 for a full listing of the definitions and axioms of *Science of Survival*.)

sequitur: something that sequentially follows another thing or a conclusion that logically follows something already stated or mentioned; connected as in thought, speech, etc. *Sequitur* is a Latin word which means "it follows." BOOK ONE, CHAPTER 1, # 5

Simple Simon: a reference to the children's story *Epaminondas,* which tells of a young boy, Epaminondas, whose mother instructs him to, "Watch out when you go outside to play. I've got six mince pies cooling on the doorstep and you be careful how you step on those pies." Taking his mother's directions literally, Epaminondas goes out onto the porch and steps, very carefully, right in the middle of each pie. BOOK TWO, CHAPTER 13, # 4

social order: the totality of structured human interrelationships in a society or a part of it; the manner in which society is organized at a specified time, the constituted social system. BOOK ONE, CHAPTER 13, # 1

solidation: a strengthening or consolidation; the act of making firm or solid. BOOK ONE, CHAPTER 27, # 4

somatic mind: that portion of the mind which, at the direction of either the reactive or analytical mind, puts solutions into effect physically. (See *Definitions and Axioms* at pages 539 to 555 for a full listing of the definitions and axioms of *Science of Survival*.)

sonic: the recall of something heard, so that it is heard again in the mind in full tone and strength. (See *Definitions and Axioms* at pages 539 to 555 for a full listing of the definitions and axioms of *Science of Survival*.)

staff of life: something which serves as a basic support or essential element of life. BOOK TWO, CHAPTER 19, # 1

stet as a phonograph record: a coined phrase meaning fixed or permanent. The word *stet* is a printer's term, meaning "let it stand": used to show that something, such as a word or grammatical symbol, at one time deleted or marked for omission is to remain in a manuscript or the like. BOOK TWO, CHAPTER 13, # 2

succumb: succumbing is the ultimate penalty of nonsurvival activity. This is pain. Failures bring pain and death. (See *Definitions and Axioms* at pages 539 to 555 for a full listing of the definitions and axioms of *Science of Survival*.)

survive: the dynamic principle of existence is *Survive*. At the opposite end of the spectrum of existence is *Succumb*. (See *Definitions and Axioms* at pages 539 to 555 for a full listing of the definitions and axioms of *Science of Survival*.)

swamp-up: a cleaning up or clearing out; a moving out of the way or road. BOOK ONE, CHAPTER 25, # 1

tactile: the recall of touch perceptics. (See *Definitions and Axioms* at pages 539 to 555 for a full listing of the definitions and axioms of *Science of Survival*.)

ten-to-the-twenty-first-power binary digits: a reference to a very large number. The word *power* means how many times a number is multiplied by itself, thus, ten to the twenty-first power means 10 multiplied by itself 21 times or 1,000,000,000,000,000,000,000. "Binary digits" are either of the digits 0 or 1 of the binary system of numbers—that system of numbering that employs only 0s and 1s. The phrase *ten-to-the-twenty-first-power binary digits* then refers to 1,000,000,000,000,000,000,000,000 of the 0s and 1s strung out one after another. BOOK TWO, CHAPTER 9, # 2

thermal: the recall of temperature. (See *Definitions and Axioms* at pages 539 to 555 for a full listing of the definitions and axioms of *Science of Survival*.)

theta (θ): thought, potentially independent of a material vessel or medium. Life force. *Élan vital.* (See *Definitions and Axioms* at pages 539 to 555 for a full listing of the definitions and axioms of *Science of Survival*.)

theta body: the personal theta entity. The soul. Evidence suggests that the theta body may, through many low tone lives, become an entheta body, but that such an entheta body might be cleared by Dianetic processing. It is probable that the theta body can, in part at least, leave the organism temporarily without causing death to the organism. (See *Definitions and Axioms* at pages 539 to 555 for a full listing of the definitions and axioms of *Science of Survival*.) BOOK ONE, CHAPTER 9

theta perceptics: communication with the theta universe. Such perceptics may include hunches, predictions, ESP at greater and lesser distances, communication with the "dead," perception of the Supreme Being, etc. (See *Definitions and Axioms* at pages 539 to 555 for a full listing of the definitions and axioms of *Science of Survival*.) BOOK ONE, CHAPTER 2

theta universe: thought matter (ideas), thought energy, thought space, and thought time, combining in an independent universe analogous to the material universe. One of the purposes of theta is postulated as the conquest, change and ordering of MEST. (See *Definitions and Axioms* at pages 539 to 555 for a full listing of the definitions and axioms of *Science of Survival*.) BOOK ONE, CHAPTER 6

Thompson, Commander: Joseph Cheesman Thompson (1874–1943), a commander in the United States Navy. He was appointed to the Navy in 1897 and became an assistant surgeon and later a surgeon. Thompson studied Freudian analysis with Sigmund Freud (1856–1939).

time track: a representation of the fact that a person exists during a period of MEST time. The present-life time track begins at the first moment of recording and ends at present time, or at death, and it includes all consecutive moments of "now" and the perceptics of those moments. The theta body evidently has a MEST time track of its own. (See *Definitions and Axioms* at pages 539 to 555 for a full listing of the definitions and axioms of *Science of Survival*.) BOOK ONE, CHAPTER 5

training pattern: a stimulus-response mechanism set up by the analytical mind to carry out activity of either a routine or an emergency nature. The training pattern may be said to be held in the somatic mind, but it can be changed at will by the analytical mind. (See *Definitions and Axioms* at pages 539 to 555 for a full listing of the definitions and axioms of *Science of Survival*.)

transorbital leukotomy: a psychiatric procedure in which the frontal lobes of the brain are separated from the rest of the brain by cutting the connecting nerve fibers. *Transorbital* means measured or drawn across between the orbits (the bony cavities of the skull containing the eyes; the eye sockets); occurring by way of or passing through the eye socket. *Leukotomy* comes from the French *leucotomie, leuco* referring to the brain's white matter (nerve tissue, particularly of the spinal column and brain) and *-tomy,* a combining form, used here to mean an incision or cutting of an organ, as designated by the initial element of the term. BOOK ONE, CHAPTER 27, # 1

vacuum tube: a glass tube normally one to six inches long and containing little to no air (a vacuum), formerly used extensively in radios, televisions, computers and other electronic devices to regulate and control electric currents or electronic signals necessary to the operation of such equipment. Because air is resistive to electrical flow, a vacuum is created in the tube so that electricity can flow inside of it. BOOK ONE, CHAPTER 1, # 3

valence-shifter: You're just like your father, don't be like Uncle Rudy, you're just like everybody else, you're exactly like Rover, you're nobody, you're not human, you're out of this world, you can't ever be yourself, I'll just have to pretend I'm somebody else or I'll never be happy again. (See *Definitions and Axioms* at pages 539 to 555 for a full listing of the definitions and axioms of *Science of Survival*.) BOOK ONE, CHAPTER 11

Validation technique: processing in which the auditor, at least for one session, concentrates exclusively on the theta side of lock chains, not allowing the preclear to run any but analytical moments on any given subject. When the preclear encounters too much entheta on a given chain, the auditor takes him to analytical moments on another subject (which moments constitute, of course, a parallel chain to the locks on that subject) obtained from the file clerk. During this type of processing somatics will turn on and off, sometimes severely, but the auditor ignores them, and keeps bringing the preclear back to analytical (not necessarily pleasure) moments. Validation technique should not be mixed with entheta technique. (See *Definitions and Axioms* at pages 539 to 555 for a full listing of the definitions and axioms of *Science of Survival.*)

visio: the recall of something seen, so that it is seen again in the mind in full color, scale, dimension, brightness and detail. (See *Definitions and Axioms* at pages 539 to 555 for a full listing of the definitions and axioms of *Science of Survival.*)

wavelength: a wavelength is a characteristic of motion. Many motions are too random, too chaotic to have orderly wavelengths. An orderly wavelength is a flow of motion. It has a regular, repeated distance between its crests. Take a rope or a garden hose and give it a flip. You will see a wave travel along it. Energy, whether electrical, light or sound, has some such pattern.

Wavelength

This is a smooth flowing wave. Its length is between crests. It is measured in units of length such as centimeters or inches or feet. —LRH

whole cloth, out of: created entirely and completely fresh. BOOK TWO, CHAPTER 18, # 1

work-dog: characterized by menial, lowly work—suitable for a dog only. BOOK TWO, CHAPTER 18, # 4

worth: if an individual's PV is high and is aligned with the dynamics toward survival, his worth may be said to be very high. A person with a high PV, however, may be aberrated so that his PV is reversed in the direction of succumbing and his worth is low. This may be computed for any one of the eight dynamics or for all. (See *Definitions and Axioms* at pages 539 to 555 for a full listing of the definitions and axioms of *Science of Survival.*)

Zeno's Apatheia: a reference to one of the central themes of the school of philosophy founded by the Greek philosopher Zeno (ca. 334–ca. 262 B.C.). It taught that man should be free from passion and indifferent to emotion, pleasure and pain, but not without rational feelings. It also taught that the universe is governed by divine will and happiness lay in conforming to such will. *Apatheia* means without feelings. BOOK ONE, CHAPTER 27, # 5

INDEX

A

D

E

FURTHER BOOKS
AND LECTURES
BY L. RON HUBBARD

THE BEST SOURCE OF INFORMATION on Dianetics and Scientology is the books and recorded lectures of L. Ron Hubbard. To guide you in learning more about Dianetics and Scientology, a selection of suggested books, lectures and videos is provided here.

The materials below have been laid out in a correct sequence for further reading and listening. The categories below begin with basic materials and progress to the more advanced or specialized.

The wisdom of L. Ron Hubbard can be found in these materials. They are available to anyone who wants them. Many of these books are available in public bookstores and libraries; the rest can be obtained at any of the churches listed on page 609, or online at the addresses at the end of this section. Many have been translated into a number of different languages.

COMPANION LECTURES TO SCIENCE OF SURVIVAL

THE SCIENCE OF SURVIVAL LECTURES • In these two companion lectures to the book *Science of Survival,* delivered just after its publication, Ron expands on his breakthroughs in understanding and predicting human behavior. In the lecture *"Theta-MEST Theory,"* Ron gives the *how* and *why* of the Tone Scale and the Chart of Human Evaluation—exactly how a person's collisions with the physical universe fix their position on the Tone Scale—and how Dianetics reverses the process. In *"The Chart of Human Evaluation,"* Ron shows you how to use the chart to cut through a person's social veneer and reach the bottom-line level that really matters—the person's ethics, truth and honesty. He demonstrates the many "tags" that are there to be observed—including the appearance of their body, their medical state and many other factors easily visible to someone who knows the chart. And he even demonstrates how you can find a person's tone level in a two-minute conversation.

SPECIAL COURSE IN HUMAN EVALUATION LECTURES • This series of ten lectures, delivered to professionals in the field of human relations, dispels the mysteries and lays out, in clear terms anyone can understand, the dynamics of human behavior. Expanding on the breakthroughs first described in his book *Science of Survival,* Ron explores the many manifestations of human behavior as laid out in the Chart of Human Evaluation. He describes the wealth of indicators one can use to locate a person on the chart, and how one can then predict their attitudes, behavior and actions. He describes exactly how one communicates to people at different tone levels to get their cooperation. If you like people and want to get along with them better, listen to these lectures and understand others as you never have before.

RECOMMENDED NEXT BOOK

SELF ANALYSIS • Here is an indispensable volume of tests and techniques that anyone can use right at home, based on the discoveries of Dianetics. This book takes the reader on the most interesting adventure of all, the adventure of self, and the realization of one's potentials, which are a great deal better than anyone ever permitted you to believe. Central to the book are self-evaluation tests, where one can plot one's improvement in tone level through the use of Self Analysis processes. The book contains processes one can do on himself—in fact, by using the book, one is being audited by L. Ron Hubbard himself. Using this handbook for just half an hour a day can dramatically improve memory, reaction time, alertness, and just the plain ordinary ability to be happy in life and enjoy things. By reevaluating oneself, an individual can see his own progress and advancement. This is the adventure of Dianetics one can employ right at home.

BOOK ONE, DIANETICS:
THE MODERN SCIENCE OF MENTAL HEALTH

DIANETICS: THE MODERN SCIENCE OF MENTAL HEALTH • The book that started it all. Hailed as a breakthrough "as revolutionary for humanity as the first caveman's discovery and utilization of fire," *Dianetics* has been a perennial bestseller for over five decades. With over 18 million copies sold, it is indisputably the most widely read and influential book on the human mind ever written. Dianetics marks a turning point in man's knowledge and understanding of himself. In this book, Ron produces the first accurate description of the human mind, reveals the single source of all human irrationality, and provides a proven effective technology to clear away the barriers to a person's full mental potential.

HOW TO USE DIANETICS, A VISUAL GUIDEBOOK TO THE HUMAN MIND • In this video, one can see the basic principles and procedures of the book *Dianetics: The Modern Science of Mental Health* clearly demonstrated, laid out step by step, so that he can apply this technology with confidence and certainty. This shows exactly how the analytical mind operates, and the negative effects of the single source of stress, unhappiness, painful emotion and psychosomatic illness—the reactive mind. And a person can see what a Dianetics auditing session looks like so he can start applying this technology right away to get rid of the reactive mind and achieve greater confidence, honesty and trust for himself, his friends and family.

DIANETICS LECTURES AND DEMONSTRATIONS • Following the release of *Dianetics: The Modern Science of Mental Health,* L. Ron Hubbard gave a special course in Dianetics to an audience in Oakland, California, eager to find out more about this breakthrough technology. In a series of four lectures, he discusses engrams, the handling of grief in a preclear, how to get preclears who are having difficulty moving again, and other new developments in Dianetics. One of these lectures includes an actual session, demonstrating the techniques of Dianetics auditing—conducted by Mr. Hubbard himself.

FURTHER DIANETICS BOOKS

THE DYNAMICS OF LIFE • Written in 1947, this book is the first formal record of L. Ron Hubbard's researches into the structure and functions of the human mind. It was L. Ron Hubbard's original thesis and includes the first description of auditing principles, including the code of conduct an auditor should follow, and the nature of engrams and their effects upon individuals. There are also case histories showing the unprecedented results of early Dianetics auditing. Not surprisingly, when it was first circulated, Mr. Hubbard was deluged with requests for more information. This led him to write his landmark manual of Dianetics procedure, *Dianetics: The Modern Science of Mental Health*—the "textbook" of Dianetics. *The Dynamics of Life* offers a more concise view of how the mind works and how Dianetics can be used to alleviate man's suffering.

DIANETICS: THE EVOLUTION OF A SCIENCE • At a young age, L. Ron Hubbard became greatly intrigued by the mystery of man and his mind. *Dianetics: The Evolution of a Science* is the story of how he came to make the breakthroughs which solve this mystery. This book reveals how Mr. Hubbard was able to recognize and isolate an individual's true basic personality and details how painful or traumatic events in life can become fused with an individual's innermost self, causing fears, insecurities and psychosomatic ills. And it shows how, by first describing the full potential of the mind, he was able to discover these impediments. Because of his work, this potential is now attainable.

ADVANCED PROCEDURE AND AXIOMS • Dianetics is the first subject to codify life into axioms. In this book one finds the fundamental principles that govern life and the mind. When one knows and uses these basic laws, one can achieve spiritual freedom. There are three points of address in any case—thought, emotion and effort. Here is their anatomy and description with exact processing for each. This book reveals for the first time the power of an individual's own thoughts and decisions in shaping life.

HANDBOOK FOR PRECLEARS • This Dianetics workbook can be used both as a processing handbook by an auditor, or as a self-processing handbook that the individual uses by himself. It is designed to raise the individual on the Tone Scale, lessening the effect of the reactive mind and restoring self-determinism, intelligence and abilities. If one wants to experience the miraculous results of Dianetics auditing, one only needs this book and one's own desire to improve.

DIANETICS 55! • This book contains a summary of the developments and breakthroughs in the five years following the publication of "Book One" (Dianetics: The Modern Science of Mental Health) in 1950. It further explores what was called in Dianetics the "awareness of awareness unit"—the person himself—and defines the components of freedom (affinity, reality and communication) and of entrapment (matter, energy, space and time). It also provides the fundamentals of communication—a subject so vital to spiritual freedom that one can state that a person is as alive as he can communicate. This text is used today in Scientology courses as the definitive manual of effective communication.

CHILD DIANETICS • Published to meet the demand from parents for a book on how to better understand and bring up children using the principles of Dianetics, Child Dianetics reveals the true cause and remedy of childhood upsets, irrationality and fears. This book shows parents how to truly understand a child and establish an honest and loving relationship based on trust and mutual respect. It is a guide no parent should be without.

NOTES ON THE LECTURES OF L. RON HUBBARD • In late 1950, Mr. Hubbard gave a series of pivotal lectures on Dianetics, the affinity-reality-communication triangle and the Tone Scale. At his request, the staff of the Hubbard Dianetics Research Foundation took detailed notes—including copies of his chalkboard diagrams—and compiled them into this comprehensive textbook. Here is some of the earliest and best material on the ARC triangle and the Tone Scale—a detailed look at how one's attitude towards life, ability to communicate with others, behavior and even physical well-being shift as one goes up and down the scale.

BASIC SCIENTOLOGY BOOKS

SCIENTOLOGY: THE FUNDAMENTALS OF THOUGHT • L. Ron Hubbard regarded *The Fundamentals of Thought* as his first Scientology book. In this work, he introduces many of the powerful basic principles of the Scientology religion. It includes a broad summary of his research and contains a complete description of Scientology's most fundamental principles: the cycle of action, the conditions of existence, the ARC triangle and the parts of man—thetan, mind and body. And one chapter consists of Scientology auditing techniques that can be immediately used to bring about changes for the better. *The Fundamentals of Thought* are, indeed, the fundamentals of life.

THE PROBLEMS OF WORK • In this book, L. Ron Hubbard isolates the problems encountered on the job—whether on the assembly line or in the executive office. He offers solutions to frayed tempers and the common feeling that one cannot possibly accomplish all there is to do. This book uncovers the way to handle the confusions that surround a job and opens the doors to efficiency.

SCIENTOLOGY: A NEW SLANT ON LIFE • A collection of thirty essays by L. Ron Hubbard on: the exact anatomy of winning or losing, the root of marital success, helping children to be successful in their own lives, two rules for happy living, what problems are made of (and what resolves them), how knowledge affects one's certainty, the importance of honesty, the preservation of freedom and more. *Scientology: A New Slant on Life* contains both a discussion of the profound principles and concepts on which Scientology is based and remarkable practical techniques anyone can use to improve his life.

SCIENTOLOGY 0-8: THE BOOK OF BASICS • This book contains all the basics and principles of Scientology. Included are the Axioms of Scientology, the Aims of Scientology, the Code of a Scientologist, the Logics, over thirty scales and charts, a description of the Scientology Symbol and more. The title means "Scientology, zero to infinity," the numeral 8 being the symbol for infinity standing upright. *Scientology 0-8* concisely provides the central, fundamental data of life.

ADVANCED SCIENTOLOGY BOOKS

SCIENTOLOGY 8-80 • The discovery and increase of life energy is a goal as old as man himself. That goal has been realized in Scientology, and this book reveals how. The "8-8" stands for "infinity-infinity" upright, the "0" represents the static, theta. In this book, L. Ron Hubbard describes how the thetan acts as a mirror. Here is the truth of man's nature as a spiritual being that *creates* and *uses* the energies of aesthetics, thought, emotion and effort to operate in the physical universe.

SCIENTOLOGY 8-8008 • The meaning of "8-8008" is that one attains infinity (the symbol 8 laid on its side) through the reduction of the apparent infinity of the physical universe to zero and the increase of one's own creative ability from an apparent zero to infinity. In other words, it is the study of how to free the human spirit from the effects of the physical universe. This is where The Factors (summations of the considerations and examinations of the human spirit and physical universe) are presented. Originally presented to attendees of L. Ron Hubbard's Philadelphia Doctorate Course lectures, they describe the native beingness of man and the interaction of theta and MEST.

SCIENTOLOGY: A HISTORY OF MAN • A fascinating look at the evolutionary background and history of the human race—revolutionary concepts guaranteed to intrigue you and challenge many basic assumptions about man's true power, potential and abilities. This book is, as L. Ron Hubbard stated in the introduction, "a coldblooded and factual account of your last sixty trillion years."

THE CREATION OF HUMAN ABILITY • This book charts the route to the ultimate human ability—operating as a spiritual being exterior to one's body. With more than eighty powerful processes, this book forms a comprehensive handbook for the rehabilitation of man's true abilities.

HAVE YOU LIVED BEFORE THIS LIFE? • With more than forty individual accounts of past lives revealed during auditing sessions, this book started a huge international upsurge of interest in the subject. It describes the life-changing benefits from recalling past lives and how this knowledge can increase spiritual awareness. It answers such questions as "What happens when a person dies?" and "Are there such things as ghosts?"

REFERENCE HANDBOOKS AND VIDEO

WHAT IS SCIENTOLOGY? • Scientology covers every aspect of life and livingness. But how do you communicate this to someone who has not experienced or seen it for himself? Those who wish to know more about Scientology or communicate the full scope of the subject to others should read *What Is Scientology?* The most comprehensive text ever assembled on the Scientology religion, this book covers its religious heritage, basic principles and practices, organizational structure, worldwide use and expansion, social betterment programs and much, much more. *What Is Scientology?* is the definitive reference for anyone who wants all the facts on the world's fastest growing religion.

THE SCIENTOLOGY HANDBOOK • A companion volume to *What Is Scientology?,* this handbook covers the basic principles anyone needs to survive. Many people want to help others and would if only they knew what to do. This book fills that need. It is the key book used by Scientology Volunteer Ministers in their crusade to do something effective about conditions on this planet. *The Scientology Handbook* provides miracle-working Scientology technology on how to preserve marriages, get delinquent children back in the fold, handle dissident elements in the society, get families out of the red, solve human conflict, handle illiteracy, resolve drug, alcohol and many other problems. With more than 950 pages of practical solutions to the real problems of life, this book is a vital survival manual to living in today's world.

AN INTRODUCTION TO SCIENTOLOGY • This one-hour filmed interview, the only one ever granted by L. Ron Hubbard, explains how he made his discoveries and breakthroughs during his explorations of the mind, spirit and life. He discusses his bestseller, *Dianetics: The Modern Science of Mental Health,* and how Scientology came about. And he answers the most commonly asked questions: What is Scientology? Why is it a religion? What is the difference between the mind and the spirit? What is man's true purpose? How do people benefit from Scientology? And what do people do in churches of Scientology?

PURIFICATION

CLEAR BODY, CLEAR MIND: THE EFFECTIVE PURIFICATION PROGRAM • Through extensive research, L. Ron Hubbard discovered that certain drugs can lodge in the fatty tissues of the body, and cause "flashbacks," tiredness, mental dullness and other adverse reactions, for years after their use ceases. He then developed the exact technology to rid an individual of the adverse effects of drugs, chemicals, radiation and toxins which can inhibit spiritual progress. This book explains that technology and provides the procedures of the Purification Rundown, the most effective program known to handle toxic residues in the body. Thousands of people from around the world have completed this lifesaving program and freed themselves from the harmful effects of drugs and toxins.

PURIFICATION: AN ILLUSTRATED ANSWER TO DRUGS • This fully illustrated book describes the Purification Rundown and exactly how it addresses the restimulative effects of drugs and toxins in the body. Included here in text and illustrations are the steps of the

Purification Rundown. The book explains how the rundown removes drugs and toxins that have been stored in the body, and how this purification restores the ability to think more clearly.

ALL ABOUT RADIATION • Written by L. Ron Hubbard and two well-known medical doctors, this book provides the facts surrounding the effect of radiation on the body and spirit and offers solutions to those harmful effects. An immediate sellout in bookstores when originally released, *All About Radiation* tells the truth about the little known and talked about subject of radiation, and introduces the Purification Rundown as the technology to handle the cumulative effects of radiation.

ETHICS

INTRODUCTION TO SCIENTOLOGY ETHICS • In *Introduction to Scientology Ethics* L. Ron Hubbard presents the first basic and workable ethics technology ever developed. Terms like *ethics, justice* and *morals* are defined, formulas to improve the survival of individuals and groups alike are provided, and codes to honest and happy living are revealed. By using these powerful principles of Scientology ethics every day a person can live a life of integrity and ever-increasing survival.

EXECUTIVE

HOW TO LIVE THOUGH AN EXECUTIVE • Recognizing that the role of the executive in an organization is planning and supervision, L. Ron Hubbard, after a broad study of communications theory and systems and a survey of many organizations, originated and composed the organizational communications system presented in *How to Live Though an Executive.* This is a communication manual for any organization. It details the exact factors an executive needs to successfully run an organization—from handling mail to raising morale to setting group goals.

PERSONAL ACHIEVEMENT SERIES LECTURES

The selected lectures by L. Ron Hubbard listed below are excellent presentations of basic Dianetics and Scientology principles and technology. Roughly one hour in length, each addresses a variety of topics, and all provide practical information for immediate use. They also give insight into L. Ron Hubbard himself, revealing his vitality, humor and enthusiasm as no written word can.

THE STORY OF DIANETICS AND SCIENTOLOGY • This is the best lecture for anyone seeking the broad overview of Dianetics and Scientology. In this personal and fascinating talk, L. Ron Hubbard introduces the people and experiences encountered during his search for the truth about man, the mind and life itself. From the friendship which sparked his interest in the mind at the age of twelve, through his travels in Asia as a teenager, and even his experiences in war, Ron describes a continuous journey of discovery culminating in the research and development of Dianetics and Scientology technology. He reveals exactly how he came to unlock the mystery of the human mind and spirit and how he finally uncovered the truth that means real freedom for mankind.

THE AFFINITY-REALITY-COMMUNICATION TRIANGLE • Here is a thorough description on the ARC triangle explained in *Science of Survival.* Contains Ron's further breakthrough about ARC which evaluates the relative importance of each of its three corners. One corner is far more important than the other two, as this lecture describes, and in fact is the most powerful item in all of life!

OPERATION MANUAL FOR THE MIND • Many people "wonder" how the mind works. Since we all have one, why is the mind not understood? This lecture, given during research following *Science of Survival,* reveals a deep-seated belief which prevents man from finding out how his own mind operates. With this "secret" exposed, the door is opened for a true understanding of oneself.

THE DYNAMICS • This lecture contains further data on attaining the goal in *Science of Survival* of assisting the individual to change for the better. Other studies before Dianetics and Scientology tried to change a person for the "benefit" of society. That is a shortsighted view as this lecture demonstrates, and shows as well how improving the individual for his *own* benefit improves society and all the dynamics to a greater degree than any other approach.

THE DYNAMIC PRINCIPLES OF EXISTENCE • Why do some people succeed while others fail? Luck? Destiny? Can one change one's own "lot" in life? Yes, one can. There is a principle which directly monitors how alive an individual is. Ron explains this principle and outlines how to apply it in life.

THE MACHINERY OF THE MIND • Whatever claims were made about the mind before Dianetics, virtually *nothing* was actually *known*. This fascinating lecture provides a clear understanding of the "machinery" of the mind, along with the processes of thought, decision-making and communication. This lecture explains how a knowledge of these factors enables anyone to regain control of his life.

INCREASING EFFICIENCY • Increased efficiency does not come from a change of diet, pills, or anything else outside the mind. This lecture describes the factors that increase efficiency and provides invaluable data to restore anyone's efficiency, effectiveness and competence.

HEALTH AND CERTAINTY • What is the connection between certainty and health? Certainty of what? In this remarkable analysis of the anatomy of certainty, Ron unlocks the door to more than physical health. Whether the health of a society or an individual, the secret is the same. The degree to which one can control one's own life depends on only one thing. That "one thing" is detailed in this lecture.

POWER OF CHOICE AND SELF-DETERMINISM • As is seen from the Chart of Human Evaluation, many factors determine one's behavior and influence the course of one's life. By far the most important is a discovery Ron made in further researches about one's own power of choice. This lecture explains how to rehabilitate this ability and how then using it could affect an individual or society.

THE ROAD TO TRUTH • What is truth? A question that has been asked since the beginning of time is now answered. In this lecture, Ron explains how to recognize the traps and half-truths that confound any who seek answers to life's most basic mysteries. And he explains what one must do to walk all the way on the "Road to Truth."

THE HOPE OF MAN • Dianetics and Scientology owe a debt to the great spiritual figures of the ages, including Siddhartha Gautama, Lao-tse, Krishna and Christ, who kept alive the flame of hope for spiritual freedom. Ron describes the role of Dianetics and Scientology in this tradition and the practical path they provide so man can at last attain this hope.

MAN'S RELENTLESS SEARCH • Man has been searching for answers to his own existence throughout recorded history. This lecture describes some of the answers provided by religions and philosophies down through the ages. And it reveals what they all missed that Dianetics and Scientology now provide.

SCIENTOLOGY AND EFFECTIVE KNOWLEDGE • The pursuit of knowledge has occupied the attention of philosophers, explorers, scholars and adventurers for thousands of years. Beyond technological advances, little of value has been learned about life itself. In this lecture several years after *Science of Survival,* Ron imparts the one simple quality an individual must assume to better understand any aspect of life. With this key, anyone can obtain effective knowledge.

THE ROAD TO PERFECTION—THE GOODNESS OF MAN • In contrast to some beliefs, but in full support of the discoveries in this book, Dianetics and Scientology view man as basically good. This lecture contains the truth about the basic nature of man and what it takes to restore an individual to a higher level of decency and ability. It is a new look to improve the good qualities that already exist in a person and to eradicate his "bad" behavior.

MAN: GOOD OR EVIL? • One question has confounded philosophers and scientists through the ages: Is man evil or is he good? No answer has ever provided any certainty—until now. Ron describes what good and evil really are and illustrates the basic nature of man. Essential information for anyone interested in human evaluation.

THE FIVE CONDITIONS OF EXISTENCE (AND FORMULAS FOR THEIR IMPROVEMENT) • There is no such thing as an unchanging condition. Whether rapidly or slowly, everything is either growing or shrinking, expanding or contracting, improving or getting worse. This lecture defines the five basic conditions and the series of actions one can take to improve any aspect of life. A job, a relationship, one's state of mind—each can be improved by applying the formula of actions appropriate to the condition it is currently in.

SCIENTOLOGY AND ABILITY • It is an old idea that teaching someone skills leading to self-sufficiency is better than charity for the recipient. Ron discovered that this idea happens to hold true for every aspect of life. The best solution to any difficulty would be to acquire the ability to solve it oneself. In this lecture, Ron describes how Scientology restores one's full inherent ability.

MIRACLES • Everybody has some idea about what would constitute a miracle. But is there really such a thing? With no appeal to faith, this lecture defines exactly what miracles are and how Dianetics and Scientology shed light on how they can be experienced.

THE DETERIORATION OF LIBERTY • People and societies throughout history have pursued freedom. Despite strong foundations like the Declaration of Independence in the United States, for example, it is possible to see our freedoms eroding. This lecture describes how to preserve high ideals in a world that desperately needs to rise on the Tone Scale.

DIFFERENCES BETWEEN SCIENTOLOGY AND OTHER PHILOSOPHIES • This lecture shatters a long-held but erroneous assumption man has made about life and which impedes and perpetuates his aberrations. Until Dianetics and Scientology, the basic problems confronting the individual had not been solved. This is but one of the essential differences between Dianetics and Scientology when compared to other studies.

WHERE TO GO
FOR DIANETICS TRAINING
AND AUDITING

THE HUBBARD DIANETICS FOUNDATION is a department within the Churches of Scientology. Every Church of Scientology has a Hubbard Dianetics Foundation.

If you would like more information about Dianetics courses, lectures, seminars or auditing, contact your nearest organization as listed below.

Or visit the Dianetics website at **www.dianetics.org** or the Scientology Global Information Center at **www.scientology.org**.

UNITED STATES

ALBUQUERQUE
Church of Scientology
8106 Menaul Boulevard NE
Albuquerque
New Mexico 87110

ANN ARBOR
Church of Scientology
2355 West Stadium Boulevard
Ann Arbor, Michigan 48103

ATLANTA
Church of Scientology
1611 Mt. Vernon Road
Dunwoody, Georgia 30338

AUSTIN
Church of Scientology
2200 Guadalupe
Austin, Texas 78705

BOSTON
Church of Scientology
448 Beacon Street
Boston, Massachusetts 02115

BUFFALO
Church of Scientology
47 West Huron Street
Buffalo, New York 14202

CHICAGO
Church of Scientology
3011 North Lincoln Avenue
Chicago, Illinois 60657-4207

CINCINNATI
Church of Scientology
215 West 4th Street
  5th Floor
Cincinnati, Ohio 45202-2670

CLEARWATER
Church of Scientology
Flag Service Organization
210 South Fort Harrison Avenue
Clearwater, Florida 33756

Church of Scientology
Flag Ship Service Organization
c/o *Freewinds* Relay Office
118 North Fort Harrison Avenue
Clearwater, Florida 33755

COLUMBUS
Church of Scientology
30 North High Street
Columbus, Ohio 43215

DALLAS

Church of Scientology
Celebrity Centre Dallas
1850 North Buckner Boulevard
Dallas, Texas 75228

DENVER

Church of Scientology
3385 South Bannock Street
Englewood, Colorado 80110

DETROIT

Church of Scientology
321 Williams Street
Royal Oak, Michigan 48067

HONOLULU

Church of Scientology
1146 Bethel Street
Honolulu, Hawaii 96813

KANSAS CITY

Church of Scientology
3619 Broadway
Kansas City, Missouri 64111

LAS VEGAS

Church of Scientology
846 East Sahara Avenue
Las Vegas, Nevada 89104

Church of Scientology
Celebrity Centre Las Vegas
1100 South 10th Street
Las Vegas, Nevada 89104

LONG ISLAND

Church of Scientology
99 Railroad Station Plaza
Hicksville, New York
11801-2850

LOS ANGELES
AND VICINITY

Church of Scientology
4810 Sunset Boulevard
Los Angeles, California 90027

Church of Scientology
1277 East Colorado Boulevard
Pasadena, California 91106

Church of Scientology
1451 Irvine Boulevard
Tustin, California 92680

Church of Scientology
15643 Sherman Way
Van Nuys, California 91406

Church of Scientology
American Saint Hill
  Organization
1413 L. Ron Hubbard Way
Los Angeles, California 90027

Church of Scientology
American Saint Hill
  Foundation
1413 L. Ron Hubbard Way
Los Angeles, California 90027

Church of Scientology
Advanced Organization of
  Los Angeles
1306 L. Ron Hubbard Way
Los Angeles, California 90027

Church of Scientology
Celebrity Centre International
5930 Franklin Avenue
Hollywood, California 90028

LOS GATOS

Church of Scientology
2155 South Bascom Avenue,
  Suite 120
Campbell, California 95008

MIAMI

Church of Scientology
120 Giralda Avenue
Coral Gables, Florida 33134

MINNEAPOLIS

Church of Scientology
  Twin Cities
1011 Nicollet Mall
Minneapolis, Minnesota 55403

MOUNTAIN VIEW

Church of Scientology
2483 Old Middlefield Way
Mountain View, California 94043

NASHVILLE

Church of Scientology
Celebrity Centre Nashville
1204 16th Avenue South
Nashville, Tennessee 37212

NEW HAVEN

Church of Scientology
909 Whalley Avenue
New Haven, Connecticut
06515-1728

NEW YORK CITY

Church of Scientology
227 West 46th Street
New York, New York
10036-1409

Church of Scientology
Celebrity Centre New York
65 East 82nd Street
New York, New York 10028

ORLANDO

Church of Scientology
1830 East Colonial Drive
Orlando, Florida
32803-4729

PHILADELPHIA

Church of Scientology
1315 Race Street
Philadelphia, Pennsylvania 19107

PHOENIX

Church of Scientology
2111 West University Drive
Mesa, Arizona 85201

PORTLAND

Church of Scientology
2636 NE Sandy Boulevard
Portland, Oregon 97232-2342

Church of Scientology
Celebrity Centre Portland
708 SW Salmon Street
Portland, Oregon 97205

SACRAMENTO

Church of Scientology
825 15th Street
Sacramento, California
95814-2096

SALT LAKE CITY

Church of Scientology
1931 South 1100 East
Salt Lake City, Utah 84106

SAN DIEGO

Church of Scientology
1330 4th Avenue
San Diego, California 92101

SAN FRANCISCO

Church of Scientology
83 McAllister Street
San Francisco, California 94102

SAN JOSE

Church of Scientology
80 East Rosemary Street
San Jose, California 95112

SANTA BARBARA

Church of Scientology
524 State Street
Santa Barbara, California 93101

SEATTLE

Church of Scientology
601 Aurora Avenue North
Seattle, Washington 98109

ST. LOUIS

Church of Scientology
6901 Delmar Boulevard
University City, Missouri 63130

TAMPA

Church of Scientology
3617 Henderson Boulevard
Tampa, Florida 33609-4501

WASHINGTON, DC

Founding Church of
  Scientology of
  Washington, DC
1701 20th Street NW
Washington, DC 20009

PUERTO RICO

HATO REY

Church of Scientology
272 JT Piñero Avenue
Hyde Park, Hato Rey
San Juan, Puerto Rico 00918

CANADA

EDMONTON

Church of Scientology
10206 106th Street NW
Edmonton, Alberta
Canada T5J 1H7

KITCHENER

Church of Scientology
104 King Street West, 2nd Floor
Kitchener, Ontario
Canada N2G 2K6

MONTREAL

Church of Scientology
4489 Papineau Street
Montreal, Quebec
Canada H2H 1T7

OTTAWA

Church of Scientology
150 Rideau Street, 2nd Floor
Ottawa, Ontario
Canada K1N 5X6

QUEBEC

Church of Scientology
350 Bd Chareste Est
Quebec, Quebec
Canada G1K 3H5

TORONTO

Church of Scientology
696 Yonge Street, 2nd Floor
Toronto, Ontario
Canada M4Y 2A7

VANCOUVER

Church of Scientology
401 West Hastings Street
Vancouver, British Columbia
Canada V6B 1L5

WINNIPEG

Church of Scientology
315 Garry Street, Suite 210
Winnipeg, Manitoba
Canada R3B 2G7

UNITED KINGDOM

BIRMINGHAM

Church of Scientology
8 Ethel Street
Winston Churchill House
Birmingham, England B2 4BG

BRIGHTON

Church of Scientology
Third Floor, 79-83 North Street
Brighton, Sussex
England BN1 1ZA

EAST GRINSTEAD

Church of Scientology
Saint Hill Foundation
Saint Hill Manor
East Grinstead, West Sussex
England RH19 4JY

Advanced Organization
Saint Hill
Saint Hill Manor
East Grinstead, West Sussex
England RH19 4JY

EDINBURGH

Hubbard Academy of Personal
Independence
20 Southbridge
Edinburgh, Scotland EH1 1LL

LONDON

Church of Scientology
68 Tottenham Court Road
London, England W1P 0BB

Church of Scientology
Celebrity Centre London
42 Leinster Gardens
London, England W2 3AN

MANCHESTER
Church of Scientology
258 Deansgate
Manchester, England M3 4BG

PLYMOUTH
Church of Scientology
41 Ebrington Street
Plymouth, Devon
England PL4 9AA

SUNDERLAND
Church of Scientology
51 Fawcett Street
Sunderland, Tyne and Wear
England SR1 1RS

AUSTRIA

VIENNA
Church of Scientology
Schottenfeldgasse 13/15
1070 Vienna, Austria

Church of Scientology
Celebrity Centre Vienna
Senefeldergasse 11/5
1100 Vienna, Austria

BELGIUM

BRUSSELS
Church of Scientology
rue General MacArthur, 9
1180 Brussels, Belgium

DENMARK

AARHUS
Church of Scientology
Vester Alle 26
8000 Aarhus C, Denmark

COPENHAGEN
Church of Scientology
Store Kongensgade 55
1264 Copenhagen K, Denmark

Church of Scientology
Gammel Kongevej 3–5, 1
1610 Copenhagen V, Denmark

Church of Scientology
Advanced Organization Saint
 Hill for Europe
Jernbanegade 6
1608 Copenhagen V, Denmark

FRANCE

ANGERS
Church of Scientology
6, avenue Montaigne
49100 Angers, France

CLERMONT-FERRAND
Church of Scientology
6, rue Dulaure
63000 Clermont-Ferrand
France

LYON
Church of Scientology
3, place des Capucins
69001 Lyon, France

PARIS
Church of Scientology
7, rue Jules César
75012 Paris, France

Church of Scientology
Celebrity Centre Paris
69, rue Legendre
75017 Paris, France

SAINT-ÉTIENNE
Church of Scientology
24, rue Marengo
42000 Saint-Étienne, France

GERMANY

BERLIN
Church of Scientology
Sponholzstraße 51–52
12159 Berlin, Germany

DÜSSELDORF
Church of Scientology
Friedrichstraße 28
40217 Düsseldorf, Germany

Church of Scientology
Celebrity Centre Düsseldorf
Luisenstraße 23
40215 Düsseldorf, Germany

FRANKFURT

Church of Scientology
Kaiserstraße 49
60329 Frankfurt, Germany

HAMBURG

Church of Scientology
Domstraße 12
20095 Hamburg, Germany

Church of Scientology
Brennerstraße 12
20099 Hamburg, Germany

HANOVER

Church of Scientology
Odeonstraße 17
30159 Hanover, Germany

MUNICH

Church of Scientology
Beichstraße 12
80802 Munich, Germany

STUTTGART

Church of Scientology
Hohenheimerstraße 9
70184 Stuttgart, Germany

HUNGARY

BUDAPEST

Church of Scientology
1399 Budapest
VII. ker. Erzsébet krt. 5. I. em.
Postafiók 701/215.
Hungary

ISRAEL

TEL AVIV

College of Dianetics
12 Shontzino Street
PO Box 57478
61573 Tel Aviv, Israel

ITALY

BRESCIA

Church of Scientology
Via Fratelli Bronzetti, 20
25125 Brescia, Italy

CATANIA

Church of Scientology
Via Garibaldi, 9
95121 Catania, Italy

MILAN

Church of Scientology
Via Lepontina, 4
20159 Milan, Italy

MONZA

Church of Scientology
Largomolinetto, 1
20052 Monza (MI), Italy

NOVARA

Church of Scientology
Via Passalacqua, 28
28100 Novara, Italy

NUORO

Church of Scientology
Via Lamarmora, 102
08100 Nuoro, Italy

PADUA

Church of Scientology
Via Ugo Foscolo, 5
35131 Padua, Italy

PORDENONE

Church of Scientology
Via Dogana, 19
Zona Fiera
33170 Pordenone, Italy

ROME

Church of Scientology
Via del Caravita, 5
00186 Rome, Italy

TURIN

Church of Scientology
Via Bersezio, 7
10152 Turin, Italy

VERONA

Church of Scientology
Corso Milano, 84
37138 Verona, Italy

NETHERLANDS

AMSTERDAM

Church of Scientology
Nieuwezijds Voorburgwal
116–118
1012 SH Amsterdam
Netherlands

NORWAY

OSLO

Church of Scientology
Lille Grensen 3
0159 Oslo, Norway

PORTUGAL

LISBON

Church of Scientology
Rua da Prata 185, 2 Andar
1100 Lisbon, Portugal

RUSSIA

MOSCOW

Hubbard Humanitarian Center
Boris Galushkina Street 19A
129301 Moscow, Russia

SPAIN

BARCELONA

Dianetics Civil Association
Pasaje Domingo, 11–13 Bajos
08007 Barcelona, Spain

MADRID

Dianetics Civil Association
C/ Montera 20, Piso 1° dcha.
28013 Madrid, Spain

SWEDEN

GÖTEBORG

Church of Scientology
Värmlandsgatan 16, 1 tr.
413 28 Göteborg, Sweden

MALMÖ

Church of Scientology
Porslinsgatan 3
211 32 Malmö, Sweden

STOCKHOLM

Church of Scientology
Götgatan 105
116 62 Stockholm, Sweden

SWITZERLAND

BASEL

Church of Scientology
Herrengrabenweg 56
4054 Basel, Switzerland

BERN

Church of Scientology
Muhlemattstrasse 31
Postfach 384
3000 Bern 14, Switzerland

GENEVA

Church of Scientology
12, rue des Acacias
1227 Carouge
Geneva, Switzerland

LAUSANNE

Church of Scientology
10, rue de la Madeleine
1003 Lausanne, Switzerland

ZURICH

Church of Scientology
Freilagerstrasse 11
8047 Zurich, Switzerland

AUSTRALIA

ADELAIDE

Church of Scientology
24–28 Waymouth Street
Adelaide, South Australia
Australia 5000

BRISBANE

Church of Scientology
106 Edward Street, 2nd Floor
Brisbane, Queensland
Australia 4000

CANBERRA

Church of Scientology
43–45 East Row
Canberra City, ACT
Australia 2601

MELBOURNE

Church of Scientology
42–44 Russell Street
Melbourne, Victoria
Australia 3000

PERTH

Church of Scientology
108 Murray Street, 1st Floor
Perth, Western Australia
Australia 6000

SYDNEY

Church of Scientology
201 Castlereagh Street
Sydney, New South Wales
Australia 2000

Church of Scientology
Advanced Organization
  Saint Hill Australia,
  New Zealand and Oceania
19–37 Greek Street
Glebe, New South Wales
Australia 2037

JAPAN

TOKYO

Scientology Tokyo
2-11-7, Kita-otsuka
Toshima-ku
Tokyo
Japan 170-004

NEW ZEALAND

AUCKLAND

Church of Scientology
159 Queen Street, 3rd Floor
Auckland 1, New Zealand

AFRICA

BULAWAYO

Church of Scientology
Southampton House, Suite 202
Main Street and 9th Avenue
Bulawayo, Zimbabwe

CAPE TOWN

Church of Scientology
Ground Floor, Dorlane House
39 Roeland Street
Cape Town 8001, South Africa

DURBAN

Church of Scientology
20 Buckingham Terrace
Westville, Durban 3630
South Africa

HARARE

Church of Scientology
404-409 Pockets Building
50 Jason Moyo Avenue
Harare, Zimbabwe

JOHANNESBURG

Church of Scientology
4th Floor, Budget House
130 Main Street
Johannesburg 2001
South Africa

Church of Scientology
No. 108 1st Floor,
  Bordeaux Centre
Gordon Road, Corner Jan
  Smuts Avenue
Blairgowrie, Randburg 2125
South Africa

PORT ELIZABETH

Church of Scientology
2 St. Christopher's
27 Westbourne Road Central
Port Elizabeth 6001
South Africa

PRETORIA

Church of Scientology
307 Ancore Building
Corner Jeppe and Esselen Streets
Sunnyside, Pretoria 0002
South Africa

ARGENTINA

BUENOS AIRES

Dianetics Association of
   Argentina
2169 Bartolomé Mitre
Capital Federal
Buenos Aires 1039, Argentina

COLOMBIA

BOGOTÁ

Dianetics Cultural Center
Carrera 30 #91–96
Bogotá, Colombia

MEXICO

GUADALAJARA

Dianetics Cultural
   Organization, A.C.
Avenida de la Paz 2787
Fracc. Arcos Sur, Sector Juárez
Guadalajara, Jalisco
C.P. 44500, Mexico

MEXICO CITY

Dianetics Cultural
   Association, A.C.
Belisario Domínguez #17-1
Villa Coyoacán
Colonia Coyoacán
C.P. 04000, Mexico, D.F.

Institute of Applied
   Philosophy, A.C.
Municipio Libre No. 40
   Esq. Mira Flores
Colonia Portales
Mexico, D.F.

Latin American Cultural
   Center, A.C.
Rio Amazonas 11
Colonia Cuahutemoc
C.P. 06500, Mexico, D.F.

Dianetics Technological
   Institute, A.C.
Avenida Chapultepec 540
   6° Piso
Colonia Roma, Metro
   Chapultepec
C.P. 06700, Mexico, D.F.

Dianetics Development
   Organization, A.C.
Avenida Xola #1113 Esq. Pitágoras
Colonia Narvarte
C.P. 03220, Mexico, D.F.

Dianetics Cultural
   Organization, A.C.
Calle Monterrey #402
Colonia Narvarte
C.P. 03020, Mexico, D.F.

VENEZUELA

CARACAS

Dianetics Cultural
   Organization, A.C.
Calle El Colegio, Edificio
   El Viñedo
Sabana Grande
Caracas, Venezuela

VALENCIA

Dianetics Cultural
   Association, A.C.
Avenida 101 No. 150-23
   (Atrás Fiat. Bolívar Norte)
Urbanización La Alegría
Valencia, Venezuela

To obtain any books or cassettes by L. Ron Hubbard which are not available at your local organization, contact any of the following publishers:

BRIDGE PUBLICATIONS, INC.
4751 Fountain Avenue
Los Angeles, California 90029

CONTINENTAL PUBLICATIONS
LIAISON OFFICE
696 Yonge Street
Toronto, Ontario
Canada M4Y 2A7

NEW ERA PUBLICATIONS
INTERNATIONAL ApS
Store Kongensgade 53
1264 Copenhagen K
Denmark

ERA DINÁMICA EDITORES,
S.A. DE C.V.
Pablo Ucello #16
Colonia C.D. de los Deportes
Mexico, D.F.

NEW ERA PUBLICATIONS
UK, LTD.
Saint Hill Manor
East Grinstead, West Sussex
England RH19 4JY

NEW ERA PUBLICATIONS
AUSTRALIA PTY LTD.
Level 1, 61–65 Wentworth Avenue
Surry Hills
New South Wales
Australia 2000

CONTINENTAL PUBLICATIONS
PTY LTD.
6th Floor, Budget House
130 Main Street
Johannesburg 2001, South Africa

NEW ERA PUBLICATIONS
ITALIA S.R.L.
Via Cadorna, 61
20090 Vimodrone (MI)
Italy

NEW ERA PUBLICATIONS
DEUTSCHLAND GMBH
Hittfelder Kirchweg 5A
21220 Seevetal-Maschen
Germany

NEW ERA
PUBLICATIONS FRANCE
E.U.R.L.
14, rue des Moulins
75001 Paris
France

NUEVA ERA
DINÁMICA S.A.
C/ Montera 20, 1° dcha.
28013 Madrid, Spain

NEW ERA PUBLICATIONS
JAPAN, INC.
3-4-20-503 Sala Mita
Minato-ku, Tokyo
Japan 108

NEW ERA
PUBLICATIONS GROUP
Ul. Kasatkina, 16, Building 1
129301 Moscow, Russia

"I AM ALWAYS HAPPY TO HEAR FROM MY READERS."

L. RON HUBBARD

THESE WERE THE WORDS of L. Ron Hubbard, who was always very interested in hearing from his friends and readers. He made a point of staying in communication with everyone he came in contact with over his fifty-year career as a professional writer, and he had thousands of fans and friends that he corresponded with all over the world.

The publishers of L. Ron Hubbard's works wish to continue this tradition and welcome letters and comments from you, his readers, both old and new.

Additionally, the publishers will be happy to send you information on anything you would like to know about L. Ron Hubbard, his extraordinary life and accomplishments and the vast number of books he has written.

Any message addressed to Author's Affairs Director at Bridge Publications will be given prompt and full attention.

BRIDGE PUBLICATIONS, INC.

4751 Fountain Avenue

Los Angeles, California 90029

USA

ABOUT
THE
AUTHOR

To know life, you've got to be part of life," wrote L. Ron Hubbard. "You must get down there and *look,* you must get into the nooks and crannies of existence, and you must rub elbows with all kinds and types of men before you can finally establish what man is."

L. Ron Hubbard did exactly that. From the open ranges of his home state of Montana to remote hills of China, from the frigid coast of Alaska to the jungles of South Pacific islands—whether working with men on explorations or teaching inexperienced naval crews to survive the ravages of a world war—L. Ron Hubbard truly learned what man and life are all about.

Armed with a keen intellect, limitless curiosity and a unique approach to philosophy and science, which emphasized workability above all else, Ron embarked upon his study of life and its mysteries while still in his teens.

Traveling extensively throughout Asia and the Pacific, he studied the wisdom of Far Eastern philosophies yet observed widespread suffering and poverty. If there was such profound wisdom in the East, he asked, then why such misery?

After returning to the United States in 1929, Ron pursued the study of mathematics and engineering at George Washington University. He was a member of one of the first American classes on nuclear physics and conducted his earliest experiments on human mental capabilities. He found that despite all of mankind's advances in the physical sciences, a *workable* technology of the mind and life had never been developed. The mental "technologies" which did exist, psychology and psychiatry, were actually barbaric, false subjects—no more workable than the methods of witch doctors.

From university, Ron next set out to find the basic principle of existence—a principle which would lead to the unification of knowledge and that would explain the meaning of existence itself—something other philosophers had attempted but never found.

To accomplish this, he studied man in many different settings and cultures. In the summer of 1932, he embarked upon a series of expeditions. The first took him to the Caribbean where he examined the primitive villagers of Martinique. Returning to the West Indies a few months later, he studied cultures of other islands, including the beliefs of Puerto Rican hill people.

Upon his return to the United States, Ron began to substantiate the basis of a theory. In 1937, he conducted a series of biological experiments that led to a breakthrough discovery which isolated the dynamic principle of existence—the common denominator of all life—SURVIVE!

Through the first weeks of 1938, and with these discoveries in hand, Ron wrote his findings in a philosophic work entitled "Excalibur." Upon completion of this historic manuscript, he allowed others to review it. Response was dramatic, and more than a few publishers eagerly sought the work. But even as the offers arrived, he knew he could not publish the book as it contained no practical therapy. That is not to imply the discoveries in "Excalibur" were not later used. Indeed, all basic formulations have since been released in other books or materials.

Much of his research was financed by his professional literary career. He became one of the most highly acclaimed authors in the golden age of popular adventure and science fiction through the 1930s and 1940s—interrupted only by active service in the US Navy during World War II. Partially disabled at war's end, he resumed his work in earnest at Oak Knoll Naval Hospital in Oakland, California where he was recovering from injuries through the spring of 1945.

Among the 5,000 naval and Marine Corps patients at Oak Knoll were hundreds of former American prisoners of war liberated from Japanese camps on South Pacific islands. In an attempt to alleviate their suffering, Ron applied what he had learned from his researches. The techniques he had developed not only helped other servicemen to regain their health, he was also able to restore his own health.

During the years that followed, Ron spent thousands of hours codifying the first-ever workable technology of the mind. He had been steadily accumulating notes on his research, in preparation for a book on the subject. To further verify his theories, he set up an office in Hollywood, California where he could work with people from all walks of life. It wasn't long before he was inundated with a variety of public, eager for his help.

By late 1947, he wrote a manuscript outlining his discoveries of the mind. It was not published at the time, but circulated amongst Ron's friends, who copied it and passed it on to others. (This manuscript was formally published in 1951 and is today titled *The Dynamics of Life*.)

In 1948, he spent three months helping deeply disturbed inmates in a Savannah, Georgia mental hospital. "I worked with some of these," he recalled, "interviewing and helping out as what they call a lay practitioner, which means a volunteer. This gave me some insight into the social problems of insanity and gave me further data in my own researches." It also restored sanity to a score of previously hopeless cases and once again proved that his discoveries were applicable to all.

As word of Ron's research spread, a steadily increasing flood of letters asked for further information and requested that he detail more applications of his discoveries. To answer all these inquiries he decided to write and publish a comprehensive text on the subject—*Dianetics: The Modern Science of Mental Health*. With the release of *Dianetics* on May 9, 1950, a complete handbook for the application of his new technology was broadly available for the first time. Public interest spread like wildfire and the book shot to the top of the *New York Times* bestseller list, remaining there week after week.

Following the release of this phenomenal bestseller, Ron's time became less his own as he was called upon to give demonstrations and provide more information on Dianetics. He launched into further research, keeping the public informed of his latest breakthroughs with lectures and a flood of published bulletins, magazines and books.

Ron continued researching, improving methods and developing techniques to advance other people's ability to apply Dianetics technology.

One of his most important discoveries is the emotional Tone Scale, and the fact that people move up or down through these emotions in a definite order or sequence. That is, Ron found that there was a completely predictable pattern of behavior for each level of the Tone Scale. After months of exacting work charting out manifestations of each level of the Tone Scale, he wrote *Science of Survival*. This book contains something never before known to man: a totally accurate method for the prediction of human behavior. By studying and using this material people are able to know with certainty what kind of behavior and actions to expect from anyone they encounter.

As 1951 drew to a close, and in spite of growing demands on his time by tens of thousands of *Dianetics* readers, he intensified research into the true identity of "life energy," which in *Dianetics* he called the "center of awareness," or the "I."

"The basic discovery of Dianetics was the exact anatomy of the human mind," he wrote. "The aberrative power of engrams was discovered. Procedures were developed for erasing them. The amount of benefit to be gained from running half a dozen engrams exceeded anything that man had ever been able to do for anybody in the history of the human race."

"The discovery of what it was that the mind was coating was the discovery of Scientology.

"It was coating a thetan. A thetan is the person himself—not his body or his name, the physical universe, his mind, or anything else; that which is aware of being aware; the identity which IS the individual. The thetan is most familiar to one and all as *you*."

These discoveries formed the basis of the applied religious philosophy of *Scientology,* the study of the spirit in relationship to itself, universes and other life. Through the application of Scientology technology, desirable changes in the conditions of life can be brought about. It incorporates Dianetics, a vital and basic branch of Scientology, and encompasses techniques which raise personal ability and awareness to heights not previously thought attainable.

It was Ron's lifelong purpose to complete his research into the riddle of man and develop a technology that would bring him up to higher levels of understanding, ability and freedom—a goal which he fully achieved in the development of Dianetics and Scientology. Ron always considered it was not enough that he alone should benefit from the results of his research. He took great care to record every detail of his discoveries so that others could share the wealth of knowledge and wisdom to improve their lives.

"I like to help others," he said, "and count it as my greatest pleasure in life to see a person free himself of the shadows which darken his days.

"These shadows look so thick to him and weigh him down so that when he finds they are shadows and that he can see through them, walk through them and be again in the sun, he is enormously delighted. And I am afraid I am just as delighted as he is."

His works on the subject of man, the mind and spirit *alone,* comprise tens of millions of published words recorded in volumes of books, manuscripts and over 3,000 taped lectures and briefings.

Today, his works are studied and applied daily in over two thousand Dianetics and Scientology groups, churches, missions and organizations around the world.

L. Ron Hubbard departed his body on January 24, 1986. His legacy is the fully completed research and codification of Dianetics and Scientology technology.

The greatest testimonies to Ron's vision are the miracle results of his technology and the millions of friends around the world who carry his legacy forward into the twenty-first century. Both continue to grow in number with each passing day.